"I have known Gulzar since our MBA days, when his clarity of thought and commitment to big ideas were already evident. To see that same conviction now reflected in The Future of Banking: A Global Blueprint for the Bank of Tomorrow is deeply inspiring. The book provides a timely and globally relevant framework for trust, resilience, and inclusion, while remaining practical and grounded in real-world experience. It is both a vision and a blueprint for the institutions of tomorrow."

Shri Vishwajit Pratapsingh Rane, *Cabinet Minister, Government of Goa, India (Health, Agriculture, Urban Development, Town & Country Planning, Women & Child Development, Forests)*

"I have known Gulzar Singh personally and professionally for many years, and have witnessed his leadership in both institutional banking and broader governance contexts. The Future of Banking: A Global Blueprint for the Bank of Tomorrow is not just a vision but a call to action - addressing financial inclusion, institutional trust, and systemic reform with rare clarity and conviction. This work is globally relevant and deeply rooted in practical experience, making it a timely and important contribution for policymakers, practitioners, and scholars alike."

Shri Karan Bir Singh *(KBS Sidhu), Indian Administrative Services, Former Special Chief Secretary, Government of Punjab, India*

"I have had the privilege of personally witnessing Gulzar Singh's leadership journey, from his role as Head of Retail Banking at HDFC Bank, where he forged innovative partnerships with public institutions, to his broader vision of trust and inclusion in finance. The Future of Banking: A Global Blueprint for the Bank of Tomorrow reflects the same integrity, conviction, and clarity I have long associated with him. It is a timely and compelling call for resilient institutions that balance financial innovation with public purpose."

Shri Jayanto Narayan Choudhury, *Indian Police Service, Former Director General, National Security Guard; Former DGP Assam Police; Independent Director Gail India*

"I have long admired Gulzar Singh's disciplined thought and leadership rooted in real-world practice. The Future of Banking: A Global Blueprint for the Bank of Tomorrow reflects his ability to blend the strategic mindset of a banker with the conscience of a public servant. His work is a timely call to design financial systems anchored in trust, ethics, and responsibility. I endorse this book not only as a mentor but as someone who believes that the future of any sector must be built by leaders who embody both competence and conscience."

Air Marshal K.S. Bhatia, *PVSM, AVSM & Bar, Former Air Officer Commanding-in-Chief, Indian Air Force*

"In every generation, a few voices rise above the noise - not by volume, but by clarity. The Future of Banking: A Global Blueprint for the Bank of Tomorrow is such a voice. Dr. Gulzar Singh has written more than a book on banking; he has authored a strategic blueprint for an age of transition where disruption, regulation, and societal expectations collide. What sets this work apart is its conscience - it never loses sight of the human element while addressing the architecture of trust. I commend this book to all those shaping the future of institutions and public life."

Major General Surjit Singh, *AVSM, VSM, FNAE, Veteran, Engineer, Member, Indian National Academy of Engineering*

"The principles of integrity, professionalism, and lifelong learning remain at the heart of banking. In an era of rapid technological change, these values provide the foundation for building trust and delivering meaningful service to customers and communities alike, ensuring the profession continues to serve society effectively.

I had the opportunity to work with Dr Gulzar Singh during his journey towards becoming a Fellow at the Chartered Banker Institute in Edinburgh. His dedication, intellectual curiosity, and ability to engage with complex issues left a strong impression on me.

This book, The Future of Banking arrives at an important time for the industry, offering perspectives on how banking can adapt to emerging challenges while remaining anchored in its core purpose. It is a timely and thoughtful contribution to the conversation on the future of our profession."

Warwick Browning, *FCBI, Assessor at Chartered Banker Institute, Scotland.*

The Future of Banking

The Future of Banking offers a global and practical blueprint for reimagining the modern financial institution. At a time when digital transformation alone is no longer sufficient, this book focuses on rebuilding trust, driving inclusive access, and enabling resilient institutional architecture.

The book brings together lived insight, global strategy, and cross-market applicability. It blends academic depth with real-world execution, offering a comprehensive roadmap for future-ready banking institutions.

The book is structured into ten chapters, each with ten modular sections, which enables clarity, flexibility, and progression. In doing so, the volume allows readers to engage with both high-level transformation themes and hands-on implementation models. It bridges the gap between academic vision and practitioner execution, offering a robust architecture for leaders navigating systemic disruption, ESG mandates, and hybrid infrastructure needs on a global scale.

Gulzar Singh is a globally respected banking leader and a UK Global Talent Visa (Exceptional Talent) recipient, with three decades of executive experience across Barclays UK, HDFC Bank India, Capgemini, and fintech ventures. Dr. Singh has held leadership roles across digital transformation, operations, financial crime, ESG strategy, and regulatory reform and is a Chartered Fellow of six leading UK professional institutes, including the Chartered Banker Institute, LIBF, and the Chartered Management Institute. He also serves on UK boards across financial services, environmental sustainability, and community care, thus making a substantial contribution to the creation of resilient, values-led institutions.

The Future of Banking

A Global Blueprint for the Bank of Tomorrow

Gulzar Singh

Routledge
Taylor & Francis Group
LONDON AND NEW YORK

First published 2026
by Routledge
4 Park Square, Milton Park, Abingdon, Oxon OX14 4RN

and by Routledge
605 Third Avenue, New York, NY 10158

Routledge is an imprint of the Taylor & Francis Group, an informa business

British Library Cataloguing in Publication Data
A catalogue record for this book is available from the British Library

Library of Congress Cataloging-in-Publication Data
A catalog record has been requested for this book

ISBN: 978-1-041-23516-3 (hbk)
ISBN: 978-1-041-23515-6 (pbk)
ISBN: 978-1-003-73754-4 (ebk)

DOI: 10.4324/9781003737544

Typeset in Sabon
by Taylor & Francis Books

To those who believe
that institutions can serve humanity.
To every thinker, reformer, and quiet leader
who shaped the idea of banking as a public good.
And to the future generations,
for whom we must build a system worthy of trust.

Contents

Illustrations

Figures

Boxes

Foreword

In a world where banking is being redefined by trust, technology, and transformation, *The Future of Banking: A Global Blueprint for the Bank of Tomorrow* stands out foremost as a stellar and timely contribution. The book is not just about where the industry is headed, but what values must accompany that journey.

Drawing on decades of leadership, Dr. Gulzar Singh brings together powerful insights from across the globe. He connects traditional banking ethos with emerging digital realities – without losing sight of what truly matters: human impact, financial inclusion, and institutional trust.

As someone who has had the privilege of leading through periods of great change, I recognise the need for frameworks that are both strategic and grounded. This book offers that. It speaks to regulators, bankers, entrepreneurs, and technologists alike – and does so with clarity, purpose, and depth.It is an invitation to help shape the next chapter of global finance – consciously, collaboratively, and credibly.

-Ram Gopal, Former CEO, Barclays India

Advance Praise

From the Global Academic Community:

Prof. Brian Charles, PhD, MBA, MS
Head Learning Facilitator-MIT
United States

In an era when the future of finance is no longer defined by technology alone – but by trust, inclusion, intelligence, and institutional character – *The Future of Banking: A Global Blueprint for the Bank of Tomorrow* emerges as a timely and essential contribution to the global dialogue. Dr. Gulzar Singh offers not just a strategic perspective on banking transformation, but a thoughtful, deeply grounded manifesto for the century ahead. I had the privilege of having Dr. Gulzar Singh as a student in one of the executive education cohorts at MIT. From the outset, his contributions reflected strategic maturity, systemic thinking, and a sincere commitment to public good. What stood out was not just his grasp of complex themes – ranging from AI to institutional trust – but his discipline, curiosity, and his instinct to translate academic insight into real-world transformation. It is no surprise that the same depth of thought and breadth of vision now informs this important work.

Across ten sharply composed chapters, Dr. Singh explores the foundations of modern finance through a forward-facing lens: modular architectures, digital identity, open ecosystems, algorithmic ethics, ESG alignment, and institutional character. But this book is not merely a survey of trends. It is a call to leadership – a roadmap for building institutions that are moreinclusive, more resilient, and more consciously designed.

What I admire most is the author's ability to balance ambition with humility. He draws not only on three decades of global experience – including senior leadership roles at HDFC Bank and Barclays – but also on the values of stewardship and service. His voice is informed, reflective, and deeply human, offering rare clarity at a time of rapid, and often confusing, change.

As we confront the urgent task of reshaping financial institutions for an intelligent and inclusive era, this book serves as both compass and catalyst. *The Future of Banking* invites leaders to act with clarity, design with conscience, and govern with foresight. In Dr. Gulzar Singh's hands, this is not merely a book about banking. It is a work of enduring relevance – an intellectual blueprint for institutions that must now rise to meet the future with intention, and not inertia.

From a Senior Voice in U.S. Banking Leadership:

Mr. Jose Delgado
Chief Banking Officer, Strategic Leadership
United States

Based in Houston, Texas, I have had the privilege of serving in senior leadership roles across the American banking sector, guiding institutions through strategic transformation, operational scale, and evolving customer expectations. The convergence of trust, technology, and governance continues to define the future of banking – not only in the US, but globally.

Over the past several years, I have come to know Dr. Gulzar Singh as a respected global leader and strategic voice in financial innovation. His writings, insights, and thought leadership consistently reflect a rare combination of institutional depth and visionary foresight. He brings together legacy banking experience with a modern understanding of inclusive, technology-enabled financial systems.

His new book, *The Future of Banking: A Global Blueprint for the Bank of Tomorrow*, is both timely and necessary. It goes beyond theoretical aspirations to offer a structured, actionable roadmap for the sector. Importantly, it holds particular relevance for the US banking ecosystem – where the call for reinvention, community trust, and digital equity is stronger than ever. This book belongs not only in the hands of CEOs and policymakers, but also in the curriculum of our leading universities and leadership programs. It is a significant contribution to the global banking discourse.

A Perspective from the Chartered Banker Institute of Scotland:

Mr. Mark Hay
Academic Associate at the Chartered Banker Institute
Scotland

Although it has been under intense scrutiny for two decades now, banking in the United Kingdom has long stood as a benchmark for professionalism, integrity, and public trust.

Its strength lies in a well-established framework of governance, customer focus, and continuous professional development that has shaped generations of bankers.

As the industry navigates a new era of digital innovation and societal expectations, the UK system offers valuable lessons in balancing heritage with transformation, ensuring that the core purpose of serving customers and communities remains unchanged.

It is in this context that *The Future of Banking: A Global Blueprint for the Bank of Tomorrow* makes such a timely and important contribution.

The book looks to draw on the discipline and principles that have underpinned UK banking traditions, integrating them into a forward-looking model that addresses global challenges. It aims to capture both the risks and opportunities facing modern banking, and offer practical pathways to strengthen resilience, enhance inclusion, and build enduring trust -principles as relevant to a local branch in Edinburgh as they are to a financial hub in Singapore or New York.

I have had the privilege of getting to know Dr Gulzar Singh during his professional journey, particularly during his successful progress through the Chartered Banker Institute's Chartered Banker program.Throughout the program he applied a rare combination of intellectual rigour, meticulous attention to detail, and genuine passion for the profession that served him well as he gained Chartered Banker status.

It was always clear that he combined deep industry knowledge with a strong commitment to doing what is right and acting in a truly ethical manner. His global perspective and ability to connect strategy with execution are evident throughout this work. This book is the outcome of decades of dedication to the banking industry and will be a valuable source of reference for leaders and practitioners shaping the industry's future.

Leadership Reflections from India's Banking Sector:

Mr. Pralay Mondal
Chief Executive Officer & Managing Director , CSB Bank

The banking sector today stands at a complex crossroads – balancing digital acceleration with deepening expectations around trust, inclusion, and long-term resilience. In such a moment, there is immense value in stepping back to reflect, reframe, and reimagine the broader institutional responsibilities we carry as financial leaders.

The Future of Banking: A Global Blueprint for the Bank of Tomorrow is a timely contribution to this ongoing dialogue. It approaches banking not just as a set of systems and products, but as a societal foundation – something that must evolve with integrity, clarity of purpose, and a future-facing mindset.

The book's strength lies in its comprehensive scope. It draws connections across technology, policy, human capital, and institutional character – recognising that transformation in finance is never just about infrastructure. It is about intent. In the years ahead, as banks navigate uncertainty and renewal, such frameworks will prove essential.

This is a work that speaks across regions and generations. It will resonate with professionals in legacy institutions, leaders in digital-first ecosystems, and policymakers seeking coherence in a shifting world. Most importantly, it reminds us that the future of banking must be designed – deliberately, responsibly, and boldly.

Message from a MD & CEO:

Vinod Easwaran
Chief Executive Officer & Managing Director, Reliance Jio Payments Bank
India

In today's evolving financial landscape, the ability to connect digital growth with long-term trust and inclusion is becoming a defining capability for institutions across markets. Strategy, regulation, customer experience, and technology are no longer operating in silos – they must converge to deliver systemic value.

I recently had the opportunity to review an early concept draft of *The Future of Banking: A Global Blueprint for the Bank of Tomorrow*, a forthcoming book that brings these ideas together in a thoughtful and globally relevant manner. Drawing on practical experience across banking, governance, and transformation, it offers a timely reflection on where the industry is headed – and what kind of leadership will be needed to build it.

Dr. Gulzar Singh presents an approach that is not just a banking playbook. It speaks to policymakers, fintech leaders, institutional innovators, and anyone involved in designing trustworthy systems – whether in Mumbai or New York.

Preface

Banking today stands at a crossroads. It is no longer what it once was – and it will never return to what it used to be. Institutions everywhere are being reshaped by technology, regulation, and society, yet one truth remains constant: while technology can transform systems, only trust can transform outcomes. This book is born from that conviction.

Drawing on more than three decades of work across continents, institutions, and disciplines, I have written this as a guide for leaders navigating disruption. It is neither a technical manual nor a nostalgic memoir, but a future-facing contribution to an industry searching for clarity, resilience, and direction.

The challenges are immense: regulatory volatility, ESG scrutiny, customer activism, geopolitical uncertainty, and the accelerating force of digital innovation. What leaders need is not more noise, but sharper navigation. This book seeks to offer exactly that.

Its format is modular yet cohesive. From AI and climate resilience to governance, trust, and inclusion, each chapter combines lived experience with strategic foresight. The aim is simple: to provide insights that are actionable.

Whether you are shaping policy, leading transformation, or simply making sense of where finance is headed, this book is for you. My hope is that it will serve as a reference, a companion, and at times, a provocation.The future does not design itself. We must design it – intentionally, inclusively, and with wisdom.

- Dr. Gulzar Singh
London

Acknowledgements

This book has been shaped by the evolving dialogue between scholars, practitioners, and institutions who continue to expand the boundaries of modern finance. I am deeply grateful to the editors, reviewers, and publishing professionals whose insight and discipline helped bring this work to life.

The chapters are built on the accumulated wisdom of those working at the intersection of governance, technology, banking, and policy. Whether through practice or research, their contributions have sharpened the arguments and strengthened the core of this book.

I wish to express heartfelt thanks to my daughters, Priya Singh and Preeti Singh, whose futures inspire every chapter of this book. May you always lead with imagination, courage, and conviction – the world needs your voice.

To my wife, Harpreet Kaur – your quiet strength and moral steadiness have been a constant anchor behind this work.

To my sisters, Nuri Singh and Gunamrit Kaur – thank you for your unwavering support across decades and continents.

To General Satbir Singh, SM, and my father-in-law – Chairman, IESM and Veteran of the 1971 War – your public service and principled leadership have left a quiet but lasting impression on this journey.

To Harbhajan Kaur, my mother, and Daljit Kaur, my mother-in-law – whose grace, quiet strength, and unwavering moral clarity remain deeply woven into the character of this work.

To the memory of Air Marshal Manjit Singh, my father – whose values, discipline, and service to the nation shaped the foundation of my own leadership journey.

To the memory of Bhai Hira Singh Ji, my great-grandfather, who was a poet, scholar, and towering figure in Sikh literature. Your wisdom, moral clarity, and literary legacy echo through these pages and remain a guiding light.

It is my hope that this work will not only serve as an analysis – but as a catalyst.

May it inspire students, regulators, academics, and executives to design institutions where trust, inclusion, and public purpose are no longer optional, but essential.

Introduction

Banks are among the world's oldest institutions, and for centuries banking has shaped economies, societies, and even our understanding of trust itself. Yet today, it faces unprecedented forces of transformation. Data-driven technology that reshapes industries overnight, global pressures on climate and sustainability, and rising expectations of fairness and inclusion are redefining what it means for banks to endure and to matter.

The real question is no longer whether banks should evolve, but how quickly and with what design. Relevance will be given to those institutions that embed trust, inclusion, resilience, and governance into their very architecture.

This book, *The Future of Banking: A Global Blueprint for the Bank of Tomorrow* sets out such a design. Written with the urgency of our times, it brings together insights from decades of practice across emerging markets and global financial hubs to propose a new framework for institutions. At its core are four essential pillars:

- Physical presence where trust is earned face-to-face
- Digital infrastructure that enables access anytime, anywhere
- ESG governance that aligns profit with purpose
- Inclusive finance that ensures no community is left behind

The aim is not to predict what might unfold, but to equip leaders, policymakers, and educators with actionable tools to shape what should unfold. Each chapter draws on lived experience and strategic foresight, combining practical insight with policy depth.

The chapters are designed to stand alone, yet together they form an integrated blueprint. Readers may read them sequentially or enter at any point, finding perspectives that are both concise and clear.

The stakes are high. Banks are being called upon not only to finance economies but to help heal them. They must remain profitable enterprises, yet also act as public assets capable of enabling prosperity for generations. This book is a call to shape that future deliberately, not to wait passively for it to arrive.The future of banking will not be inherited. It must be designed intelligently, inclusively, and purposefully.

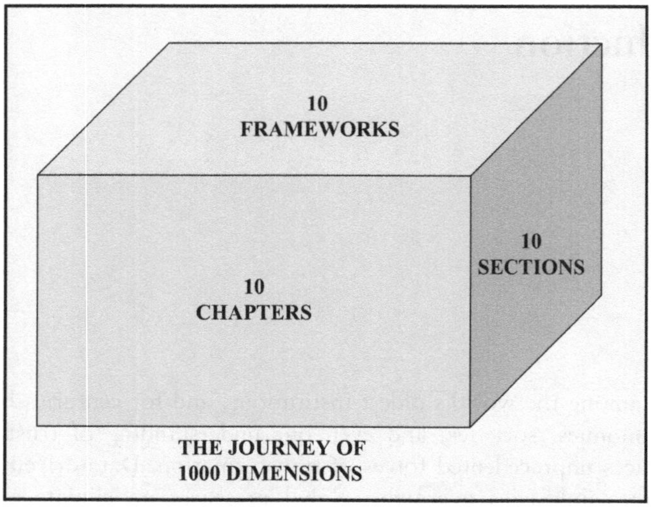
10
FRAMEWORKS
10
SECTIONS
10
CHAPTERS
THE JOURNEY OF
1000 DIMENSIONS

1 The Changing Bank

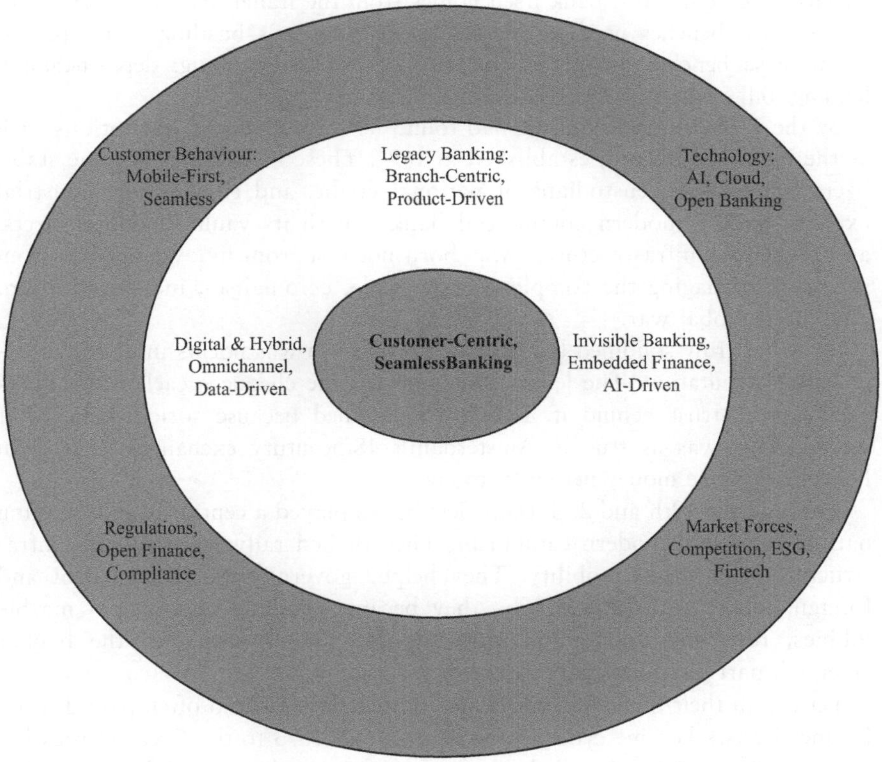

Figure 1.1 Banking evolves from legacy branch networks to digital hybrid models and finally to invisible, ecosystem-driven finance – converging on a seamless customer experience.

DOI: 10.4324/9781003737544-1

1 The Roots of Modern Banking

The origins of banking are far more human than digital. Long before we had algorithms or mobile apps, societies were exchanging trust in the form of grain, gold, and goodwill. In ancient Mesopotamia – often credited as the birthplace of accounting – temple priests safeguarded harvest surpluses and issued early forms of credit against stored goods. These were not just economic transactions; they were acts ruled by the social contract, built on mutual dependence and moral duty. Long before there was finance, there was faith.

As trade routes spread across Babylon, Egypt, India, and China, the role of money changers, goldsmiths, and early lenders emerged. In Classical Greece and Rome, rudimentary financial systems facilitated taxation, warfare, and commerce. Yet banking, in its truest form, took institutional shape in the Italian Renaissance. The word bank itself comes from the Italian banca – referring to the wooden benches used by merchants in Florence's bustling marketplaces. From these benches arose the blueprint of modern banking: deposit-taking, lending, bill exchange, and risk management.

By the 17th century, banking had found its formal seat in institutions such as the Bank of England, established in 1694. These institutions became stabilizers for empires, custodians of national credit, and engines for industrial expansion. The modern commercial bank – with its vaults, balance sheets, and regulatory infrastructure – was born not just from innovation, but from necessity: managing the complexities of trade, colonialism, industrialization, and, later, global war.

But what truly solidified banking as a profession was not its infrastructure – it was its reputation. The ledger, the contract, the cheque – each was only as good as the trust behind it. Banking functioned because society believed it would. This was as true in Amsterdam's 18thcentury exchanges as it is in Nairobi's mobile money networks today.

Through the 19th and 20th centuries, banks played a central role in shaping nation-states and modern capitalism. They fuelled railways, factories, infrastructure, and social mobility. They helped governments manage debt and foreign policy. And increasingly, they became symbols of power – marble lobbies, revolving doors, and global logos. The mystique of the banker emerged: part guardian, part gatekeeper, part elite.

Yet for all their grandeur, banks also absorbed risk – and often passed it on. Financial crises became cyclic: from the panic of 1873 to the Great Depression of the 1930s and later the oil shocks of the 1970s. Each time, banks were either the catalyst or the casualty. And with each cycle, their role in society was questioned more deeply. By the end of the 1900s, banking had changed completely. What used to be simple and personal became complicated and hard to understand. Banks moved away from knowing their customers personally to just selling products to anyone who walked in.

As computers, global business, and looser rules prevailed, banks got bigger and bigger – but they also grew more distant from the people they served.

Something important got lost along the way: the personal connection between the bank and the person, between what banks said they wanted to do and what actually happened.

Here's what we shouldn't forget: banking didn't start with computers and apps – it started with people. Trust was built when bank managers sat down for tea with customers in small town branches. It grew through firm handshakes and real relationships. It was passed down through families when fathers told their sons, "You can trust this bank."

That human trust – that's what made our entire financial system possible in the first place.

The introduction of technology in banking, while transformative, was initially administrative. Computers automated ledgers. ATMs extended reach. Credit cards replaced cash. But these were tools of efficiency – not yet instruments of reinvention. The digital age did not challenge banking's foundations; it digitized them.

However, the seeds of disruption were sown. By the 1990s, online banking had begun to erode the spatial monopoly of the branch. By the 2000s, mobile banking liberated finance from fixed locations. And by the 2010s, fintech and platform economies began challenging the very assumptions of who could bank, how, and through whom. Suddenly, the roots of modern banking – once so deep and institutional – were exposed to new weather.

Crucially, the crisis of 2008 marked a psychological turning point. The public began to question not just how banks operated, but why they existed in the first place. For many, banking became synonymous with risk, excess, and detachment from real-world consequences. The trust that had taken centuries to build was eroded in a matter of months. And yet, paradoxically, it was in this moment of reckoning that the future of banking began to emerge. For to understand where we are going, we must first understand where we've come from – not just at a functional but at a philosophical level.

The roots of modern banking teach us that finance has always been a mirror of society. It reflects our priorities, our technologies, and our values. When society becomes unequal, so too does access to finance. When innovation flourishes, finance follows. And when trust is broken, banks lose not just customers – but their social license to operate.

As we stand at the edge of a new financial era – defined by AI, decentralization, embedded services, and ethical demands – it is worth returning to the roots. Not to replicate them, but to rediscover the core human mandate of banking: to protect, to empower, and to invest in possibility. In doing so, we don't find nostalgia – but guidance. For while the tools may change, the purpose remains: banking is, and must always be, a system for enabling the future.

2 The Global Turning Point

The 2008 financial crisis was more than a failure of the banks – it was the disintegration of a type of confidence. In boardrooms and living rooms alike, individuals started questioning not only whether financial institutions had failed, but whether the concept of banking had shed its moral compass. During those months, trust – banking's currency of first resort – was destroyed on a worldwide basis. What then ensued was not only economic devastation but a permanent change in public opinion, political focus, and institutional salience.

For decades, banks had become larger, more remote, and more dominant. They had been transformed from community-based institutions into multinational firms, extensively involved in everything from property to sovereign bonds. The sophistication of their products, the obscurity of their risk models, and the divide between their services and the everyday lives of ordinary people had all increased. When the crisis struck, it wasn't merely a financial system in meltdown – it was a cultural awakening. It exposed the fact that far too many institutions had favoured engineering over empathy, scale over safety, and profit over people.

In the aftermath, banking lost its automatic legitimacy. Governments needed to bail out banks that had proclaimed themselves too big to fail. Regulatory authorities hastened to impose new regimes – from Basel III to Dodd-Frank – aimed at preventing future meltdowns. But regulation, as it turned out, could not, by itself, restore trust. That would require time, action, and a new vision of what a bank should be.

This moment post 2008 marked a global turning point. In emerging markets, it catalysed innovation. In mature economies, it demanded reinvention. And in every corner of the financial system, it forced an uncomfortable but essential question: What are banks for in the 21st century?

The crisis coincided with a parallel revolution – the rise of digital connectivity. While the physical world was struggling with institutional collapse, the virtual world was speeding up. smartphones became ubiquitous. Cloud computing came of age. Social media remade public conversation. And a new generation of digitally native consumers arrived – wary of old authority, impatient with inefficiency, and eager for instantaneity. They did not want to be treated like a bank's customers. They aspired to be enabled by money tools as responsive and intuitive as the apps they used to manage their lives.

This technological and generational change created a second fault line. Banks were no longer able to depend on legacy systems or legacy reputations. Fintech start-ups emerged, not merely to contest pricing or design, but to contest the very architecture of financial service delivery. Digital wallets, peer-to-peer lending platforms, robo-advisors, and alternative credit scoring mechanisms demonstrated that banking functions could be reimagined – faster, cheaper, and more personalized.

Notably, however, this was not solely disruption from the outside in. Within big banks, executives started dealing with their own inertia. Organizational silos, dated IT infrastructure, waterfall project lifecycles, and internal politics were all brakes on innovation. The culture that had previously shielded stability was now slowing down agility. The question was no longer whether banks had to change, but whether they could, and would they do so before legacy became irrelevant.

At the same time, regulatory landscapes also changed. In the UK, the Financial Conduct Authority (FCA) implemented a more innovation-accommodating stance. In India, the Reserve Bank of India (RBI) encouraged the growth of digital payment platforms. In Africa, governments collaborated with telcos to grow financial access through mobile money. These developments indicated that agility, access, and accountability were not competing priorities – and that regulators themselves also had a part to play in transforming the financial sector.

Then something big shifted – and it was no longer just about the cash. People began to discuss ESG (that is, Environmental, Social, and Governance issues), but these issues weren't the next checkbox on an application. They resulted in an entirely new way of considering the real risks for business. Suddenly, banks began to fret over such things as: Will global warming damage our investments? Are we diverse enough? Are our computer algorithms discriminating against anyone?

Instead of just caring about how much money the banks brought in each quarter, everyone – investors, government regulators, and regular customers –now wanted to know: What do you do? How are you contributing to the world? Banks realized they could no longer appear to be simply taking from individuals and communities without giving back. They needed to demonstrate that they were doing more than just supporting their clients – they were strengthening society, stabilising the economy, and protecting the planet. It was not sufficient to simply generate money; they had to show that they made the world a better place.

This moment of change revealed a greater truth: that banking is not a neutral practice. The kind of systems the banks create, the credit they offers the information they accumulate – all these actions have real-world results. Whether they invest in green infrastructure or in fossil fuels, whether they open up opportunities for micro-entrepreneurs or shut them off by using old models, whether they insure customer data or market it for profit – each choice a bank makes is a choice about the future we are creating.

Some institutions responded by changing. Digital transformation shifted from pilot schemes to board-level priorities. Chief Innovation Officers became central to executive teams. Legacy systems were broken up into modules. Agile approaches were embraced. Banks started investing in fintechs, developing APIs, and remaking customer journeys around customer needs, rather than internal organization. Others slowed down – stuck between quarterly pressures and old habits.

This turning point, therefore, is not a moment in time. It is a continuous reorientation – requiring clear vision, humble leadership, and bold design. Banks need to decide if they will be custodians of a dying model or designers of a new model.

Today we stand in a world which is still defined by that turning point. Crypto currencies are pushing the boundaries of monetary sovereignty. Artificial intelligence is transforming the definition of credit and fraud. Climate threats are rewriting balance sheets. And financial inclusion is no longer an act of charity – it is a market necessity. Each of these forces requires banks to redefine what it means to serve, to lead, and to survive. The tipping point was never merely about survival. It was, and remains, about relevance. And in a world characterized by choice, change, and challenge, relevance must be earned - not taken.

3 Changing Expectations, Changing Roles

The role of the bank has always been a reflection of the society it serves. In an era of agricultural trade, it was a storehouse. In the age of empires, it was a financier of war and trade. During industrialization, it became an institutional enabler of mass expansion. But today, in the midst of digital saturation, ecological strain, and social transformation, the expectations placed on banks are no longer historical – they are immediate, urgent, and deeply personal.

In markets such as the UK and US, this shift is especially stark. Where once customers accepted queues, forms, and fixed hours, they now demand 24/7 access, intuitive interfaces, and real-time decision-making. In the past, people adapted their lives to the bank's processes. Now, they expect the bank to adapt to theirs. This is not a minor operational tweak – it is a fundamental change in positioning: from institution to enabler, from gatekeeper to partner.

Look at what happened with banking apps. In the UK, banks such as Monzo and Starling didn't just make prettier apps – they completely changed what banking could feel like. In the US, Chime became hugely popular, not because they invented some fancy new financial product, but because they got rid of the annoying stuff that everyone hated – like those brutal overdraft fees and filling out endless forms just to open an account.

These newer banks succeeded because they kept things simple and focused on what people actually care about: getting things done quickly, knowing exactly what's happening with their money, being treated fairly, and having services that fit into their real lives. It wasn't rocket science – it was just common sense.

But changing expectations go beyond UX design or faster transactions. Customers now want intelligent service – services that anticipate, contextualize, and respond. A bank that informs you when a subscription fee is increasing or one that flags unusual spending before you notice it is no longer impressive – it is expected. Personalization is no longer a luxury; it is the new benchmark for credibility.

These expectations are being shaped by platforms outside of finance. When consumers experience the real-time personalization of Netflix, the delivery precision of Amazon, or the conversational ease of WhatsApp, they instinctively carry those standards into their financial lives. They ask, often subconsciously: Why can't my bank do this? And increasingly, they are turning to those who can. This is where the role of banks must evolve. It is no longer enough to be a reliable vault or a compliant lender. Today's bank must be a financial life companion – an interpreter of data, a filter for decisions, a coach for wellbeing, and a curator of opportunities. The institution must shift from being product-led to needs-led, from being passive to proactive.

This change also impacts the way trust is earned. In the past, a grand building or a long history was enough to imply solidity. Today, trust is digital, dynamic, and earned in moments. If your app crashes when someone is trying to make a payment overseas, you lose trust. If your chatbot gives evasive or generic responses in a moment of need, you lose trust. The threshold for disappointment is low – but the bar for loyalty is high.

We are also witnessing a shift in what people expect banks to care about. It is no longer enough to talk about shareholder returns or regulatory compliance. Customers – especially younger generations – want to know where their money is going. Are their savings funding fossil fuels or sustainable energy? Are their mortgages aligned with environmental risk zones? Are their credit models biased or inclusive?

Here's the thing – banks don't get to choose whether they want to change or not. It has become a survival issue. Traditional banks aren't just competing with those slick fintech startups anymore. Now they're up against Apple, Google, and Amazon – companies that also handle your money but do it so smoothly you barely notice.

Get this: Starbucks in the US actually handles more prepaid money than a lot of local community banks. Think about that. Your coffee shop is basically doing banking. These tech companies have figured out something important – they know how you actually live your day-to-day life. So they've made financial stuff just … happen. You buy something with Apple Pay without thinking twice. You split a dinner bill through an app. You don't even realize you're doing "banking".

That's what traditional banks are up against: money stuff that's so smooth and invisible you forget it's even happening. If banks want to survive, that's the bar they have to meet. To meet these expectations, banks must revisit how they define value. Historically, value was measured in deposits, assets, and net interest margins. But in the emerging model, value lies in utility, data insight, and continuous engagement. A bank that helps a customer avoid debt is more valuable than one that simply offers a high-interest loan. A bank that enables a small business to grow sustainably is more valuable than one that just extends overdraft protection.

Crucially, this changing role also demands internal cultural transformation. Banks cannot simply hire a Chief Innovation Officer and expect relevance. They must re-skill teams, dismantle silos, empower decision-making at the edge, and embrace experimentation. They must recognize that relevance is earned through behaviour, not branding. Some banks are already figuring this out, and they're doing it in really interesting ways.

Take Capital One in the US – they're building actual cafés and co-working spaces. Not just places to do banking but places where the community actually wants to hang out. They have realized that people need more than just somewhere to deposit checks. In the UK, Lloyds is using AI to help customers faster while also making sure they're reaching people who usually get left out of the financial system. They're basically saying, "Let's get smarter AND more inclusive at the same time."

In India, banks such as ICICI and Axis have become really clever – they've woven their financial services right into farming and rural life. Instead of expecting farmers to come to the city bank, they brought banking to the farmers. And in Nigeria, digital lenders are doing something amazing: they're giving loans to people who've never borrowed money before, just by looking at how they use their phones. No credit history? No problem – they'll figure out if you're trustworthy in other ways.

What all these banks have in common is that they're not just sitting in marble buildings waiting for customers to show up. They're going to the people, solving real problems, and fitting into how people actually live their lives. What motivates them is a simple truth: people no longer need banks for access to money. They need banks for confidence, clarity, and continuity. The institutions that deliver this will not only survive – they will lead. The role of banking is being rewritten in real-time. It is moving away from legacy structures and toward life integration. And this transformation – from provider to partner, from process to presence – is the defining opportunity of our financial century.

4 From Branches to Digital Journeys

There was a time when the bank branch was more than just a financial service point – it was a symbol of security, permanence, and trust. Whether in the high streets of the UK, the suburban towns of the US, or the rural heartlands of India, a branch represented credibility. A physical place where names were remembered, cheques were processed, and human reassurance was available on demand. The design of branches – with their columns, counters, and vaults – spoke of safety, hierarchy, and legacy.

But in the last two decades, that symbolism has been steadily eroded. The digital revolution didn't just give customers new channels; it redefined the meaning of access. The smartphone, more than any policy or innovation, became the new front door to banking. In markets like the UK, app-based banks such as Monzo and Starling have demonstrated that trust can be earned without bricks and mortar. In the US, the COVID-19 pandemic accelerated this shift dramatically: during 2020 alone, mobile banking adoption surged by over 30%, while foot traffic in branches fell by as much as 50%.

And yet, the debate around the future of branches is not about disappearance – but transformation. The question is not whether branches should exist, but what they should become. The transactional function – depositing cheques, transferring funds, paying bills – has largely migrated online. What remains are the complex, emotional, or community-oriented functions: mortgage consultations, business financing discussions, financial planning, and inclusion support for the digitally excluded.

In this context, branches must evolve into experience hubs, not remain transaction centres. Some progressive banks are already doing this. Capital One's "Cafés" in the US offer co-working spaces, financial workshops, and lifestyle services alongside traditional banking. In the UK, Nationwide has committed to maintaining a high-street presence while redesigning its branches for a more flexible, advice-led service. These are not just nostalgic moves; they are strategic responses to a new type of customer: one who expects both digital convenience and human guidance.

But the real revolution is not in the branch redesign – it is in the journey architecture. In the digital world, what matters is not the channel but the continuity. A customer should be able to start an account application on their phone, complete verification with a biometric ID, speak to a human advisor over video, and receive approval – all without repeating information. This seamless, multi-touch, omnichannel flow is the foundation of customer trust in the modern era.

Designing digital journeys means rethinking how processes are triggered, how data is used, and how customers are understood. Banks must move away from legacy siloed systems, where each department or product operates in isolation, and move toward integrated platforms where customer context is continuous. When a customer logs into an app, their recent transactions, pending goals, and risk alerts should shape what they see. When they call a helpdesk, the advisor should know not just their balance but their journey – what they tried to do, where they got stuck, and which solution fits their need.

Inclusion must also guide the digital shift. Not all customers have equal digital literacy or access. Elderly customers, those with disabilities, migrants, and low-income populations face barriers that can't be solved by apps alone. In the UK, initiatives such as the Banking Framework Agreement and the Access to Cash Review have tried to ensure that physical alternatives remain available. In the US, some community banks are pairing digital onboarding with in-person support, especially in underserved areas. Globally, hybrid models – combining agent banking, voice interfaces, and community hubs – are emerging as more resilient than pure digital setups.

Importantly, the digital journey is not just about replicating old forms online. It is about rethinking the entire customer experience through the lens of value and simplicity. For example, rather than asking a customer to choose from a list of loan products, a bank might present tailored options based on real-time cash flow, spending behaviour, and life events. Instead of forcing users to navigate menus, smart assistants and chatbots can guide them conversationally. This is not just user interface design – it is customer empathy, encoded in technology.

The technical infrastructure behind this evolution is equally vital. APIs, cloud-native platforms, and microservices allow banks to break away from rigid monolithic systems and adopt more flexible, scalable architectures. This enables faster deployment of new features, better integration with third-party services, and real-time responsiveness to user needs. Banks such as JPMorgan Chase and Lloyds Banking Group have publicly committed to multibillion-pound investments in digital transformation – not because it is fashionable, but because it is existential.

With this shift, the role of employees also changes. Frontline staff are no longer tellers – they are advisors, educators, and sometimes technologists. They must be trained not only in products but in emotional intelligence, digital literacy, and problem-solving. Leadership must also evolve: digital transformation is not an IT project – it is a cultural redefinition of how a bank sees itself and serves its people.

The journey from branch to digital is also a journey from control to co-creation. In the past, banks dictated how customers would interact with them. Today, customers shape those interactions. Feedback loops, usage analytics, social listening – these are not add-ons; they are the heartbeat of service design. Banks that listen well adapt faster. And those that adapt faster are seen as more trustworthy.

Finally, digital journeys create a new kind of risk – one of invisibility. If a customer never sees a person, never walks into a building, and never pauses to reflect – will they still feel loyalty? Will they still feel seen? This is why even the most digitized banks must build digital intimacy – not through gimmicks but through relevance, proactivity, and care. From branches to digital journeys, the lesson is clear: presence is no longer physical – it is contextual. The future bank does not wait for the customers to arrive. It goes to the customers, when and where they need it most.

5 Innovations Reshaping Everyday Finance

Finance, once a slow-moving and conservative domain, is now at the centre of a quiet revolution. No longer confined to monthly statements and branch visits, financial services have become embedded, invisible, and increasingly intelligent. Innovation is no longer an event; it is a constant. From how we pay to how we plan, the entire rhythm of money has changed – driven by technologies that reshape behaviour, expectation, and possibility.

In the UK, open banking has set the tone for how innovation can be democratized. By mandating that banks share customer data securely with licensed third parties, the UK has enabled a new generation of apps and platforms that help users track spending, manage debt, optimize savings, and even negotiate bills on their behalf. This shift – from closed systems to open ecosystems – has sparked a wave of creativity. Platforms such as Plum, Emma, and Snoop have turned budgeting into a dynamic, gamified, real-time experience.

Meanwhile, the US took a different approach – they just let the market go wild, and some pretty cool stuff happened. Companies such as Stripe, Square (now called Block), and Robinhood completely changed the game. Stripe made it dead simple for any website to take payments. Square let tiny coffee shops accept credit cards with just a little device plugged into their phone. Robinhood made stock trading feel like playing a game on your phone instead of calling some intimidating Wall Street broker.

But here's where it gets really interesting: financial stuff started showing up everywhere, not just in banks. We call this "embedded finance", but what it really means is that money management just became part of everything else you do. For example, if you drive for Uber in California, you don't have to wait two weeks for a paycheck – the money just shows up in your app wallet every day. If you run a small online shop, you can get a business loan right from the same dashboard where you track your sales. Going to the doctor and can't afford the bill? The healthcare app can offer you a payment plan right there on the spot.

Finance isn't this separate, scary thing anymore. It's just woven into your regular life, happening when and where you actually need it. At the centre of this change is data, not just large amounts of data but smart data. Banks and fintechs are learning to analysebehavioural patterns, contextual triggers, and life-stage indicators to offer hyper-relevant nudges. Did a customer's electricity bill spike unusually? Did they shop at a furniture store, possibly indicating a move? Are their spending patterns aligning with financial distress or opportunity? Algorithms can now surface insights once buried in the fine print. Done well, this is not surveillance – it is service with intuition.

Consider the rise of predictive finance. Some challenger banks can now alert customers before they go into overdraft, suggest transfers to savings when income spikes, or recommend cancelling dormant subscriptions. In effect, financial services are becoming proactive advisors, not just passive recorders. This is a radical departure from the traditional model where the bank waited for the customer to ask.

Biometric authentication is another area where everyday finance has changed irreversibly. Facial recognition, fingerprint scanning, and behavioural biometrics (such as how you type or hold your phone) are replacing passwords and PINs. In the UK, voice-based verification is already used by major high street banks, while in India; Aadhaar-linked authentication has enabled millions to access banking without paperwork. In the US, Apple's Face ID has made biometric security a standard expectation. These innovations don't just enhance convenience – they reduce fraud and build psychological trust in digital channels.

Payments, too, have evolved from being an action to being an experience. Contactless cards, QR codes, and mobile wallets have removed the friction from everyday transactions. In China, Alipay and WeChat Pay have made digital payments near-universal – even street vendors accept them. In Africa, M-Pesa has transformed how households manage remittances, savings, and loans. In the West, "Buy Now, Pay Later" (BNPL) solutions are now embedded into checkout flows, often without involving a traditional credit card or bank.

Yet innovation is not just about adding more tools. It is about rethinking how value is created and delivered. Traditional banks have often equated innovation with product expansion: a new credit card, a new investment option, a new mortgage variant. But the real innovation today lies in simplification and empowerment. A budgeting app that helps a teenager manage their first paycheck. A micro-loan platform that approves funds in minutes for a street vendor. A savings feature that rounds up purchases and invests the difference. These are not glamorous features – but they change lives.

Innovation is also driving financial inclusion. In developing economies, low-cost smartphones and simplified KYC ("Know Your Customer") processes have brought millions into the formal financial system. In the UK and US, underserved communities are being reached through prepaid debit cards, second-chance banking, and community fintech initiatives. In Latin America, digital banks like Nubank have used UX simplicity and low-cost structures to attract over 70 million users – many of whom were previously unbanked. Innovation, in this context, is not just technical – it is moral.

Not all innovation is necessarily a good thing. The rise of high-interest "Buy Now, Pay Later" schemes, addictive trading apps, and data-hungry financial platforms has sparked growing concern. Regulators are starting to question the psychological and systemic risks that come with this era of hyper-convenience. Too often, financial literacy can't keep up with the pace of innovation – leaving a dangerous gap between what people can do and what they truly understand. This is where banks need to step up – not just by adopting new technologies, but by taking responsibility for how they are used and ensuring that they are introduced in a thoughtful, ethical way.

Cybersecurity is another critical frontier. As financial services become more digitized, the attack surface widens. The challenge is to create systems that are secure by design, not just patched after a breach. AI-based fraud detection, multi-factor authentication, decentralized ID solutions – all play a role in safeguarding customer trust. Banks must treat security not as a technical requirement but as a core user experience.

Culturally, innovation demands a new mindset. Banks can no longer think in five-year product cycles. They must operate in agile sprints, co-create with users, test and learn continuously. Institutions that once prided themselves on stability must now learn how to evolve in real-time. This is not chaos – it is capability.

The future of everyday finance is not about grand disruption – it is about subtle, continuous reinvention. It is about using technology to return banking to its roots: helping people manage uncertainty, plan their futures, and navigate complexity with confidence. When innovation is done right, it fades into the background. It makes finance feel simple, supportive, and even empowering. It doesn't just change how we bank – it changes how we live. Trust is not inherited; it must be consciously designed into every layer of banking.

6 Fintechs, Superapps, and Platform Disruption

A decade ago, financial institutions viewed technology companies as enablers – partners that could help modernize legacy infrastructure or enhance online services. But today, those same technology firms have become direct competitors. The emergence of fintechs, superapps, and platform-based ecosystems has not merely disrupted the edges of banking – it has begun to redefine the centre.

In the UK and US, the fintech boom emerged from post-2008 disillusionment, regulatory openness, and a hunger for alternatives. Entrepreneurs saw inefficiencies in everything from remittances to credit scoring. Investors saw margins, user growth, and untapped demographics. And customers – weary of fees, friction, and bureaucracy – were willing to try something new. This is how challenger banks such as Monzo, Chime, and N26 found their footing: not by copying traditional banks, but by reimagining what banking could feel like.

These fintechs focused obsessively on the user journey. They built mobile-first interfaces, eliminated unnecessary steps, and made onboarding frictionless.

They offered early wage access, spending analytics, savings automation, and fee transparency. For many younger users, their first interaction with finance was not through a high street branch but through a bright, friendly app that "just worked".

But the disruption didn't end with traditional banking. The rise of superapps – platforms that bundle multiple services into one seamless experience – has started to redefine what a financial institution actually is. In Asia, apps such as WeChat in China and Grab in Southeast Asia combine messaging, ride-hailing, payments, insurance, and investing – all within a single interface. Users can chat with friends, order food, book flights, transfer money, and pay their utility bills without ever leaving the app. In this world, finance is not a separate task – it is quietly embedded into everyday life.

In India, Paytm and PhonePe have become financial ecosystems, offering lending, insurance, mutual funds, gold investment, and utility payments to hundreds of millions. In Africa, platforms such as M-Pesa have grown beyond mobile money into savings, credit, and merchant solutions – often in areas where traditional banks had little reach. The model is simple: if you control the interface, you control the relationship. And once you own the relationship, you can layer on services, gather data, personalize offerings, and build stickiness that even large banks struggle to match.

This platform dynamic is not just technological – it is strategic. Banks historically organized themselves around products – deposits, loans, credit cards, mortgages. Platforms organize around needs – mobility, housing, communication, shopping. A user doesn't log onto Grab to apply for a loan; they do it to get somewhere. The loan is embedded in that experience. This shift – from product-centric to need-centric design – is the crux of the disruption.

In the US and UK, banks are starting to respond. Goldman Sachs' Marcus initiative and its Apple Card partnership reflect a move toward platform partnerships. JPMorgan has invested in numerous fintechs and built out API ecosystems. In the UK, HSBC Bank has explored open banking collaborations, and Lloyds has pushed forward with digital identity and data portability. But these are still adaptations. The real challenge lies in rethinking the core business logic: What does it mean to be a bank when your customers don't see "banking" as a separate activity?

The rise of platform finance also creates regulatory complexities. Superapps blur the lines between industries, jurisdictions, and accountabilities. Who regulates a platform that offers credit, stores value, delivers groceries, and enables messaging? What happens when a payments function is embedded within a social network prone to misinformation or data leaks? These questions are being debated actively in the US, EU, and across Asia – with no simple answers.

There is also the question of data dominance. Superapps and fintech platforms accumulate vast behavioural datasets. They know not just how much a user spends but when, where, why, and with whom. This allows for unprecedented personalization – but also raises issues around privacy, consent, and algorithmic bias. In 2023, regulators in India and Europe began cracking down on non-transparent credit scoring models and nudging platforms toward clearer consent architecture. But enforcement lags innovation.

From a competition standpoint, banks face a difficult choice: build, buy, or partner. Building platforms from scratch requires cultural transformation and tech fluency that many institutions lack. Buying fintechs can be expensive and politically sensitive. Partnering introduces new risks – reputational, operational, and strategic. Yet doing nothing is not an option. Customers now expect financial services to be instant, embedded, and intelligent.

The future of banking may lie in composable architecture – where banks provide regulated infrastructure, and platforms orchestrate the experience. In this model, banks are the "pipes" and platforms are the "interface". This is not necessarily a loss. If done well, it allows banks to focus on what they do best: risk management, regulatory compliance, and capital stewardship – while leaving experience innovation to more agile partners.

But this requires humility, interoperability, and trust. Banks must open up their APIs, rethink data ownership, and embrace modularity. In turn, platforms must respect financial integrity, customer protection, and long-term sustainability.

Some institutions are already starting to blur the boundaries. Take Revolut, for example – headquartered in the UK but serving customers around the world – it positions itself as both a fintech and a platform, offering everything from banking and crypto to travel insurance and trading. Stripe, while not a bank, handles billions in transactions and provides banking-as-a-service to platforms across the globe. In the US, Plaid connects users to hundreds of fintech apps through secure data aggregation. These companies are not just disrupting banking – they are reshaping the very infrastructure behind it.

For traditional banks, the lesson is not to panic but to search for clarity. Clarity about what value they offer, what role they want to play, and how they can participate in ecosystems without losing their identity. Not every bank must become a platform. But every bank must become platform-ready.

The era of linear competition is over. Banks are no longer competing just with each other – they are competing with ecosystems. The winners will not be those with the biggest balance sheets, but those with the clearest sense of purpose, the strongest partnerships, and the deepest user understanding. In the platform era, the bank that thrives will not be the one that shouts most loudly – but the one that listens best, integrates most deeply, and adapts most quickly.

7 New Frontiers in Financial Access

Financial access has long been treated as a static measure – a binary condition of having or not having a bank account. But in today's world, that view is no longer sufficient. Access is not only about availability; it is about meaningful participation. It is not just whether someone can open an account, but whether that account improves their life. It is not simply about onboarding users but about enabling them to transact, save, borrow, insure, and grow.

In many ways, financial access is the new infrastructure – as fundamental as roads, electricity, or clean water. And as it is the case for these services, its design and distribution are deeply unequal. As of 2024, more than 1.4 billion adults globally remain unbanked. The vast majority of them live in Africa, South Asia, and parts of Latin America. But even in advanced economies such as the UK and US, there are millions of people who are underbanked, excluded, or underserved – often due to credit invisibility, geographic isolation, or systemic bias.

What is changing, and changing quickly, is the boundary of what's possible. Technology, data, and policy are converging to push the boundaries of financial inclusion in unprecedented ways. From mobile-based credit scoring in Kenya to blockchain-enabled micro-insurance in Colombia, the 21st century is witnessing a reimagining of how financial systems reach out to the marginalized.

Mobile as the Gateway

The most dramatic transformation has come through the mobile phone. In countries such as India, Nigeria, and the Philippines, mobile penetration exceeds banking penetration by a wide margin. This disconnect has given rise to mobile-first financial ecosystems. Services like M-Pesa in Kenya, bKash in Bangladesh, and Paytm in India have enabled millions to send and receive money, pay bills, and even access loans – all through simple mobile interfaces.

In the UK, mobile-first banking has been instrumental in reaching younger populations, gig workers, and migrants who may find traditional banks inaccessible. Challenger banks such as Monzo, Starling, and Revolut have stripped away paperwork and branches, focusing instead on instant onboarding, intuitive interfaces, and real-time support. For someone arriving in London from abroad, being able to set up an account in minutes can mean the difference between participation and exclusion.

In the US, platforms such as Chime have addressed similar gaps – targeting those excluded from mainstream credit systems, such as people with thin credit files, low incomes, or irregular employment. Their features – early wage access, no overdraft fees, and fee-free ATMs – are more than conveniences. They represent a reconfiguration of financial dignity.

Beyond Banking: Ecosystems of Access

But access goes beyond banking. It includes the ability to store value, transact securely, build assets, and protect against risk. In this sense, ecosystems matter. In Latin America, platforms such as Nubank offer not just accounts but savings tools, personal finance education, and small business support. In Indonesia, GoPay (part of the Gojek ecosystem) embeds payments, credit, and insurance into a lifestyle app. These ecosystems reduce friction, lower cost, and create relevance.

Insurance is one of the most under-penetrated areas in the developing world-yet one of the most essential. Micro-insurance schemes, often delivered through mobile networks, are beginning to address this. For example, in Ghana, BIMA offers life and health insurance for as little as 2 USD per month, bundled with mobile airtime. These innovations do not just offer protection – they create a culture of planning, resilience, and forward-looking behaviour.

Credit is another frontier. Traditional credit systems have relied on backward-looking data: employment history, address stability, past repayment. But in many countries, such data is absent, inaccurate, or exclusionary. New models use alternative data – such as mobile top-ups, utility payments, geolocation, and even social network behaviour – to build credit profiles. In Kenya, Tala and Branch have provided micro-loans to millions using smartphone data. In Brazil, Creditas is experimenting with AI-driven risk models that factor in non-traditional indicators.

These new frontiers are not without challenges. Over-indebtedness, data privacy, and algorithmic bias are real concerns. In markets such as India, the unregulated growth of digital lending led to aggressive recovery practices, prompting regulatory crackdowns. Innovation must be matched with consumer protection, ethical design, and transparency.

Financial Access in Crisis and Conflict

One of the most compelling areas of innovation is in crisis response. Displaced populations – refugees, migrants, and internally displaced people – often lose access to their financial identities. Without documents, fixed address, or national IDs, they are rendered invisible to traditional banking. Technology is beginning to bridge this gap.

Blockchain-based identity solutions are enabling secure, portable, and verifiable IDs for people on the move. The World Food Program, for example, has used blockchain to deliver cash assistance to refugees in Jordan, without intermediaries or physical infrastructure. In Ukraine, digital wallets have been used to distribute emergency funds. These examples reflect a future where access is not just national – it is portable and programmable.

In the UK, the COVID-19 pandemic exposed the fragility of access. Elderly citizens, those without smartphones, and low-income households struggled with digital-only service delivery. Community banks, postal banking, and agent networks have since gained renewed attention as resilient complements to digital innovation.

Inclusion by Design, Not as an Afterthought

A key insight from all these innovations is that financial inclusion must be designed in from the start. Retrofitting access is expensive and ineffective. Whether it is the interface language, the size of transaction fees, the availability of customer support, or the structure of KYC – every design decision either includes or excludes.

This is where regulatory frameworks play a crucial role. In the UK, the FCA has promoted "financial lives" research to understand lived experiences of underserved customers. In the US, the Community Reinvestment Act (CRA) mandates that banks must serve all parts of the community, not just profitable ones. Globally, initiatives such as the Alliance for Financial Inclusion (AFI) are helping regulators share best practices and build inclusive policies.

But policy alone is not enough. Financial access must be part of the business strategy. It is not only part of Corporate Social Responsibility (CSR) – it is a market opportunity. The unbanked represent not just social need but economic potential. Financial institutions that ignore them do so at their own peril. As McKinsey has shown, closing the gender gap in financial inclusion could add trillions to global GDP.

Toward Financial Citizenship

Ultimately, financial access is about agency – the ability of individuals to make informed choices, pursue goals, and weather shocks. It is about becoming a financial citizen – not just a customer. This requires not only tools and products but education, dignity, and trust. The frontier, then, is not only technological or geographic. It is conceptual. It lies in rethinking what it means to be included. It lies in designing for complexity, context, and community. It lies in shifting from financial access to financial empowerment.

As banks navigate their digital transformation journeys, this must remain central. The future bank is not just efficient – it is inclusive. Not just profitable – but purposeful. And as we move toward a world where algorithms, apps, and APIs dominate the landscape, we must remember that the true measure of innovation is not how advanced our systems are – but how many people they genuinely serve.

8 Invisible Banking in a Connected World

In the early days of banking, every transaction was visible, deliberate, and deeply personal. Customers walked into branches, spoke with tellers, signed paper ledgers, and left with a tangible record. Trust was built through routine and face-to-face interaction. Today, that model has been completely flipped. In our hyper-connected world, banking is becoming almost invisible – woven into our devices, platforms, and habits so seamlessly that people often forget a bank is even involved.

But this shift toward invisibility is not about removing banks – it is about embedding them. It is about creating financial services that are ambient, automatic, and in tune with real-life needs. Modern consumers don't want to "do banking". They want to get things done – buy something, book a service, manage their money – and banking is just the infrastructure that makes it all possible. The smoother the experience, the better.

In the UK, this trend is playing out in real-time. Take Transport for London (TfL) – millions of commuters tap in and out of the underground using contactless debit cards or mobile wallets. No ticket purchase, no top-up, no banking app opened. The financial transaction is there, but it is almost imperceptible. Similarly, utilities, council taxes, and even charity donations can be set to auto-debit – quietly managed in the background of daily life.

In the US, Amazon's "Just Walk Out" stores take this further. Customers pick up items and leave – payments are processed automatically through pre-linked accounts. Apple Pay and Google Wallet allow frictionless in-store and online payments with biometric security. In both markets, banking is shifting from a noun to a verbless experience – something that happens for the customer, not by the customer.

The Role of APIs and Ecosystem Integration

This invisibility is possible through application programming interfaces. (APIs). APIs allow different platforms to speak to each other securely and in real-time. Open banking frameworks – pioneered in the UK and increasingly adopted across Europe and the US – have enabled third-party providers to plug directly into the banks' infrastructure, with customer consent. This means that budgeting apps, mortgage brokers, investment platforms, and e-commerce portals can now offer banking services without becoming banks themselves.

In the background, banking-as-a-service (BaaS) providers such as Solaris bank (Germany), Railsr (UK), and Synapse (US) are quietly powering these integrations. Their APIs allow fintechs, retailers, and even airlines to offer savings accounts, loans, and cards within their own ecosystems. The result: users interact with the brands they trust, while banks become the financial backbone, often invisible.

This architecture of invisibility is not just efficient – it is scalable. It allows banks to reach new customers, new markets, and new use cases without direct acquisition costs. It also changes the economics of banking: the unit cost of serving a customer falls, while the volume of interactions rises. For customers, the benefit is clarity – fewer logins, fewer decisions, and fewer delays.

Contextual and Predictive Finance

The next layer of invisibility is contextual finance. This is where the system anticipates needs and responds proactively. Imagine this: your rent is due in three days, your balance is running low, and your app nudges you with an offer to temporarily extend your overdraft – not as a penalty but as a courtesy. Or your wearable device notices increased physical activity and offers discounts on health insurance premiums. These scenarios are no longer theoretical. They are happening in leading-edge markets.

In Asia, Ant Group's Alipay is embedding insurance offers based on transaction behaviours. In Latin America, RappiPay (linked to Rappi's delivery platform) offers credit limits based on real-time income from gig work. In the UK, apps like Clearscore use credit history and behaviour to recommend pre-approved offers – often without the customer needing to apply in the traditional sense.

This invisible banking is also predictive. AI and machine learning models analyse streams of data – from transaction histories to location pings – to forecast needs and mitigate risk. If a customer shows signs of financial distress (missed bills, rising overdraft usage, reduced income), the system can offer support before a crisis hits. Done ethically, this becomes a form of digital empathy.

Trust in the Absence of Touchpoints

But invisibility poses a paradox: the less visible banking becomes, the harder it is to maintain trust. Traditionally, trust was built through eye contact, handshakes, and service rituals. In the digital age, trust must be engineered – through design, responsiveness, transparency, and security.

Customers need confidence that systems are working in their interest, not merely on their behalf. They need reassurance that data is safe, that permissions are clear, and that algorithms are fair. In the UK, the Consumer Duty regulations introduced by the FCA have emphasized this – requiring firms to demonstrate that outcomes are beneficial, comprehensible, and not misleading.

This invisible era also challenges brand identity. If customers never see your logo, enter your branch, or speak to your staff, how do you stay relevant? Some banks are responding by creating micro-moments – helpful nudges, alerts, or content that reinforces the brand's voice. Others are investing in emotional design – using tone, visuals, and gestures to convey warmth and personality, even in automated channels.

The Ethical Dimension of Invisibility

With great invisibility comes great responsibility. When banking decisions are automated, there's a risk of opacity. Why was a loan denied? How was a credit score adjusted? What data is being used, and by whom? These questions are essential – and increasingly being asked by regulators, academics, and advocacy groups.

In the US, the Consumer Financial Protection Bureau (CFPB) has scrutinized algorithmic lending for potential bias. In the EU, the AI Act includes provisions for transparency in high-risk systems – including those used in financial decision-making. Globally, there is growing recognition that algorithmic accountability must be embedded, not retrofitted.

Banks must embrace this proactively. Clear disclosures, explainable models, consent layers, and opt-outs are not barriers – they are trust enablers. The most successful invisible banking systems will be those that remain ethically visible – transparent about how they work, and why.

Human Touch in a Digital World

Finally, invisibility does not mean absence. The most sophisticated digital banks understand that customers still want human connection – especially in moments of uncertainty. This is why many leading fintechs are reintroducing live chat, video consultations, and hybrid models. The best systems let customers choose their level of engagement – from fully automated to fully personal.

Even in an invisible system, banks must show up when it matters – during fraud, bereavement, hardship, or life events. The future is not either/or. It is a spectrum of visibility, calibrated to customer needs.

In a connected world, banking must become something you feel, not something you do. It must be ambient, secure, intelligent, and compassionate. Invisible banking is not about hiding – it is about integrating. It is about creating a world where financial tools support people silently, faithfully, and always. And as banks redesign themselves for this new reality, they must remember: invisibility is not the absence of service – it is the ultimate form of trust.

9 Banking as a Public Good

Banking has always walked a fine line between two roles: part private enterprise, part public infrastructure. On the one hand, banks are commercial players – competing in markets, managing risk, and aiming to deliver returns for shareholders. On the other, they play a critical public role: safeguarding deposits, providing credit, facilitating payments, and helping to maintain economic stability. It is in times of crisis that this public role becomes most visible – and most essential.

In the 21st century, the balance between profit and public value is being redefined. In the aftermath of global shocks – from the 2008 financial crisis to the COVID-19 pandemic, from climate change to ongoing cost-of-living pressures – the question is no longer whether banks should serve society, but how they must serve it. The future of banking is not just about innovation or efficiency – it is about accountability, purpose, and responsibility.

The Moral Contract of Modern Banking

At its heart, banking relies on trust – not just between customer and institution but between institutions and the societies in which they operate. This trust is not earned by quarterly earnings reports but by consistently good behaviour. Do banks support small businesses in downturns? Do they serve rural and marginalized communities? Do they invest in extractive industries, or in renewable futures? These are not soft questions – they are structural.

In the UK, institutions like the Bank of England have long emphasized the role of financial stability as a public good. The Financial Services and Markets Act 2023 introduced specific mandates to promote financial inclusion and consumer protection. The British Business Bank – a state-owned development bank – exists to improve access to finance for SMEs across the UK, particularly in underserved regions.

In the US, the Community Reinvestment Act (CRA), first enacted in 1977, was designed to encourage banks to meet the credit needs of all segments of their communities, including low – and moderate – income neighbourhoods. Recent proposals aim to modernize the CRA for the digital age, ensuring that online-only banks are held to the same standards of community contribution.

These efforts reflect an emerging principle: banking is not neutral. Where banks choose to lend, invest, and operate shapes economies and societies. And therefore, how they define success must go beyond financial metrics.

Inclusion is an Obligation, Not an Option

For decades, financial inclusion was framed as charity or outreach – a peripheral effort, not a core responsibility. Today, that narrative is shifting. Inclusion is now seen as an economic imperative. Unbanked populations represent not only moral obligations but untapped markets. Serving them is not about doing good – it is about doing banking better.

Digital tools have made this possible. Biometric identification, mobile onboarding, and simplified KYC processes have lowered barriers. Governments are leveraging these tools for direct benefit transfers, pensions, and relief payments. In India, the Jan Dhan Yojana scheme brought over 400 million people into the banking system, linking accounts with mobile numbers and national IDs. In the UK, the Post Office plays a vital role in offering basic banking access to underserved populations.

The question for banks is not whether they can serve these groups, but whether they choose to. Do they invest in the infrastructure, partnerships, and customer support required to do so ethically and effectively?

Public-Private Synergy in Crisis Response

The COVID-19 pandemic revealed the indispensable role of banks in national crisis response. From processing furlough payments to disbursing emergency loans, banks became conduits of public policy. In the UK, the Bounce Back Loan Scheme (BBLS) and Corona virus Business Interruption Loan Scheme (CBILS) were channelled through commercial banks – who suddenly found themselves executing government priorities at a large scale.

In the US, the Paycheck Protection Program (PPP) similarly relied on banks to deliver emergency funding to small businesses. Yet both programs exposed disparities: smaller businesses, minority-owned firms, and low-income communities often faced longer delays, higher rejection rates, or limited access. The lesson: banks are essential infrastructure – but that infrastructure must be equitable.

Looking forward, governments and banks must design systems that are ready not only for profit cycles but for public shocks. This requires scenario planning, resilient digital infrastructure, and inclusive design. It also requires alignment of incentives – ensuring that public service is rewarded, not penalized, within financial models.

Climate, ESG, and the Purpose-Driven Bank

Perhaps the most profound expression of banking as a public good is in the domain of climate finance and ESG. Banks allocate capital. Where that capital flows – to fossil fuels or green infrastructure, to extractive industries or regenerative agriculture – determines the fate of the planet.

In the UK, leading banks have committed to net-zero targets, and the Bank of England has integrated climate risk into its regulatory framework. In the US, despite political contention, institutions like Blackrock and JPMorgan have increased their ESG disclosures and green financing commitments. Globally, the Glasgow Financial Alliance for Net Zero (GFANZ) now includes over 500 firms managing $130 trillion in assets.

Yet ambition must be matched with accountability. Green washing, inconsistent metrics, and voluntary standards cannot drive systemic change. Public trust will depend on real-world outcomes – lower emissions, improved resilience, and inclusive transition financing. Banks must view themselves as more than just sources of capital. They should see themselves as participants in the fight against climate change. This includes supporting businesses and communities in decarbonization, funding adaptation in vulnerable regions, and investing in the skills and jobs of the green economy.

Rethinking Profit, Value, and Measurement

To serve the public good, banks must rethink how they measure success. Profitability remains essential – but it must be balanced with other forms of value. What if we measured banks by their impact on small business formation, financial literacy, environmental resilience, or generational wealth transfer? This requires new metrics, new disclosures, and new mindsets. Integrated reporting – combining financial, environmental, social, and governance data – is gaining traction. So is stakeholder capitalism, which positions employees, communities, and ecosystems as central to business decisions.

Some institutions are going further. In New Zealand, Kiwibank operates with a public purpose mandate. In Canada, Vancity Credit Union incorporates social audits into its annual review. In the UK, Triodos Bank publishes a detailed impact report alongside its financial statements. These models are not fringe – they are prototypes of a future where banking is measured by what it enables.

Toward a Banking Charter for the 21st Century

To fully realize banking as a public good, we must move toward a shared charter – a new social contract between banks, governments, and citizens. This charter would affirm that:

- Financial access is a right, not a privilege.
- Profit must serve people, not displace them.

- Innovation must be inclusive by default.
- Risk must be shared, not shifted.
- Trust must be earned continuously.

Such a charter would not be imposed – it would be co-created. It would recognize diversity across models, regions, and institutions – but insist on common principles. It would position banks not as relics of the past but as architects of a sustainable, inclusive, and just future.

The next generation of banks will not be judged solely by their apps or branches but by their impact. They will be measured not just by the value they extract but by the value they deliver – to customers, communities, and the planet. Banking as a public good is not a political idea. It is a human one. It asks a simple question: What are banks for? And the answer, if we get it right, will echo for decades.

10 A Vision for the Century Ahead

The arc of financial history has always bent toward reinvention. From the invention of coinage and the rise of trade guilds to central banking and digital wallets, finance has adapted to meet the evolving needs of society. But rarely has a single century demanded as much transformation as the one we are entering now. The next hundred years will not be defined merely by technology or capital flows – but by the values we embed into our systems, and the futures we choose to finance.

To design the future of banking is not just to optimize services. It is to reimagine them. It is to ask: What should the financial system look like in 2125? Who will it serve? What will trust mean in a world of AI, climate volatility, demographic change, and post-national governance? These are not hypothetical questions – they are strategic imperatives.

The End of the Industrial Model

Most of today's banks still operate according to a logic born in the Industrial Age – built around fixed infrastructure, product silos, and risk containment. These models were not wrong; they were appropriate for their time. But they are increasingly unfit for an era defined by fluidity, decentralization, and networked systems.

In the century ahead, banking must become adaptive by design. Institutions will need to evolve as ecosystems – modular, open, and responsive. Organizational charts will be replaced by networks of capability. The most successful banks will be those that do not define themselves by size or tradition but by agility, relevance, and trust.

Intelligence, Not Just Information

We're entering an era where artificial intelligence will influence nearly every aspect of financial decision-making. AI will underwrite loans, optimize investment portfolios, detect fraud, and even model complex economic futures. But the real question is not what machines can do – it is what they should do. In this landscape, governance, ethics, and human oversight will become core responsibilities for banks.

In the UK, regulators are already piloting AI sandboxes to test models in controlled, secure environments. In the US, the White House's blueprint for an AI Bill of Rights outlines key principles like transparency, fairness, and accountability. Globally, banks will need to invest not just in powerful algorithms but in AI literacy, explainability, and meaningful user consent. The future bank will not be a tech company. It will be a wisdom institution – curating data, interpreting signals, and making decisions that balance precision with principle.

From Ownership to Stewardship

Traditional banking has been grounded in ownership – of capital, assets, and outcomes. But the emerging century will demand stewardship. Banks will not only manage funds – they will steward futures. They will be expected to take long-term responsibility for the social, environmental, and psychological consequences of their operations.

This is already visible in climate finance. Banks are under pressure to align lending with 1.5°C pathways, to decarbonize portfolios, and to support just transitions. But stewardship will go further. It will include biodiversity, mental health, intergenerational equity, and algorithmic safety. In this future, metrics will change. Return on equity will sit alongside return on ecosystem. Value at risk will include social volatility. And shareholder primacy will be reframed as stakeholder legitimacy.

Platforms of Trust, Not Just Providers of Credit

Trust will remain the cornerstone of banking – but it will take new forms. In an age of deep fakes, misinformation, and cyber-threats, banks will be called upon to act as digital fiduciaries. They will verify identity, protect privacy, mediate truth, and anchor belief.

This is not a hypothetical shift. Already, banks in the UK and EU are investing in digital identity infrastructure – enabling customers to access services securely across platforms. In the US, partnerships between banks and Big Tech are changing how authentication functions. In emerging markets, digital identity is often the first step toward economic participation. The banks that succeed will not be those with the loudest brands – but those with the deepest trust reserves.

Inclusion as a Systemic Mandate

The future will not be worth inheriting unless it is inclusive by default. The next hundred years will see unprecedented urbanization, ageing populations, climate displacement, and automation-driven job disruption. Financial systems must not only respond to these trends – they must pre-empt and shape them.

This means designing for cognitive diversity, for neurodivergence, for linguistic pluralism. It means ensuring that digital tools are accessible to the elderly, the undocumented, the remote, and the digitally hesitant. It means seeing inclusion not as a policy or initiative – but as a design philosophy.

In the UK, initiatives such as the Access to Cash Review, financial capability strategies, and community finance schemes offer models. In the US, fintechs targeting underbanked communities – such as MoCaFi, Daylight, or CapWay – are proving that inclusion is innovation. Globally, the new frontier is not just access – it is agency.

Rethinking Education, Memory, and Legacy

One of the quiet revolutions of the coming century will be in financial education. But education cannot be static – it must be embedded. Learning will happen through usage, through simulation, through intelligent interfaces. Banks will not just serve – they will teach.

Institutional memory will also evolve. As leadership transitions, regulatory frameworks shift, and data archives expand, banks will need to preserve knowledge systemically. This means investing in collective intelligence, knowledge graphs, and ethical storytelling. Most importantly, the future of banking will be measured by the legacies it leaves. Did it improve the resilience of a community? Did it finance a healthier planet? Did it build platforms of opportunity, not just extract value?

Designing a Future Worth Inheriting

The century ahead is not yet written. But one thing is clear: banks will not be spectators. They will be co-authors. They will shape the energy transition, the AI economy, the architecture of digital life. They will influence how cities evolve, how families build wealth, how democracies function. This is not about mission statements. It is about design choices – in products, policies, partnerships, and priorities. If we are to build a future worth inheriting, banks must be more than institutions. They must be moral engines. They must be places where power meets purpose, and where capital becomes capacity.

A century from now, no one will recall today's interest rates or marketing slogans – but what will be remembered are the systems we built, the futures we enabled, and the people we chose to serve. Let this be the century when banking did not just digitize but humanize – when banks became moral engines, where power met purpose, and where capital was transformed into capacity. Above all, let this be the century when banks fulfilled their highest calling: to be architects of possibility.

Strategic Framework Box: Chapter 1. The Changing Bank Framework: From Historical Institution to Dynamic System

Key Insight

The 21st-century bank is no longer a static institution built on vaults and branches. It is a living system – shaped by trust, technology, history, and public purpose. To understand where we must go, we must first confront what banking has been.

Strategic Takeaway

The future of banking requires more than digital transformation. It requires institutional imagination. We must move from preserving legacy to building legacy.

Dimension	*Legacy Paradigm*	*Future Paradigm*
Purpose	Custody, credit, and compliance	Inclusion, innovation, and regeneration
Architecture	Branch - based, siloed, paper - intensive	Digital, modular, real-time
Trust Model	Institutional authority	Distributed, transparent, earned
Customer Role	Passive consumer	Active co - creator
Regulatory Context	Reactive, static, national	Adaptive, real-time, cross - border
Societal Role	Enabler of capital markets	Enabler of dignity and resilience

This chapter proposes that banking must be seen as infrastructure – not in the traditional sense of capital allocation but as a foundation for human agency, economic mobility, and institutional continuity. The future bank must serve not only shareholders but also societies.

Bibliography

World Economic Forum (2018). *The Future of the Global Financial System: A Near-Term Outlook and Long-Term Scenarios*. Geneva: World Economic Forum.

2 The New Leadership

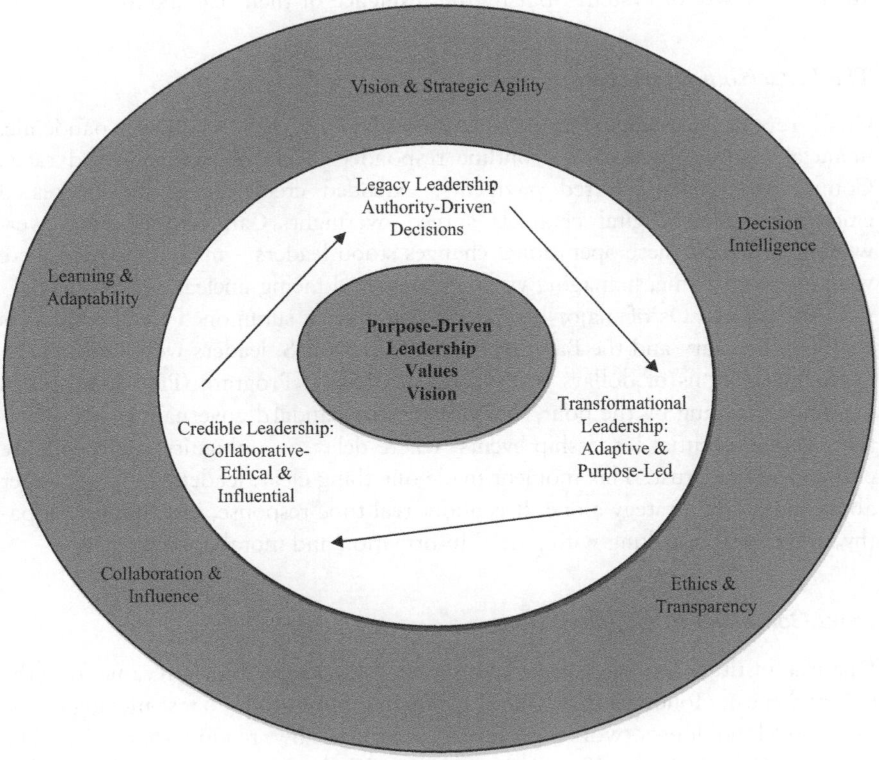

Figure 2.1 Leadership in financial institutions evolves from authority-driven to purpose-led, transformational leadership -built on agility, ethics, and societal impact.

DOI: 10.4324/9781003737544-2

1 Leadership in Crisis and Transition

In finance, leadership has always mattered – but lately, it is taken on a new sense of urgency. With crises coming faster and harder – from the 2008 financial crash to COVID-19, inflation spikes, geopolitical tensions, cyber threats, and climate change – for a bank today, good leadership is not only of strategic importance, but essential for survival.

In earlier decades, leadership often meant long-term planning, regulatory stewardship, and managing change through orderly processes. Today, it means absorbing shocks in real-time, communicating under pressure, and making systemic decisions amid uncertainty. This transition is not theoretical. It has reshaped boardrooms, forced retirements, created new C-suite roles, and exposed a core truth: that the financial institutions of tomorrow will be defined not by their size or systems, but by the resilience of their leadership.

The Leadership Stress Test

Crisis reveals character. During the early days of the COVID-19 pandemic, financial institutions became frontline responders. Central banks slashed rates. Commercial banks deferred payments, extended credit lines, and processed emergency relief. Digital channels surged overnight. Call centres were overwhelmed. Behind these operational changes stood leaders – many of whom were working from home, managing virtual teams, and facing unclear policy signals.

In the UK, CEOs of major high street banks were summoned for weekly calls with the Treasury and the Bank of England. In the US, leaders were tasked with deploying trillions of dollars in Paycheck Protection Program (PPP) loans, with guidance changing by the hour. These were not standard governance scenarios – they were existential leadership events, where delay or ambiguity could collapse entire chains of trust. This moment made one thing clear: leadership is no longer about long-term strategy alone. It is about real-time response, institutional empathy, and decision-making with partial information and moral consequence.

From Command to Collaboration

Financial institutions once relied on top-down leadership – direction came from the top, and culture followed the chain of command. But in today's fast-moving crises, that model no longer works. Complex decisions now require shared insights, because no single leader has all the answers. Modern leadership is about collaboration – working across departments, regions, and partners to get things done.

This shift has reshaped how financial leadership works. Crisis teams are now permanent fixtures. Boards are expected to engage in continuity planning. And roles such as like Chief Financial Officer, Chief Operating Officer, and Chief Risk Officer now work alongside the CEO as equal partners in navigating high-stakes moments. Even previously "soft" roles – such as Chief People Officer and Chief Sustainability Officer – are now central to business resilience. In practice, today's leaders have to juggle a lot: responding to regulators, managing culture, tracking economic signals, listening to customers, and keeping tech up to speed. The era of solo leadership is over. We're now in the era of networked leadership.

Adaptive Leadership in Action

Crises don't follow scripts. When Silicon Valley Bank collapsed in 2023 – driven by a digital-age bank run sparked by a single tweet – traditional crisis responses fell short. In only 48 hours, $42 billion was withdrawn. It wasn't just a failure of risk management – it was a failure to adapt quickly.

Now contrast that with banks that responded more effectively. In Singapore, DBS rolled out contactless onboarding and fast relief programs within days of pandemic-related government moves. In the UK, TSB rapidly revamped remote work and focused on supporting vulnerable customers. These responses weren't flawless – but they were fast, transparent, and aligned. Adaptive leaders don't wait for certainty. They move forward through ambiguity, guided by values, experience, and active listening. They communicate clearly, build trust, and bring in diverse perspectives.

Leadership Beyond the Crisis Moment

Often, the most dangerous part of a crisis is what comes after. Complacency, burnout, and finger-pointing can erode an institution from within. Strong leaders know recovery needs to be built into the response. They ask: What do we rebuild? What do we let go? And what did we learn?

Post-crisis leadership is not about reacting – it is about shaping what comes next. The best leaders focus first on rebuilding morale, knowing that trust can't be demanded; it must be earned through clarity, empathy, and presence. Instead of rushing ahead, they create time to reflect – turning lessons into new strategies without blame. They also plan for the next crisis, not just the last one. Resilient leaders treat disruption as a constant. They embed lessons into culture, align values with everyday actions, and prepare their teams for whatever's next.

Take COVID-19. Leaders who stayed curious, open, and engaged emerged stronger. Others, eager to "go back to normal", now face disengaged teams, damaged reputations, or regulatory pressure. Real leadership is not about performing under pressure. It is about creating the conditions for long-term resilience and growth.

The Human Side of Crises

In the middle of reports, metrics, and market reactions, it is easy to forget that leaders are human too. They face stress, fatigue, and personal disruption – just like everyone else. But they are still expected to stay calm, make tough decisions, and communicate constantly.

That's why mental health and emotional intelligence have become essential parts of leadership today. In the US, financial sector execs reported rising burnout and disengagement after 2021. In the UK, some banks have made executive coaching and resilience programs permanent – not just crisis responses. The strongest leaders are not those who pretend to be invincible. They show calm without denial, empathy without losing control, and confidence without ego. That's not weakness – it is what earns trust in uncertain times.

Preparing for What's Next

Crises are not going away. We're now facing overlapping disruptions – climate, finance, energy, geopolitics, AI – all shifting at once. The next challenge might come from anywhere: artificial intelligence, supply chains, or new regulations.

Leaders need more than one-time fixes – they need real, adaptive resilience. That means proactive scenario planning, cross-training teams in ethics, tech, and stakeholder engagement, and building diverse leadership across gender, background, and experience. Resilient leadership is a shared effort, not something that rests on one person. The banks that thrive will treat leadership development as part of risk management – not just as talent strategy.

Leadership today is not about predicting every crisis. It is about making sure your organization can survive, learn, and grow through whatever comes next. It is not about the title – it is about the responsibility. Not about personal style – but about building a system. Not about one leader – but about how the whole organization shows up under pressure.

2 The Shifting Nature of Authority

In the past, authority in banking was clear-cut. It came from job titles, boardrooms, and regulatory stamps – rooted in hierarchy, control, and status. But that model no longer fits today's fast-changing financial world. Now, authority is shifting – from positional to relational, from fixed to earned, from centralized to shared. This is not just a new leadership style – it is a complete redefinition of what it means to lead in an era of constant visibility and fluid power.

Banks can no longer rely on trust by default. Customers expect seamless, transparent experiences. Employees want purpose. Regulators move at digital speed. Authority today must be built – and rebuilt – through behaviour, culture, credibility, and alignment, not just titles or structure.

The Breakdown of Hierarchical Certainty

Historically, financial institutions were built on a model of command – and – control. Decision – making was linear. The CEO or managing director set the tone; the rest followed. This worked – for a time – because systems were slow, environments were stable, and the flow of information was predictable.

Several forces have chipped away at traditional leadership structures. Digital transformation has raised the bar – customers now expect 24/7 access, instant solutions, and personalized service, putting frontline teams in the spotlight over long chains of command. Hybrid work has also changed the game, making hierarchy less relevant and highlighting the need for trust, clarity, and coordination. Meanwhile, reputational risks have grown – in a world of social media, a single misstep or delay can go viral in seconds. And with generational shifts, younger employees don't automatically respect titles; they look for transparency, purpose, feedback, and real credibility. All of this is redefining leadership – today, authority is not granted by position, it is earned every day through competence, clarity, and integrity.

These forces are reshaping what effective leadership looks like. A senior executive may still have formal authority – but unless they demonstrate competence, listening, and ethical clarity, that authority will be undermined or ignored. In today's environment, respect must be lived, not demanded.

Distributed Leadership: Empowering Without Abdicating

One of today's biggest leadership challenges is learning to lead without controlling everything. Distributed leadership is not about dodging accountability – it is about enabling smart decisions at every level. In fast-paced environments, no one person has all the answers. This is especially true in banking, where risk, compliance, digital innovation, and ESG teams need to operate semi-independently, yet stay aligned. Leaders today are more like conductors than commanders.

We're already seeing this shift in action. Digital banking agents are empowered to solve issues without waiting for approval. Innovation teams are testing products in regulatory sandboxes, moving fast while staying compliant. During crises, cross-functional pods bring together experts from risk, tech, compliance, and customer service to respond quickly and effectively.

What all this shows is that modern leadership is not about micromanaging – it is about setting clear decision rights, smart escalation paths, and strong feedback loops. The focus moves from control to building culture, clarity, and trust. This shift requires trust, clear decision rights, robust escalation protocols, and continuous feedback. The leader's job is not to micromanage – but to set standards, create clarity, and build culture.

Authority Through Credibility, Not Control

In the 2020s, institutional authority is shaped by personal credibility. Stakeholders – whether customers, regulators, employees, or the public – ask not just: What role do you have? But: What have you done? What do you stand for? Can I trust your judgment? Credibility is earned through:

- Consistency – Does the leader's behaviour match their values and words?
- Competence – Do they understand the business, the risks, and the context?
- Courage – Will they make difficult decisions, admit error, and speak up?
- Connection – Are they accessible, empathetic, and real?

In the UK, this is increasingly visible through public accountability. Bank CEOs appear before Parliament. Senior executives are personally named in Financial Conduct Authority (FCA) enforcement cases. Boards are assessed not just on profitability but on how they handle fraud, inclusion, and digital literacy.

In the US, reputational risk has become a key driver of executive compensation and performance evaluation. Leaders are judged not only on financial return but on environmental, social, and governance outcomes. In both markets, the age of invisible leadership is over. Authority is now transparent, measurable, and interactive.

The Rise of Horizontal Influence

In today's financial institutions, many critical roles – such as heads of ESG, innovation, risk analytics, or digital ethics – don't come with direct authority. These leaders must drive change through trust, influence, and coalition-building, not command. This reflects a broader shift toward horizontal leadership – where authority is earned through expertise, integrity, and the ability to mobilize people across teams and silos.

For institutions, this shift brings real challenges. It means developing leaders not just for technical skill, but for their ability to persuade, align, and lead collaboratively. High-potential talent must learn to navigate competing priorities, listen actively, and frame ideas to build consensus – not just push decisions. Boards also need to evolve – recognizing and rewarding those who lead laterally, especially in fast-moving areas such as green finance, AI governance, and global regulation, where no single person or team has all the authority. In these spaces, progress depends on shared leadership and collective accountability.

Regulatory and Public Authority

Finance leadership now operates in a web of accountability – not just to shareholders but also to regulators, governments, customers, and communities. That brings complexity but also opportunity. Regulations such as the UK's Senior Managers and Certification Regime (SMCR) or the EU's Digital Operational Resilience Act (DORA) don't just demand institutional compliance – they assign personal responsibility. Executives need to understand not just the rules but their own direct obligations.

At the same time, public scrutiny is changing how authority works. With growing concerns around inequality and financial access, banks are increasingly viewed as public actors – whether they like it or not. Today, leadership needs moral legitimacy, not just a legal mandate.

To meet these expectations, banks must engage more openly with both regulators and the public. That means maintaining active dialogue with oversight bodies, not just checking compliance boxes. It also means clearly stating your values and living by them – embedding them into the organization's culture, and being ready to explain decisions publicly. As the line between financial leadership and social responsibility continues to blur, leaders must be able to hold both roles at once.

The Future of Financial Authority

The nature of authority in banking is changing – it is becoming more dynamic, more transparent, and more collaborative. Leadership is shifting in four key ways:

- From power over others to power with others
- From chasing status to committing to service
- From keeping a distance to encouraging dialogue
- From rigid formality to real authenticity

These are not surface-level changes – they demand a deep cultural shift in how leadership is practiced and understood. Titles will matter less. What will matter more are contribution, credibility, and consistency. Financial institutions that embrace this shift – and invest in leadership models that reflect it – will be better equipped for the systemic changes ahead.

In the modern bank, authority is not something you inherit or declare. It is something you earn – through your actions, your words, and how you show up every day. Leadership is not defined by where you sit on the org chart. It is defined by what others experience when you lead. This is the future: visible, accountable, empowered – and earned.

3 Leading With Values, Not Just Vision

For years, financial institutions were driven by vision – bold growth plans, strategic forecasts, and innovation goals. But today, vision is not enough. In a world facing inequality, climate crises, social division, and waning trust, leadership is now measured by values. It is not just about what leaders achieve but how – ethically, inclusively, and transparently.

Around the world – from the UK and US to emerging markets – leaders are under growing pressure to show not just what they believe, but what they stand for. In financial services, where trust is a public good and risk affects society at large, leading with values is not just the right thing to do – it is a strategic must.

The End of the Neutral Leader

Traditionally, bank leaders were expected to be neutral. They were to avoid politics and personal opinions while focusing on performance and compliance with regulations. Values were implied, not spoken. But this attitude is no longer tenable. Events such as the 2008 financial crisis, the racial justice movements of 2020, the war in Ukraine, and the growing urgency of climate change have shifted public expectations. Silence is now interpreted as complicity. Ethical ambiguity is seen as weakness. In this environment, the notion of the "value-neutral" leader is obsolete.

Around the world, financial leaders are facing growing public scrutiny – and staying silent is no longer an option. In the UK, banks are under pressure to align lending with net-zero goals, as customers push for climate-conscious portfolios and fossil fuel divestment. In the US, top executives are being called to Congress to answer tough questions on racial equity, ESG standards, and crypto ethics. Across Asia and Europe, leadership credibility now hinges on clear public commitments to gender equality, data privacy, and inclusion. Leadership has moved out of the boardroom – it is now about taking a visible stand on issues that matter.

Values as Operating Infrastructure

Leading with values is not about occasional public statements or glossy ESG reports. It is about how decisions are made, people are treated, and resources are allocated – every day.

For values to carry weight in banking, they must be embedded into the daily fabric of decision-making rather than relegated to aspirational statements. Values show their true power when they shape hiring and promotion policies, inform how credit is priced and risks are managed, and guide the design of algorithms and data use. They must also influence how institutions select suppliers and partners, as well as how they respond to misconduct or failure. In this sense, values are not cosmetic gestures or side issues but the operating infrastructure of a modern financial institution.

For example, when a bank decides to offer preferential rates to certified eco-friendly businesses, or to limit exposure to extractive industries, it is making a value-led commercial decision. When a fintech builds tools that explain credit decisions for customers with low digital literacy, it is demonstrating inclusion by design. These are not acts of charity. They are expressions of what the institution believes is right and necessary – embedded into core systems, not side issues.

Leadership Alignment: Personal and Institutional

One of the most powerful – and difficult – aspects of leading with values is the alignment between personal convictions and institutional commitments. Leaders who model courage, empathy, and integrity set the tone for the entire organization. But if the institution fails to reflect those same values in its incentives, culture, or behaviour, the result is cynicism.

True alignment between personal conviction and institutional commitment demands four kinds of discipline. It begins with clarity – being explicit about what the institution stands for and which values are non-negotiable. It requires consistency, ensuring those values are upheld not just in isolated teams or regions but across every level of the business. It also means facing consequences: when values are violated, even by senior people, accountability must be visible and uncompromising. Finally, alignment calls for honest communication – treating values as operating principles rather than public-relations language.

An example from the UK: One high street bank that champions inclusion recently declined to renew relationships with clients whose public conduct conflicted with the bank's stated values. This generated short-term controversy – but long-term credibility. Customers and employees took note. In contrast, when values are vague, leaders default to convenience. Ethics becomes selective. And the cost is reputational erosion.

Navigating Trade-offs and Tensions

Leading with values does not mean every decision is easy. It often means navigating real tensions – between profitability and ethics, innovation and inclusion, speed and oversight. Living by values also means confronting trade-offs. Should a bank launch a high-margin lending product if it risks deepening indebtedness among vulnerable customers? Should it continue in a high-risk but profitable market when governance or human rights concerns are unresolved? These are not abstract debates – they are daily leadership choices. In such moments, values serve as a compass rather than a script, guiding institutions to debate, surface, and resolve tensions in line with declared principles rather than chasing quarterly results.

In these scenarios, values act as a compass, not a script. The role of leadership is to ensure that the trade-offs are surfaced, debated, and resolved in line with declared principles – not just quarterly targets. It also means creating decision environments where diverse perspectives are welcomed. Value-driven leadership is not authoritarian. It is inclusive, deliberative, and morally grounded.

Embedding Values in Culture

Culture is where values either thrive – or fade. No executive speech can replace what people actually experience day to day. To truly embed values, institutions need more than slogans. It takes consistent, intentional action. That means hiring and promoting not just for performance but for integrity. It means recognizing ethical choices – even when the outcomes aren't ideal – and creating space for dissent, whistle blowing, and honest dialogue.

Leaders at all levels should be trained in ethical decision-making and bias awareness, so responsibility becomes part of everyday behaviour. And values shouldn't be limited to HR – they should guide how AI, data, and tech are governed too. Some US banks are now using "culture dashboards" that track metrics such as employee voice, ethics complaints, inclusion, and internal mobility – right alongside financial KPIs. The message is clear: culture isn't a side issue. It is a leadership responsibility.

The Business Case for Values

Sceptics may ask: Is this not too idealistic? Doesn't leading with values come at a commercial cost? The data suggests otherwise. Studies show that institutions with strong ethical cultures:

- Retain top talent longer
- Face fewer regulatory penalties
- Recover faster from crises
- Generate stronger brand loyalty
- Outperform peers in long-term profitability

Customers increasingly choose brands aligned with their beliefs. Employees seek meaning, not just pay. Investors track ESG performance as a proxy for resilience. Values are not soft. They are strategic assets.

A New Leadership Narrative

Leading with values is not about being morally perfect – it is about having moral clarity. It means being open about what you stand for, owning the gap between ideals and reality, and doing the work to close it. Most importantly, it is about building a culture where doing the right thing is expected and supported, not punished.

The future of finance won't be shaped by leaders who just repeat mission statements – but by those who live their values, even when it is hard. The old leadership model asked: Where are we going? The new one asks: Who are we becoming? In uncertain times, values are the anchor. They guide action when strategy stumbles, rally teams under pressure, and build lasting trust beyond the headlines. Leading with values is not a trend – it is the foundation of strong, credible, human-centred leadership in finance.

4 Institutional Trust and Personal Credibility

Trust is the lifeblood of finance. Without it, markets stall, customers pull back, and institutions fail. But trust is not fixed – it is earned and re-earned through every decision, crisis, and interaction. Today, trust is not just about the institution; it is tied directly to individual leaders. A leader's credibility and a bank's trustworthiness are inseparable.

In the 20th century, trust came from stability, brand, and size. A big, established bank felt reliable simply by existing. But that has changed. Now, trust depends on transparency, ethics, responsiveness, and authenticity – not just history or scale. This shift demands more from leaders. They must manage their institution's finances and embody its values, explain decisions clearly, and handle scrutiny personally. Strong leadership credibility boosts strategy; weak credibility can undermine even the best plans.

Why Institutional Trust is Fragile

The 2008 financial crisis shattered public trust worldwide, revealing systemic failures and a gap between executives and customers. Since then, banks have worked hard to rebuild trust through regulation, governance reforms, and cultural change.

Yet trust remains weak. Surveys in both the UK and US consistently show that while people rely on financial institutions, they do not fully believe in them. Many customers feel alienated, underserved, or misunderstood. Institutional statements about purpose or ESG are often met with scepticism. And even minor scandals – a data breach, a mis-sold product, a poorly handled complaint – can cascade into reputation damage. This is because trust is no longer abstract. It is deeply personal. And it is dynamically formed – shaped by social media, peer influence, and the 24/7 news cycle. Institutions are judged not by intentions, but by the lived experiences they create.

The Rise of Leadership as a Trust Builder

In this context, leaders must now act as trust architects. Their actions, tone, and visibility directly impact how the institution is perceived. This is true not only for CEOs but for board members, regional heads, and function leaders. Consider:

- A CEO's letter to customers during a crisis
- A senior executive's comments on inclusion or climate finance
- A board chair's statement following a misconduct investigation
- A CFO's explanation of risk exposure in an earnings call

Every public statement from a financial leader is not just communication – it is a leadership moment. It either builds trust or weakens it. Take 2023, when a major UK retail bank faced backlash over account closures tied to political views. The issue wasn't just the policy – it was the leadership's response. A lack of clarity, transparency, and personal accountability turned a policy decision into a full-blown trust crisis. The lesson? Institutional trust is now inseparable from personal credibility.

Trust Is Local, Global, and Layered

In large financial institutions, trust must be built on multiple fronts: Internally, it powers performance. Teams innovate and collaborate more when they trust their leaders. Fairness, humility, and consistency create the psychological safety needed for an ethical culture. Externally, trust is a license to operate. Regulators expect transparency. Customers stay loyal when they feel respected. Partners seek alignment in values – not just profit.

Globally, trust depends on context. In some regions, it is about compliance. In others, it is about empathy and service. Leaders must adapt without compromising core integrity. Credibility is not a script. It is how leaders show up – in real-time, across cultures and systems.

Five Levers of Personal Credibility

To build personal credibility – and by extension, institutional trust – leaders need five key elements:

1. Transparency: Be open about actions and decisions. When you don't communicate, doubt fills the gap.
2. Competence: Know your stuff – and explain it clearly. People trust leaders who handle complexity with confidence.
3. Consistency: Align actions with stated values. When words and behaviour match, trust grows.
4. Empathy: Listen and show you understand. In moments of uncertainty, empathy makes leadership human.
5. Responsibility: Own the outcomes, good or bad. Deflecting blame damages credibility. Owning mistakes builds respect.

Together, these form a trust equation that is greater than the sum of its parts. They create a leadership presence that people can rely on – not just when things go well, but especially when they do not.

The Dangers of Delegated Trust

One of the silent risks in large organizations is the delegation of trust – the belief that "someone else" is handling the institution's credibility. Sometimes it is the corporate affairs team. Sometimes it is compliance. Sometimes it is the brand.

But real trust can never be outsourced or delegated – it has to live at the very core of leadership. It must be embodied by leaders in the way they conduct themselves, modelled consistently in meetings, reflected in the decisions they make, and validated through the scrutiny of stakeholders. Trust, in this sense, is not a communications exercise but a lived reality.

When trust is treated as a messaging problem, rather than a leadership function, credibility gaps emerge. Customers sense dissonance. Employees disengage. Regulators raise concerns. Instead, trust must be owned at the top – and operationalized across the whole leadership ecosystem.

Institutional Trust in the Age of AI and Automation

As financial services become more digital, algorithmic, and opaque, new questions of trust emerge. Customers no longer simply ask: Do I trust the bank? They ask: Do I trust the systems behind the decisions? This introduces a new layer of leadership credibility. Senior leaders must be able to:

- Explain how credit scoring algorithms work
- Justify why certain data is used or not used

- Demonstrate that AI tools are fair, unbiased, and auditable
- Commit to governance that protects customer rights

In short, the move toward AI and automation does not reduce the need for trust – it amplifies it. Because when systems make decisions, it is leaders who remain accountable. In the US, several bank CEOs have recently spoken directly about their AI ethics frameworks – not as technical white papers but as leadership commitments. In the UK, regulators are beginning to assess algorithmic governance as part of institutional culture. This is the next frontier of credibility: Can your institution be trusted when no human is watching?

From Trust Repair to Trust Advantage

Trust is not just something to fix after a crisis – it is something leaders must actively build every day. When done right, trust becomes a real competitive edge.

A trusted bank holds onto customers, attracts mission-aligned talent, and works more smoothly with regulators. It can take risks, recover faster from setbacks, and move forward with confidence. Trust is not a soft concept – it is a strategic asset that fuels resilience, loyalty, and growth. Building trust is slow, often invisible work – until pressure hits. Then, it becomes a leader's most valuable currency.

In today's financial world, trust is not built top-down. It is built from the inside out – through the leaders' daily behaviour and credibility. This is not just about communication. It is a core leadership responsibility. Because when trust is broken, no strategy works. And when trust is strong – even uncertainty becomes manageable.

5 Learning from Global Leadership Failures

Leadership failure in finance is not usually about lack of skill – it is more often about blind spots, unchecked egos, cultural disconnects, or ethical missteps. When banks fall – whether through scandal, collapse, or reputational damage – it is usually because of leadership decisions, not just flawed strategy. To move forward, institutions need to face these failures honestly – and learn from them.

The Myth of the Lone Visionary

One of the most damaging myths in financial leadership is the "flawless visionary" CEO – the kind who centralizes decisions, shuts down dissent, and treats caution as disloyalty. It may sound bold in theory, but in practice, it is led to major failures. During the US subprime mortgage crisis, several high-profile collapses exposed what happens when leaders chase growth at any cost. Internal warnings were ignored, regulators were dismissed, and governance failed to provide guardrails. The result: disaster.

In the UK, aggressive sales strategies led to widespread mis-selling scandals – driven by short-term goals, weak board oversight, and leadership that didn't question systemic misconduct.

The lesson? Vision alone is not enough. Effective leadership also requires humility, ethical judgment, and the courage to welcome challenge. It is not about the one person at the top – it is about collective wisdom, accountability, and culture.

Failure to Adapt to Culture and Context

Leadership that's too rigid or compliance-driven can backfire – especially in agile, innovation-focused teams such as those in fintech. In relationship-based markets, overly centralized leadership can erode trust by sidelining local perspectives. And in cultures where empathy drives loyalty, a strict hierarchy can feel out of touch.

One global bank, known for operational strength, struggled in its Asia-Pacific business for exactly this reason. Senior leaders in London made decisions with little local input. Employee turnover rose, customer trust dropped, and eventually, the whole senior management team had to be restructured to restore local empowerment. The takeaway: leadership is not one-size-fits-all. To succeed globally, institutions need leaders who listen, learn, and adapt – not those who apply one single model everywhere.

Ethical Drift and Normalization of Deviance

Leadership failures often don't come from one big mistake but from a slow slide in standards – what behavioural scientists call the "normalization of deviance". Small lapses get accepted, justifications pile up, and systems look fine on the surface but are hollow underneath.

This happens when organizations set aggressive sales targets that encourage harmful behaviour or excuse exclusionary cultures for the sake of performance. Technical risks such as unresolved cybersecurity issues or growing tech debt go unaddressed. Worst of all, silence takes over – leaders don't speak up even when decisions clash with public commitments. These are not just technical problems – they are leadership failures where accountability gets lost and ethics take a back seat.

A clear example is the Wells Fargo scandal, where millions of unauthorized accounts were opened to hit unrealistic sales goals. Leaders ignored whistleblowers and red flags, and the culture drifted away from stated values. The fallout is still felt today. This shows why ethics must be baked into leadership, governance, and culture – not just pushed through regulations.

The Silence of the Boardroom

Leadership failures often happen because those who should speak up stay silent. Boards, responsible for oversight, can enable failure by being passive – accepting limited info, avoiding tough questions, or prioritizing loyalty over learning.

Post-crisis reviews in several transatlantic institutions revealed that some directors lacked the financial knowledge to challenge complex strategies. Others simply deferred to powerful CEOs. Conflicts of interest, poor diversity, and close social ties also hurt board independence.

Effective boards need to be curious, informed, independent, and brave. They should foster a culture where oversight is meaningful, and challenge is seen as a valuable contribution – not a confrontation. This is crucial in areas such as climate risk, cybersecurity, AI governance, and digital ethics – fields that demand both technical expertise and moral clarity.

The Risk of Short-Termism

Many leadership failures are caused by focusing too much on short-term wins – quarterly results, share prices, or personal bonuses – while ignoring the institution's long-term health. This shows up in poor succession planning, avoiding inclusive business models, or delaying climate expenditure to boost immediate profits. These moves might look good now but weaken resilience and risk reputational and regulatory damage later on.

Chasing quick growth can bring strong returns in the short term but often leads to brand damage, penalties, or strategic failure later. The fix? Leadership that thinks long-term – making decisions that may not pay off immediately but ensure the institution's future strength. Regulators in the UK and US are increasingly focused on how leaders handle long-term risks and sustainability, not just short-term capital efficiency.

Failure to Listen

Another common leadership failure is not listening deeply or often enough to employees, customers, and other stakeholders. Many crises start with ignored warnings – from staff alerts, customer complaints, or frontline insights – dismissed by insulated or overconfident leaders.

A European bank, for example, faced a major scandal after repeatedly ignoring anonymous staff reports about unethical sales practices. Action only came after public outrage – too late to prevent the damage.

On the other hand, institutions that build strong listening systems – safe reporting channels, customer feedback loops, and direct board engagement with employees – are better at spotting risks early and strengthening their culture. Listening is not passive. It is an active leadership skill that uncovers risks, drives inclusion, and builds trust.

From Case Studies to Cultural Learning

To turn leadership failures into growth, institutions need to treat them as ongoing learning opportunities – not just moments of blame. This means using failure reviews to redesign systems and embedding those lessons into training so that they become part of the organization's DNA. Encouraging honest stories from current and former leaders helps create a culture where vulnerability is strength. Most importantly, building a strong institutional memory prevents repeating mistakes and builds resilience.

The US military's after-action reviews offer a great model – financial institutions could adopt similar practices as a matter of routine, not just after a crisis. Normalizing learning from failure is key. If it is stigmatized, lessons are lost and history will repeat itself.

Toward a Culture of Humble Leadership

The real solution to leadership failure is not perfection – it is humility. Great leaders welcome dissent and challenge because diverse perspectives make decisions stronger. They admit when they don't have all the answers instead of hiding behind false confidence. True strength comes from sharing power and building collective ownership, rather than clinging to control. They commit to continuous learning, seeing every change as a chance to grow. Most importantly, humble leaders are driven by purpose, not ego – taking decisions that serve both their institutions and society. These are not just "soft skills" – they are essential survival skills for a sector constantly under scrutiny and evolving fast.

As financial institutions face AI, climate change, geopolitical shifts, and rising social demands, a measure of good leadership is how well we learn from these challenges. The best leaders are not those who avoid mistakes. They are the ones who own their fallibility, put ethical guardrails in place, and create systems where truth surfaces quickly. Failure can teach us – if we're willing to listen.

6 Adaptive Leaders in Financial Systems

In today's fast-changing, hyper-connected world, financial leadership is not just about technical know-how or straightforward planning anymore. It requires adaptability – the ability to navigate uncertainty, handle complexity, and lead with resilience through constant change. As regulations evolve, technologies advance, customer needs diversify, and geopolitical risks grow, old leadership models simply don't cut it. The leaders who succeed are the ones who can continuously make sense, respond, learn, and adjust on the fly.

Adaptability is not a "soft" skill – it's a vital strategic competence that banking institutions must deliberately cultivate. Throughout the UK, US, and worldwide, adaptive leadership is the new gold standard for navigating complexity without compromising values, performance, or accountability.

Adaptability has never been more critical. Today's leaders must contend with digital disruption and fierce fintech competition, in addition to rising climate-related financial risk and pressure to achieve ESG objectives. Geopolitical turbulence and economic uncertainty probe the strength of institutions, while changing regulations and cross-border compliance rewrite the rulebook. Clients demand transparency, velocity, and access, increasing the stakes for trust and service. And yet, path-breaking technologies – such as AI, quantum computing, and decentralized finance – are reshaping what leadership is required to deliver in the moment.

Each of these changes is difficult in and of itself. In combination, they are system-level challenges that cannot be addressed by one department or one leader alone. Old-style leadership – based on predicting, controlling, and command – is simply not designed for them. Adaptive leaders, on the other hand, function as orchestrators, learners, and connectors. They do not regard uncertainty as a threat, but rather as a new reality to adapt to.

Key Traits of Adaptive Leaders

Adaptive leadership is not merely about rapid response – it's about transforming with prudence. Effective adaptive leaders are good at sense-making through decoding signals from varied sources: market trends, employee input, customer feedback, and geopolitical movements. The constant sense-making assists them in constructing a real-time and qualitative picture of their context.

Equally vital is resilience under pressure. Adaptive leaders stay calm during crises, making thoughtful, timely decisions and guiding their organizations through setbacks with clarity and steady resolve. Ultimately, adaptive leaders are defined less by what they know and more by their ability to learn, unlearn, and continuously reframe challenges.

Case Study: Adaptability in Action

In 2020, when the COVID-19 pandemic led to worldwide lockdown, some UK banks needed to shift operations quickly:

- Entire call centres were shifted to home working within a few days.
- Digital channels were scaled to levels never seen before.
- Fresh lending programs (such as the UK government's CBILS) were rolled out in record time.
- Customer support lines were reconfigured to support vulnerable segments.

These answers were not driven by pre-written playbooks. They were facilitated by leaders who were able to coordinate emergent responses, reallocate resources, and learn in real-time.

In the US, adaptive leadership was seen in the reaction of certain institutions to the racial justice reckoning of 2020 – re-examining internal diversity pipelines, investment in community finance initiatives, and creating new governance positions for equity and inclusion. In each instance, flexibility was not merely a reaction. It was strategic positioning in the face of adversity.

Adaptive Systems Demand Adaptive Leaders

No leader is an island. Adaptive leadership requires supporting systems that encourage flexibility, decentralization, and intelligent risk-taking. This entails flattening hierarchies to speed up decisions and leveraging real-time data to react quickly. Rewards for performance must encourage learning and improvement, not merely rigid compliance. Leadership development must cherish curiosity, collaboration, and diverse input. Cross-functional and international assignments encouraged by leaders help them break silos, while "experimentation zones" provide protected environments for trying out new ideas. Without these enablers, even the most adaptive leaders are bogged down by bureaucracy and fear of failure.

The Role of Psychological Safety

Adaptive leadership flourishes when individuals are safe to share, challenge assumptions, and acknowledge uncertainty without risking penalty. Vulnerable leaders build space for teams to point out risk and propose innovative ideas.

Especially in fields such as AI and digital finance, rapid change can conceal danger. A low-ranking analyst who detects credential bias in algorithms or an out-front agent who recognizes patterns of fraud needs to feel empowered to flag a problem. This requires active listening, validating input, and accepting dissent as valuable – not disruptive.

Developing Adaptability in Leadership Development

Adaptability is not an innate quality – it's developed through focused leadership training. Leaders develop this ability by working in various markets, functions, and customer segments, which enhances their perspective and hones their flexibility. Methods such as scenario planning allow them to rehearse responses to unknown futures in risk-free environments. Peer learning promotes mutual reflection and development, while immediate feedback enables leaders to adapt and refine processes in real-time. Coaching and mentoring are also crucial in enhancing emotional intelligence and rapid decision-making, enabling leaders to remain effective under pressure.

Nowadays, some of Europe's and Asia's leading organizations are adding flexibility into leadership reviews. One of Singapore's top banks, for instance, doesn't just judge senior managers on performance but on their ability to manage complexity and change. This is evidence of a new wisdom: the way leaders deal with in ambiguity is now a key performance measurement.

Avoiding the Pitfalls of Adaptation

Flexibility is key – but it must be anchored. Not all pivots are wise, and not all experiments are moral. Adaptive leaders must remain watchful for these threats.

Organizations which promote true adaptation view failure as a learning experience, not the end of the road. They embrace uncertainty, resupply their minds frequently, and combine innovative problem-solving with robust collaboration. Diversity counts – disparate opinions inform better thought. Here, leadership is not about tight control; it's about giving space for new thinking and systems to originate at any point in the organization.

The greatest adaptive leaders find balance: they remain flexible without losing direction. They test but in defined parameters. And they lead with self-knowledge and a high sense of values.

Leading Adaptive Institutions

Adaptive leadership must ultimately move beyond the individual. It must be embedded in the way the institution perceives itself. An adaptive institution:

- Learns from failure
- Embraces uncertainty as strategic terrain
- Updates its mental models and strategy regularly
- Encourages lateral thinking and collaboration
- Infuses its adaptive responses with inclusivity

Leadership here is less about command and control, and more about laying the groundwork for the emergence of the best ideas, solutions, and systems anywhere in the organization. This frame of mind will be critical as banks navigate AI disruption, climate-related transition finance, geopolitically fragmented markets, and more.

In the age of complexity, fixed leadership is brittle. Adaptive leadership is not a style – it is a survival mechanism. It enables institutions to stay coherent amidst chaos, values-based in a rapidly changing world, and relevant in a world that will not wait for them. The future of finance won't be about people who have all the answers – but about those that know how to keep asking the right questions.

7 Governing Through Complexity

In the 21st century, leadership and governance are inseparable – and governance is no longer just a box to check. It is a strategic, moral, and public expression of institutional integrity. As financial systems grow more complex and interconnected, governance demands have changed fundamentally. Today's leaders must navigate ambiguity, uncertainty, and competing priorities without losing sight of core values or coherence. This is not just a technical update – it is a fundamental shift.

Traditional governance was designed for predictable, stable environments with clear cause and effect and centralized authority. Today, risk can come from anywhere – a cyberattack in Asia, a regulatory change in Brussels, a social media crisis in New York. Climate change, geopolitical tension, and AI failures all impact governance in real-time. In such a world, leaders need governance frameworks that are not only compliant but also intelligent, adaptable, and trustworthy.

Governance Beyond Compliance

For years, governance in banking was mostly about compliance – checking regulatory boxes, reviewing risks, and ensuring financial controls were in place. If the rules were followed, governance was considered solid. But that's no longer enough. In today's fast-changing world, governance must shift from passive oversight to active, forward-looking stewardship.

This means asking deeper questions: Are we just managing risk, or also aligning governance with a meaningful purpose? Are we reacting to challenges, or preparing for what's ahead? Are we including diverse, emerging voices in decision-making? And beyond control – do we have ethical clarity guiding our actions? Today, strong governance is not just about avoiding failure. It is about creating the conditions for resilient, ethical success.

The Complexity Challenge

Complexity in financial systems arises from four interrelated factors:

1. Pace of Change: Regulations, technology, and customer expectations evolve constantly, making it difficult to plan in multi-year cycles.
2. Interdependence: Financial services are entangled with tech, telecom, energy, and public policy. A decision in one domain can have cascading effects.
3. Stakeholder Diversity: Leaders must consider regulators, investors, employees, customers, communities, activists, and ecosystems – often with conflicting interests.
4. Data Overload and Algorithmic Risk: Decisions are now mediated by AI, automation, and predictive models – many of which are opaque or evolving.

In this environment, governing is no longer about finding the "right" answer. It is about creating processes that can navigate trade-offs, tensions, and transformation without losing legitimacy.

From Boards to Dynamic Governance

Traditional board structures – quarterly meetings, fixed committees, and siloed roles – are not built for today's complexity. Forward-thinking institutions are moving toward more dynamic governance models. They are using real-time dashboards for continuous oversight and faster decisions. Joint committees, like Risk and ESG or Audit and AI Ethics, are tackling cross-cutting issues. To avoid groupthink, many are forming external advisory boards, which bring fresh, critical perspectives. And instead of just aiming for compliance, they are using scenario-based rehearsals to build real preparedness for uncertainty.

In both the UK and US, some of the most adaptive financial institutions have embedded "complexity-aware governance" – combining traditional prudence with dynamic sensing. This does not mean abandoning structure. It means designing governance that can flex without fragmenting.

Ethical Governance in Ambiguous Terrain

Complexity doesn't lessen accountability – it raises it. In tough trade-offs, institutions need to act with ethical clarity. Ethical governance matters most in moments of uncertainty. Decisions like protecting privacy in digital banking, managing fossil fuel exposure during the climate transition, or setting limits on AI in credit scoring are not just technical – they require ethical judgment. Even choices around layoffs or restructuring in the face of automation are governance issues, not just management calls.

That's why governance must go beyond risk checks to include serious ethical reflection. This means involving ethics officers in strategic decisions, ensuring diverse voices are at the table, and clearly documenting the values behind tough calls. Just as important, these processes should be transparent – so stakeholders see not only what was decided, but how and why.

Governance as Culture, Not Just Structure

Transparency today is a governance tool – not just a PR tactic. Modern leadership understands that governance is not confined to the boardroom. It is woven into culture, decisions, and relationships across the entire organization.

In adaptive institutions, governance is everyone's responsibility. Middle managers help bridge strategy and daily operations. A strong risk culture supports smart decision-making and innovation. Employees are trained to spot and raise ethical concerns, and frontline staff feel empowered to flag risks – building integrity from the ground up. This distributed model relies on clear communication, accessible policies, and leaders who walk the talk. Because no matter how good governance looks on paper, it only works if people actually live it.

Digital Systems and Governance Accountability

The rise of AI, machine learning, and algorithmic platforms introduces profound governance challenges. Leaders must now govern systems they may not fully understand – but for which they remain publicly accountable.

Governing Algorithms and Automation

As finance leans more on algorithms, tough ethical and accountability questions emerge. If an algorithm unfairly denies someone a loan, who's responsible – the developers, the company, or the tech itself? Bias in automated systems is a real risk, and fixing it takes more than good intentions. It requires regular audits, transparent data practices, and continuous monitoring to ensure fairness.

Transparency with users is another concern. Many customers don't even realize they are interacting with virtual agents, which can affect trust and service quality. Beyond ticking compliance boxes, organizations need to ask: Do our data practices truly reflect our values?

Regulators in the UK and EU are already setting digital governance standards, with the US close behind. But leadership shouldn't wait for regulation. Institutions must proactively build governance frameworks that anticipate risks, explain decisions clearly, and prioritize fairness – especially in an increasingly automated world.

Organizations are taking steps to manage the ethical use of AI. One way is by creating AI and data ethics committees to guide responsible practices. Some are also including technical experts on their boards to help make better decisions around technology. Algorithms are being audited regularly, and impact assessments are published to show how these systems affect people. Leaders are also being trained in algorithmic accountability so they understand the risks and responsibilities involved. Governing through complexity means governing through systems, not just over them.

Multi-Jurisdictional Complexity

For global institutions, governance gets more complex as laws and norms vary across regions. A product that works in the US might raise privacy issues in the EU, require new licenses in Asia, or trigger political pushback in emerging markets.

Leadership must strike a balance – upholding global values while adapting to local rules. That means empowering regional teams to make context-specific decisions, staying current with policy shifts worldwide, and coordinating governance across jurisdictions in real-time.

One global bank in London manages this with a federated model: global ethics and risk standards, paired with local governance tailored to market needs. In short, governing across borders requires both consistency and flexibility.

Governing with Future Generations in Mind

The most challenging aspect of complexity is time. Financial institutions are often measured by short-term results – but governance decisions on climate, AI, infrastructure, and inclusion shape the long-term.

True leadership looks beyond today's shareholders to tomorrow's stakeholders. It means choosing resilience over short-term wins, investing in systems that reduce future risks, and building sustainable – not just profitable –

operations. In this way, governance becomes a legacy: not just what you permit now, but what you leave behind.

To govern through complexity doesn't mean controlling every outcome. It means leading with clarity, agility, and integrity – so the organization can face uncertainty without losing its values. In an age of AI, climate disruption, and social change, governance is leadership. And leadership is governance – made visible, intentional, and accountable.

8 The Inner Life of Financial Leaders

When we talk about leadership in banking, the focus is usually on strategy, governance, and shareholder returns. But behind every high-stakes boardroom decision is something more personal – the inner life of the leader. This includes their values, fears, habits of thought, emotional patterns, and ethical instincts – the often-unseen forces shaping how they lead.

In today's complex world, leadership can't be fully understood through résumés, KPIs, or performance reviews alone. We need to look deeper – at the inner structure that drives decision-making under pressure. And this is not a soft topic – it is a strategic one. The quality of leadership, especially in moments of crisis or ethical trade-offs, depends on what happens inside the leader before it shows up in policies.

Why the Inner Life Matters More Than Ever

Leadership is not just about delivering short-term results – it is about making decisions that hold up over time. That requires resilience, long-term thinking, and a commitment to sustainable practices. But the real challenge is not just external. It is psychological. Leaders without inner clarity often react impulsively, lose sight of their values, and erode trust.

Those with self-awareness and emotional discipline, on the other hand, stay grounded. They lead with integrity, empower others, stay calm under pressure, and learn from setbacks instead of deflecting blame. This kind of inner strength is critical – not just for CEOs but for anyone in high-stakes roles, from regulators to risk and innovation leaders.

Emotional Intelligence and Self-Regulation

At the heart of inner leadership is emotional intelligence – the ability to understand and manage emotions in yourself and others. For financial leaders, this is not a bonus skill – it is an essential one. Leaders with high emotional intelligence (EI) recognize their stress triggers, read emotional dynamics in meetings, face discomfort head-on, and foster empathy and open dialogue. They empower others instead of dominating them.

Without EI, leadership becomes brittle. Dissent gets shut down, conflict escalates, anxiety hides behind control, and toxic cultures take root – bringing real reputational risk. That's why institutions in the UK and US are increasingly integrating EI into executive development programs. Because technical skills without self-awareness are not just incomplete – they're a liability.

Stress, Burnout, and the Cost of Performance

One of the most overlooked risks in financial leadership is chronic stress and burnout. The constant pressure to perform, stay visible, and navigate change takes a real toll - on well-being, decision-making, and ethics. Burnout is not just a personal health issue - it is a systemic risk.

Under pressure, even experienced leaders can lose empathy, clarity, and judgment. They may become reactive, disengage from collaboration, or detach from the organization's values. In some cases, they compromise ethical standards just to keep pace. When leaders burn out, institutions lose more than productivity - they lose trust.

Cognitive Bias and Reflective Practice

Financial leaders rarely have perfect information. Decisions often rely on judgment – shaped by biases and mental shortcuts. Common traps include confirmation bias (seeking info that supports existing beliefs), overconfidence (underestimating risk), status quo bias (resisting change), and groupthink (valuing harmony over challenge).

The antidote? reflective practice. This includes habits such as journaling, coaching, peer learning circles, or "pre-mortems" that explore what could go wrong before decisions are finalized. Ironically, these practices are often dropped when the pressure is high – exactly when they are most critical.

Moral Clarity and Ethical Grounding

Some of the hardest decisions in finance aren't about what's legal – they are about what's right. Should a profitable product be pulled if it risks harming consumers? Is it okay to delay ESG reporting for convenience? How do you define fairness in AI-driven lending? These are not just compliance questions – they require moral clarity.

Ethical leadership is about having the courage to do the right thing, especially when no one's watching. That clarity often comes from a leader's inner life: shaped by personal values, role models, exposure to diverse perspectives, and grounding practices such as reflection, faith, or philosophy. Without this inner compass, even high-performing leaders can falter when the stakes are high. Banks that overlook this inner dimension may find that their leaders succeed – until the moment they don't. In both London and New York, a growing number of financial organizations are rethinking the pace and pressure of leadership – not out of altruism but to ensure long-term coherence.

The Role of the Inner Life in Crisis Leadership

Crises are the ultimate test of leadership. In moments of reputational threat, system failure, or public outrage, the inner life of the leader becomes visible to all. Those who panic, blame, or deny erode trust. Those who speak with composure, admit uncertainty, and act ethically inspire confidence-even amidst chaos.

Crisis leadership is not a script. It is an expression of preparation, discipline, and self-awareness. Leaders who have cultivated their inner lives are less likely to be hijacked by ego or fear. They act with maturity, empathy, and strategic calm. This was evident during the early weeks of the COVID-19 pandemic, when some financial leaders demonstrated remarkable composure and community responsiveness – while others faltered under pressure.

Institutions that Support the Leaders' Inner Lives

Finally, leaders can't do this work alone. Organizations need to build environments that support the inner lives of their leaders. This means encouraging reflection and ethical conversations at every level, creating space for vulnerability and learning within senior teams, rethinking what leadership development really means, and valuing character and consistency just as much as charisma or credentials.

One UK bank now includes "reflective agility" as a criterion in its leadership reviews. A North American investment firm offers mindfulness and resilience training for its entire executive bench. These are not fringe examples – they are signals of where leadership is going. The outer success of an institution is shaped by the inner clarity of its leaders.

In a future where complexity is constant and expectations are high, financial leadership must be grounded in more than intelligence, ambition, or expertise. It must be grounded in character. And character begins on the inside.

9 Cultivating the Next Generation

Succession leadership is no longer a behind-the-scenes, low-key undertaking. Creating the next generation of leaders is now an open responsibility, a strategic imperative, and a moral obligation. As experienced leaders retire or transition, financial institutions need to invest proactively in bringing forward successors – not only to preserve the status quo but to lead in a significantly altered world.

This new generation is confronted with a complicated, digital, global, and ethically challenging world. Equipping them is more than imparting skills – it's transferring vision, courage, and the capacity to create substantial change.

In the past, banks promoted people based on length of service, allegiance, and technical expertise, advancing them along a clear-cut ladder from analyst to executive. Training primarily emphasized operations and regulations, and there was little attention paid to diversity or innovative thinking.

But the velocity of change has overtaken that model. Experience alone will no longer be sufficient. Leaders today require cross-disciplinary competencies and systems thinking to manage complexity, in addition to a strong commitment to inclusion – fuelled by customer, regulator, and societal imperatives. To address finance, technology, climate, and ethics challenges, institutions need to rethink how they spot, develop, and groom their next leaders.

Characteristics of the Emerging Financial Leader

Tomorrow's finance leaders will not be younger editions of today's – they'll have new mindsets forged by having grown up in a digitally native world where tech comes instinctively. They'll have broader views and greater exposure to diverse cultures and perspectives through their global experiences. Strong social and environmental focus will make them more conscious of the broader implications of their actions.

They'll tend to challenge rigid hierarchies, favouring flatter, more collaborative structures. Comfortable with ambiguity, they'll embrace iterative processes and actively seek input from diverse sources. Effective emerging leaders are great at systems thinking, looking outside silos to see the broader picture. They influence and connect through networks rather than give directions top-down. Inspired by purpose, they pursue roles that matter to them, embedded in their values. They are also highly agile learners, quickly adapting to rapidly changing situations.

Most importantly, they act with moral purpose – seeking not only profit but justice and enduring results. Identifying and fostering these qualities early on is essential in developing solid leaders for the future.

Rethinking Leadership Development

Leadership development can no longer be a disconnected function provided late in life. It needs to start sooner, go deeper, and look more like the world of today. Below a few strategies to develop leadership:

- Rotate high-potential staff across various regions, products, and functions – such as ESG, technology, risk, and community finance
- Match older leaders with younger staff to familiarize both with intergenerational and digital fluency deficits
- Apply real-time problem-solving situations (such as handling a cybersecurity incident or media emergency) to develop decision-resilience
- Let emerging leaders have strategic conversations with executives to bring in new perspectives while ensuring accountability and visibility
- Instil life-long learning with short courses in ethics, digital transformation, AI governance, and behavioural finance
- Have future leaders work on sustainability, DEI (Diversity, Equity, Inclusion), and public engagement initiatives to expand their vision

UK-based institutions such as Lloyds Banking Group and Nationwide have started to pilot such models. In the US, companies such as Blackrock and JPMorgan are incorporating environmental leadership modules and ethical dilemma case studies into management training.

The Value of Inclusion in Developing Leaders

Leadership cannot emanate from a homogeneous group. In order to be representative of society, institutions need to actively create diverse pipelines – differing by gender, race, socioeconomic status, and experience.

This involves hiring outside the conventional elite schools and appreciating diverse career routes, including returners and career changers. Organizations need to establish transparent sponsorship schemes to aid underrepresented groups and address bias in promotions and appraisals. Most importantly, diversity work must be monitored not only at recruitment but across all leadership tiers to secure long-term momentum.

Representation is not sufficient. Inclusive spaces must be built where diverse leaders can succeed – with visibility, influence, and support. Developing the next generation is not merely about ability. It's about legitimacy and credibility.

Intergenerational Leadership Dynamics

One of the less obvious leadership succession challenges is intergenerational transition management. Older leaders might find the younger generation impatient or undisciplined. Younger leaders might find their seniors risk-averse or disconnected. This is a chasm to be crossed, not through paternalism, but through mutual learning. Effective institutions foster:

- Intergenerational dialogue-forums where stories and strategies are shared
- Shared models of leadership – temporary co-leadership of projects or committees
- Respect for values – with openness to evolution, not rigidity

When these bridges are intentionally constructed, the leadership culture is being enriched instead of divided.

Cultivating Ethical Courage

Tomorrow's leaders will face complex dilemmas with no clear playbook, requiring judgment beyond traditional rules. They will need to decide tough questions – such as whether to pause AI systems that improve performance but harm fairness, or whether to avoid profitable clients who pose serious ESG risks.

In a globally turbulent world characterized by political instability and social turmoil, they will also need to reconcile their fiduciary responsibilities with their larger social responsibility: the influence their institutions have on society.

Ethical courage will be needed to meet these challenges honourably. These are not problems to be solved with spreadsheets. They are ethical dilemmas. Shaping the next generation must involve ethical courage: the strength to act with discernment when rules are uncertain and the pressure is intense.

This type of ethical leadership may be developed by embedding ethics across all leadership courses – not as a separate module, but as an ongoing filter through which choices are considered. It also entails creating open spaces where ethical argument and opposition are encouraged, helping developing leaders to reflect on genuine moral dilemmas. Organizations need to move beyond rewarding results and start honouring decisions taken with integrity, even if they come at a price. Lastly, showcasing leaders who set an example of acting in line with principles and taking risks provides compelling examples of how to combine ethical conviction and bold action. In conclusion, we need to raise a generation not just of capable leaders, but of good ones.

The Role of Technology in Leadership Development

Technology is now an ally in leadership development. AI, machine learning, and behavioural analytics are more commonly applied to recognize core characteristics and trends among emerging talent. This allows organizations to understand their workforce more clearly. The insights are used to personalize the learning pathways to a greater degree, based on individual needs and interests. Behavioural analytics also allow for tracking developmental milestones, giving continuous visibility of progress. By examining dynamic data sets, organizations can also predict leadership potential better, enabling more effective talent decisions.

This presents opportunities; however, it must be handled with care. Technology should support human judgment – not be a substitute for it. Leadership is more a matter of presence, emotion, and relationships than of data. Digital tools should enable a human-centred leadership journey.

Beyond the Institution: Leadership for Society

Financial leadership no longer exists in a vacuum. The next generation needs to be trained to lead in society, not merely within banks. This involves being an active participant in public policy discussions to impact and direct regulatory systems. It also entails interaction with civil society organizations and community-based finance models to sustain inclusive economic growth. Clear communication with the public and media is fundamental to establish trust and accountability. Leaders also need to bridge commercial goals with wider national or global aspirations, and align business strategies with social and environmental goals.

In both the US and the UK, next-generation leaders are more driven by mission – looking for roles in which to combine personal and professional values.

Institutions that support this aspiration will attract, retain, and raise the best of the next generation

10 Leadership for a Changing World

The world that banks and financial institutions must navigate today is unlike the world in any previous era. The assumptions that underpinned traditional leadership models – stability, predictability, control – have all been eroded. We now face a world that is volatile, interconnected, morally contested, and technologically disruptive. This demands not an evolution in leadership, but a reimagination of it.

Financial leadership is no longer confined to profit, regulation, and organizational loyalty. It must encompass societal context, planetary boundaries, and generational stewardship. The leaders of tomorrow must be system thinkers, ethical anchors, adaptive stewards, and humble learners. In short, they must be designed for a world in flux. This final section of Chapter 2 is not a conclusion. It is an invitation – to lead not only with skill, but with vision and conscience.

The Collapse of Linear Leadership

Leadership in traditional banking used to follow a straightforward path: climb the ladder, learn the rules, deliver results, inherit authority, and retire with a solid reputation. This model assumed that the environment was stable, that the future looked like the past, and that leadership was primarily about execution and control.

But that old model doesn't work anymore. Today's financial world is shaped by accelerating climate risks, widespread digitization and AI disruption, a decline in trust toward institutions, changing public expectations, and growing polarization and geopolitical uncertainty. Leaders who attempt to manage the future using yesterday's paradigms risk irrelevance – or worse, collapse. What is needed now is non-linear, generative, purpose-led leadership that grows not from authority but from authenticity and alignment.

Defining Leadership for This Moment

What kind of leadership can hold space for ambiguity while advancing clarity? The following capacities are emerging as essential:

- Narrative Intelligence: The ability to frame meaning in chaos and to help institutions and societies make sense of uncertainty
- Moral Imagination: The courage to act ethically beyond compliance, envisioning what justice and inclusion could look like in emerging systems
- Systems Thinking: Understanding that risks and opportunities span across borders, disciplines, and generations

- Emotional Roundedness: The capacity to remain composed, empathetic, and humble in moments of volatility and critique
- Distributed Empowerment: Moving from command-and-control to platforms of shared ownership, where leadership is practiced across the institution

These are not optional extras. They are the backbone of legitimacy and relevance in a changing world.

Leadership Across Generations and Geographies

As financial institutions globalize, leadership must become multicultural, multigenerational, and multilingual – not just in language but in values. A CEO in London must understand digital payment cultures in Lagos, regulatory debates in Brussels, and political shifts in Washington. A rising leader in Mumbai must navigate cross-border ESG standards, AI ethics in global credit scoring, and financial inclusion metrics shaped by Latin America and Southeast Asia.

Global leadership calls for curiosity about different cultures, respect for local context and history, humility in making decisions, and the ability to truly listen – not just speak. Likewise, cross-generational leadership requires leaders to engage deeply with the concerns of younger generations – around sustainability, fairness, voice, and long-term stewardship. If leadership is not intergenerational and international, it risks becoming obsolete.

From Heroic to Humble Leadership

The myth of the lone, charismatic leader who "saves" the institution is fading. In its place, a more grounded model is taking shape: the humble, principled, collective leader. This is not a passive posture. Humility in leadership means knowing what you don't know, creating space for dissent, admitting mistakes openly, sharing success while welcoming scrutiny, and leading by example – not by ego.

Humble leadership is especially powerful in high-stakes environments. It builds trust faster, defuses polarization, and fosters psychological safety – a key ingredient for innovation and adaptive performance. Financial institutions that elevate humble leadership create cultures of collective intelligence, not personality cults.

Building Leadership at Every Level

One of the greatest shifts underway is the democratization of leadership. Leadership in a changing world is not confined to boardrooms or executive committees. It is enacted in branches, contact centres, product teams, data science labs, and community partnerships. Everyone has a role to play in building trust, solving problems, and representing institutional values.

This means training frontline staff in ethical decision-making, empowering product managers to question exclusionary features, valuing operational insight just as much as strategic planning, and recognizing that every employee plays a role in protecting the organization's reputation. The future of leadership is distributed – not diluted.

Resilience as a Leadership Mandate

A changing world also means greater exposure to shocks: pandemics, cyber-attacks, regulatory ruptures, AI system failures, political unrest. Resilience is no longer just a technical function – it is a leadership imperative. Leaders must ask:

- Can our systems recover quickly and fairly from failure?
- Are we prepared for unknown risks, not just known ones?
- Do we have adaptive governance, not just compliant structures?

Resilience must be built not only into systems, but into cultures, relationships, and leadership mindsets. It is not just about bouncing back. It is about bouncing forward – learning, growing, and reimagining better systems through crisis.

Rebalancing Power and Responsibility

With leadership comes power. But in the 21st century, leadership power must be held differently – with transparency, with accountability, and with purpose. Financial leaders must find a new balance – between power and service, authority and listening, growth and responsibility, and autonomy and regulation.

This new contract of leadership asks not just: What can we do? but: What should we do? – not just: How can we win? but How can we serve? Ethical leadership is not just an idea. It forms a strong base for lasting institutions.

The Legacy Question

Ultimately, every leader must ask: What am I leaving behind? What kind of institution, culture, or precedent will I pass on to those who follow? In a changing world, legacy is not measured by status, exits, or personal brands. It is measured by the systems a leader helps to strengthen, by the people they enable to grow, by the values they protect under pressure, and by the risks they face with courage. It is also reflected in the integrity they model, even when invisible to others.

This is what will define leadership in the decades ahead. The future does not demand perfect leaders – it demands present, principled, and prepared ones. It calls for individuals and teams who are willing to hold uncertainty, build trust, and move with courage. Leadership for a changing world is not forged in isolation. It is built in relationships, in questioning, in reflection, and in action. Let us raise a new generation of financial leaders – not just to adapt to the world, but to help shape a better one.

Strategic Framework Box: Chapter 2. The Leadership Shift: From Command to Credibility in Financial Systems

Key Insight

Leadership in the financial sector is no longer defined by titles or control. It is defined by trustworthiness, adaptability, and the ability to govern complexity with moral clarity. The next generation of financial leaders must build institutions that inspire confidence, not compliance.

Strategic Takeaway

Future-ready leadership in banking must balance institutional gravity with emotional intelligence. The bank of tomorrow will be shaped not by the most powerful executive, but by the most trustworthy one.

Leadership Axis	*Traditional Model*	*Transformational Model*
Authority Base	Formal hierarchy	Values-driven legitimacy
Response to Crisis	Procedural enforcement	Ethical accountability
Decision-Making	Risk-averse and siloed	Adaptive, consultative, transparent
Public Engagement	Minimal, cautious	Visible, credible, mission-led
Cultural Role	Enforcer of performance	Cultivator of character and inclusion
Time Horizon	Quarterly targets	Generational stewardship

This chapter argues that the role of a financial leader has shifted from being a gatekeeper to being a guide. In an age of digital complexity and institutional fatigue, leadership must emerge not from charisma, but from coherence – the alignment of action, vision, and values.

Bibliography

Kotter, J. P. (2012). *Leading Change*. Harvard Business Review Press.

3 The Everyday Bank

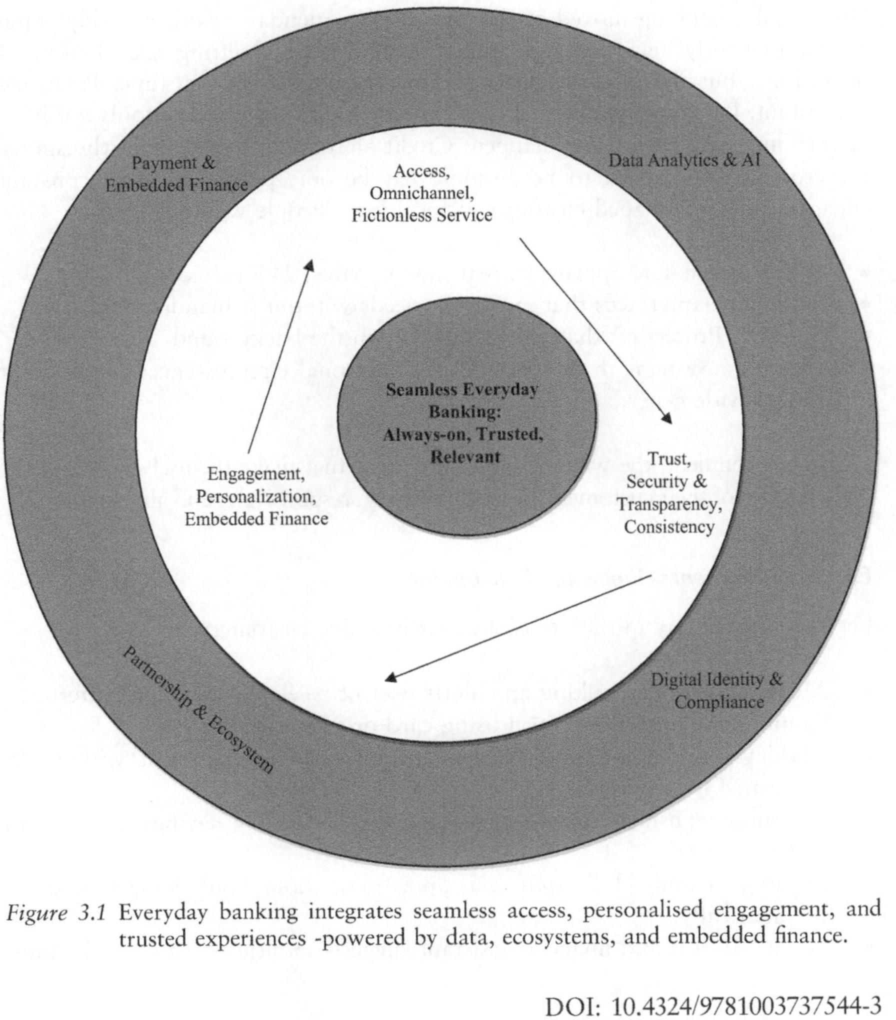

Figure 3.1 Everyday banking integrates seamless access, personalised engagement, and trusted experiences -powered by data, ecosystems, and embedded finance.

DOI: 10.4324/9781003737544-3

1 The Bank in Everyday Life

Banking used to be an occasional task – opening an account, applying for a loan, or updating a passbook at the branch. It was transactional and infrequent. But in today's digital world, that has completely changed.

Now, banking is part of daily life. Whether it is shopping online, commuting, splitting bills, or subscribing to services, people interact with banks constantly – often without even realizing it. Banks are no longer just places we visit; they are a part of how we live.

This shift is changing not just how banks function, but how they're viewed. In a fast-paced world with high expectations, banks need to be seamlessly integrated into everyday life – relevant, invisible, and essential all at once.

From Occasional Interactions to Constant Engagement

Historically, banking moved at the pace of the calendar – with monthly statements, quarterly reviews, and annual loan renewals setting the rhythm of operations. But the modern customer journey unfolds in real-time. Payments are instant. Balances are checked multiple times a day. Budgeting tools notify us of spending patterns as they happen. Credit alerts ping the moment thresholds are crossed. What used to be periodic has become persistent. This constant engagement has reshaped customer expectations. People want:

- Speed: Immediate approvals, real-time updates, 24/7 service
- Simplicity: Interfaces that anticipate needs without demanding effort
- Security: Protection that works invisibly in the background
- Empathy: Systems that reflect people's personal circumstances – and don't just provide generic offers

In this environment, the winning banks are those that make themselves part of the daily rhythm of their customers' lives – intuitively, responsively, and almost invisibly.

Everyday Moments, Financial Touchpoints

Let's consider a day in the life of a digitally active customer:

- Morning: Mobile banking app alerts user of weekend spending pattern.
- Commute: Contactless travel using card or phone wallet.
- Midday: Online shopping triggers instant one-click payment with bank-integrated loyalty rewards.
- Afternoon: Push notification recommends optimising savings account for better interest.
- Evening: Family bill split via app; joint household budget updated automatically.
- Night: AI-powered financial assistant suggests monthly cash flow planning.

Each of these touchpoints reflects a micro-interaction with the banking system. None of them resemble the traditional notion of "going to the bank". Yet all of them deepen the bank's role in the user's everyday life. Banks that see these micro-moments as key opportunities become relevant not by force, but by being present.

The Shift from Product to Presence

In the old model, banks sold products: savings accounts, mortgages, insurance, and loans. Marketing was geared around pushing these offerings at points of perceived need. But in the new paradigm, banking must be present before the need arises. It must understand behaviour, anticipate transitions, and offer contextual value – all without being seen as overwhelming or intruding.

This shift calls for a change in mindset – from campaigns to ongoing conversations, from selling to sensing needs, from product launches to designing customer journeys, and from one-off touchpoints to delivering continuous value. The modern customer does not ask: Which bank has the best savings account? They ask: Which banking app understands my spending habits, helps me plan, and lets me live my life more easily?

Banking in a Multichannel, Multimodal World

Today's customers move fluidly between apps, devices, and ways of interacting. This creates both challenges and opportunities for banks. Modern banking needs to be mobile-first – but not mobile-only. Banks should work seamlessly across platforms such as superapps, fintech APIs, and messaging apps. Voice functionality is increasingly important too, allowing users to ask quick questions or make transactions naturally. And across every channel – whether it is an app, website, branch, or chatbot – the experience should feel consistent and connected.

Examples are everywhere: Monzo and Starling in the UK are known for real-time, mobile-led experiences. In the US, Capital One's voice assistant "Eno" brings natural language to everyday banking. In Singapore, DBS uses AI to embed banking into daily digital routines. In all of these, the bank is not just a tool – it is a companion.

Emotional Resonance and Habit Formation

Money is emotional. It affects how we feel about safety, identity, goals, and even self-worth. So, banks that are part of everyday life must go beyond functions – they need to make people feel good about themselves. That means designing gentle nudges to build good habits without guilt, offering flexibility in tough times (such as overdraft relief), celebrating milestones such as landing a first job or buying a home, and enabling shared financial goals – whether that's budgeting as a family or saving as a group.

Habit plays a big role here. People don't always choose what's best – they stick with what feels familiar. If your banking app becomes the go-to device for checking finances or getting advice, switching away from it becomes harder. The goal is not to create dependence – it is to build trust and routine.

The Risk of Overreach

With everyday presence comes a new kind of risk: overreach. If banks are always watching, always suggesting, always nudging – they can become invasive. Customers sometimes feel tracked instead of supported, manipulated rather than guided, and stressed by constant notifications or upselling.

The key is to design graceful presence – where the bank is there when needed, silent when not, and respectful of personal rhythms. This means offering opt-in layers of support, giving users control over notifications and data sharing, avoiding dark patterns or guilt-based nudges, and being transparent about how insights are generated. Being part of people's daily lives is a privilege – not something a bank is entitled to.

Reimagining Value in Everyday Contexts

Ultimately, the everyday bank is not just a utility. It is a partner adding value to the customer's life journey. This can include wellness insights such as financial health reports linked to lifestyle goals, micro-investments such as round-up features that help build wealth passively, geo-aware offers such as discounts or alerts based on local behaviour, and community initiatives that support local businesses, circular economy platforms, or volunteering opportunities.

In developing regions, mobile money platforms such as M-Pesa have turned basic phones into lifelines – enabling daily commerce, bill payments, and even health interventions. In mature markets, banks that lean into sustainability, inclusion, and real-life challenges (e.g. cost of living support) build deeper emotional equity. The future of banking is not just functional. It is formational.

Banking in everyday life is no longer a concept – it is a necessity. As money becomes embedded into digital environments, banks must either evolve into ambient, trusted companions – or risk being replaced by those that do. To remain relevant, banks must understand how people live – not just how they transact. They must design for life, not just for lending. They must earn the right to be present – and then use that presence wisely.

2 The Mobile as the New Branch

There was a time when a bank's identity was tied to its physical branch – grand buildings, marble counters, and a visible presence in the community symbolized trust and stability. But that centre of gravity has shifted. Today, for billions of people, the mobile phone is the bank – always open, always on, always personal.

This is not just a tech upgrade – it is a cultural shift. Mobile banking has transformed how people interact with financial institutions, and even how they define what a bank is. To understand today's banks, we have to see the mobile device as more than a tool – it is the new front door, the service desk, the product shelf, and the face of the brand.

From Physical Space to Digital Interface

The decline of brick-and-mortar branches is well documented. In the UK, more than 5,000 branches have closed over the past decade. In the US, over 3,000 branches have shuttered, especially in rural and low-income urban areas. Similar patterns are evident across Europe and Asia. Yet this is not simply about cost-cutting. Customers are voting with their thumbs. According to a Deloitte global survey:

- Over 70% of banking interactions now begin on mobiles.
- More than 50% of millennial and Gen Z customers never visit a physical branch.
- Even high-net-worth individuals prefer mobile access for daily transactions and investment updates.

The mobile app has become the primary interface between bank and customer. But it is not just a smaller version of online banking. It is a reimagined branch experience – portable, proactive, and profoundly personal.

Redefining the Customer Experience

The mobile-first model pushes banks to ask new questions: How can we offer instant answers without human delay? Can we replicate the warmth and empathy of a branch visit through a screen? How do we keep security and compliance strong without hurting the user experience? And what should it feel like to have the bank right in a customer's pocket? The answer lies in blending design intelligence, AI-powered interaction, and human fallback channels. For instance:

- NatWest in the UK uses biometric login and one-tap customer service call-backs.
- Nubank in Brazil offers a conversational user interface with real-time financial advice.
- DBS in Singapore uses predictive nudges to help users save and spend smarter.

These are not just features. They are behavioural redesigns – turning the branch experience into a continuous digital relationship.

The Power of Push, Not Pull

In a traditional branch model, the customer initiates the interaction – they visit the bank to ask for help or complete a transaction. In mobile banking, the relationship flips. The bank can send smart, real-time nudges like: "You've just been paid – would you like to save some now?" or "You spent 18% more this month – here's a breakdown." It might say, "Your credit score improved – unlock better rates," or remind you, "A subscription you no longer use is due tomorrow – cancel now?"

These nudges can be frictionless, context-aware, and deeply valued. But they also require ethical boundaries, personalization, and user control. When done well, the mobile becomes not just a service channel, but a trusted financial coach.

Inclusion Through Mobiles

In many emerging economies, mobile phones have become the only bank branch. Physical infrastructure is expensive and inaccessible in remote or underserved regions. Mobile banking leapfrogs this by offering:

- Account opening via video KYC
- QR-code payments at local markets
- Peer-to-peer transfers via phone numbers
- Micro-insurance and credit based on mobile usage data

Examples include:

- Kenya: M-Pesa transformed a feature phone into a banking platform.
- India: Paytm, Phonepe, and government-backed Unified Payments Interface (UPI) have connected rural populations to digital finance.
- Philippines: GCash and Maya offer loans, payments, and investments – all mobile–first.

In these contexts, the mobile is not just the new branch. It is the first branch ever opened for millions of people.

The Role of the Mobile App as an Ecosystem

Leading banks are now treating their apps as ecosystems rather than just service channels. This means integrating lifestyle services such as travel booking and utility payments, marketplace features such as insurance comparisons and gold buying, third-party tools such as carbon footprint trackers and budgeting apps, and conversational agents or virtual assistants.

In China, Alipay and WeChat have made banking ambient – embedded in social, retail, and everyday services. In the West, Revolut, Monzo, and Chime are emulating similar models by creating financial "hubs", where users can do far more than just move money. The mobile bank is no longer just a portal, it is becoming a platform.

Designing for Trust and Empathy

A physical branch builds trust through smiles, eye contact, and familiarity. A mobile app must create that trust differently – using a warm, clear, and respectful tone of voice, offering help instead of blame when errors happen, ensuring accessibility with large fonts and screen reader support, and providing feedback loops so users feel heard when they report problems or ask for help. Design is not decoration. It is the emotional infrastructure of mobile banking. Trust is not just built on encryption. It is built on felt experience.

Challenges and Responsibilities

Going mobile has its downsides. Not everyone is comfortable with digital tools, and too much automation can leave people feeling unsupported – especially in complex situations. Security features such as biometrics and OTPs can feel intrusive, and constant connectivity raises real concerns about privacy and data use. Banks have a responsibility to handle these issues with empathy and clarity. The future of mobile banking is not just about adding features – it is about creating a more human-centred design.

The Future: Ambient, Adaptive, Autonomous

The next generation of mobile banking will be everywhere – on watches, in cars, through smart assistants. It will adapt to users, learn from their habits, and even take action on their behalf, like adjusting budgets or offering pre-approved services without being asked. But with this power comes responsibility. People will only trust banks that prove they deserve it – through real, meaningful experiences, not marketing slogans.

The mobile branch is not a step down. It is the next step forward – bringing banking closer to everyday life than it has ever been before. It is with us, learns from us, and – if designed well – works for us. The real question is not whether the mobile will replace the branch. It is: How can we make it better than the branch has ever been?

3 Designing Seamless Customer Journeys

In today's banking world, competitive advantage is not just about pricing or branch networks – it is about delivering a smooth, connected customer journey. Customers now interact with banks across many touchpoints: apps, websites, ATMs, branches, call centres, and even third-party platforms. The real challenge is not access – it is making that access effortless, smart, and emotionally satisfying.

A great customer journey is not a nice-to-have – it is a strategic must. It builds trust, drives loyalty, and influences whether customers stay, leave, or disengage. In a world where attention is scattered and expectations are high, banks need to shift from thinking about transactions to thinking about journeys.

From Channels to Journeys

Traditional banking was built around separate channels – branches, websites, call centres – each with its own systems and data. Customers had to fit into that structure. Now, it is time to flip that model. Banks must design around the customer journey, not internal silos. But in today's customer-centric world, this structure is inverted. Customers expect:

- Consistency: Information and tone should not vary between channels
- Continuity: A conversation started on chat should continue on the phone
- Control: The ability to pick up where they left off, at their convenience
- Context-awareness: Systems that remember preferences, history, and intent

This means designing cross – channel, longitudinal experiences that reflect the flow of real life – not the legacy silos of the institution. Banks must orchestrate experiences, not just deliver services.

Understanding the End-to-End Journey

A seamless journey starts with deep understanding. Banks must map:

- Trigger moments (e.g. changing jobs, buying a house, receiving a large payment)
- Decision points (e.g. choosing between account types or loan options)
- Emotional peaks and valleys (e.g. anxiety about credit approval, delight at a successful payment)
- Common pain points (e.g. repeated identity verification, lost documentation, lack of clarity)

These insights allow banks to design experience flows rather than isolated interactions. Consider the journey of a customer applying for a mortgage:

1. Discovery: Browsing rates on a mobile app
2. Simulation: Using a calculator to assess affordability
3. Pre-approval: Uploading documents digitally
4. Support: Chat assistant answers queries at 10pm
5. Human handover: Seamless transition to an advisor call
6. Finalization: E-signing on the app
7. Post-loan: Personalized tips on home ownership and repayments

At no point should the customer be forced to repeat themselves, re-authenticate unnecessarily, or "start over" on a different channel.

Frictionless Design: More Than Just User Experience UX

A seamless journey is not just about good-looking design – it is about making every step feel easy and intuitive. That means cutting out unnecessary steps, avoiding repeated logins or forms, using plain language, and anticipating what the customer needs next. For example, if someone already shared their employment info for a loan, they shouldn't have to re-enter it when applying for a credit card. If a salary hits their account, a savings suggestion should show up immediately – not days later. And error messages should be clear and helpful, like "Try uploading a JPEG under 5MB" instead of something cryptic like "Error code 204".When a journey is well designed, it feels effortless. The customer remembers what they achieved – not what they had to do to get there.

Personalization Without Intrusion

Smart personalization makes the experience feel tailored – but it should add value, not feel invasive. That means greeting users by name without making assumptions about their income or goals. It is about offering helpful tips, not pushy advice. Suggesting relevant products, but always giving the option to opt out. And learning from behaviour without crossing privacy lines. In practice, it is as simple as asking:

> "Want to see weekly spending insights?"
> "Prefer chat, email, or a call-back?"
> "Need help planning for a holiday?"

Put the customers in control – and make the journey working with them, not at them. Empowerment, not intrusion, is the hallmark of seamless design.

Human Moments Still Matter

Personalization works best when it is thoughtful – not invasive. Digital ease shouldn't come at the cost of emotional connection. Even the smoothest journey needs human moments – designed with care and empathy. Take First Direct in the UK, often rated top in customer satisfaction thanks to its blend of digital convenience and human warmth. In Asia, the OCBC Bank's AI chatbot can sense frustration and hands over to a real person – an important gesture of respect.

Systems That Talk to Each Other

Behind every great journey is great tech. Seamless experiences depend on integrated systems: unified customer profiles, real-time data syncing, connected

APIs, and cloud-native infrastructure that can scale and adapt. This is where many banks hit a wall – struggling with legacy systems, data silos, and disconnected platforms. And when the backend is messy, customers feel it fast: repeating the same info, getting mixed messages, or hitting dead ends when switching channels. Tech is not the journey – but it is what makes a great journey possible.

Metrics That Reflect Reality

Old-school banking metrics focus on parameters easy to measure, such as call durations, logins, or downloads. But smooth journeys need better indicators:

- Time to resolution – how quickly a customer achieves their goal
- Drop-off points – where users abandon the process
- Emotional satisfaction – how confident and respected they feel
- Cross-channel continuity – whether they can pick up where they left off, no matter the channel

If you want to design better journeys, you need to measure what actually matters. Banks must measure what matters to the customer, not just what is convenient for operations.

Journey Thinking as a Culture

Ultimately, seamless design is not a project – it is a culture. It means listening to customers with humility, empowering cross-functional teams to solve end-to-end problems, incentivizing collaboration over departmental key performance indicators, and seeing the bank not as a collection of products but as a service ecosystem woven into the customer's life.

The best journeys are not created in design sprints. They are co-created through lived experience, feedback, iteration, and deep empathy. To design seamless customer journeys is to honour the customer's time, emotion, and intelligence. It is to say: "We see you. We understand your intent. And we are here to help – without making you work for it." This is the new benchmark. Not speed, not slickness – but seamlessness.

And the banks that get it right will not just keep customers. They will earn trust, affection, and advocacy in a noisy, competitive world. The digital banking journey evolves from mobile onboarding and embedded payments to real-time personalization and invisible financial services. Each layer deepens engagement and reduces friction in everyday life.

4 Embedded Payments and Smart Wallets

Payments used to be obvious points of friction – standing in line at the bank, writing cheques, or entering long card numbers online. Now, they are becoming instant, invisible, and intelligent. And this shift is not just about convenience – it is changing the role banks play in our everyday lives. At the heart of this change are two key ideas: embedded payments and smart wallets. Together, they are breaking down traditional banking boundaries and redefining how we exchange value – by embedding payments directly into the apps, platforms, and experiences people already use. For banks, these are not just new features – they are strategic foundations for staying relevant in everyday life.

What Are Embedded Payments?

Embedded payments refer to the seamless integration of payment capabilities within non-financial platforms, so users can transact without switching apps or interfaces. Think of:

- Paying for an Uber ride without handling cash or card
- Ordering groceries from a smart fridge
- Making a one-click donation during a live stream
- Settling invoices directly from accounting software

These experiences blur the line between banking and living. The payment becomes an invisible enabler, not a separate event. From a banking viewpoint, this changes where the control lies. Instead of owning the front-end experience, banks provide secure payment rails in the background – a utility layer powering commerce across contexts.

Smart Wallets: Beyond Storage

The term "wallet" once evoked a leather pouch filled with notes and cards. Today's smart wallets are digital containers that:

- Store and manage multiple payment instruments
- Prioritize sources (e.g. credit, debit, loyalty, Buy Now, Pay Later) dynamically
- Offer contextual nudges (e.g. "Use this card to earn cash back")
- Integrate with biometric authentication and device security
- Enable seamless tap-to-pay, scan, or voice-triggered actions

Examples include:

- Apple Wallet and Google Wallet: Aggregating cards, tickets, passes, and IDs
- Paytm and Phonepe in India: Offering QR payments, gold purchases, transit top-ups
- Alipay and WeChat Pay in China: Turning chat apps into full commerce ecosystems

A smart wallet is not just a digital version of the old one. It is a decision engine for how and when value is exchanged.

The Convergence of Banking and Platforms

The rise of embedded payments is a by-product of a broader trend: platformization. Tech platforms are increasingly integrating financial features. Retailers, logistics companies, content creators, and social networks are embedding payments to remove friction, boost conversion rates, enable micro-transactions, and monetize new kinds of interactions. Banks, in turn, are shifting roles – from being the destination to becoming the rails.

Forward-looking institutions are embracing Banking-as-a-Service (BaaS), offering APIs that integrate with partner ecosystems. They are focusing on payment orchestration to route, optimize, and secure transactions in real-time. They are also powering third-party apps with white-labelled wallets, providing branded or unbranded financial layers. In this model, the bank's value is not diminished – it is distributed.

Relevance in Real-time

Embedded payments let banks be present right at the moment of intent. For example, when a customer books a flight, travel insurance is offered as part of the same transaction. When buying coffee through a food delivery app, a loyalty discount is automatically applied. And when a user checks their budget after shopping, a prompt encourages them to save. This real-time relevance is critical. In a world of short attention spans and hyper competition, timing is everything. Banks that operates on yesterday's logic – offering products post-fact – risk irrelevance.

Invisible Does Not Mean Impersonal

As payments become ambient, banks face a paradox: How to remain trusted when no longer visible? Trust in this environment must be built into the interface through clarity, confirmation, and the ability to reverse actions. It should be reinforced by experience – zero errors, instant support, and intelligent defaults. And it must be anchored in brand memory, so customers recognize who powers their payments, even if it is behind the scenes. This requires banks to shift from attention-seeking to presence-building. Not loud, but reliable. Not flashy, but foundational.

The Power of Data and Context

Smart wallets and embedded systems use data – ethically and securely – to provide budgeting insights such as spending patterns and forecasted shortfalls, detect fraud through behaviour analysis, offer personalized deals, and deliver timely financial coaching. For instance, a wallet might suggest a Monday reset after high weekend spending or give health-related budgeting tips based on late-night food orders. It could even provide forex rates and insurance when detecting travel abroad. The aim is support, not surveillance.

Around the world, embedded payments have taken different forms. China's WeChat and Alipay blend chat, payments, Social Media, and commerce seamlessly. India's UPI uses government-backed infrastructure to fuel fintech innovation. Sweden's Swish and Norway's Vipps gained popularity through easy peer-to-peer payments. In the US, Cash App, Venmo, and Square have built apps that simplify payments within communities. Meanwhile, the UK's Open Banking lets third-party wallets offer bank-linked services – with user permission. Each context reflects regulatory nuance, cultural preferences, and legacy infrastructure – but the common thread is convenience and control for the user.

Risks and Responsibilities

Convenience brings challenges. One-click payments can lead to impulse buys, more access points increase fraud risk, and data trails raise ethical concerns about surveillance. Plus, not everyone is digitally savvy, which can cause exclusion. Banks and platforms need to balance smooth experiences with necessary safeguards – such as extra checks on big or unusual payments. They should mix automation with user control, support innovation while ensuring inclusivity, and combine speed with protection. Most importantly, banks must avoid becoming passive service providers. Owning the wallet means owning the customer relationship.

The Future: Ambient, Interoperable, and Intelligent

Payments are expanding into new areas such as the Internet of Things – fridges reordering groceries, cars paying tolls automatically, and voice-activated buys. Wearables such as rings, watches, and even biometric implants will enable contactless payments. Cryptographic wallets will handle digital currencies, NFTs (non-fungible tokens), and programmable money. Global wallets will support cross-border use, currency switching, and multiple languages.

Banks need to prepare for both tech merging and diverse user needs across regions and groups. The winners will offer flexibility, security, and seamless experiences everywhere. As payments fade into the background, banks have a huge opportunity: to be everywhere, invisible, yet essential. Embedded payments and smart wallets are not just new tech – they are about staying relevant in customers' everyday lives. Not every payment will be noticed, but every experience builds trust. Get it right, and you'll be trusted – even when unseen.

5 Personalization Beyond Products

In a world where digital interactions are abundant and attention spans fleeting, personalization has become the defining battleground in banking. Yet, for many institutions, personalization still means little more than offering the right product to the right segment. This approach, while familiar, is fundamentally limited. True personalization goes beyond products – it touches context, behaviour, emotion, timing, and tone.

The banks that win loyalty in the digital age will not be those with the widest portfolio, but those who demonstrate deep relevance – treating each customer as a unique individual with evolving needs, not just a data point in a marketing funnel. This section looks at how financial institutions are shifting from transactional relevance to contextual intelligence. It explains why this change is both strategic and ethical.

The Limitations of Product-Centric Personalization

For years, banks have used segmentation based on income, age, location, or job to tailor offers – such as mortgages for homeowners or student loans for young adults. While this works broadly, it often misses individual nuances. It overlooks life changes such as career breaks or caregiving, personal values such as sustainability or culture, financial habits, and emotional factors such as anxiety or trust. Product-centric personalization risks being impersonal. It answers the question: What can we sell you? The better question is: How can we help you live the life you value?

Personalization as Experience Design

Modern personalization is about creating an experience, not just pushing a sale. This means adjusting tone and language – some customers want formal reassurance, others prefer a friendly, informal approach. It involves customizing interfaces, with simple dashboards for beginners and advanced views for power users. It respects channel preferences, whether that's SMS, email, app notifications, or no notifications at all.

Timing matters too – knowing when to suggest, when to pause, and when to listen. And it includes feedback loops that let customers shape the interaction as it happens. For example, a customer saving for a home might appreciate motivational nudges and visual trackers. A retiree worried about fraud may prefer in-person verification instead of fast onboarding. Meanwhile, a gig worker could want flexible credit lines that adjust to their fluctuating income. Personalization is not an algorithm. It is respectful design that adapts to the individual.

Behavioural Insights and Financial Wellbeing

Behavioural economics shows that small nudges can have a big impact on financial outcomes. Banks can use behavioural data to encourage saving through round-up programs, milestone trackers, or matching incentives. They can promote healthier habits by categorizing spending, showing monthly trends, or gamifying budgets. They can help prevent harmful actions with alerts for unusual transactions and gentle nudges before overdrafts. And they can offer emotional reassurance with messages such as, "You're on track," "You've saved more than last month," or "Well done".

These interventions may seem small, but they humanize banking. They speak to emotion as well as logic. For instance, Monzo in the UK famously introduced spending controls for gambling – a feature driven by empathy and widely praised for supporting mental health. It is personalization not for profit, but for protection.

With regard to ethics, personalization means greater responsibility for the banks. Banks must be transparent about what data is used and why. Personalized services should always be an opt-in, not the default. They need to set clear boundaries to avoid manipulation or surveillance. Inclusivity is key – algorithms should never reinforce bias or exclusion. Finally, choice architecture should guide users gently, nudging without ever coercing. Personalization should be empowering, not exploitative. A personal experience should leave the customer feeling seen – not under surveillance.

Localization as a Layer of Personalization

In global banking, personalization must also mean localization. This includes respecting language and dialect preferences, using culturally relevant images and references, accommodating religious or ethical financial practices such as Shariah-compliant banking, and accounting for local tax rules, regulatory disclosures, and holidays.

For example, users in India may prefer festive savings plans aligned with Diwali or Eid. In the UK, climate-conscious customers may seek green banking options. In the US, Black or Hispanic communities may respond to culturally fluent engagement and representation. Personalization that ignores culture becomes tone-deaf.

Personalization and the Role of AI

As banking moves into ecosystems, personalization needs to follow the user. This means context-aware APIs that offer relevant banking features within partner platforms, federated identity for seamless logins and consistent preferences across services, data portability that lets customers control their information across apps, and invisible orchestration to create unified experiences throughout embedded journeys.

For instance, a ride-hailing app might integrate micro-savings after each trip; a freelance platform might suggest tax-saving investments in-app; a travel app might auto-adjust currency wallets. In each case, personalization is not tethered to the bank's app – it is ambient, adaptive, and embedded.

But AI must be governed carefully. It needs fairness to avoid discriminatory outcomes. Customers deserve transparency – knowing why a decision was made. And while machines assist, humans must remain accountable as the ultimate fallback.AI can power personalization. But humane intelligence must guide it.

Measuring What Matters

Traditional metrics – click-through rates, product uptake – only tell part of the story. Modern personalization success should be measured by customer satisfaction – do users feel truly understood? It also includes the quality of engagement – are features used consistently and meaningfully? Behavioural outcomes matter too – are customers better off financially? And finally, trust indicators – are customers willing to opt into deeper services? The goal is not just to personalize, but to build long-term, values-aligned relationships.

Personalization as a Cultural Competence

Finally, personalization is not a toolset. It is a mindset and a culture. Banks must empower their teams to empathize, not just optimize. They need to listen closely to customer voices throughout their journeys and keep improving them based on real experiences. Success should be measured by customer wellbeing, not just product sales. A personalized bank is not one that only knows your name. It is one that knows when to speak, what to say, and when to stay silent.

In the end, personalization beyond products is not just a digital strategy. It is a philosophy of care. It means recognizing that every customer brings not just financial needs, but life stories, aspirations, fears, and dreams. To serve them well, a bank must do more than remember what they bought. It must remember who they are becoming – and walk alongside them with intelligence, humility, and grace.

6 Building Everyday Relevance with Data

In today's digital world, relevance is not achieved through sporadic campaigns or flashy offers. It is achieved through ongoing, context-aware, and data-driven engagement. The modern bank must become an institution that is not only present at moments of need – such as applying for a mortgage or recovering from fraud – but also woven into the customer's daily life with subtle utility and consistent value.

This is where data has a significant impact. Not merely as a tool for analytics, but as a means to build meaningful, real-time relationships that evolve with each interaction. Data is no longer the backend exhaust of transactions. It is the engine of relevance.

From the Collection to the Daily Application of Data

Banks sit on vast reservoirs of data: transaction histories, location patterns, device information, credit usage, savings behaviour, customer service logs, and even sentiment captured through chatbots and surveys. But too often, this data remains underutilized or poorly integrated – trapped in silos or used only for compliance and risk. To create daily relevance, banks must shift from:

- Retrospective analysis to real-time responsiveness
- Generic insights to hyper-contextual nudges
- Product targeting to lifestyle alignment

The goal is to anticipate needs, remove friction, and add value before the customer asks for it.

Enabling Proactive Engagement

Traditional banking is largely reactive: a customer asks, the bank responds. Data can create personalized, helpful moments throughout the day. For example, a morning update might say, "You're 12% under budget this week." Alerts could warn, "Your usual bill is higher – want to review or set a limit?" Spending patterns might highlight deals, such as cashback for your Friday dining.

Savings nudges could suggest putting aside a portion of a bonus, while cash flow reminders warn if income and bills don't line up. Travel alerts might offer easy insurance activation, and recurring habits could prompt setting up automatic donations. For instance, a new parent might get tips on child savings plans, someone nearing retirement could see pension projections, and a spike in online shopping might trigger fraud alerts. Proactive engagement builds a sense of care and partnership, not just service delivery.

Making Data Usage Visible and Valuable

One of the biggest concerns customers have about data is opacity. They know banks collect information, but they rarely see the benefit. To earn trust and stay relevant, banks must show clearly how their data use is of value to the customer. Customers should have control over what's collected and how it is applied. Transparency around algorithms and data logic is essential. And just as important – banks must avoid overreach; not every insight needs to become a notification. For instance:

> "We used your spending history to recommend this card with higher cash back in your preferred categories. You can adjust these settings anytime."

Empowered customers are more willing to share – when they understand the benefit.

Real-time Infrastructure: The Hidden Enabler

Behind the scenes, daily relevance requires robust infrastructure. Event-driven architecture allows systems to respond to life events as they happen. A unified customer view breaks down silos across departments and platforms. Edge computing and APIs enable fast, localized decision-making. And AI and machine learning ensure systems continuously learn and adapt to individual behaviour.

This is not easy. Many banks are still dependent on batch processing, nightly reconciliations, and legacy systems of customer relationship management. Building daily relevance requires reimagining data infrastructure as strategic infrastructure. Cloud-native banks – such as Revolut, Nubank, and Starling – have demonstrated how real-time data flow enables customer-centric innovation.

Data Ethics and Daily Trust

With increased data use comes greater moral responsibility. Banks must commit to purpose limitation – using data only to benefit the customer, not for extractive gain. They must ensure non-discrimination, making sure data-driven decisions are fair and inclusive. Upholding digital dignity means avoiding profiling that feels invasive or exploitative. And customers should always have recourse and the ability to review or challenge algorithmic outcomes.

Trust is fragile. A single misstep – a denied loan without explanation, a targeting mistake based on sensitive history – can undo months of good work. Building daily relevance is not just technical. It is ethical and cultural.

Global Trends in Data-driven Banking

Different regions are showcasing innovative approaches:

- UK and EU: Open Banking has unlocked consent-based data sharing, enabling smarter personal finance apps.
- US: Fintechs such as Plaid and Intuit enable consumers to stitch together multiple sources of financial data.
- Asia: Superapps such as Gojek and Grab integrate lifestyle and banking data for real-time value.
- Africa: Mobile money platforms use usage patterns to offer micro-loans and real-time credit scoring.
- Latin America: Neo-banks use behavioural data to help users build creditworthiness in informal economies.

Each of these models reflects a broader truth: data is not the product – relevance is.

Building a Culture of Relevance

Daily relevance can't just come from dashboards. It requires a team effort to truly listen, design systems that adapt, and create experiences that evolve in real-time. It also means using feedback to improve continuously – and measuring success by how useful you are in customers' daily lives, not just by Return-on-investment figures.

Banks need to shift from one-time campaigns to ongoing conversations that go beyond selling to helping and celebrating progress. Building daily relevance means being part of customers' lives – not just as a provider, but a quiet, trusted presence adding value every day. It is saying:

> "We see you. We understand your rhythms. We respect your privacy. And we're here whenever you need us."

7 Trust at the Point of Service

In today's world of ambient finance – where banking happens seamlessly in the moment – trust is built or lost instantly. A failed payment, a security alert, a denied credit, or a misunderstood chatbot can all shape how customers feel right away. Service trust, unlike brand trust built over time, relies on being consistent, clear, and reliable every single time, across all devices and channels. This section looks at how trust is earned – not through slogans, but through everyday customer experiences.

The New Frontline: Invisible, Digital, Instant

Banking's frontline used to be the branch – where trust grew through personal interactions.

Now, it is everywhere: a tap-to-pay on the metro, a balance alert, a fraud warning at the pump, a 2 am chatbot password reset, or a savings tip right after payday. These micro-moments shape how customers see their bank and require a new kind of excellence – built on digital trust and reliability.

The Five Pillars of Service Trust

To deliver trust at the point of service, banks must operationalize five pillars:

1 Reliability

- The app must load.
- The payment must go through.
- The balance must be correct.
- The transaction history must sync.

Failures here don't only cause inconvenience – they erode credibility. In a digital-first world, uptime is trust.

Clarity

- Instructions must be simple.
- Error messages must explain, not obscure.
- Terms must be understandable.

Uncertainty breeds fear. Clarity reassures.

Speed

- Customers expect real-time actions.
- Delays feel like neglect.

Whether confirming a transfer or issuing a card replacement, slowness signals weakness.

Empowerment

- Customers should be able to act without friction.
- Limits, controls, and permissions must be transparent.

A trusted bank is one that lets the user feel in control.

Recovery

- Mistakes will happen.
- But the response must be human, swift, and sincere.

Trust is often strengthened by how a bank recovers from failure.

Real-time trust signals are essential in modern banking – just like e-commerce platforms use badges and ratings to build credibility. Banks must embed these signals directly into service interactions. Messages such as "Secured with Face ID", "This payment is protected under our guarantee", or "Chat with a human anytime" build confidence. Others such as "You can undo this transaction for the next 60 minutes" or "No impact on your credit score – this is a soft check" help users feel safe, informed, and in control. These messages reduce anxiety and reinforce confidence in the moment. Trust is not just felt. It is communicated deliberately.

Consistency Across Channels

Customers expect a smooth experience whether they start on the app, switch to email, or call support. Having to repeat info or re-authenticate hurts trust. Building real-time trust means having unified profiles, seamless data syncing, and smart orchestration across all channels – so every interaction feels smooth and reliable. When a bank forgets, the customer feels forgotten.

With more people using AI tools such as chatbots and robo-advisors these must be accurate, respectful and clear, and always offer an easy way to reach a human when needed. A chatbot that offers a flawless experience still erodes trust if it refuses to hand over to a human when required. Automation should enhance trust, not gatekeep it.

Design for Reassurance

In banking, good design builds trust. Visual cues, clear language, and animations help users feel safe, avoid mistakes, and understand what's happening. Designers should use progress indicators such as "Step 2 of 3," confirmations such as checkmarks, and undo options to give users confidence. Helpful tooltips guide them through tricky steps, and accessible design ensures everyone can use the service comfortably. A well-designed interface doesn't just feel good. It feels trustworthy.

Preventive Trust vs. Reactive Trust

Traditional risk management focused on response – fraud detection, complaints handling, dispute resolution. Modern trust is built on prevention. This means deploying anomaly detection systems that instantly flag unusual behaviour, setting spending caps to halt problems before they escalate, and using smart nudges to remind users of limits or upcoming bills. Identity verification should be adaptive – scaling with risk levels while minimizing user burden. Trust is strongest when the user never experiences failure in the first place.

Regional Trust Norms and Cultural Sensitivity

Trust is never culturally neutral. In Germany, stringent data privacy laws make explicit opt-ins and user control essential. In India, trust hinges on reassuring customer service combined with mobile-first simplicity. In the US, guarantees around security and rapid service foster confidence. Meanwhile, the UK prioritizes fairness, transparency, and clear resolution channels. In the Gulf countries, trust is shaped by local language support and adherence to Shariah-compliant financial principles. A global bank must design for local trust expectations.

Institutional Trust at the Service Layer

Finally, trust at the point of service connects to trust in the institution. Every failed login, denied payment, or unhelpful chatbot contributes to a narrative:

> "This bank doesn't care. This bank is unreliable. This bank doesn't get me."

Conversely:

> "That was fast. That was simple. That felt safe."

These are not only UX wins – they are reputational wins. Trust is no longer earned just through heritage, ads, or awards. In a digital world, trust is earned one interaction at a time. Trust is earned in moments of seamless service: when a customer logs in and instantly finds what they need, when a payment is processed effortlessly without hesitation, when an alert warns the customers of risk before they even notice it, and when a chatbot responds with empathy – "I understand, let me connect you to someone who can help." This is not just operational excellence. It is the new foundation of customer loyalty. In an age of ambient banking, the point of service is the point of trust.

8 Serving the Invisible Customer

Across all markets, there's a group of customers who are invisible – not by choice, but by design. They remain on the sidelines and are often overlooked by traditional systems, marketing, and products. They are not "non-customers", just under-engaged and under-served. Invisibility goes beyond income or location – it is influenced by culture, disability, digital skills, gender, immigration, and life situations. The bank of the future can't call itself inclusive if it doesn't recognize and serve these millions of invisible customers. This section explores the hidden faces of modern finance and how visionary banks are redesigning services to reach, respect, and empower them.

Who Are the Invisible Customers?

Invisible customers are not only the unbanked or the underbanked. They include:

- Elderly users unfamiliar with digital tools
- Low-income gig workers who avoid formal products out of fear or mistrust
- Refugees and migrants with limited documentation
- Caregivers, mostly women, who manage family finances but are not the primary account holder
- Neurodivergent individuals overwhelmed by complex interfaces
- People with disabilities navigating inaccessible apps
- Individuals with poor credit histories who receive no proactive engagement
- Young adults just entering the financial system but not yet recognized by traditional scoring

These users fall through the cracks – not because they are unreachable, but because we haven't tried hard enough to reach them.

Visibility Begins with Listening

To serve the invisible, the first step is to truly see them by listening deeply to their needs and barriers. This requires inclusive user research that reaches beyond urban, affluent groups, along with field studies involving vulnerable communities. It also means building partnerships with NGOs and advocacy groups, and creating feedback loops that capture lived experiences.

For example, some visually impaired customers prefer audio banking interfaces, but these are often not well integrated. Others prefer visiting branches – but find physical spaces poorly designed or intimidating. Understanding these preferences is not just about empathy – it is strategic design.

Rethinking Onboarding and Access

Making banking visible starts with easier onboarding, especially for marginalized users. This means accepting alternative IDs for migrants, offering digital literacy help, supporting multiple languages, providing no-fee, zero-balance accounts, and using agent-assisted sign-ups in underserved areas.

India's Aadhaar-enabled micro-banking shows how biometrics and mobile tech can boost access at scale. In the UK, challengers such as Monese serve migrants without credit history or proof of address. Keeping onboarding simple, flexible, and local makes all the difference.

Designing for Digital Literacy and Confidence

Invisibility often comes from a lack of confidence, not of access. Banks should focus on clear, simple language, offer tutorials or demos, and reveal features gradually as users become familiar with the service. Helpful prompts should guide without overwhelming, and users should always be able to reach a human for support. Banking shouldn't test intelligence – it should build financial confidence.

Some customers prefer simplicity, rarely check balances, avoid promos, and like paper statements or in-person help. Respecting their pace means honouring their style without pushing engagement. These quieter users are not disengaged – they just use banking differently. Banks should avoid penalties for inactivity and over-soliciting, offering low-clutter, low-pressure options that deliver what's needed without noise. Supporting quietly confident users shows true maturity in banking.

Trust and Dignity at the Margins

Invisibility is often reinforced by fear – of judgment, rejection, or surveillance. Many low-income or immigrant users steer clear of formal banking due to confusion over terms, fear of penalties, feelings of ineligibility, and past experiences of prejudice. Building their trust means providing culturally competent support, setting privacy-respecting defaults, ensuring fair and inclusive algorithms, designing without discrimination, and offering compassionate dispute resolution. It is about creating a space where everyone feels seen, safe, and valued. When customers feel safe, they begin to step forward. Dignity leads to visibility.

Data Gaps and Invisible Behaviour

Invisibility is also a data problem. Customers who rely heavily on cash, share accounts with family, avoid digital tools, live in multi-occupancy housing, or lack credit histories often fall through the cracks of algorithmic decision-making. As a result, they frequently receive poor product recommendations, face inaccurate risk assessments, and miss out on proactive support – making them invisible in a system designed for data-rich profiles. Addressing their needs means rethinking how data is gathered and used to include these diverse financial realities. Banks must move beyond proxy data and invest in contextual models – models that use alternative data sources, community signals, and longitudinal understanding. For instance:

- Mobile top-up frequency as a proxy for income consistency
- Rental payment patterns as indicators of creditworthiness
- Savings club participation as a measure of financial discipline

Smart banks look beneath the surface to see the full story.

Serving with Simplicity and Grace

The design challenge in serving invisible customers is not one of complexity – it is one of humility. Services must be:

- Simple, but not simplistic
- Powerful, but not overwhelming
- Respectful, not patronizing

In Nigeria, services such as Piggy Vest allow users to save money via text messages, making it accessible to non-smartphone users. In Latin America, BBVA's "Simple Accounts" provide basic financial services without the burden of documentation. These are not stripped-down products – they are elevated essentials, built with care.

The Power of Community Touchpoints

Many invisible customers place their trust more in their communities than in corporations. To reach and support them effectively, banks can build partnerships with trusted local institutions such as churches, mosques, and temples, as well as cooperatives, women's groups, disability rights organizations, youth clubs, and shelters. These collaborations not only foster trust but also create more culturally sensitive and accessible financial services tailored to community needs. Community-based financial literacy, service delivery, and trust-building are powerful. When institutions show up in the spaces people already trust, they extend their own credibility.

From Metrics to Meaning

Traditional success metrics – active users, product uptake, transaction volumes – don't always reflect progress in inclusion. Banks must track:

- Growth in first-time account holders from underserved segments
- Use of accessibility features
- Drop-off rates during onboarding
- Resolution times for vulnerable customers
- Customer satisfaction across diversity cohorts

Inclusion is not a campaign. It is a cultural practice embedded in daily service. To serve the invisible customer is not just a moral obligation – it is a strategic imperative. The markets of tomorrow will be defined not by the affluent few but by the billions whose financial lives are now emerging. Seeing them is not enough. Serving them – simply, respectfully, and reliably – is the future of everyday banking.

9 Rethinking Retail at the Global Scale

Retail banking has traditionally been built on local relevance – tailored to geography, regulation, currency, and culture. But in today's hyperconnected world, a new dynamic is emerging: local intimacy delivered through global infrastructure. The retail bank of the future must simultaneously operate at personal depth and planetary scale.

As customer expectations converge across borders – expecting instant payments, invisible onboarding, 24/7 access, and personalized services – banks must reimagine how they scale intelligently, ethically, and inclusively. Retail is no longer just physical proximity – it is digital intimacy, powered by intelligence and trust, capable of reaching billions without diluting values.

This section explores how globalization is reshaping the design, delivery, and governance of retail banking – and what it takes to serve the everyday needs of people from London to Lagos, Singapore to São Paulo.

The Shifting Shape of Scale

In the old model, scaling retail banking focused on expanding physical presence – more branches, bigger ATM networks, broad advertising, and standardized products across regions. Today, scale looks very different: it is about leveraging APIs rather than ATMs, prioritizing personalized experiences instead of one-size-fits-all products, investing in robust data infrastructure over physical locations, and building real-time platforms that replace slower batch processing systems. The shift is from tangible expansion to digital agility and customer-centric innovation.

Modern banks now think like digital platforms – where core capabilities are centrally designed, but interfaces and offerings are dynamically adapted to local contexts. This is "global" banking – global in architecture, local in empathy.

From Headquarters to Hubs

Legacy banks often centralize decision-making in headquarters – typically in capital cities or financial centres. But this limits agility and cultural responsiveness.

The future demands a shift to multi-nodal models: Regional hubs with product ownership, localized compliance interpretation, decentralized customer research, and cross-border design studios are becoming common strategies. These approaches are illustrated, for example, by HSBC's adaptive teams in the Asia-Pacific region, Santander's regional fintech partnerships in Latin America, and Standard Bank's hub-and-spoke model across Africa. They don't dilute control – they distribute innovation.

Global Infrastructure, Local Experience

Delivering at the global scale without losing local soul requires a layered model: The Core Layer (Global) includes cloud-native core banking, real-time data analytics, shared security protocols, and a unified API architecture. The Platform Layer (Regional) features localized workflows and integrations, country-specific compliance engines, and adaptations for currency, tax, and language. The Experience Layer (Local) focuses on interfaces in local languages, cultural references in design, support hours aligned with the region, and trust-building through local norms. This modular architecture enables consistency without rigidity.

Regulatory Complexity as a Design Opportunity

Going global means dealing with many regulations – such as GDPR in Europe, PSD2 in the UK, AML rules in the Gulf countries, data laws in India, fair lending rules in the US, and KYC standards in Africa. Instead of seeing this as a headache, smart banks build privacy-by-design systems, use explainable AI, offer dynamic consent tools, and embed compliance into the user journey. Trust at scale comes from proactive governance.

Harmonizing Product Portfolios

At scale, products need core consistency (such as fraud protection), flexible modules (interest rates, loan terms), and local customization (language, credit scoring). This requires a design system – not just a product list. Think of it like LEGO blocks: global standards assembled locally.

Building Intelligence That Travels

AI must be trained globally on diverse data, fine-tuned for local markets, and checked for bias. For example, a London credit model might unfairly penalize informal incomes in Nairobi. Ethical scaling means using local data, testing fairness, and involving local experts. Retail banking must respect cultural and cognitive diversity everywhere.

Embedded finance as a global vector allows retail banks to extend global reach by embedding their services into third-party platforms such as retail checkout financing, ride-hailing driver payments, insurance integrated into travel bookings, and salary-linked micro-loans. This strategy lets banks scale without direct customer acquisition and helps reach previously invisible customer groups, especially in informal economies. Examples include Grab Financial micro-investment tools in Southeast Asia, Mercado Pago's credit offerings in Latin America, and Apple Card's partnership with Goldman Sachs in the US. Embedded finance enables retail reach without retail footprint.

Scaling is not just about revenue – it is about responsibility and resonance. To grow inclusively, banks must focus on underserved regions, avoid colonial tech approaches, invest in local financial education, keep services affordable, and co-create products with local communities. A global bank should be truly invested in the markets it serves.

Global banks face challenges such as political instability, currency swings, natural disasters, regulatory changes, and cyber-threats. Meeting these requires distributed infrastructure, market-specific planning, real-time risk monitoring, and quick emergency responses. Scale without resilience is risky; continuity planning is a promise to customers. Success is not just numbers – of customers, countries, or data. It is about retaining customers, uplifting communities, fostering innovation, and maintaining trust through change.

Global scale is not about being everywhere. It is about being meaningfully somewhere – in every life you touch, every day. To rethink retail at the global scale is not to build a bank that conquers geographies, but a bank that adapts to them with humility, intelligence, and purpose. It is the bank that says:

> "Wherever you are, we're already there – in your language, with your values, at your service."

10 Making Banking Effortless

The most powerful user experience is often the one a customer doesn't even notice. When banking becomes seamless – integrated into the flow of daily life, free of friction or confusion – it transitions from a service to an invisible utility, quietly enabling goals, reducing stress, and building confidence.

Effortless banking is not just about removing complexity. It is about designing around the customer's time, attention, and intent, while anticipating needs before they arise. It is an aspiration that sits at the intersection of technology, trust, empathy, and operational excellence.

In a world of always-on digital lives, the bank that removes friction wins not only business – but loyalty.

From Process to Presence

For decades, banking has required processes: forms, passwords, branch visits, paperwork, and multi-step approvals. These processes may have been secure and thorough, but they were also time-consuming, opaque, and intimidating.

Effortless banking moves beyond rigid processes to focus on being genuinely present for the customer – there when needed, invisible when not. It delivers the right service exactly when and where it matters most. Interactions require minimal effort from users, with crystal-clear guidance and no room for confusion, making banking feel natural and seamless. When the user feels in control, without feeling burdened, effortlessness emerges.

The Architecture of Simplicity

Behind that simple, clean interface is a complex, powerful system. Effortless banking depends on modular platforms designed to pivot fast, APIs that blend banking smoothly into other apps, real-time infrastructure for immediate updates, automated decisions to cut delays, and event-driven journeys that react dynamically to what users do. It is a finely tuned engine built for speed, flexibility, and user-centricity.

For example, rather than asking the customer to search for a service, the bank can detect a salary deposit and offer a savings suggestion or investment nudge – in real-time. Effortless does not mean minimal. It means intelligently orchestrated. An effortless experience must be:

- Consistent across mobile, desktop, voice, and in-person
- Continuously synced across platforms
- Intuitive regardless of the channel

A task started on the mobile app should be completed via smart speaker or a support agent without repetition. A query logged via chatbot should be visible to the call centre. All this hinges on solid foundations: unified customer identity systems to know who you are across channels, shared event logs so every interaction is tracked and accessible, and channel-agnostic design frameworks that let support flow seamlessly whether you're chatting, calling, or video banking. Together, these ensure help is not just available but truly connected and personalized. Customers don't think in terms of channels. They think in terms of tasks. Effortless banking follows the task.

The Role of Automation and AI

Effortless banking thrives on silent intelligence – systems working quietly behind the scenes to understand what the user wants, which fast-track approvals, adapt workflows on the fly, tailor the experience instantly, and keep risks in check continuously. AI plays a central role by spotting fraud as it happens, anticipating needs with predictive prompts such as "Did you mean to…?", streamlining onboarding automatically, and powering conversational assistants that smoothly hand over to humans when needed.

It is a seamless blend of smart tech and thoughtful design making banking feel effortless and intuitive. But this intelligence must be transparent, explainable, and ethical. A denied loan or a frozen account must be accompanied by clear reasons and easy resolution paths. Simplicity without fairness is deception, not effortlessness.

Reducing Cognitive Load

The human brain is finite. Every additional choice, form field, term, or delay adds cognitive friction. Designing for effortlessness means focusing on clarity and simplicity. It is about showing users just what they need, speaking in plain language, keeping screens clean, guiding them through steps in a natural order, and offering smart defaults to reduce decision fatigue.

For example, messages such as "You're nearly done – just one more step" reassure and encourage progress; "No need to upload ID again – we have it from last time" saves time and frustration; and "Based on your spending, you may not need this feature right now" helps keep the experience relevant without overwhelm. It is all about making banking feel smooth, intuitive, and respectful of the user's time and attention. Small touches compound into big relief.

Proactive Support, Not Reactive Apology

Effortless service anticipates needs before they become problems:

- A card about to expire? Offer renewal proactively
- A payment failed? Suggest the most likely fix – not just an error code
- A change in travel detected? Pre-authorize global card use or recommend temporary limits

Effortless banks do not wait for complaints. They pre-resolve friction – using data, design, and empathy.

Human Help, Friction-Free

Even in a digital world, human support is crucial. Effortless banking means help is always nearby – quick, relevant, and empathetic. Call agents can see your full digital history, so you never have to repeat yourself. Chatbots pick up right where you left off, and video banking offers face-to-face support when it really counts. Effortless doesn't mean less human – it means human when it matters most.

Some of the best effortless banking features work quietly: subscription managers cancel unused services automatically, auto-sweeps move money to savings for you, and round-up programs nudge you to save without thinking. For freelancers, real-time tax tools simplify tough tasks. Shared wallets help families manage money transparently, and smart bill payers schedule payments based on actual cash flow to avoid overdrafts and fees.

These use cases showcase how banking is evolving from reactive service to proactive, almost invisible support. These features work quietly, in the background. They make customers feel looked after, not locked in.

What Effortlessness Signals

Effortless banking sends a clear message: The bank respects your time by cutting friction, understands your daily life, and keeps things simple. Trust grows not by being flashy, but by quietly fixing pain points so you barely notice. Customers don't remember flashy dashboards – they remember when things "just worked". No repeated questions, no extra hassle. Most of all, it made them feel confident and in control of their finances.

Strategic Framework Box: Chapter 3. Banking in Motion: Designing Relevance in Everyday Financial Life

Key Insight

The most successful banks of the future will not be those with the most branches or features – but those that become invisible enablers of daily life. Relevance is no longer about product depth; it is about being present at the moment of need.

Strategic Takeaway

To remain essential in a platform-driven world, banks must transcend their own boundaries and become useful without being noticed. This is the essence of modern trust.

Touchpoint Dimension	*Legacy Bank*	*Everyday Bank*
Customer Interface	Physical branches, static portals	Mobile - first, Omni - channel, embedded UX
Product Logic	Account - centric, siloed offerings	Journey - centric, contextual services
Engagement Model	Periodic interactions (e.g. monthly)	Continuous presence, embedded flows
Data Use	Back - end reporting	Front - end personalisation in real time
Service Visibility	Explicit and separate from life events	Embedded into commerce and routines
Trust Building	Face - to - face, relationship manager	Frictionless, predictive, value - aligned

This chapter highlights a key design principle: The everyday bank must be less visible, but more valuable. By embedding services into the rhythms of life – shopping, commuting, care giving, working – banks can transform from service providers into seamless infrastructure.

Bibliography

Deloitte (2022). Global Digital Banking Survey: Reimagining the Customer Experience. Deloitte Insights.

4 The Human Foundation

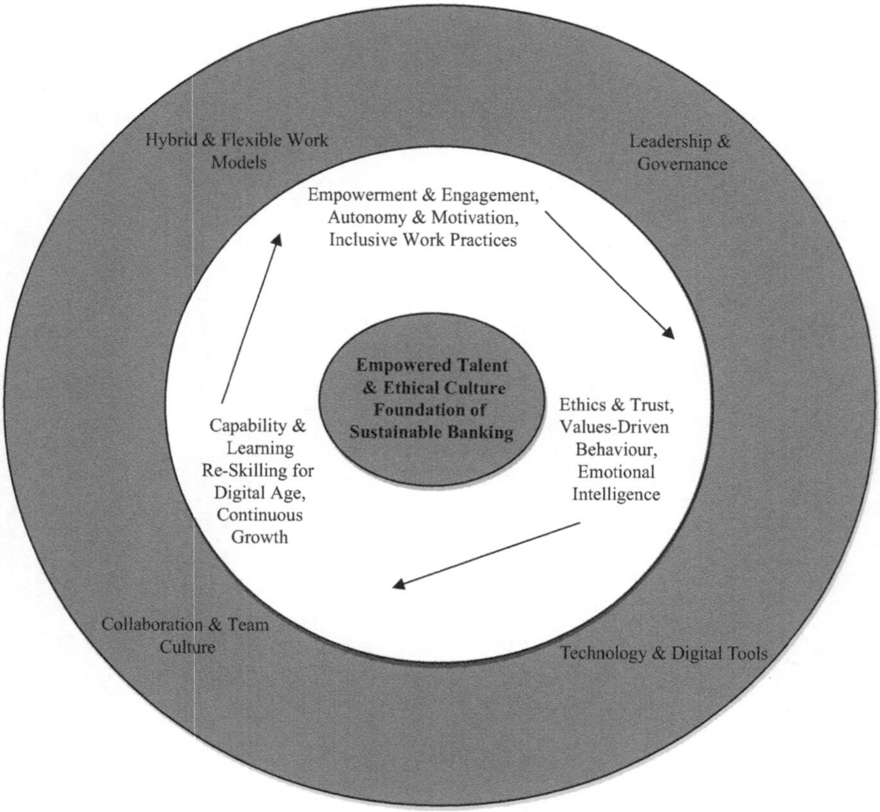

Figure 4.1 Future-ready banks are built on empowered talent, continuous learning, and ethical culture – supported by flexible, technology-enabled workplaces.

DOI: 10.4324/9781003737544-4

1 The Culture Beneath the Strategy

Every bank has a strategy – planned in boardrooms and shared in reports – but success often depends more on the culture behind it. Culture is how things really get done when no one's watching. In banking, where trust matters most, culture is not just a "soft" issue – it is the core operating system. This section highlights the crucial role of culture as banks adapt to a digital, inclusive, and fast-changing world. Culture is not an afterthought; it comes before strategy, supports it, and ultimately decides if the strategy will thrive or fail.

What really sets banks apart is what customers feel – how they are treated in tough moments, how transparently their problems get solved, and how consistent their experience is across every touchpoint. This customer experience is shaped not by mission statements, but by the cultural norms of the institution:

- Do relationship managers feel empowered to resolve issues, or are they afraid of overstepping their remit?
- Is frontline empathy encouraged or treated as inefficiency?
- Are service failures seen as opportunities to rebuild trust or threats to be suppressed?

In short, culture seeps through the service – shaping everything from the tone of emails to decisions about credit.

Strategy Without Culture is Decoration

When strategic transformation fails, it often is not because the ideas behind it are weak, but because the bank's culture pushes back against them. A bank may commit to becoming agile, customer-centric and innovative – yet falls short to do so. The reasons for this are the big barriers to innovation often present in organizations: When hierarchies limit initiative, people hesitate to take ownership. Risk aversion kills creativity, because failure is feared rather than seen as a learning opportunity. Silos block collaboration, so knowledge stays trapped inside them instead of spreading to other departments. And fear-based cultures shut down honest feedback, making it impossible to improve the organization.

When transformation is treated more as a process than a cultural journey, it becomes fragile – producing dashboards instead of genuine shifts. Culture is not just a backdrop to strategy. It is what drives the strategy. Moving from a rules-based mindset to one grounded in values shifts the focus from policing behaviour to empowering people. Placing trust over control encourages autonomy and accountability, judgment over rigid procedures allows for adaptability and nuance, and purpose over pure profit reminds everyone why the work matters beyond the numbers.

This cultural evolution supports innovation, resilience, and genuine customer focus. But how do you see this playing out in the teams or organizations you're involved with? Banks that embed values – such as empathy, transparency, and fairness – into everyday decision-making find themselves more resilient, more adaptive, and more aligned with customer expectations.

The Problem of the Cultural Inheritance

Many legacy banks inherit cultures built in another era – shaped by industrial models, geographic monopolies, and a homogeneous workforce. These cultures may persist even when the leadership changes or the strategy pivots. Examples include rewarding seniority over insight, tolerating toxic behaviour from high performers, equating compliance with ethical conduct, and valuing perfection over learning.

Cultural debt, in the same way as literal debt, accumulates invisibly – until it is suddenly too big. Cultural transformation starts with acknowledging the inheritance – and deciding what to keep, what to develop, and what to abandon.

Leadership as a Cultural Signal

Every action a leader takes – whom they promote, how they respond to failure, what they measure – sends out a cultural signal. Banks traditionally have strong formal structures, which means that informal cues are even more powerful. When the CEO praises a junior analyst for surfacing a risk early, it fosters a culture of speaking up. Conversely, when a senior manager tolerates corner-cutting to meet targets, it fuels a culture of silence. Additionally, when diversity targets are met without allowing for real inclusion, it leads to tokenism rather than true transformation. Culture is not a poster on the wall. It is the outcome of accumulated choices by those in power.

Micro cultures, Macro Impact

Banks rarely are monolithic. The culture in the retail banking division may differ from the one in corporate banking; the call centre may embody different norms than the trading floor. These micro cultures must be understood, respected, and aligned – not forcibly homogenized. Modern cultural transformation involves:

- Listening deeply across layers
- Mapping subcultures through qualitative and quantitative data
- Creating cultural guardrails rather than enforcing one-size-fits-all norms

The goal is alignment, not uniformity. A resilient banking culture enables diversity of thought within a shared purpose.

Metrics That Matter

In order to shift culture, you must measure it, but not through vanity indicators such as staff engagement scores alone. Instead, banks should track parameters such as psychological safety levels in teams, time-to-resolution for ethical concerns, rates of upward challenge during risk reviews, inclusion based on peer behaviour, and alignment between stated values and observed actions. Culture becomes real when it is observable, discussable, and accountable.

As banks digitize, cultural assumptions must evolve from paper trails to digital transparency, from physical presence to trust-by-default, and from control over devices to enablement through platforms. Hybrid work, remote onboarding, and algorithmic decision-making all require new cultural fluency.

For example, how does a team maintain cohesion when working asynchronously across time zones? How does a junior analyst escalate a concern in a Slack-based workflow? What happens when AI decisions replace human discretion? Digital transformation without cultural adaptation leads to drift, disconnection, and disenchantment.

Culture can be reinforced not only through speeches and training, but also through design choices. Onboarding journeys can celebrate shared values, while performance reviews assess collaboration, not just delivery. Risk systems can reward early alerts instead of incident responses only, and internal communications can highlight the importance of learning from failure. Systems are never neutral. They either amplify or erode culture. The bank of the future designs systems that institutionalize its best values – even when humans are not watching.

Conclusion: Culture as Core Infrastructure

In a future defined by automation, open finance, and algorithmic complexity, culture becomes the irreducible human core. Strategy may define where a bank wants to go. Technology may define how it gets there. But culture determines whether anyone will follow – and whether anyone will stay. The strongest foundation for transformation is not technology. It is a culture that says:

> "We listen. We learn. We act with integrity. We evolve together."

This is the real blueprint for the bank of tomorrow.

2 From Control to Empowerment

The traditional architecture of banking was built on control – of processes, people, risk, and reputation. Hierarchies were rigid, decisions centralized, compliance enforced through surveillance and standardization. In an era shaped by industrial logic and regulatory caution, this made sense. But as the world has shifted – technologically, socially, and philosophically – so too must the foundations of financial institutions.

The modern bank must operate with distributed intelligence, not centralized command. This requires a pivot from control to empowerment – a culture where people are trusted to act, learn, and lead at all levels. In this section, we explore what this shift truly entails, and how institutions can transition from legacy mindsets of oversight to frameworks of autonomy, creativity, and ownership.

Why Control No Longer Works

Control-based systems rely on predictability – fixed routines, repeatable tasks, and linear chains of command. But today's financial ecosystem is anything but predictable. Markets shift rapidly, customer expectations evolve in real-time, and competition comes from unexpected places – fintechs, platforms, AI start-ups, even retailers. This fluidity creates three problems for control-driven models:

1. Bottlenecks: Centralized decisions slow down innovation. Frontline staff, which are closest to the customer, often have the fewest decision rights.
2. Disengagement: Employees treated as cogs lose motivation. Creativity is suppressed. Learning stagnates.
3. Mismatch with talent expectations: New generations of professionals value purpose, autonomy, and agency. They do not thrive under micromanagement.

In short, the control model is not just inefficient – it is culturally obsolete.

Empowerment Is Not Chaos

Critics of empowerment worry about chaos. However, empowerment does not mean there is no structure. It means designing smart frameworks where individuals have the information, authority, and support to act responsibly.

In empowered organizations, strategy is clear and cascaded transparently. Roles are defined but not confined, allowing for flexibility and adaptability. Feedback loops operate constantly, fostering continuous improvement. Mistakes are viewed as opportunities for learning rather than grounds for blame, encouraging a growth mindset throughout the organization. Empowerment does not mean relinquishing leadership. Instead, it reimagines it – from directing to facilitating, from gatekeeping to enabling.

Case Study: Nordic Banking Culture

Nordic banks have long embraced models of employee autonomy, reflecting broader societal norms around trust and responsibility. In several Swedish and Finnish banks, frontline staff are trained to make credit decisions up to a certain threshold without managerial approval. This is not recklessness – it is trust in competence. The result? Faster service, higher employee satisfaction, and better risk calibration because the employee taking the credit decision has more knowledge about the applicant's circumstances. Empowerment here is not a slogan, but an operational reality.

Psychological Safety as Infrastructure

Empowerment cannot flourish without psychological safety – the belief that one can speak up, admit mistakes, and propose ideas without fear of punishment. This is particularly crucial in banking, where error-aversion has long been culturally entrenched. To shift this mindset, leaders must model vulnerability – for example, by openly admitting what they don't know. Teams should be trained in the art of constructive dissent, creating space for challenge and dialogue. Most importantly, feedback must be de-risked so that speaking up doesn't feel like a threat to one's career.

In high-trust teams, junior analysts can flag anomalies in transactions. In low-trust teams, silence prevails – until it becomes a compliance issue. Empowerment without safety is performative. Safety without empowerment is paternalism. Together, they unlock true agency.

Digital Tools for Empowerment

Technology can reinforce control or enable autonomy. It depends on the design. For example:

Dashboards give employees visibility into performance by making metrics accessible rather than hiding them within management layers. AI assistants are designed to support human judgment, enhancing decision-making rather than replacing it. Workflow tools enable self-directed task management and foster transparent collaboration among teams.

When thoughtfully deployed, digital platforms can democratize access to information, reduce dependency on hierarchy, and accelerate responsiveness. However, tools alone do not empower. The surrounding mindset and processes matter just as much.

Redesigning Risk Ownership

In traditional models, risk is "owned" by control functions: compliance, audit, legal. But in empowered models, risk awareness becomes a collective discipline. This requires a major cultural reset. Key shifts involve embedding risk thinking directly into product design rather than limiting it to post-launch reviews. Customer-facing teams are trained in regulatory literacy to better understand compliance requirements. Additionally, organizations recognize and reward the early identification of risks to encourage proactive management. The empowered bank treats risk not as a specialist domain, but as a shared mindset.

From Command Chains to Decision Circles

Command chains work in military settings. But in dynamic, interdependent environments such as financial services, decision-making is best when distributed and contextual. High-performing banks are experimenting with cross-functional squads that are empowered to solve problems from end to end. They implement a rotating leadership to build empathy and ownership across teams. Additionally, decentralized approval processes are adopted to accelerate innovation while maintaining the necessary control. This is not decentralization for its own sake, but a design choice aligned with complexity.

The Empowered Customer Mirrors the Empowered Employee

Interestingly, empowered cultures internally often translate to better experiences externally. A bank that trusts its staff to act independently also tends to design better for customer autonomy. This manifests in self-service journeys that provide real control, transparent fees and choices, and support that respects dignity rather than fostering dependency. Empowerment, thus, is cultural coherence – inside and out.

The Leadership Challenge

Empowerment requires a very different kind of leader – one who listens more than talks, who coaches rather than commands, and who creates space instead of occupying it. This is deeply uncomfortable for many leaders raised in command-and-control systems. It requires humility, systems thinking, and emotional intelligence. Training alone won't suffice. Incentives are also needed to support the shift. Leaders must be evaluated on how well they build leaders around them, not just on deliverables.

Conclusion: From Control to Confidence

Empowerment is not the absence of control. It is the presence of confidence – in people, in systems, in culture. It is a wager that, with the right tools, clarity, and support, people will rise to the occasion. And over time, that trust compounds into a workforce that is faster, smarter, more fulfilled – and more aligned with purpose. In the bank of tomorrow, control is not abandoned. It is reimagined as trust-enabled governance. And empowerment is not a risk. It is the foundation of resilience.

3 Talent in the Age of Automation

The banking industry is undergoing a seismic shift – not merely digital, but human. As automation, AI, and machine learning become core infrastructure, banks must not only redesign systems, but reimagine the roles, capabilities, and purposes of their employees. Talent in the age of automation is not defined by what humans can do better than machines, but by what only humans can do at all. This is not the end of human talent in banking – it is its redefinition. Tasks are disappearing, roles are evolving, and capabilities are becoming fluid. And for banks that understand this transformation there is an opportunity to unlock a new era of creativity, empathy, and strategic value.

The Myth of Replacement

Much of the public discussion about automation presents it as a replacement. Machines are taking over human jobs. While true for some routine functions, this narrative is overly simplistic .In reality, it is tasks that are being automated, not whole jobs. New roles are emerging, especially in oversight, orchestration, and exception handling. Augmentation is outpacing replacement in many knowledge-intensive functions.

For example, AI can process loan applications at scale – but human judgment is still needed for borderline cases, ethical dilemmas, and customer empathy. Robotic process automation can streamline compliance checks – but it cannot interpret ambiguous regulatory changes. Thus, the winning question is not: Which jobs will disappear? but: How will work be reimagined to create more value, more meaning, and more resilience?

The New Talent Equation

Talent strategies must now answer three questions:

1 Which work will be done by machines?
2 Which work must remain human?
3 How can the two complement each other intelligently?

This leads to a new design of roles:

- From processors to interpreters
- From compliance enforcers to risk navigators
- From task executors to system thinkers
- From order followers to value creators

For banks, this means a shift from hiring for functional repetition to cultivating human distinctiveness: empathy, judgment, ethics, design, and foresight.

Core Human Capabilities in Banking

As automation expands, the value of what is uniquely human grows. Among the most critical emerging competencies are:

1 Ethical Reasoning: With AI making decisions that affect credit, fraud, and access, ethical interpretation becomes vital. Humans are needed to set parameters, challenge outcomes, and ensure alignment with values.
2 Empathy and Communication: Especially in retail banking and customer service, the human ability to listen, reassure, and contextualize will remain irreplaceable – particularly during moments of stress (e.g., bereavement, fraud, financial hardship).

3. Foresight and Scenario Thinking: Machines optimize for known patterns. Humans explore possible futures. Strategic roles increasingly demand the capacity to imagine unintended consequences and take long-term decisions under uncertainty.
4. Collaboration and Influence: Working in cross-functional teams – often across geographies and cultures – requires the ability to use soft power and persuasion and to find shared meaning, not just to follow instructions. These are not "nice to have" traits. They are the new foundations of competitive advantage.

Rethinking Talent Pipelines

In this context, traditional approaches to recruitment and workforce planning no longer suffice. Banks must hire for potential, not just credentials. They need to retrain at scale, moving employees from legacy roles to future-fit capabilities. Investing in learning infrastructure is crucial, including developing internal academies and encouraging peer-to-peer teaching. Additionally, partnering with education providers helps shape curricula and align them with evolving industry needs. For example, Singapore's DBS Bank has invested heavily in digital upskilling for all employees, with programs that include data literacy, coding boot camps, and design thinking. Talent becomes a renewable resource – not a static asset.

Inclusivity in the Talent Shift

Automation presents a paradox: it can deepen exclusion if poorly managed, or expand opportunity if designed inclusively. To ensure the latter, access to reskilling must be broad and not limited to elite talent. Job redesign should consider all levels within the organization, from call centres to compliance departments. Additionally, digital tools need to be accessible and intuitive to avoid alienating employees.

Diversity also becomes a strategic asset. Heterogeneous teams are better at identifying blind spots in algorithms, stress-testing models, and interpreting nuanced human behaviour. Inclusive talent strategies are not only fairer – they are smarter.

Managing the Emotional Landscape

The shift to automation often causes emotional dislocation, including anxiety over job security, fear of irrelevance, and resistance to new technologies. These reactions are rational and require empathetic management. Leaders must be transparent about what is changing and why, celebrate human contributions alongside technical upgrades, and create safe spaces for employees to express their questions and fears and to navigate transitions. Culture cannot be an afterthought. It must lead the change.

The Rise of the Hybrid Workforce

As automation progresses, the future workforce will be hybrid – humans and machines working in tandem. Banks must design for collaboration between humans and AI agents, employees and bots, and teams and data models. This changes everything from team structure to interface design. Employees need not only digital skills, but machine partnership literacy: knowing when to rely on AI, when to override, and how to explain outcomes. This is not science fiction. It is already happening in areas such as fraud detection, credit underwriting, and wealth management advice.

Global Perspectives: India, UK, and US

- India: Massive investment in fintech and back-office automation is reshaping talent needs, with an emphasis on data skills and multilingual support. Banks are blending human support with chatbots for vernacular outreach.
- UK: Traditional banks are reskilling staff at scale, often in partnership with tech platforms. Lloyds and Santander Bank have both launched major internal learning programs, recognizing the shift from transaction handling to customer service.
- US: The shift is more market-led, with high demand for product designers, AI trainers, and risk interpreters. JP Morgan and Capital One are among those leading the integration of machine learning teams with frontline operations.

In all markets, the trend is clear: the human role is not shrinking – it is evolving.

Leadership for Talent Transformation

Finally, leaders must treat talent not as a cost centre, but as a core strategic differentiator. This means:

- Moving from seeing HR as admin to talent as strategy
- Linking workforce planning to innovation and customer goals
- Measuring success not by headcount, but by human impact

Boards and executives must understand that the future of the bank depends not just on its systems – but on how it invests in, protects, and unlocks its human capital.

Conclusion: Redefining the Human Advantage

Talent in the age of automation is not about resisting change. It is about reclaiming the essence of being human in a digital world. Banks that thrive will be those that:

- Redesign work to amplify human strengths
- Retrain workers with empathy and vision
- Build cultures that honour both technology and humanity

This is not a race against machines. It is a race to become more deeply human – in a way that no machine can replicate.

4 Rethinking Roles and Capabilities

The shift toward automation, platform banking, and AI-assisted decision-making is not simply reshaping workflows – it is fundamentally reconfiguring how banks define, assign, and develop roles. The 20th-century model of stable job titles and narrowly defined functions is giving way to an era of fluid capabilities, dynamic teams, and lifelong learning. Banks must now rethink their internal architecture not only around what gets done, but around who does it, how, and why. This section examines the strategic redefinition of roles in the modern financial institution – and the shift from a world of fixed job descriptions to a culture of adaptive capabilities.

From Functions to Capabilities

Historically, banks were built around departments: operations, treasury, lending, marketing, compliance. These silos defined not just reporting lines but identities – people were "credit officers" or "tellers" or "relationship managers". In today's landscape, rigid boundaries often inhibit performance. Customers expect cross-functional service, products are developed through agile, multidisciplinary teams, and technologies disrupt role boundaries faster than organizational charts can keep up. Modern banks are shifting from focusing solely on functions to emphasizing capabilities – concentrating not just on a person's title, but on what they can actually contribute.

Capabilities are transferable across roles and domains, upgradable through learning and experience, and viewed as strategic assets rather than mere HR formalities. For example, the ability to understand customer data is important for marketing, risk, compliance, and product design, regardless of the job title of the employee.

Designing for Adaptability

Rethinking roles requires a shift in design principles. The goal is not to define a static position, but to design a dynamic ecosystem where people grow with the business. This involves:

1. Modular role structures: Breaking jobs into key tasks and capabilities, allowing people to plug into projects based on fit, not just title.

2 Flexible career pathways: Enabling movement across functions – e.g., from risk to product to ESG – based on transferable skills and evolving interests.
3 Role evolution by learning: Redefining progression not as promotion, but as capability deepening – learning something new, applying it in real settings, and expanding influence. This architecture fosters agility and unlocks human potential.

Case Study: Capabilities in Practice

Standard Chartered has adopted a "skills-first" approach in parts of its HR and operations teams. Instead of advertising jobs, it advertises projects that require specific capabilities: data visualization, stakeholder engagement, regulatory scanning. Employees then self-nominate based on interest and skill.

This approach increases internal mobility, boosts motivation through ownership, and allows the bank to respond quickly to changing needs. It also fosters a more empowered, entrepreneurial mindset.

The Role of Learning Ecosystems

You cannot rethink roles without rethinking learning. Banks must build capability academies – internal platforms where employees continuously develop skills aligned to strategic needs.

These ecosystems should include on-demand learning modules that are digital and bite-sized, cross-functional projects serving as learning labs, mentorship and coaching opportunities, peer-to-peer teaching, and certification pathways recognized both internally and externally.

Importantly, learning must be incentivized – through recognition, performance metrics, and visible career advancement. The bank of tomorrow is a learning organism – without a fixed hierarchy of tasks.

Rethinking Managerial Roles

Automation also reshapes management by shifting the manager's role from supervision to enablement. This involves facilitating team learning, navigating ambiguity, coordinating between humans and machines, and curating experiences that build capability. Leadership development must prepare managers to be systems thinkers, not just task assigners. Capability-based organizations need capability-building managers.

Bridging the Gap: Capability Frameworks

To put these ideas into practice, banks are now deploying capability frameworks. These frameworks map the key competencies needed across the organization, link those competencies to business goals, and offer tools for self-assessment and growth planning. A good framework includes both technical (e.g., data analysis, AML regulation) and human capabilities (e.g., influencing, adaptability, ethical reasoning).Importantly, these frameworks are not static – they must be updated annually to reflect market, regulatory, and technological shifts.

Aligning Capabilities with Strategic Themes

As financial institutions evolve, certain thematic capabilities are becoming particularly critical:

1. Digital Fluency: Not every employee must be able to code, but all must be comfortable working alongside digital systems, understanding data flows, and using platforms effectively.
2. Customer Empathy: With growing focus on experience and trust, human-centred thinking is a core business asset.
3. Sustainability and ESG: Understanding how environmental, social, and governance principles integrate into business decisions is no longer optional.
4. Crisis Resilience: The ability to adapt under pressure, recover from disruption, and lead through volatility is essential across functions.

Banks that bake these capabilities into roles – from onboarding through to executive development – will have an edge in agility, trust, and impact.

Global Snapshot: Role Reinvention across Markets

- UK: Banks such as NatWest and Lloyds are redefining branch and contact centre roles to be more advisory, empathetic, and data-savvy, blending traditional customer service with digital fluency.
- US: Institutions are designing "fusion" roles – blending product, technology, and compliance knowledge – to support agile development and innovation.
- India: With a younger workforce and rapid fintech growth, banks are embedding learning into daily operations, offering rotation-based development and gamified skill platforms.

In all those regions the core message is the same: Roles must evolve faster than hierarchies.

Technology as an Enabler – Not a Replacement

Digital platforms can support role reinvention when thoughtfully applied. AI can suggest learning pathways based on career goals and performance. Internal mobility tools can match employees with short-term projects that stretch their capabilities. Smart dashboards can track not only what employees do, but how they grow. However, this requires trust – the technology must be transparent, supportive, and non-punitive, enabling people rather than monitoring them.

Conclusion: The Rise of Capability-Centric Institutions

To thrive in the age of constant transformation, banks must stop designing for roles and start designing for resilience – through people who can adapt, grow, and lead in ambiguity. This means:

- Viewing each employee not as a job title, but as a portfolio of capabilities
- Creating space for curiosity, learning, and reinvention
- Building systems that flex with people – not people who break under systems

The future bank will not be defined by headcount, but by capability density – the aggregate potential of its people to respond wisely, act ethically, and deliver value in a world that refuses to stand still.

5 Building Ethical and Inclusive Teams

In the era of rapid digital transformation and systemic complexity, banking is no longer judged solely by profitability or efficiency. Increasingly, trust, fairness, and integrity have become the defining attributes of sustainable institutions. At the heart of this evolution is a fundamental shift: Organizations must build teams that are not just high-performing, but also act ethically and are inclusive by design.

Inclusion and ethics are no longer just about following rules or managing reputation. They are essential strategic assets. Financial institutions must foster environments where diverse voices are valued, where decisions are made with care and accountability, and where every team member contributes not only skill but conscience. This section explores the organizational foundations of such teams and how they underpin long-term performance in the banking sector.

Ethics and Inclusion – Why Now?

Ethical and inclusive teams offer measurable advantages. They bring better risk awareness, as diverse perspectives help flag hidden dangers. They build stronger customer trust, as institutions begin to reflect the communities they serve. They foster greater innovation, driven by the collision of different lived experiences. And they lead to improved retention, as employees feel seen, heard, and valued.

These outcomes are crucial in financial services, where misjudgment or exclusion can result in systemic harm – from denied credit access to algorithmic bias and cultural misalignment. In an interconnected, digitally transparent world, ethical failures are amplified. Conversely, ethical leadership and inclusive design are rewarded with loyalty, brand equity, and regulatory goodwill.

Inclusion as a Strategic Imperative

Inclusion is not simply about representation; it is the active design of systems where everyone can contribute meaningfully. This means implementing equitable hiring practices that diversify talent pipelines beyond elite institutions or traditional networks. It requires making development opportunities – such as promotions, training, and mentorship – accessible across all backgrounds and geographies. Psychological safety must be prioritized, so that team members feel free to challenge assumptions, admit mistakes, and propose ideas without fear. Finally, inclusion means designing for belonging – not settling for tokenism, but ensuring all employees genuinely feel part of a shared mission. Financial services have historically preferred homogeneity in leadership. Shifting this requires a deliberate architecture, not just well – meaning slogans.

Embedding Ethics into Everyday Practice

Ethics must move beyond codes of conduct and become part of operations. That means:

- Values-based decision frameworks: Equipping teams with tools to evaluate trade-offs in product design, data use, and customer engagement
- Real-time escalation channels: Allowing employees to flag concerns without career risk
- Ethical performance metrics: Tracking not just outcomes, but how outcomes are achieved

For example, ethical underwriting might involve assessing not just default risk, but the social consequences of a loan product's structure. Ethical AI requires human oversight, fairness audits, and mechanisms for customers to challenge algorithmic decisions. Inclusion without ethics is fragile. Ethics without inclusion is blind. The two must reinforce each other in practice.

The Leaders' Behaviour Sets the Tone

Culture is not shaped by policy documents – it is lived through behaviour. Leaders must model transparency in their own decision-making, demonstrating that openness builds trust. They should be willing to admit uncertainty, acknowledging that ethics is a continuous journey rather than a fixed destination. Sponsoring diverse voices is essential – not just in hiring, but in strategic conversations where real influence is exercised. Most importantly, leaders must hold themselves accountable for ethical blind spots and cultural exclusions, recognizing that leadership carries the responsibility to listen, learn, and adapt. Ethical leadership is not about perfection – it is about humility, courage, and consistency.

Inclusive Design in Technology and Products

As banks digitize, inclusion must extend to digital interfaces and product strategies. Accessibility is essential – mobile apps, websites, and interfaces must be designed to accommodate users with disabilities, low literacy levels, or limited internet connectivity. Multilingual support is equally critical, particularly in diverse or multilingual markets such as India, South Africa, or the UK, where language can be a barrier to financial participation. Product strategies must also prioritize low-cost access to ensure that pricing models do not inadvertently exclude low-income segments. Additionally, bias auditing should be a standard practice to identify and mitigate discriminatory patterns in AI systems, underwriting processes, or customer profiling, ensuring fairness is built into every digital experience. Technology is never neutral. Ethical and inclusive design requires intentionality at every stage.

Case Studies: Global Practices

1 Standard Chartered

The Bank has introduced inclusive design principles across its digital products, including tools for customers with visual, auditory, and cognitive impairments. The company's internal "Accessibility Lab" tests services against real user scenarios.

2 ICICI Bank (India)

ICICI has launched programs to increase rural and female participation in its workforce, including flexible roles for women returning from career breaks and language-sensitive customer service models in rural regions.

3 Bank of America (US)

The company's "Responsible Growth" framework integrates ESG, racial equity, and ethics into performance assessment for senior leaders. Inclusion is not an HR goal – it is embedded in the business strategy.

Each of these examples demonstrates how inclusive ethics becomes a competitive differentiator.

The Role of Data in Ethical Inclusion

Modern banks are data-rich, which presents a double-edged sword. On the one hand, data offers opportunities – it can uncover patterns of exclusion, highlight service gaps, and expose systemic inequities. On the other hand, it introduces risk – poor data practices can breach customer privacy, entrench bias, and create opaque systems that customers don't understand or trust. Ethical teams approach data with discernment. They practice data minimization by collecting only what is necessary, and build consent architecture that gives customers clear understanding and control over how their data is used. Bias monitoring is a continuous task, ensuring that models are regularly tested for discriminatory patterns. Transparency is equally critical – customers should be able to query and challenge decisions, particularly those made by automated systems. Ultimately, inclusive banking is data-aware, not data-dependent – it values the human context behind the numbers.

Global banks must also consider cultural inclusion, as their teams increasingly span regions, languages, and diverse social norms. Effective collaboration in such environments demands more than just shared goals – it requires intentional design. Cultural fluency training helps employees navigate differences in communication styles, decision-making, and expectations. Time zone-aware planning ensures that collaboration doesn't consistently burden one region over another. Equity in voice and influence is essential, particularly in hybrid teams where remote members can easily be sidelined in discussions and decisions. At the same time, respect for local customs must be balanced with adherence to core ethical standards, ensuring that inclusion does not mean compromising on integrity. A globally inclusive team recognizes difference – and builds strength through it.

Metrics That Matter:

- Demographic representation at all levels.
- Inclusion sentiment scores, gathered anonymously.
- Ethical incident reporting trends.
- Impact metrics (e.g., increase in credit access for underserved populations).
- Attrition and promotion patterns across gender, race, ability, and background.

What gets measured gets managed – and what gets shared builds accountability.

Conclusion: From Compliance to Conscience

The most forward-looking banks are those that understand inclusion and ethics not as restrictions, but as release mechanisms: unleashing the full potential of human capital, earning customer trust, and building systems that reflect the societies they serve. In order to build ethical and inclusive teams, banks must be deliberate in their design. They must invest in capacity, not just compliance. They should honour differences as a source of strength. And they must align products and policies with values. In an age of scrutiny, complexity, and accelerated change, the foundation of long-term success is simple: do the right thing, and bring everyone along.

6 Learning as a Core Organizational Function

In an age of unrelenting technological change, evolving regulations, and shifting customer expectations, financial institutions can no longer treat learning as a peripheral function. Learning is not a benefit, an afterthought, or a cost centre. It is the engine of strategic renewal.

For banks to thrive in an environment defined by complexity and disruption, they must become learning organizations – institutions where knowledge creation, adaptation, and application are continuous and embedded into the fabric of everyday work. This section explores what it means to place learning at the core of the bank's operating model, and how this shift transforms not only talent development but also the institution's resilience, relevance, and purpose.

From Training to Learning Ecosystems

Traditional banks have long equated learning with training – typically classroom-based, HR-managed, and compliance-focused. While such training remains necessary, it is insufficient. Modern banking demands a move from episodic training to continuous capability development, delivered through learning ecosystems.

A learning ecosystem is always-on, accessible anytime, anywhere. It is contextual, aligned with real-time tasks and strategic priorities. It is multimodal, blending digital platforms, live coaching, peer learning, and stretch assignments. It is democratized, enabling self-driven learning journeys, not just top-down courses. In these ecosystems, employees do not wait for training. They actively seek growth as part of their job.

Why Learning Must Be Strategic

Embedding learning as a core function allows banks to react faster to disruption, whether regulatory, technological, or market-based. It helps close capability gaps at scale, especially in areas such as digitalization, ESG, data, and customer centricity. It drives innovation, as teams that learn are more likely to experiment and iterate effectively. It also helps retain top talent – people stay where they can grow.

Banks that underinvest in learning often find themselves playing catch-up – hiring expensively, reorganising reactively, and suffering from internal stagnation. By contrast, banks that encourage learning adapt proactively and competitively.

Learning Aligned to Organizational Purpose

Strategic learning begins with a simple question: What capabilities will we need tomorrow that we don't have today? The answer should be based not solely on trends but also on the bank's mission, market dynamics, stakeholder needs, and long-term risk scenarios.

For example, a bank committed to financial inclusion must teach frontline teams not just customer service, but cultural sensitivity, behavioural economics, and accessible tech design. Sustainability-focused banks must up skill teams in ESG frameworks, climate finance, and impact measurement. When learning aligns with purpose, it becomes transformational.

Case Studies: Learning-centric Cultures

1 ING (Netherlands)

The Dutch bank has restructured large parts of its workforce into agile squads with embedded learning loops. Employees use the "Pace" platform to set growth goals, access micro-learning content, and receive continuous feedback.

2 DBS Bank (Singapore)

DBS launched the "Be My Guest" shadowing program and internal "Gandalf Scholars" to promote cross-pollination of knowledge. Its AI-powered learning hub curates personalized content pathways for each employee based on their role and aspirations.

3 Goldman Sachs (US)

With its "Pine Street" leadership development initiative, Goldman emphasizes experiential learning for senior executives through live problem-solving and multi-stakeholder simulations – helping leaders adapt to ambiguity and scale impact.

Each of these examples treats learning as a strategic enabler, not a compliance necessity.

The Manager as Learning Coach

Managers need to transition from simply assigning tasks to becoming learning coaches. This involves actively identifying learning opportunities in everyday work, offering timely and constructive feedback, fostering curiosity and experimentation, and collaborating with team members to develop growth plans.

When learning becomes a shared priority, performance and development reinforce each other. Organizations can support this by embedding learning KPIs into managerial evaluations – making capability-building part of leadership accountability.

Technology as an Enabler – Not the End

Learning platforms, AI tutors, VR simulations, and digital academies provide unparalleled scale and personalization, but technology alone cannot ignite the desire to learn. Banks must cultivate a growth mindset culture, acknowledge and reward learning behaviour, and prioritize learning by making dedicated time for it rather than treating it as something to be done after work. Blending tech-enabled and human-led learning unlocks the best of both worlds – scalability with empathy.

Social and Peer Learning

In high-performing learning cultures, knowledge does not flow only top-down. Peer learning is powerful:

- Communities of practice allow people to share experiences, mistakes, and hacks.
- Reverse mentoring connects junior digital natives with senior leaders.
- Open forums and town halls make organizational knowledge visible and participatory.

Knowledge sharing must be incentivized, instead of knowledge being hoarded. A learning organization sees every employee as both teacher and student.

Governance and Measurement

To elevate learning to a core function, strong governance is essential. This involves appointing dedicated learning officers at senior level, establishing clear capability maps aligned with the organization's strategy, and allocating budgets that prioritize development rather than just headcount or systems. Additionally, tracking the impact of learning by measuring how it translates into business value is crucial. Relevant metrics may include time to productivity in new roles, rates of internal mobility and promotion, employee learning indexes based on self-reported confidence and growth, and improvements in business KPIs following training, such as net promoter scores, risk incidents, and product innovation. Learning must be visible and valued at the board level.

Equity in Access to Learning

Learning must be accessible to everyone, not just those in head office or designated as high-potential. Inclusive learning involves providing mobile access for frontline staff, offering language support and localization, creating modular options to accommodate varying bandwidth and time constraints, and designing tailored pathways that address different starting points. Without measures to promote equity, learning systems amplify inequality. Democratizing development is a matter of both fairness and long-term resilience.

Building a Culture of Curiosity

Perhaps the most important shift is cultural. A true learning organization is not built through platforms or courses – but through a shift of the mindset. This approach emphasizes encouraging questions rather than simply providing answers, viewing mistakes as opportunities for learning instead of failures, celebrating curiosity, experimentation, and the courage to embrace change, and sharing stories of growth alongside achievements. In a curious culture, people feel safe to explore, stretch, and reinvent – and the organization evolves with them.

Conclusion: The Learning Bank

The bank of the future is not the one with the best strategy – but the one best equipped to learn, unlearn, and relearn at scale. It is a place where growth is not episodic, but happens every day. Where development is not delegated to HR, but owned by every leader and learner.

Embedding learning as a core organizational function requires strategic alignment, cultural transformation, technological enablement, equity of access, and strong governance supported by committed leadership. The journey begins not with a platform, but with a mindset: that learning is not an add-on – it is the business itself.

7 Reinventing the Workplace Experience

The workplace is no longer just a location – it is an ecosystem of interactions, tools, expectations, values, and possibilities. For the banking sector, which has traditionally relied on formality, hierarchy, and physical presence, the transformation of the workplace is not merely a matter of logistics. It is a question of identity and purpose.

Reinventing the workplace goes beyond hybrid schedules or digital tools. It is about building a work environment where people can thrive, contribute meaningfully, and feel part of something larger. As employee expectations evolve – especially among younger generations – banks must rethink how they design, govern, and cultivate the experiences that define daily work.

From Headquarters to Human-Centred Hubs

In the past, workplace design often revolved around central control, supervision, and symbolism – large buildings with corporate lobbies, corner offices, and fixed seating plans. Today, the shift is clear: functionality and humanity trump formality. Leading financial institutions are reimagining the workplace as:

- Collaboration hubs, not monitoring zones
- Fluid spaces that support deep focus, creativity, and informal exchange

- Wellbeing-oriented environments, with attention to lighting, ergonomics, and mental health
- Hybrid-enabling locations, designed for both in-person and virtual cohesion

This shift requires integrating physical, digital, and cultural elements to create a coherent and inspiring employee experience.

The Rise of the Hybrid Banker

Hybrid work is no longer just a temporary response to the pandemic but has become a sustained expectation. However, hybrid models introduce new challenges, such as ensuring equal visibility and voice for remote participants, building culture and trust without informal interactions such as water cooler moments, and designing meetings, projects, and feedback loops that accommodate different time zones, bandwidth limitations, and work-from-home realities. To address these challenges, banks must move beyond binary thinking of office versus home and focus on intentionality by identifying which work benefits from co-location, determining when synchronous communication is more effective than asynchronous, and leveraging digital tools to promote inclusion rather than isolation. The hybrid banker is not just mobile – they are empowered by design.

Culture Is Still Local – Even When Global

Multinational banks must recognize that workplace expectations vary by geography. For example:

- In Japan, hierarchy and consensus may shape workplace rhythms differently than in the Netherlands.
- In Nigeria or India, family obligations may influence work hours and location choices.
- In the US or UK, flexibility and autonomy may be stronger talent attractors than salary alone.

Reinventing the workplace requires sensitivity to local norms and adaptability in global policies. One-size-fits-all rarely works. The best institutions build frameworks that allow flexibility within shared values.

Technology as an Experience Layer

The digital layer of the modern workplace is where most interactions now occur. As such, banks must treat tech not just as infrastructure, but as employee experience. This includes:

- Frictionless tools: Integrated, intuitive platforms for communication, documentation, and task management
- Choice and autonomy: Allowing employees to personalize their digital workspace
- Security without surveillance: Balancing compliance needs with privacy and trust
- Well -being prompts: Features that nudge breaks, discourage after-hours overload, and support mental health

When technology is thoughtfully deployed, it reduces noise, increases clarity, and amplifies connection.

The Manager as Experience Designer

In a distributed and digitized workplace, the manager's role is central to fostering culture and cohesion. Managers move beyond simply assigning tasks to becoming designers of the daily work experience. This involves setting clear expectations and boundaries, fostering connection through regular check-ins, appreciation, and shared rituals, and recognizing contributions even when they may go unnoticed. Effective managers are emotionally intelligent, digitally fluent, and people-first leaders. They shape how work feels – not just how it is performed.

Belonging in a Dispersed World

One of the greatest risks of modern work is isolation. When people do not feel seen, heard, or included, their engagement erodes – even if they are performing tasks efficiently. Banks need to build a sense of belonging at scale by implementing peer mentoring and buddy systems, fostering cross-functional communities such as women in fintech and LGBTQ+ banking networks, promoting inclusive storytelling through channels such as internal newsletters that highlight diverse voices, and encouraging transparent decision-making paired with two-way dialogue. Belonging is the emotional infrastructure of high-performing teams. Without it, even well-paid professionals will leave.

Case Studies in Workplace Reinvention

1 Standard Chartered (Global)

With its "Future Workplace, Now" program, Standard Chartered redesigned office spaces in multiple cities to support hybrid work – with flexible desks, collaboration zones, and wellness facilities. It also piloted a 3-day work-from-anywhere model for select teams.

2 Capital One (US)

Capital One eliminated assigned seating and encouraged hybrid rhythm-setting at the team level. Its "Workplace of the Future" integrates employee feedback loops and technology upgrades in every refresh cycle.

3 NatWest (UK)

NatWest invested in "Colleague Listening" platforms and redesigned employee journeys to emphasize empathy and simplicity. From onboarding to exit, each touchpoint is treated as a human experience, not just a transaction.

These banks show that reinventing the workplace can be strategic, iterative, and culture-led.

Performance without Burnout

Modern banks must decouple performance from presenteeism. Outcomes matter more than hours. At the same time, performance must not come at the cost of burnout. Achieving this requires setting realistic goals, tracking well-being metrics such as workload fairness, recovery time, and team morale, providing managers with training on balancing workloads, and fostering a time-off culture that encourages taking breaks and holidays, and offline recovery. Wellness is no longer an HR initiative. It is a core driver of sustainable productivity.

Designing Work Around Life – Not the Other Way Around

Employees increasingly want work to fit into their lives – not to dominate them. Banks that support this are not just attractive – they are future-proofing their talent model. They offer:

- Flexible schedules
- Part-time or phased return options
- Support for care giving and life transitions
- Remote-first policies where feasible

...When people can bring their whole selves to work, they bring more energy, creativity, and loyalty.

Conclusion: The Workplace as a Living System

The future of work in banking focuses not on policies but on experiences. Reinventing the workplace involves continuously asking whether initiatives help people thrive, align with organizational values, and support both performance and humanity.

Reinvention requires courage. It asks leaders to challenge legacy norms, listen deeply, and design with care. The most human workplaces will attract the most human talent – and in the end, that will be the source of enduring advantage.

8 Leading with Emotional Intelligence

In an ever-more algorithm-driven, analytics-driven, automated world, the most lasting leadership trait is likely to be the most human one: emotional intelligence (EQ). Technical ability is required for banks that are subject to transformation, regulation, and reinvention – but emotional capability breeds trust, unity, and resilience.

EQ is not a nice-to-have, soft skill – it's a crucial ability. It enables leaders to relate to teams, manage uncertainty, and make data-informed decisions that also reflect human values. As financial institutions are being transformed, so should the leadership models driving them – and EQ needs to be at the heart of that transformation.

Understanding EQ

EQ consists of five main domains:

1. Knowing one's emotions, triggers, and effect on others
2. Controlling disruptive feelings, remaining calm and responsive
3. Being driven by internal values instead of external incentives
4. Recognizing and sensing the feelings of others
5. Handling relationships, influence, teamwork, and conflict

In banking, these skills impact everything from boardroom conversation to customer service culture.

Why EQ Matters in Banking

Banking at its core is still a people business, even in the age of technology, and EQ is playing an important role in it. Emotionally intelligent leaders navigate through change by sensing, acknowledging, and tackling fear and resistance. They lead diverse teams with cultural sensitivity and empathy, and they create an environment of inclusion. In times of crisis, calm and attuned leadership maintains confidence under fire. Client relationships are built not just on competence but on emotional connection. Additionally, EQ facilitates ethical decision-making because it enables leaders to know the effect of financial decisions on people.

Banks which focus on EQ create institutions that are perceived to be safe, inclusive, and high-performing.

Case Study: Satya Nadella and Microsoft's EQ Renaissance

Though Microsoft is a bank, Satya Nadella's tenure there teaches us some important lessons. He transformed Microsoft's corporate culture from one of internal competition to one of cooperation – rooted in empathy and a growth mindset. Market value skyrocketed on his watch, and so did employee satisfaction and creativity.

Nadella's success was not based on additional strategy decks, but on emotional clarity, humility, and human connection – all essential for banking leaders facing similar challenges.

The EQ Deficit of Traditional Banking

Throughout history, banking leadership has been associated with values such as decisiveness, reasonableness, control, and objectivity. Although these are still valuable, an overemphasis on them has tended to lead to hierarchical silos, a deficiency in psychological safety, blind spots to risk, and responses to customer or employee issues that can be tone-deaf. The financial crisis of 2008 exposed not only governance failures but EQ failures as well. Institutional actors had no idea of the consequences of their actions in the real world.

Developing EQ: It Can Be Taught

The good news is that EQ can be acquired and quantified. Banks can cultivate it through 360-degree feedback processes, leadership mentoring and coaching, reflective exercises such as journaling or the discussion of scenarios, role-playing and simulation – particularly ethical dilemmas or client dialogue – as well as mindfulness and resilience programs. Institutions that approach EQ as a formal development objective – rather than an ancillary characteristic – construct a deeper, more resilient leadership bench.

EQ and Inclusive Leadership

Empathy is the backbone of inclusion, and emotionally intelligent leaders engage deeply with marginalized voices, challenge their own assumptions and biases, listen for dissent and dialogue, and see how systemic inequity plays out in behaviour and policy. Inclusion does not come about through numbers. It is felt – or not – in day-to-day interactions. EQ is the gateway to a fully human-centred model of leadership.

Measuring EQ in Leadership

To raise emotionally intelligent leaders, one needs to quantify and reward such behaviour. This means integrating EQ metrics – including team trust, quality of feedback, and emotional climate – into performance appraisals, assessing leaders on results, but also on how they get there, including EQ-driven behaviour such as coaching, listening, and facilitating as part of promotion criteria, and regularly measuring organizational culture through engagement and psychological safety surveys. Banks need to desist from treating empathy and listening as intangibles – and begin treating them as essential leadership skills.

Boards and top executives have a key role to play in role-modelling EQ from the top. They lead by example with humility and openness, restore a sense of fairness and justice in response to crises, create structures that encourage listening throughout the organization, and acknowledge mistakes, which has the effect of reinforcing trust rather than undermining it. When top leaders model EQ, it trickles down. When they do not, no amount of HR training can make up for that.

AI, Automation, and the Human Advantage

While automation can take over more of the banking industry's operational work, EQ is all about human interactions. While AI can refine processes such as credit scoring, it cannot assure a panicked customer, coach a struggling colleague, or sense the emotional currents in a negotiation. EQ therefore becomes a competitive advantage. Banks with a high EQ culture retain more talent, serve customers more effectively, and handle risk better.

Instilling EQ into Leadership Pipelines

To really instil EQ, banks need to reimagine their leadership development pipelines:

- Early career: Train emotional self-awareness and communication skills in addition to technical expertise
- Mid-career: Provide coaching, a supportive peer network, and feedback-rich experiences
- Senior levels: Encourage narrative leadership, trust-building, and systemic empathy

Recruitment processes must filter not just for experience, but for emotional maturity as well. That is about being "nice", it's about being effective, aware, and human in high-stakes settings.

Conclusion: EQ as Leadership Infrastructure

As banking becomes more global, digital, and complex, it is tempting to think that leaders need to become more technical. But the reverse is true too: the more intelligent and knowledgeable the systems become, the more emotionally intelligent the leaders need to be. EQ isn't a nicety – it's infrastructure. It keeps culture, trust, inclusion, and agility together. It's the human connection that stitches data to action, decisions to outcomes, and strategy to people. The future bank will be guided not only by razor-sharp intellects – but by open hearts.

9 Returning to Institutional Character

Beneath every financial institution's strategy, structure, and service lies something more fundamental: character. While performance can be measured by quarterly returns and market share, character reveals itself in times of ambiguity and crisis, and in long-term stewardship. In the fourth industrial revolution, where algorithms and global capital flows often dictate outcomes, the question of institutional character may seem quaint – but in truth, it has never been more urgent.

Character is not about public relations or mission statements. It is about the deep-rooted values that guide action when no one is watching. In banking, it determines how trust is earned, how decisions are made under pressure, and how the institution relates to society at large. As the industry confronts ethical dilemmas, societal inequality, climate challenges, and digital opacity, a return to institutional character is both a moral and a strategic imperative.

What Is Institutional Character?

Institutional character represents the enduring moral and cultural identity of an organization. It encompasses core values that are reflected in behaviour rather than merely stated, consistency between words and actions, accountability for unintended consequences, and a sense of duty that extends beyond profit. Unlike brand or reputation, which can be curated, character is earned slowly and revealed suddenly – especially during stress, scrutiny, or scandal.

The Erosion of Character in Modern Finance

Over the past two decades, banks have significantly failed on several occasions, with examples including mortgage fraud and the sale of misleading products, manipulation of benchmarks such as the LIBOR scandal, discriminatory lending practices, and the awarding of excessive bonuses even during times of public bailouts.

These were not simply regulatory lapses – they were failures of institutional integrity. Policies existed, but character was absent. Decisions favoured expediency over ethics, and risk was detached from human consequence. Such moments not only lead to hefty fines, but they also pose serious risks to legitimacy.

The Role of a Bank's Founding Purpose

Many historic banks were founded with a clear social mission. Mutual building societies in the UK aimed to help working-class families save money and own homes. Credit unions in the US were established to serve local communities that were underserved by traditional banks. Similarly, Islamic banks, community development financial institutions (CDFIs), and cooperative lenders were created based on values of justice, transparency, and inclusivity. Over time, scale and profit imperatives diluted these origins. Returning to institutional character means reconnecting with a bank's founding purpose, adapting it to today's context, and placing it at the heart of culture and strategy.

Character-Driven Leadership

A bank's character is most directly shaped by its leadership. This encompasses board-level decisions regarding risk-taking, customer focus, and responses to failure. It also includes executive behaviour, particularly in times of public pressure or media scrutiny, and the tone set from the top, where authenticity, humility, and courage hold greater importance than charisma.

Leaders with institutional character ask whether a decision is the right thing to do, even if it is inconvenient, whether it will stand the test of time, and whether their actions serve society as a whole rather than only servicing the shareholders. These questions do not replace strategy – they inform it.

Embedding Character into Culture

To operationalize institutional character, banks must:

1. Hire for values, not just skills
2. Reward integrity, even when it costs short-term gains
3. Create space for ethical dialogue – including dissent
4. Build feedback loops from customers, communities, and employees
5. Maintain consistency between marketing and operations

Institutions with strong character build cultures where people feel safe to speak, motivated to serve, and aligned to something meaningful.

Institutions as Citizens

The concept of the corporate citizen has evolved, and today banks are expected to go beyond mere legal compliance. They are called upon to contribute to financial literacy, take meaningful action on climate change and sustainability, promote diversity and inclusion, support local communities and small and medium-sized enterprises (SMEs), and avoid investments that harm society or the planet. These are not CSR checkboxes. They are expressions of institutional character. Customers, especially younger ones, are watching closely – and choosing brands that reflect shared values.

Case Study: Triodos Bank (Netherlands)

Triodos Bank offers a compelling example. Founded in 1980, it lends exclusively to projects that add cultural, environmental, or social value. Its investment criteria include transparency, sustainability, and long-term impact. Triodos proves that profit and principle can coexist - and that institutional character can be a source of loyalty, differentiation, and resilience.

Character in the Age of AI and Automation

As decisions become increasingly data-driven, the importance of human character grows rather than diminishes. Questions arise such as whether lending algorithms should be allowed to deny credit solely based on risk models, how to ensure fairness when AI systems mirror societal biases, and who is held accountable when automation causes harm to customers. Institutions with strong character address these challenges by designing ethical guardrails for technology, establishing transparent review processes, maintaining human override capabilities, and ensuring that decision-making aligns with foundational values – not just efficiency. Technology without character becomes dangerous. With character, it becomes empowering.

The Long Arc of Trust

Trust is earned through consistent behaviour rather than branding. When banks act with integrity and character over time, they become trusted stewards, which fosters regulatory goodwill, improves talent retention, lowers the cost of capital, and builds enduring customer relationships. In contrast, when trust is broken, it can take years – or decades – to rebuild. Warren Buffett once said, “It takes 20 years to build a reputation and five minutes to ruin it.” Institutional character protects reputation by anchoring action in values that outlast trends.

Conclusion: Legacy as a Leadership Mandate

At some point, every institution must ask itself: What do we want to be remembered for? Legacy is not just about assets under management or technological innovation. It is about the mark left on society – the lives improved, the communities supported, the principles upheld.

Returning to institutional character is not nostalgic – it is future-oriented. In an era of climate urgency, global inequality, and trust deficits, banks must act not only as economic engines but as moral institutions. Those that lead with character will not only endure – they will inspire.

10 A Human-Centred Future

As the banking industry charges forward into a future defined by digital infrastructure, artificial intelligence, climate adaptation, and platform economies, a critical question arises: Will we build systems that elevate humanity – or sideline it? This chapter closes with a clear answer: The future of banking must be human-centred by design, not just intention.

This is not a philosophical nicety – it is a strategic necessity. Banks that lose sight of the human experience, the emotional reality, and the ethical responsibility at the heart of finance will struggle to sustain trust, talent, and long-term relevance. As technology becomes ubiquitous, the differentiator will not be innovation alone – but integration with human need, dignity, and aspiration.

The Case for Human-Centred Design

Human-centred banking means designing products, systems, services, and cultures around the real lives of customers, employees, and communities. It values:

- Empathy over efficiency
- Inclusion over abstraction
- Clarity over complexity
- Experience over control

It is not about slower processes or lower profits – it is about smarter, more sustainable growth, where people feel seen, heard, and supported.

Reframing the Purpose of Banking

At its core, banking is about enabling people to build secure lives, helping entrepreneurs create livelihoods, supporting institutions to function and flourish, and contributing to the stability and prosperity of societies. A human-centred bank focuses on understanding what customers are trying to achieve rather than just finding out which products they want. It designs services with not only its mainstream customers but also those at the margins of society in mind, measures success by well-being outcomes instead of transaction volumes, and treats staff as creative, ethical collaborators rather than mere resources.

This approach transforms customer journeys into human journeys by redesigning processes that reflect real life – for example, a loan process that supports first-generation students by acknowledging both financial risk and social mobility potential, mortgage systems that recognize non-traditional employment like gig work and freelancing as valid, and recovery frameworks that approach debtors with compassion rather than punishment. This approach needs us to listen to real experiences, work together with users, and make improvements based on emotional, cultural, and behavioural insights.

Technology as a Tool – Not a Proxy

There is a common temptation to view digital systems as neutral or all-knowing, but technology inherently reflects the values of its creators. Human-centred banking ensures that algorithms are explainable and open to challenge, personalization does not cross into surveillance, automation enhances rather than replaces human decision-making, and digital experiences are built on trust, clarity, and informed consent. A human-centred bank uses AI to amplify empathy and efficiency, not to remove the human from the equation.

Redesigning Work in Banking

Human-centred banking extends beyond customer experience to begin within the organization itself. This involves prioritizing psychological safety and emotional well-being, providing flexibility, autonomy, and a sense of purpose in roles, acknowledging the human cost of burnout, monotony, and exclusion, and designing hybrid work environments that support flow, focus, and fairness. The bank of the future must attract people not just through compensation – but by offering meaningful, respectful, empowering work.

Inclusive by Design, Not Default

Human-centred banks embrace inclusivity from the very beginning, rather than treating it as a retrofitted compliance requirement. This means designing interfaces accessible to users with disabilities, offering products in multiple languages or dialects, identifying and eliminating algorithmic bias, and proactively serving underbanked groups such as migrants, refugees, and informal sector workers. This is not merely good ethics – it is good economics. Inclusion expands the total addressable market and unlocks new sources of value and loyalty.

Ethics as a Daily Practice

A human-centred bank approaches ethics not as a yearly report item but as a constant design consideration. It questions whether a savings app's gamification might increase anxiety rather than motivation, whether interest rates for vulnerable customers should be higher just because data enables it, and whether a digital assistant should nudge users toward more expensive products. A human-centred mindset places long-term trust above short-term margin. It seeks not only what can be sold to customers – but also what should be offered to them.

Global Lessons in Human-Centred Models

- In the UK, challenger banks such as Monzo and Starling Bank have differentiated themselves through user-friendly interfaces, real-time support, and transparent language – proving that clarity and empathy can coexist with scale.

- In the US, Capital One's design transformation placed human experience at the centre of both branch innovation and digital experience, with cross-disciplinary teams anchored in user empathy.
- In India, fintech platforms such as Paytm and Jan Dhan have expanded access by simplifying mobile experiences, recognizing local needs, and partnering with government programs.
- In Africa, services such as M-Pesa and Tala have embedded themselves into the rhythms of daily life by building trust and usability from the ground up.

These examples show that human-centred design is not about geography or GDP – it is about intention and execution.

Human-Centred Governance

The shift to human-centredness must extend to leadership and governance. This involves listening to customer and employee voices at the board level, appointing chief design or customer officers with genuine authority, embedding ethics, behavioural insights, and cultural intelligence into oversight, and viewing complaints not as liabilities but as valuable design intelligence. Governing for human outcomes means going beyond shareholder value to ask: What kind of impact are we creating? Who benefits – and who is left behind?

The Moral Dividend

Ultimately, human-centred banking pays a moral dividend – restoring belief in finance as a force for good. In a world of mistrust and dislocation, institutions that place humans at the centre:

- Attract deeper loyalty
- Inspire better policy relationships
- Weather reputational storms
- Leave a lasting social footprint

The best technology can scale. The best strategies can optimize. But only human-centred design can build the kind of finance the world actually needs.

Conclusion: Designing from the Heart

In closing this chapter – and the foundational part of the book – we return to a timeless truth: finance is a human invention, and it must remain a human endeavour. The bank of the future will not be defined only by its digital platforms, cloud-native systems, or AI engines. It will be defined by the human outcomes it creates – safety, inclusion, agency, and dignity.

To build a truly resilient, ethical, and future-ready financial system, we must lead not only with intelligence and power – but with compassion, clarity, and care. This is the human foundation, from which everything else must rise.

Strategic Framework Box: Chapter 4. From Control to Character: Rebuilding the Human Core of Banking

Key Insight

Institutions don't transform – people do. The long-term future of banking will be determined not by technology or regulation, but by the culture, character, and capabilities of the people who lead and sustain it. Strategy without humanity will always fall short.

Strategic Takeaway

True transformation begins with people. When the human foundation is strong, strategy becomes sustainable – and trust becomes natural.

Human Factor	*Legacy Approach*	*Future - Centred Approach*
Organizational Culture	Control, hierarchy, fear	Empowerment, trust, shared ownership
Talent Philosophy	Process - oriented, compliance - driven	Purpose - led, multi - skilled, diverse
Learning Model	One - off training, top - down compliance	Continuous, peer - led, adaptive learning
Ethical Foundation	Rule - based conduct policies	Values - based behavioral integrity
Workplace Design	Transactional, monitored environments	Human - centred, hybrid, emotionally aware

This chapter reframes banking not as a machine of compliance, but as a human institution. It explores how culture is not what leaders say – but what people do when no one is watching. The future bank must attract, retain, and nurture individuals who see banking as a vocation, not just a profession.

Bibliography

Schein, E. H. (2017). *Organizational Culture and Leadership*. 5th Edition. Wiley.

5 The Core Transformed

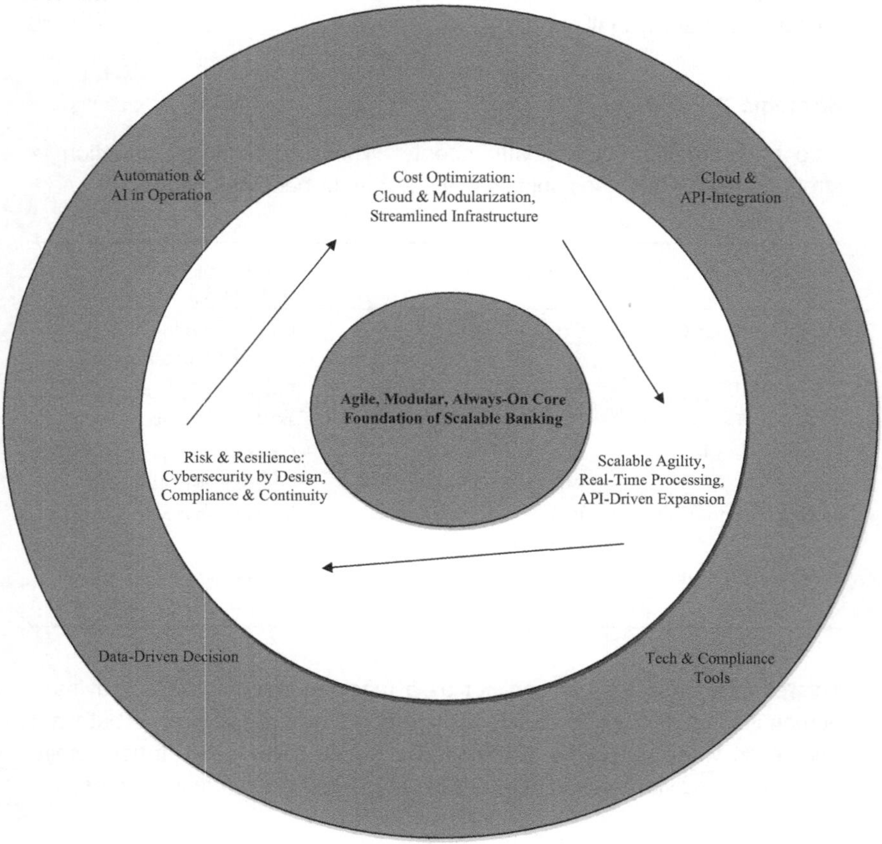

Figure 5.1 Core transformation optimizes cost, strengthens resilience, and enables scalable agility – powered by cloud, APIs, and intelligent automation.

DOI: 10.4324/9781003737544-5

1 Breaking Free from Legacy Constraints

Modern banking systems were not designed for the digital age. Their architecture reflects an era of batch processing, siloed operations, and cautious centralization. What was once strength – the stability of tried-and-tested mainframes and dependable core systems – has become a weight on innovation, flexibility, and competitiveness. Breaking free from these legacy constraints is not simply a technical upgrade; it is a strategic transformation that defines whether a bank is ready to operate – and thrive – in a real-time, platform-driven, customer-centric world.

For over four decades, legacy systems formed the operational backbone of banking institutions. They processed transactions, housed customer data, enforced compliance, and connected multiple lines of business. In many cases, these systems have been patched and extended beyond their original design intent, creating complexity, brittleness, and deep dependency. The challenge now is how to modernize without breaking trust, security, or continuity – and how to do so at speed.

The Weight of Technical Debt

Legacy systems carry a heavy load of technical debt. Past design choices restrict both current and future capabilities. Banks may rely on outdated programming languages such as COBOL, lack internal expertise to maintain or develop them, and operate in a rigid monolithic structure where a single update risks impacting dozens of dependent functions.

This technical debt affects several critical areas: speed to market is slowed because launching new features often requires months of backend coordination; customer experience suffers as friction in digital channels is frequently linked to core system limitations; compliance becomes costly and slow due to the difficulty of adapting to new regulatory standards; and security is compromised because patching older systems can create vulnerabilities in cyber resilience. To build for tomorrow, banks must first confront the invisible cost of maintaining yesterday's code.

Operational Rigidity and the Inflexibility Problem

Legacy constraints extend beyond technical issues to deeply affect operations. For example, settlement cycles that depend on overnight batch processing hinder real-time services, static customer data models limit the ability to generate personalized insights or segmentation, the inability to integrate with third-party Application Programming Interfaces (APIs) restricts participation in broader ecosystems, and fragmented architectures create data silos that undermine the goal of seamless customer journeys.

In effect, legacy systems limit a bank's ability to act with agility, test rapidly, integrate externally, and deliver value at speed. In a competitive market shaped by cloud-native challengers and fintech disruptors, this rigidity can be fatal.

The Strategic Imperative for Transformation

The imperative to modernize is no longer optional – it is existential. In jurisdictions such as the UK, US, and EU, digital regulation, open banking mandates, and customer expectation curves have shifted decisively.

For example, in the UK, open banking APIs require fast and standardized data access. In the US, the emergence of real-time payment infrastructures such as FedNow and RTP calls for modern core banking systems. Globally, the demands of ESG reporting and ethical AI governance frameworks necessitate integrated and responsive systems. Staying on a legacy system is like trying to build a skyscraper on a crumbling foundation. The taller your ambition, the more unstable your future.

Psychological and Cultural Lock-In

Interestingly, one of the biggest barriers to transformation is culture rather than technology. Leadership teams often fear disrupting mission-critical services, show reluctance to retire familiar but inefficient systems, underestimate the customers' tolerance for change – especially among older demographics – and tend to underinvest in change management and upskilling.

This creates what behavioural economists call "status quo bias" – a tendency to stick with the familiar, even when it is failing. Breaking free from legacy means breaking old mental models, not just IT infrastructure.

Learning from Global Leaders

Some banks have made the leap – and reaped the rewards:

- DBS Bank (Singapore) re-platformed over several years, moving core components to cloud-native microservices and embracing Agile-at-scale. This enabled them to launch new services rapidly and become a global digital leader.
- BBVA (Spain and Mexico) committed early to full-stack transformation, investing over a decade to modernize their data architecture, APIs, and customer platforms – becoming one of Europe's most digitally mature banks.
- Goldman Sachs (US) separated digital products from legacy systems through modularization – enabling the launch of Marcus and transaction banking APIs independently.

These examples show that transformation is possible – but requires clear vision, long-term investment, and courageous execution.

Phased vs. Big Bang Approaches

A key question in modernization is whether to pursue:

1 A "big bang" replacement, where the old core is decommissioned entirely and a new system takes over; or
2 A phased, modular strategy, where legacy and modern systems run in parallel as capability is gradually migrated.

Most banks now prefer the second approach because it reduces risk by avoiding single points of failure, enables ongoing learning and adjustment, allows legacy and new systems to coexist during the transition, and aligns better with real-world operational constraints. However, it demands strong architectural governance, robust APIs, and clear service-level interfaces between old and new systems.

Cloud as an Exit Strategy from Legacy

Many institutions are leveraging cloud adoption as a catalyst to break free from legacy constraints. Transitioning to cloud-native platforms provides elastic scalability for compute-intensive processes, standardized APIs and containerization, real-time data streaming and analytics, and zero-downtime deployments. But the move to cloud must be strategic, not superficial. "Lifting and shifting" legacy workloads into virtual servers replicates the same problems in a different place. The goal must be to recreate the architecture, not to re–host it.

Regulatory Considerations

Regulators closely monitor core transformation efforts, focusing on issues such as operational resilience – whether the bank can maintain service continuity during migration, data localization and sovereignty – where sensitive data is stored, vendor risk – if the bank is overly reliant on a single cloud or platform provider, and auditability – ensuring changes to decision engines or core logic can be fully traced. This means that transformation requires constant regulatory dialogue, robust testing, and fail-safes built into every stage.

Building a Case for Change

Successful core transformation starts with a shared recognition of the costs of inertia. These include opportunity costs from delayed product launches, brand risk stemming from poor digital experiences, talent drain caused by uninspiring technology environments, and the risk of becoming irrelevant in a rapidly evolving market ecosystem. Leaders must communicate that transformation is not a project – it is a strategic re-anchoring of the business model itself.

Conclusion: The Liberation of Modern Banking

Breaking free from legacy constraints is about more than updating software. It is about liberating the bank's imagination, unlocking agility, resilience, and innovation. It enables a future where:

- Real-time data powers proactive advice.
- Modular services can be assembled on demand.
- Partners can plug in via secure, standardized APIs.
- Risk and compliance are embedded, not retrofitted.

In essence, the bank stops being a fortress – and becomes a platform. But this future only arrives when institutions have the courage to confront their past. Breaking free from legacy is not easy – but staying trapped in it is far more dangerous.

2 Designing Modular Core Architectures

For centuries, bank architecture reflected the banks themselves – centralized, hierarchical, and monolithic. But as customer demands, regulatory requirements, and competitive forces changed, the fault lines in traditional banking architecture started to appear. Now, with a sense of urgency, banks have to shift from rigid, vertically integrated systems to modular, composable architectures that provide flexibility, speed, and interoperability without trading off trust or resilience.

A modular core architecture is not merely a set of APIs or cloud services. It is a deliberate redesign of the structure, links, governance, and development of banking functions over time. It unmoors the permanent from the temporary, the robust from the provisional, and the secure from the scalable. And by doing so, it empowers banks to react quickly to change, integrate across ecosystems, and free up innovation at scale.

What Is Modular Architecture?

Fundamentally, a modular banking architecture breaks down the historic "core banking system" into autonomous but interoperating components, each with the responsibility of a single business capability – for example, customer onboarding, payments processing, risk scoring, product configuration, or compliance checking.

These modules are speaking to each other via APIs and message queues instead of depending on hardcoded integrations. They can be deployed individually so that frequent updates are not affecting the whole system. Even if they're being sourced from best-of-breed players or are being developed in-house, they're running on explicit data contracts so there is governance and clarity. It's similar to constructing with Lego blocks – every component is purpose-built yet reconfigurable – compared to conventional concrete structures where a change involves disassembling the whole.

Why Modularity Matters

Legacy monolithic core systems, though proven over time, have serious disadvantages: resistance to change from risky and time-consuming updates, scalability chokepoints where expansion in one area impacts the entire system, vendor lock-in through heavily customized solutions, and innovation drag, with new digital channels unable to integrate effectively.

A modular core design solves these problems by providing agility and resilience. New products can be tried out without affecting core processing; partners can attach to specific modules without having access to the full system; and cloud or new technology migrations are possible to be carried out in stages. And perhaps most crucially, this allows banks to move at the speed of digital innovation and not be constrained by legacy release schedules.

Strategic Principles for Modular Design

Effective modular architecture will demand more than a technical breakdown of the core banking system into components. It must be based upon a collection of strategic design principles:

- Domain-driven design (DDD): Modules should be aligned with business domains (e.g., loans, cards, KYC), not technical layers.
- Decentralized governance: Each module will have an "owner" accountable for performance, upgrades, and the roadmap.
- API first: All modules need to expose and use APIs – with good versioning, throttling, and security.
- Loose coupling and strong cohesion: Modules need to depend on other modules as little as possible but operate smoothly within the system.
- Observable: It should be possible to monitor every module, with good logging, metrics, and failure tracing.

These rules help avoid turning modularity into fragmentation.

The Role of Microservices

Microservices are a practical example of modular architecture widely used by banks – these are small, autonomously deployable services that communicate with each other via APIs or event streams. Microservices have several major benefits: granular scalability by enabling banks to scale up only the parts that need to be scaled up, diversity in technology by allowing use of the most appropriate tools for a given single service, parallel development through several independent teams, and resilience, since a failure in one service will not take the whole system down.

However, microservices add complexity into orchestration, testing, security, and data consistency. Hence, many banks take a hybrid approach – applying microservices to high-change domains and more stable modules to core ledger or compliance workloads. Here are a few examples from global leaders:

- Standard Chartered Bank rolled out digital-only brand Mox in Hong Kong with a cloud-native, modular core from Thought Machine. This facilitated fast market launch, agile product innovation, and complete digital onboarding from day one.
- ING adopted a multi-layer architecture where customer engagement, product engines, and transaction processing were all isolated from each other. This facilitated each layer to develop at its own speed with fewer dependencies and greater resilience.
- JPMorgan Chase made significant investments in developing internal platforms and service architectures that created separation between legacy mainframe systems and contemporary digital products – particularly in payments, risk, and trading infrastructure.

These banks demonstrate that modularity is not a nice-to-have but a strategic facilitator – even for the world's largest and most complicated financial organizations.

Data as a Modular Asset

Real modularity relies not just on system architecture but also on data modularity. In legacy systems, data is generally inextricably linked to applications so that it cannot be easily extracted, analysed, or shared. In contrast, in contemporary architectures, data is exposed and made available through APIs, events – for example, customer logins or transactions – are streamed in real-time, a shared data model exists between systems, and data lineage as well as consent tracking is inherent.

This method allows for real-time personalization, combined ESG and compliance reporting, and cross-functional insights that are valuable to credit, fraud, and product teams .Modular data infrastructure is needed to prevent modular applications from going blind.

Modularity and Ecosystem Integration

One of the biggest benefits of modularity is that it allows for ecosystem collaboration. In a time of embedded finance, open banking, and platform partnerships, no institution can do it alone.

A modular architecture can be used to:

Enable fintechs to embed with chosen services (e.g., onboarding, payments)
Enable banks to white-label or rebrand third-party products
Enable regulatory tech modules (e.g., AML scoring) without changing core systems

For example, a bank could embed a specialist ESG scoring engine on its SME lending platform through APIs – improving sustainability metrics without having to rebuild the underlying logic. This composability is the basis of the bank-as-a-platform architecture.

Controlling the Transition to Modular

Moving to a modular architecture is an evolutionary process and not a sudden change. It needs a target state design that fits into the overall business strategy, defined milestone stages such as decoupling KYC or externalizing the product catalogue, investment in developer tools, DevOps (development operations) skills, and API gateways, and the creation of new roles such as module product owners and platform architects to lead and direct the transformation. Most importantly, it requires executive commitment. Without that, modularity is just a technical endeavour – not a strategy for transformation.

Risks and Trade-offs

Although modularity can provide great benefits, it also comes with some new challenges for banks to navigate very carefully. Governance complexity arises as there are distinct ownerships and standards to be maintained for a variety of different modules. Integration testing is more challenging, with many moving pieces needing to be coordinated very tightly. Change is necessary, as developers and business units must learn new, more flexible methods of working. Moreover, modular sourcing can cause vendor sprawl, raising operating complexity if not managed well. These are risks that can be controlled through good architectural discipline, platform thinking, and business sponsorship.

Conclusion: Future-Proofing through Modularity

Modular core architecture isn't merely about building quicker – it's about building for change. In a world of relentless regulatory change, shifting customer requirements, and emerging technological horizons, the only constant strategy is one that can adapt. A properly designed modular system allows banks to constantly innovate without jeopardizing core operations, partner extensively while retaining control, react rapidly to changing regulatory mandates, and materially lower time-to-market for new products.

3 APIs, Integration, and the Digital Backbone

In the digital economy, a bank is only as strong as its connections. No longer confined to internal systems and proprietary technologies, the modern financial institution operates in an ecosystem – of partners, platforms, customers, regulators, and machines. In this networked environment, APIs are the connective tissue, enabling secure, standardized, and scalable interaction between systems, services, and stakeholders. APIs are no longer just a technical enabler; they are the strategic infrastructure underpinning the future of finance.

For banks transitioning from legacy systems to digital-first operations, APIs and integration capabilities serve as the digital backbone – the essential infrastructure that binds together modular components, external partnerships, real-time services, and cloud-native platforms. Without a robust integration strategy, even the most modern applications become isolated silos.

Why APIs Matter in Banking

Historically, banking systems communicated through point-to-point integrations – hard-coded pipelines designed for stability, not flexibility. These worked well in a closed, tightly controlled environment but failed to scale in the face of external partnerships, mobile apps, or real-time data flows. APIs reverse this logic. They offer:

- Reusable interfaces: Any authorized system can access defined services (e.g., payments, KYC).
- Secure access control: Using tokens, encryption, and consent mechanisms.
- Version control: New functionalities can be introduced without breaking existing integrations.
- Real-time interaction: Events can be consumed and acted upon instantly.

In short, APIs change a static bank into a programmable platform. This new platform can extend, evolve, and interact across boundaries.

Internal vs. External APIs

A modern bank typically operates with three tiers of APIs:

1. Internal APIs: These connect different internal services, such as the customer profile service linking to the risk engine or the credit scoring module interacting with the product catalogue.
2. Partner APIs: These give trusted partners access to selected services – for example, enabling an insurance firm to offer embedded credit products using the bank's infrastructure.
3. Public/Open APIs: Mandated in regions such as the UK and EU under open banking regulations, these allow third parties (with customer consent) to access data or initiate payments.

Each type demands a different security approach, governance model, and monitoring strategy – but all of them are part of the same architectural shift toward composable, collaborative banking.

The Open Banking Catalyst

The 2018 introduction of the Revised Payment Services Directive (PSD2) and open banking in the UK and EU represented a turning point. Banks were required to expose customer account and transaction data (with consent) and enable third-party payment initiation – all via secure APIs. While initially seen as a compliance burden, open banking unleashed a wave of innovation:

- Fintechs such as Yolt, Plum, and Emma offered intelligent money management by aggregating data across banks.
- Challenger banks such as Monzo and Starling built their platforms API-first, enabling modular growth and agile integration.
- Incumbents such as Lloyds and HSBC created developer portals and sandbox environments to foster partnerships.

Crucially, open banking shifted APIs from backend tools to frontline strategic assets. Today, regions from Australia to India and Brazil are adopting similar frameworks – pushing banks globally toward API maturity.

Building an Integration Layer

To manage the complexity of APIs at scale, banks typically implement an API management layer – a suite of tools and platforms that facilitates authentication and authorization (e.g., OAuth2), traffic management and throttling, monitoring, analytics, and logging, developer onboarding and sandboxing, as well as policy enforcement and version control.

Platforms such as Mule Soft, Apigee, Kong, or WSO2 are often deployed as enterprise API gateways, sitting between internal services and external consumers. This not only standardizes access but also simplifies compliance and scalability. Integration also requires attention to event-driven architecture – where systems communicate through streams of events (e.g., "payment received", "loan approved") rather than synchronous calls. Tools such as Kafka or Amazon Event Bridge are increasingly used to support real-time, decoupled integration patterns.

Microservices and API Contracts

In a modular architecture, microservices expose their functionalities through APIs, and their effectiveness relies on clear, stable API contracts. These contracts define input and output parameters, error codes and exception handling, rate limits and performance SLAs, and security protocols.

Strong API contracts allow different teams – often spread across countries or continents – to build independently yet coherently. This is especially vital in banks with global operations or federated IT structures. APIs also support test automation, continuous integration and continuous deployment (CI/CD) pipelines, and canary deployments – enabling software to be released faster, safer, and with measurable feedback loops.

Monetizing APIs and Creating Platforms

Beyond technical enablement, APIs can become revenue-generating assets. Banks use them in different ways:

- BBVA (Spain) offers APIs for identity verification, payments, and account aggregation through a commercial developer portal.
- DBS (Singapore) has launched over 300 APIs, enabling partners to build digital journeys embedding DBS services.
- Goldman Sachs offers APIs for transaction banking and treasury services to institutional clients.

This marks a shift from banking as a product provider to banking as a platform – a model where the bank's capabilities are delivered as services to an ecosystem of builders, innovators, and intermediaries.

Challenges in API-Driven Integration

Despite its potential, API-centric integration comes with notable pitfalls. Many banks wrap legacy systems in APIs without redesigning the underlying logic, which can result in poor performance. Governance gaps – such as inconsistent documentation, versioning, and unclear ownership – can lead to uncontrolled API proliferation. Publicly exposed APIs also introduce security risks if not properly secured and monitored. Additionally, shifting from traditional project-based IT to productized API teams demands a significant cultural and mindset change across the organization. Overcoming these requires sustained investment in API strategy, education, tooling, and leadership.

APIs in the US and UK

In the UK, open banking has driven a mature ecosystem with hundreds of third-party providers leveraging APIs for PFM (Personal Finance Management), lending, and SME tools. Regulatory support, strong developer engagement, and a fintech-friendly culture have made the UK a global leader.

In the US, although not mandated at a federal level, market-driven adoption of APIs is strong. Banks such as Chase, Wells Fargo, and Bank of America provide APIs to partners for data sharing and payments. The Financial Data Exchange (FDX) has emerged as a voluntary standard to harmonize APIs across institutions. The US approach demonstrates that even without regulation, API-first banking is becoming the norm, especially due to the rise of customer expectations for interconnected services.

The Future of the Digital Backbone

As banks progress in their transformation, APIs and integration platforms will evolve to support hyper-personalized banking journeys orchestrated through dynamic APIs, cross-industry ecosystems that integrate with sectors such as telecommunications, retail, and mobility, AI and machine learning models that depend on real-time data flows and decision hooks, and green and ethical finance platforms that use APIs for carbon tracking, ESG scoring, and sustainable investing. In this future, the bank is not just a service provider – it becomes an intelligent infrastructure layer embedded into the lives, businesses, and platforms of its customers.

4 Cloud as Strategic Infrastructure

Cloud computing is no longer a future vision or a peripheral IT consideration – it is now the strategic foundation upon which the modern bank is built. From powering scalable platforms to enabling real-time analytics and AI – driven decisioning, cloud infrastructure has become central to how banks operate, innovate, and compete. What began as a shift in technology delivery has evolved into a redefinition of organizational agility, cost efficiency, resilience, and ecosystem integration.

This section explores why the cloud is not just about data centres or storage, but a fundamental enabler of new business models and customer experiences – and why banks that treat it merely as a cost-saving tactic risk missing the full scale of its transformative potential.

From Infrastructure to Innovation Engine

Traditional banking systems were built on specific premises. Their infrastructure was scaled for peak load and managed internally. The systems also faced long procurement cycles. This model constrained change. Every new feature required provisioning, hardware upgrades, and significant downtime. Maintenance costs went up while agility remained elusive.

In contrast, cloud infrastructure – particularly public cloud platforms such as Amazon Web Services (AWS), Microsoft Azure, and Google Cloud – provides on-demand scalability, allowing capacity to expand or contract instantly. It offers global reach, enabling services to be deployed across multiple regions within minutes. Managed services, ranging from databases to machine learning, help reduce operational complexity. Additionally, elastic pricing with pay-per-use models optimizes cost efficiency. But the true advantage of cloud is not just infrastructure savings – it is the ability to innovate faster, respond to change dynamically, and build new capabilities at scale.

Cloud as Strategic Infrastructure

When positioned strategically, cloud goes beyond being just a hosting environment to becoming the digital substrate that powers platform banking models, enabling APIs and microservices to be composed and deployed dynamically. It supports real-time decisioning through scalable data pipelines and streaming platforms, ensures resilient architectures with automated failover, redundancy, and high availability zones, and unlocks advanced AI and machine learning capabilities by providing access to cutting-edge toolkits, GPU infrastructure, and scalable computing resources.

For example, a fraud detection model can investigate millions of transactions per second and retrain in real time on cloud-native infrastructure. A new product can be soft-launched in one market and scaled globally in days. These capabilities would be unthinkable on static legacy infrastructure.

Cloud-Native vs. Cloud-Hosted

One of the common misconceptions in banking transformation is equating the use of cloud technology with simply migrating legacy systems to hosted environments. While "Lift and shift" strategies can deliver some cost benefits, they often retain the inefficiencies and rigidity of the original system.

The real breakthrough comes from cloud-native design:

- Containerized applications using tools such as Docker and Kubernetes
- Serverless computing, enabling functions to execute on-demand without pre-provisioned servers
- CI/CD pipelines, allowing automated testing, deployment, and rollback
- DevOps culture, blending development and operations for continuous delivery

Banks such as Capital One, ING, and Standard Chartered have embraced cloud-native approaches to modernize their core systems, improve developer velocity, and reduce time-to-market.

The UK and US Cloud Landscape

In the United Kingdom, the Financial Conduct Authority (FCA) has taken a balanced approach, encouraging cloud adoption while emphasizing due diligence, operational resilience, and supplier risk. The Bank of England's supervisory statements outline the need for exit strategies, data governance, and oversight of material outsourcing arrangements. UK banks such as NatWest, HSBC, and Lloyds have partnered with major cloud providers to drive digital transformation – often in hybrid or multi-cloud setups to reduce the concentration risk.

In the United States, cloud adoption has accelerated, particularly among regional and challenger banks seeking agility. Regulatory clarity from bodies such as the Office of the Comptroller of the Currency (OCC) and the Federal Reserve has supported this trend, though risk management and cybersecurity remain top priorities.US-based bank JPMorgan Chase, for example, committed to a multi-year journey to build an internal cloud platform, while leveraging public cloud capabilities to deliver AI-powered client experiences and real-time risk analytics.

Cybersecurity and Compliance in the Cloud

Security in the cloud is a shared responsibility – while cloud providers secure the infrastructure, banks must secure their applications, data, and access controls. Key considerations include:

- Encryption at rest and in transit
- Identity and access management (IAM)
- Zero trust architectures
- Continuous compliance monitoring
- Audit trails and logging

Leading banks implement cloud security posture management (CSPM) tools and carry out regular threat simulations to ensure defences are adaptive. Compliance requirements such as GDPR, PCI-DSS, and sectoral regulations must be embedded into the design from day one. Crucially, cloud infrastructure allows banks to react more quickly to threats – spinning up new security policies or isolating workloads in minutes rather than days.

Cloud and Resilience by Design

Operational resilience has become a critical priority in today's always-on banking environment, where outages, latency, or regional failures can directly impact customers and damage reputations. Cloud technology supports this by enabling multi-region redundancy to mitigate data centre outages, automated backup and disaster recovery processes, proactive failure testing through chaos engineering, and dynamic traffic rerouting combined with auto-scaling to maintain seamless service availability. Regulators increasingly require resilience by design, not just recovery plans. Cloud-native architectures make this feasible at scale.

Cost Management and FinOps

While cloud technology offers cost efficiency, its uncontrolled usage can cause expenses to escalate rapidly. To manage this, banks are adopting FinOps (Financial Operations) practices that include real-time monitoring of consumption, allocating costs to specific teams or business units, optimizing resource usage by, for example, right-sizing compute power, and implementing budgets, alerts, and automated shutdowns to keep spending under control. Cloud cost transparency enables better alignment between business value and technology spend – reinforcing strategic decision-making.

Cloud Partnerships and Ecosystems

As banks shift their focus from infrastructure to capability building, cloud providers evolve into strategic partners rather than mere vendors. These collaborations encompass co-development of AI tools and use cases, access to global fintech ecosystems, joint innovation labs and accelerators, as well as migration support and skill development programs.

For instance, Deutsche Bank's partnership with Google Cloud includes not just infrastructure modernization, but data science enablement and cultural transformation. Similarly, Goldman Sachs launched a financial data cloud on AWS to support institutional clients. These partnerships redefine the bank's competitive landscape – offering platform advantages that legacy-only rivals cannot match.

Moving Beyond the Data Centre Mindset

Perhaps the most profound shift in moving to the cloud is psychological. Banks must let go of traditional control models, prioritize speed over certainty, transition from rigid IT governance to business-enabled engineering, and embrace experimentation and failure as essential components of innovation. This cultural transformation is often harder than the technical migration. It involves reskilling, change management, and a redefinition of leadership accountability.

The Cloud as a Public Good Enabler

Cloud infrastructure plays a vital role in advancing financial inclusion and supporting ESG outcomes. It enables digital onboarding for underserved customers through mobile-first channels, promotes green cloud practices as hyperscalers shift toward renewable energy, facilitates scalable distribution of government payments and humanitarian aid, and supports real-time climate risk modelling essential for sustainable finance initiatives. Thus, the cloud becomes more than infrastructure – it turns into a platform for societal impact, enabling banks to extend their reach and responsibility at scale.

Toward Cloud-Mature Banking

Banks that treat cloud technology as strategic infrastructure are no longer asking: Should we move to the cloud? but: How do we fully leverage it? Cloud-mature banks demonstrate a strong alignment between their business goals and cloud architecture, supported by unified cloud governance frameworks that span across teams. They adopt DevSecOps (Development Security and Operations) practices to seamlessly integrate security into the development process and manage cross-border deployments in compliance with local data sovereignty regulations.

They are not just more efficient – they are more adaptive, inclusive, intelligent, and secure. In the century ahead, as banking becomes more embedded, distributed, and intelligent, the cloud is not an optional infrastructure – it is the invisible foundation enabling institutions to evolve and endure.

5 From Static Systems to Agile Platforms

Traditional banking systems were designed for control, predictability, and centralization. In an era when product cycles spanned years and customer expectations evolved slowly, these static systems were sufficient. But today's financial landscape demands speed, adaptability, and collaboration. As the market shifts toward digital ecosystems and real-time delivery, banks must move from rigid systems to agile platforms – changing not just the technology, but also their culture and governance. This section looks at the structure, operations, and strategy of platform-based banking. It explains why agility is not just a trendy word but a crucial strategy for survival.

The Legacy Trap

For decades, banks relied on vertically integrated systems that tightly coupled products, processes, and data. These monolithic structures created many challenges: Banks often faced slow innovation cycles caused by system interdependencies, along with high change-management costs that demanded extensive months of testing. They also contended with vendor lock-in, where reliance on proprietary technologies limited flexibility, and operational risks arose from code bases that were no longer well understood internally.

Most legacy systems were not built to interact with the outside world – let alone integrate with third-party services, support mobile-first banking, or ingest real-time data streams. As new entrants – fintechs, neobanks, and platform-native firms – entered with composable, cloud-native architectures, the rigidity of traditional systems became a liability.

Defining an Agile Platform

An agile platform is not a product, but an architectural and operational model. Modern architectures feature decoupled microservices that can evolve independently, with APIs serving as interfaces rather than mere integrations. They leverage reusable capabilities such as payments, KYC, and credit scoring, supported by developer-first infrastructure incorporating CI/CD pipelines. These systems enable dynamic orchestration of services across both internal and external boundaries. This modular approach allows banks to respond quickly to market needs, plug into new ecosystems, and deliver experiences that evolve continuously.

UK and US Case Studies

In the United Kingdom, banks such as like Monzo and Starling built their platforms from scratch using microservices, APIs, and real-time event architectures. Their ability to launch features rapidly – for example spending insights, instant card freezing, or connected savings pots – reflects the power of agile platforms. Meanwhile Lloyds Banking Group undertook a multi-year transformation program, moving core services to modular platforms and embedding agile delivery practices within its technology and business teams.

In the United States, Goldman Sachs's Marcus platform offers APIs to fintech partners, enabling new product lines such as Apple Card or embedded savings. Bank of America uses agile pods and integrated delivery models to accelerate customer-facing innovation across its digital channels. These shifts are not just technical – they require new mindsets, governance models, and skill sets.

Organizing Around Capabilities

One of the most powerful enablers of platform agility is capability-based design. Rather than organizing technology around products or departments, banks increasingly structure platforms around capabilities such as:

- Onboarding
- Authentication
- Payments
- Lending
- Notifications

Each capability can be developed, deployed, and scaled independently. This separation reduces dependencies, accelerates delivery, and enables capabilities to be reused across journeys or business lines. For example, a customer authentication service designed for retail banking can also support wealth or SME channels – improving consistency, reducing cost, and simplifying compliance.

Platform Governance and Product Thinking

With agility comes complexity. Managing hundreds of microservices, APIs, and capabilities requires new forms of governance. Leading banks apply:

- Domain-driven design (DDD) to align architecture with business concepts
- API lifecycle management, including versioning, security, and usage analytics
- Service ownership models, where teams manage their components end-to-end
- Product management disciplines, treating capabilities as evolving offerings

The shift from "project" to "product" thinking means teams own the full lifecycle – from strategy and build to operate and evolve. Product managers become key to prioritizing features, aligning with customer needs, and measuring success.

APIs and Internal Marketplaces

Agile platforms succeed when internal teams behave like external service providers. That means offering APIs, publishing documentation, monitoring usage, and charging for consumption. Some banks establish internal developer marketplaces, where teams can discover and reuse capabilities without duplicating effort. For example:

- A Chatbot team can call the KYC API instead of revalidating identity.
- A loan origination engine can use the credit scoring service already in place.

This platform mindset encourages reuse, reduces duplication, and creates a culture of collaboration.

Agile Delivery and Ways of Working

Technology platforms enable agility – but it is the organizational culture which determines whether they will be successful. Agile teams are organized into squads or pods that bring together product, design, and engineering expertise. They follow Scrum or Kanban methodologies with two-week sprints, supported by CI/CD practices. Automated testing and observable tools ensure quality and transparency, while regular retrospectives and learning loops foster continuous improvement.

In the UK, banks such as TSB and Nationwide have reorganized around these principles, embedding agile delivery into business strategy. In the US, firms such as Capital One transitioned their entire workforce to agile methodologies to unlock responsiveness and customer focus. Agility is not a tech function – it is a leadership function.

Ecosystem Integration and Platform Banking

Agile platforms extend beyond organizational boundaries. Banks increasingly partner with fintechs, retailers, and government services – embedding financial services into broader journeys. This requires open banking, which relies on APIs that enable secure and standardized data access, often protected by OAuth and other secure authorization protocols. Effective implementation includes clear data-sharing agreements and user consents, supported by API monetization strategies and developer portals to encourage ecosystem participation.

For example, an SME accounting platform might integrate a bank's invoicing and lending APIs. A ride-sharing app might embed driver insurance, powered by a bank's underwriting engine. These ecosystem plays are only possible with agile, modular platforms.

Platform Resilience and Observability

With agility comes the risk of instability. Distributed platforms must be observable, testable, and resilient. Modern systems use distributed tracing to track customer journeys across multiple services, ensuring visibility and performance monitoring. Feature flagging allows the safe rollout of new functionalities by controlling exposure. Chaos engineering practices test system resilience by simulating failure scenarios, while service meshes manage communication between services and enforce security and operational policies effectively. Real-time dashboards and telemetry allow operations teams to respond proactively – maintaining trust while enabling change.

ESG and the Inclusion Lens

Agile platforms are also enablers of inclusive and sustainable finance: They allow for a quicker rollout of features tailored for underserved groups, with modular design reducing the costs associated with experimenting and creating niche products. APIs facilitate the extension of financial services such as credit, insurance, and savings into rural or informal markets, while agile methodologies foster participatory design, allowing community input to continuously shape and improve services. In this sense, platforms are not just technical – they are ethical. They help institutions move from one-size-fits-all banking to adaptive, human-centred solutions.

Platform Maturity and Strategic Impact

Mature platform organizations demonstrate:

- Platform thinking at the board level.
- Enterprise architecture aligned to capability maps.
- Shared language across IT and business teams.
- Clear metrics for velocity, reuse, uptime, and business impact.

They also invest in platform enablement teams – not to build features, but to empower others through tools, libraries, and standards. As platform maturity deepens, banks shift from delivery to orchestration – not doing everything themselves, but enabling others to build, connect, and innovate.

Conclusion: Agility as Strategy

To thrive in the century ahead, banks must be more than stable institutions – they must be adaptable organisms. This adaptability is achieved with platforms, which create the foundations for:

- Rapid innovation
- Embedded finance

- Scalable resilience
- Inclusive growth

From London to San Francisco, from Nairobi to Singapore, tomorrow's leading banks will be those for which agility is not an initiative, but part of their identity.

6 Cybersecurity and Resilience by Design

In the digital age, a bank's most valuable currency is trust – and that trust is increasingly under attack. With the rise of open banking, cloud-native architectures, and API-led ecosystems, the threat surface for financial institutions has expanded dramatically. Banks no longer operate within closed environments; they are deeply connected to fintechs, partners, regulators, and customers through real-time, distributed systems. In this landscape, cybersecurity can no longer be an afterthought. It must be built in – by design – into every layer of the banking architecture. This section looks at the principles and practices that support secure and resilient banking systems in a rapidly changing world full of cyber risks.

The Shift from Reactive to Proactive Security

Historically, banks approached cybersecurity as a compliance function – a set of controls, audits, and perimeter defences focused on reacting to incidents. But modern banking demands a proactive stance. Threats now originate from:

- Nation-state actors targeting critical infrastructure
- Sophisticated fraud rings using deep fake technology
- Insider threats in hybrid work environments
- Supply chain vulnerabilities via third-party integrations

Banks must assume that breaches will occur – and design systems to anticipate, contain, and recover swiftly. The mantra is no longer "secure the perimeter" – it is "assume breach" and design for resilience.

Zero Trust Architecture in Practice

One of the foundational shifts in security strategy is the adoption of zero trust architecture (ZTA). Instead of assuming internal systems are safe, ZTA enforces continuous verification, based on:

- Identity: Every user, device, and workload must authenticate.
- Least privilege access: Permissions are minimized and context-aware.
- Segmentation: Data and services are isolated to prevent lateral movement.
- Monitoring and analytics: Real-time telemetry drives adaptive responses.

Banks such as JP Morgan Chase and Santander UK have moved toward zero trust models, particularly for remote work, cloud workloads, and API gateways. This architecture reduces the blast radius of an incident and supports dynamic, real-time governance.

Cloud Security and Shared Responsibility

As banks migrate to the cloud, they must embrace a new paradigm: shared responsibility. Cloud providers (e.g. AWS, Azure, GCP) secure the infrastructure, but banks are responsible for:

- Identity and access management (IAM)
- Data encryption and key management
- Configuration management
- Monitoring and logging

Misconfigured cloud services – such as public S3 buckets or exposed APIs – are among the most common causes of breach. To mitigate this, leading banks implement:

- Infrastructure as Code (IaC) with built-in security policies
- Automated compliance checks using tools such as Sentinel or Open Policy Agent
- Cloud security posture management (CSPM) platforms to detect drift

Cloud-native security is not optional – it is mission-critical.

API Security and Open Banking Risks

The rise of APIs – particularly through open banking mandates in the UK, EU, and beyond – creates new risks. APIs expose core functions such as authentication, payments, and account data to third parties. Without strong API security, banks face threats such as broken object-level authorization, insecure authentication flows, excessive data exposure, rate-limiting bypasses and DDoS attacks.

To manage this, modern banks implement API gateways with strict policy enforcement, OAuth 2.0 and Open ID Connect for secure authorization, token expiry, refresh, and revocation logic, and runtime anomaly detection using AI/ML for behavioural monitoring. Firms such as Starling Bank and N26 have demonstrated leadership in secure open banking, offering developer portals with layered access and robust documentation.

Operational Resilience: Beyond Uptime

Cybersecurity is only half the equation. Banks must also ensure operational resilience – the ability to deliver critical services even amid disruption, whether caused by cyberattacks, system failures, cloud outages, natural disasters, or supply chain interruptions.

Regulators in the UK (e.g. PRA, FCA) have introduced resilience mandates, requiring banks to: define important business services, map dependencies, set impact tolerances, run scenario tests and tabletop exercises, and demonstrate recovery within defined timeframes. Banks such as Lloyds, Nationwide, and Bank of America are investing in resilience engineering, business continuity playbooks, and cross-functional incident response.

Secure DevOps and Shift Left Security

Security is strongest when embedded early – not bolted on at the end. This is the principle of shift left security, which integrates security practices into DevOps pipelines: Static and dynamic code analysis is conducted during development, along with security scans in CI/CD pipelines. Container scanning is performed to detect vulnerabilities, while secrets management helps prevent credential leaks. Additionally, dependency tracking is used to monitor open-source risks. This DevSecOps approach ensures that security is part of the build process, not just the audit process. Banks that adopt it reduce both risk and rework.UK challenger banks such as Monzo and Atom Bank have pioneered secure DevOps at scale – pushing hundreds of secure deployments per week.

AI, Fraud Detection, and Behavioural Biometrics

Modern cyber defence also relies on intelligent systems. Banks now use AI and machine learning to detect payment fraud using pattern recognition, monitor employee behaviour for anomalies, analyse device fingerprints and location data, and identify phishing and social engineering attempts. Behavioural biometrics – such as keystroke dynamics, swipe speed, and app navigation – adds a layer of silent security, improving detection without friction.

For example, HSBC and Wells Fargo have deployed AI-driven platforms that detect abnormal transactions in milliseconds – helping pre-empt attacks before customers notice any suspicious activity.

Cross-Border Threats and Global Coordination

Cybersecurity is a global issue. Banks operating across borders must deal with fragmented regulatory environments, differing data residency laws, varying definitions of "critical systems," and transnational cybercrime networks. This situation calls for global coordination, including:

- Information sharing through ISACs (information sharing and analysis centres) and FS-ISACs (financial services information sharing and analysis centres)
- Participation in cross-border cyber drills (e.g. Cyber Storm)

- Alignment to frameworks such as NIST, ISO 27001, and the EU DORA (Digital Operational Resilience Act)

As the digital economy becomes more interconnected, cyber risk becomes systemic. A single breach can ripple through markets – making resilience a shared responsibility.

Ethics, Transparency, and the Human Dimension

Cybersecurity is not only a technical issue – it is an ethical one. Customers deserve transparency about data usage, clarity on their rights in case of breach, and consent that is informed, not buried in legalese.

Banks that treat Cybersecurity as a trust enabler, not just a control, differentiate themselves in crowded markets. Training frontline staff, educating customers, and engaging transparently with regulators all build social capital. Moreover, inclusive design ensures that security mechanisms – such as two-factor authentication – also work for elderly, disabled, or low-tech users.

Toward Cyber-Resilient Banking

To build cyber-resilient banks, leaders must bring together an organizational culture which considers security as everyone's responsibility, not just a matter of IT, design which embeds security from infrastructure to UX, a governance approach which ensures clear roles, escalation paths, and KPIs, and investment which provides sustained funding for tools, talent, and training.

The future of banking is not just digital – it is secure by design. Resilience is not about never failing, but about failing safely, recovering quickly, and learning continuously. Banks that embrace this mindset will be trusted stewards of the financial future.

7 Enabling Always-On, Real-Time Finance

The modern economy never sleeps – and neither can the infrastructure that powers it. As digital lifestyles expand across time zones and devices, customers expect 24/7 access, zero-delay transactions, and uninterrupted service. The traditional concept of banking hours has been rendered obsolete by a new paradigm: always-on, real-time finance.

This section explores how banks are reengineering their technology and operating models to meet the demands of an always-connected, latency-intolerant world. It delves into the enablers, challenges, and future pathways of real-time banking.

The End of Batch Processing: A Generational Shift

For decades, banks depended on batch processing. This system queued transactions throughout the day and reconciled them overnight. This architecture worked in the era of physical branches, cheques, and end-of-day settlement cycles. But in today's world of mobile wallets, open APIs, and instant payments, batch systems are a liability.

Customers nowadays expect instant fund transfers (e.g. Faster Payments, UPI), real-time account updates and alerts, immediate loan or credit decisions, and seamless e-commerce payments without delay. Banks must replace their batch-dependent cores with architectures that are event-driven, real-time, and elastic. This shift is not just technical – it is a transformation of the underlying business thinking.

Real-Time Payments and Global Momentum

The global wave of real-time payments has accelerated dramatically across markets: In the United Kingdom, the Faster Payments Service (FPS) has transformed personal and SME transactions; in the United States, Fed Now enables real-time clearing and settlement for financial institutions. India's UPI has revolutionized peer-to-peer and merchant payments, while Brazil's PIX, launched by the Central Bank, has seen explosive adoption. Singapore and Thailand use FAST and Prompt Pay to interlink cross-border real-time payments.

These systems require banks to operate with high availability, low latency, and zero downtime, around the clock. The technology stack must support millions of concurrent messages, intelligent routing, and fraud detection at millisecond speed.

Architecture for Real-Time Banking

- To deliver true real-time capabilities, banks are adopting a layered, modular architecture built on several core enablers: Event-driven design allows systems to trigger actions based on events (e.g. payment received, loan approved) using message queues and pub/sub models.
- Streaming platforms such as Apache Kafka and Pulsar enable real-time data ingestion, processing, and analytics.
- Microservices, which are independent and loosely coupled, allow updates and scaling without full system shutdowns.
- Real-time databases such as Redis, Aerospike, and Cassandra ensure sub-second reads and writes.
- APIs and webhooks enable real-time integration with partners, apps, and user-facing channels.

Banks such as ING, BBVA, and DBS have re-platformed core services using these patterns to achieve sub-second response times across multiple channels.

Resilience in a 24/7 World

Always-on systems must also be always-resilient. This includes:

- Active-active data centres across geographies providing failover, supported by continuous replication and self-healing infrastructure
- Real-time monitoring and observable going beyond mere logging
- Chaos engineering simulating and hardening systems against failure
- Blue-green and canary deployments enabling continuous upgrades without outages

For example, Capital One in the US has invested heavily in site reliability engineering (SRE) and automated rollback systems to maintain 99.999% uptime across mobile and web platforms.

Real-time Analytics and Personalization

Real-time finance is not only about speed – it is about relevance. Streaming analytics enables banks to detect fraud as it happens, not after, offer personalized product recommendations instantly, alert users to unusual spending or low balances, and enable financial nudges ("you're about to exceed your budget"). This requires an intelligent backbone that combines customer data platforms (CDPs) for unified views, machine learning models for real-time inference, and contextual decision engines triggered by behaviour, location, or device. Banks such as HSBC and Citi have piloted intelligent alerting systems that help customers avoid fees, track spending, and adjust their financial plans in real time.

The Operational Model: Continuous Delivery and 24/7 Support

Technology alone is not enough. Banks must also reinvent their operating models to support always-on delivery: DevOps and Site Reliability Engineering (SRE) teams manage uptime and automation, supported by follow-the-sun support across geographies to handle issues without delay. Real-time incident response protocols are integrated with monitoring tools, and cross-functional war rooms facilitate high-impact event resolution.

Institutions such as Goldman Sachs and Standard Chartered have shifted toward continuous delivery pipelines, enabling code releases multiple times per day – without interrupting the service.

Compliance, Risk, and Real-Time Governance

Regulatory frameworks are catching up with real-time operations. In the UK, the Bank of England and FCA have outlined operational resilience requirements, including impact tolerances for critical services, real-time monitoring of service health, and immediate customer communication protocols.

Similarly, in the EU and US, stress testing now includes scenarios involving digital outages and cyber incidents with instant regulatory reporting requirements. Banks must embed real-time governance mechanisms into their architecture, ensuring audit ability, traceability, and decision logging – especially when using AI for real-time decisions.

The Cost of Downtime: A Strategic Risk

The business case for real-time banking is not only customer experience – it is risk mitigation. Downtime now translates into customer churn and reputational damage, regulatory fines and supervisory scrutiny, and loss of competitive position to fintechs and neobanks. Research suggests that an hour of outage for a major retail bank can cost upwards of $500,000 in direct and indirect impacts. Real-time resilience is no longer optional – it is strategic.

Real-Time Beyond Payments: Credit, Wealth, and Insurance

The principles of real-time banking are expanding beyond payments: Customers applying for credit are given instant decisions regarding eligibility, approval and disbursal (e.g. Klarna, Affirm); wealth management provides real-time portfolio updates and micro-investing; insurance features usage-based pricing and instant policy issuance; and SMEs benefit from live cash flow dashboards, invoice factoring, and credit line adjustments. Firms such as Revolut and Chime have shown that real-time user experiences can redefine product categories, not just channels.

Future Frontiers: 5G, Edge, and Embedded Finance

Looking ahead, real-time finance will be shaped by5G and edge computing enabling latency-sensitive use cases in wearables, IoT, and AR/VR, embedded finance integrating real-time financial functions into non-bank platforms (e.g. ride-hailing, e-commerce), and programmable money, including CBDCs and smart contracts, automating real-time transactions based on conditions. Banks must prepare to be real-time nodes in larger digital ecosystems – responsive, intelligent, and interoperable.

Conclusion: Becoming a Real-Time Institution

To thrive in the real-time era, banks must shift from:

- Static processing to dynamic interaction
- Isolated systems to event-driven ecosystems
- Periodic decision-making to continuous responsiveness

This is not just a tech upgrade – it is an institutional reimagining. Banks must embed speed, intelligence, and agility into their DNA, making real-time not just a feature, but a foundation.

Those that do will not merely keep pace with developments – they will define the rhythm of modern finance.

8 Rethinking Cost, Risk, and Scale

The traditional trade-offs between cost, risk, and scale in banking are no longer fit for the digital age. Historically, banks operated on the assumption that in order to reduce risk, one had to increase cost; and to achieve scale, institutions had to centralize and consolidate operations. But in a world of modular architectures, cloud-native infrastructure, and smart automation, these assumptions are changing.

This section explores how leading banks are rethinking the operating equation – achieving scale without centralization, lowering cost without compromising control, and managing risk as a dynamic capability rather than a compliance artefact.

Breaking the Cost-Risk Binary

Banking infrastructure has traditionally been expensive and brittle. Legacy systems are often vertically integrated, bespoke, and difficult to maintain – leading to rising technical debt and mounting operational risk. In the past, the assumptions were clear:

- Cheaper systems meant higher operational risk
- Secure systems demanded significant capital expenditure
- Scalable infrastructure required long lead times and monolithic design

Today, that trade-off is no longer necessary. With cloud, automation, and microservices, banks can build resilient, low-cost, scalable systems that are more agile than their predecessors. Take the case of Starling Bank in the UK: its cloud-native platform allows it to operate at a fraction of the cost of legacy institutions, while achieving real-time updates, high availability, and continuous compliance

Cost Transformation: From Fixed to Variable

One of the most dramatic shifts enabled by digital infrastructure is the move from fixed cost structures to variable, usage-based models. Key enablers include public cloud platforms (e.g. AWS, Azure, GCP) offering pay-as-you-go pricing, serverless computing eliminating idle infrastructure, low-code and no-code platforms allowing rapid development, and open-source software replacing proprietary licensing.

By transitioning from capital expenditure (CapEx) to operational expenditure (OpEx), banks gain flexibility to experiment, scale, or contract based on demand. For instance, Goldman Sachs' Marquee platform uses elastic cloud resources to serve both retail and institutional clients without duplicating infrastructure. Moreover, automation of processes such as KYC, AML, credit scoring, and fraud detection reduces the cost per customer – enabling cost-effective growth into underserved markets.

Risk as a Real-Time, Adaptive Function

Risk management is no longer a quarterly process buried in spreadsheets and after-the-fact reviews. Today's banking environment demands real-time, predictive, and contextual risk frameworks. Modern approaches include machine learning models anticipating fraud or credit default, behavioural analytics detecting anomalies in customer activity, scenario simulation engines testing thousands of stress cases instantly, and dynamic limits adjusting exposure thresholds based on real-time conditions.

For example, BBVA uses AI to run continuous risk assessments across its retail and SME portfolios, enabling proactive intervention before risk materializes. The architecture to support this includes streaming data pipelines enabling instant signal processing, centralized risk data lakes being fed by all business units, and cross-functional model governance teams ensuring explainability and compliance. This shift enables banks to move from a defensive posture to a strategic one – managing risk as an enabler of value, not just a cost.

Scaling Through Modularity

Traditional approaches to scale required monolithic systems and centralized operations – often resulting in rigidity, bottlenecks, and high sunk costs. Digital-native banks are now achieving global scale through modular, decentralized components. For example, modular microservices allowing the scaling of specific features (e.g. payments, onboarding) independently, containerization (e.g. Kubernetes) ensuring scalable, portable deployments, APIs enabling services to be reused across products, countries, and partners, and decoupled data stores letting banks scale reads and writes separately based on usage patterns.

This approach not only supports horizontal scaling across customer bases but also vertical scaling across new products, channels, and geographies. Standard Charterer's nexus platform, for instance, allows the bank to plug into e-commerce and telecom ecosystems across Asia, leveraging its modular core to scale financial services through partners – not branches.

Cost, Risk, and Scale in the Age of ESG

Environmental, Social, and Governance (ESG) mandates are reshaping the banks' cost-risk-scale calculus. Cost now includes the responsibility to invest sustainably in green infrastructure; risk involves assessing climate exposure across portfolios; and scale focuses on expanding inclusive finance without increasing inequality.

This requires integrating ESG metrics into core systems, including climate-adjusted credit scoring models, carbon footprint dashboards for retail and SME clients, and ESG-aligned investment algorithms in wealth management. Institutions such as NatWest and BNP Paribas are building dedicated ESG data layers within their architecture to manage these mandates at scale – turning compliance into competitive advantage.

Rethinking Legacy Cost Structures

Many banks are still locked into contracts and service models from a pre-digital era – large outsourcing arrangements, proprietary licensing, on-premises hardware, and manual reconciliation processes. Modernization involves sunsetting legacy contracts and renegotiating vendor terms, re-platforming core services on modern, extensible foundations, eliminating data silos to reduce redundancy and data duplication costs, and investing in in-house capability to replace expensive third-party dependencies.

It is not just about reducing cost – it is about regaining control over strategic assets. Banks like OCBC and Rabobank have pursued deliberate in-sourcing strategies, building cloud-native developer teams and reducing reliance on external IT vendors.

Data-Driven Unit Economics

To manage cost and risk dynamically, banks must establish granular, real-time unit economics for every product, channel, and customer. This requires integrating activity-based costing systems into core operations, profitability heat maps identifying subscale or high-risk segments, dynamic pricing engines reflecting cost and risk in real time, and embedding customer lifetime value (CLV) analytics in CRM tools. Such transparency empowers better decisions – whether to invest in a product, automate a service, or sunset an offering. It transforms strategy from reactive to proactive.

Organizational Implications

The rethinking of cost, risk, and scale extends beyond technology – it redefines how banks organize themselves. Agile cross-functional teams reduce coordination costs, platform operating models scale innovation without bloating bureaucracy, cloud financial operations (FinOps) bring discipline to cloud usage and cost control, and governance by design ensures compliance is embedded into the build process.

Banks like Lloyds have adopted platform-based business units (e.g. "Home Buying Platform") that align technology, product, risk, and finance teams – enabling speed without sacrificing governance.

Conclusion: The New Equation

The old equation was linear:

Scale = Centralization; Risk Control = High Cost; Innovation = Optional

The new equation is dynamic:

Scale = Modularity; Risk = Adaptive Intelligence; Cost = Elastic Infrastructure

By redesigning this equation, banks can build operating models that are scalable, sustainable, and strategically aligned to a fast-moving world. Cost, risk, and scale are no longer constraints to be traded off – they are dimensions to be optimized together. The banks that master this new balance will not just survive disruption – they will set the pace for what banking can become.

9 Navigating the Core Transformation Journey

Transforming a bank's core is among the most ambitious and high-stakes undertakings in modern financial services. It involves rewiring the very systems, processes, and operational DNA upon which every product, service, and regulatory obligation is built. For many banks, the question is not whether to modernize their core, but how to do it without jeopardizing stability, compliance, or customer trust.

This section offers a pragmatic blueprint for navigating core transformation: from framing the journey to overcoming common roadblocks, selecting technology approaches, and managing change across legacy and digital environments.

From Legacy Burden to Strategic Imperative

Legacy core systems, often built decades ago, are deeply embedded, costly to maintain, and hard to modify. They hinder innovation, delay product launches, and increase operational risk. However, wholesale replacement can feel too risky or too costly.

The modern approach is not about "rip and replace". Instead, successful banks treat core transformation as a strategic, staged journey, guided byclear business outcomes (e.g. faster time to market, lower cost per transaction), modular architecture principles, agile delivery and iterative value realization, and deep alignment between IT and business functions. DBS Bank, for example, navigated its transformation by replacing key components incrementally while maintaining business continuity – evolving toward a platform architecture without destabilising its operations.

Framing the Transformation: Vision and Roadmap

The starting point is strategic clarity. Without a shared vision, core transformation becomes a technical project rather than a business-led reinvention. Leaders must address why they want to transform the bank (speed, resilience, growth, regulation), what the end state should look like (cloud-native, modular, API-first), and what the non-negotiables are (regulatory uptime, customer data integrity), and set a realistic timeline and budget.

A robust roadmap should break down the transformation into phases (e.g. decoupling, modernization, migration), prioritize high-impact areas (e.g. payments, customer onboarding, reporting), align with regulatory windows and product cycles, and include milestones for internal capability building. Transparency and consensus at this stage set the tone for governance, stakeholder commitment, and pace.

Choosing the Right Path: Four Core Strategies

Banks today adopt one or more of the following core transformation approaches:

1. Encapsulation
   - Wrap legacy systems with APIs or middleware to improve usability
   - Quick wins, but long-term limitations
2. Coexistence (Progressive Modernization)
   - Run legacy and modern systems in parallel, gradually migrating functions
   - Balances risk and value realization
3. Greenfield Build
   - Build a new core from scratch while maintaining the old one for continuity
   - High innovation, often used by digital subsidiaries (e.g. Marcus by Goldman Sachs)
4. Full Replacement (Big Bang)
   - Decommission the old core and go live with a new one at once
   - High risk, only suitable in select contexts (e.g. smaller banks or new entrants)

Many leading institutions opt for coexistence, where they create a digital core alongside the legacy environment, progressively shifting customers, products, and workloads.

Key Enablers: Technology and Architecture

Regardless of the chosen approach, several enablers are foundational to successful transformation: API-first design ensures services are modular and interoperable; event-driven architecture enables real-time responsiveness; cloud-native platforms support elastic scaling and rapid deployment; containerization and orchestration provide agility and resilience; and decoupled data and process layers help avoid lock-in.

Partnering with specialized fintechs or core providers such as Thought Machine, Mambo, or Tremens can accelerate development, but banks must retain architectural control to ensure sustainability.

Managing Risk and Continuity

The biggest fear in core transformation is disruption – service outages, compliance failures, or data loss. Mitigating these risks requires parallel run environments and shadow testing, dual-write and reconciliation engines to ensure data integrity, rollback protocols for migration stages, regulatory sandboxing where allowed, and simulation of production scenarios before cutover.

Banks such as ING and BBVA used "canary deployments" – releasing new features or systems to a small subset of users – to test performance and safety before a wider rollout. Importantly, regulators must be engaged early, especially for mission-critical migrations (e.g. core ledger systems). Building regulator confidence is key to avoiding showstoppers.

Culture and Capability

Transformation is as much about people as it is about platforms. Success depends on cross-functional teams blending business, technology, risk, and compliance, product thinking over project thinking, agile ways of working with sprints, backlogs, and retrospectives, and upskilling programs for legacy staff and new hires alike. For example, NatWest invested heavily in training programs for platform engineering and cloud capability – ensuring talent could sustain the transformation beyond vendor support. Moreover, senior leadership must embody the change: celebrating iteration, accepting setbacks, and avoiding micromanagement.

Metrics that Matter

Measuring transformation success cannot rely solely on technical metrics. Banks should track the time to launch new products, customer onboarding duration, change failure rates, cost per transaction, API usage rates, platform uptime and latency, and revenue per feature released. These metrics shift the focus from internal milestones to external value delivery – the true benchmark of transformation.

Lessons from the Field

Several global banks offer lessons in navigating this journey. Citi adopted a layered architecture, decoupling frontend channels from the legacy core while progressively building a microservices foundation. Standard Chartered launched SC Ventures to experiment with new cores in greenfield digital subsidiaries. Bank of America spent over a decade and billions of dollars to re-architect its systems, creating an integrated, in-house platform with unmatched scalability. What unites successful transformations is not just technology – it is leadership commitment, iterative delivery, regulatory collaboration, and cultural resilience.

Building Institutional Memory

A key risk in large-scale transformation is losing institutional memory – knowledge of past systems, customer histories, exception handling rules, and undocumented processes. Banks should document legacy processes thoroughly, use knowledge graphs to link past and present systems, preserve test cases and decision logs, and retain transition teams during and after cutovers. Without this, even well-designed platforms can stumble due to operational blind spots.

Conclusion: Transformation as a Live Journey

Core transformation is not a one-off project. It is a live journey of continuous renewal. The banks that succeed treat it not as a destination but as a strategic discipline – evolving their platforms, people, and processes in alignment with customer needs and technological possibilities. In a volatile, fast-moving world, the core must become a platform for constant change. This requires courage, clarity, and craft. Those who embrace it will not only survive disruption – they will define the future of finance.

10 Building a Living Financial System

The future of banking does not lie in static systems but in living, evolving financial infrastructures. As customer expectations, regulatory demands, and technological capabilities shift continuously, banks must reimagine their core systems not as fixed assets, but as living platforms – flexible, adaptive, resilient, and responsive. A living financial system is not simply a modern core. It is an institutional philosophy: a commitment to change, embedded in architecture, talent, governance, and culture. This concluding section brings together the principles from earlier discussions. It also presents a forward-looking plan for how financial institutions can create and maintain a living financial system.

What Is a Living Financial System?

A living system is one that can continuously adapt and evolve while maintaining integrity. In the context of financial services, this means real-time responsiveness to customer and market events, continuous deployment of code, products, and fixes, modular design allowing components to be upgraded independently, data-driven intelligence that grows smarter over time, policy-aligned controls that evolve with regulation, and human-centric workflows that flex with internal capabilities. Such a system is dynamic and proactive, rather than reactive. It can pivot in the face of crises, scale with growth, and regenerate after disruption.

Beyond Modernization: The System as a Living Organism

Most core transformation projects focus on replacing legacy technology. But a living system requires more than technology – it demands a different kind of thinking. In biology, living organisms evolve through interaction with their environment. Likewise, banks must design their platforms to evolve through interaction with customers (preferences, behaviour, feedback loops), partners (APIs, embedded finance, platform ecosystems), regulators (dynamic compliance, open data, shared audits), and data (real-time telemetry, machine learning, risk signals).This philosophy shifts the mindset from building systems to cultivating ecosystems. Static roadmaps are replaced by continuous sensing and response.

Pillars of a Living Financial System

To move from aspiration to execution, financial institutions must address six foundational pillars:

1 Architecture: Modular and API-Centric

- Decompose monoliths into services that can evolve independently
- Use API gateways and service meshes to enable secure interconnection
- Design for failure and recovery, not just uptime

2 Infrastructure: Cloud-Native and Elastic

- Move to containerized workloads and orchestration (e.g., Kubernetes)
- Implement auto-scaling based on real-time load
- Prioritize infrastructure as code for agility and repeatability

3 Data: Real-time, Interoperable, and Ethical

- Establish event-driven pipelines and streaming architectures
- Design data models that support consent, lineage, and auditability
- Embed privacy and bias-detection mechanisms in AI workflows

4 Security and Governance: Embedded and Adaptive

- Shift from perimeter security to zero-trust architectures
- Enable real-time threat detection and dynamic policy enforcement
- Align governance with operational velocity without creating bottlenecks

5 Talent: Cross-Functional and Continuously Learning

- Upskill teams in platform engineering, DevOps, cloud, and ML

- Promote T-shaped talent with depth and breadth
- Embrace a culture of experimentation, retrospectives, and growth

6 Culture: Resilient and Transparent

- Foster psychological safety and open communication
- Make learning from failure an institutional habit
- Align incentives with long-term sustainability, not short-term delivery

Case Study: A Living Core in Practice

ING Group, a pioneer in digital banking, offers a strong case study. Their core transformation strategy focused on building a "banking platform as a service," enabling:

- Continuous software releases (several per day)
- Cross-border reuse of digital components
- Real-time customer analytics
- End-to-end process observability

This living core empowered ING to scale new services, integrate third - party offerings, and meet regulatory demands flexibly – all while keeping operations resilient and customer experience seamless.

Designing for Evolution, Not Just Efficiency

A common trap is designing systems for current requirements alone. A living financial system must be designed with evolution in mind: Temporal architecture accommodates feature flagging, rollback paths, and dual-versioning; decoupled delivery enables teams to innovate without cross-team dependencies; feedback instrumentation builds telemetry and observable into every layer; governance pipelines automate controls to evolve in tandem with services. By embedding change-readiness into every layer, banks can respond to volatility without resorting to reinvention.

Aligning with ESG and Societal Goals

A living system is also a more responsible system. It enables:

- Real-time ESG tracking including the carbon footprint per transaction and supply chain transparency
- Financial inclusion insights identifying underserved populations through AI
- Dynamic policy enforcement adapting lending criteria or sustainability thresholds on demand Crisis responsiveness enabling rapid deployment of relief schemes, grants, or tailored support during economic shocks

This aligns with the broader role of banking as a public good – supporting not only markets but also social stability and environmental stewardship.

Institutional Longevity in the Digital Age

Banks with living systems are not just digital – they are durable. In an age of disruption, the ability to learn, adapt, and improve continuously is what defines longevity.

Living systems help institutions:

- Absorb shocks without system collapse
- Launch new services without scaling failure
- Comply with evolving regulations without rework
- Engage customers with relevance and trust
- Attract top talent with modern workflows

This is not just about infrastructure. It is about the bank's immune system – its ability to respond to threats, heal itself, and grow stronger over time.

Leadership in a Living System

None of this is possible without leadership alignment. Executives must invest in foundational capability, not just front-end innovation, set vision and guardrails but empower decentralized decision-making, prioritize resilience over speed when trade-offs emerge, and continuously ask: Are we learning fast enough? Boards and regulators must also adapt, recognizing that the new normal is not stability but continuous motion.

Conclusion: The Future of Banking, Not Repeating the Past

The next decade will belong to financial institutions that build systems capable of learning, adapting, and thriving in uncertainty. Static systems – even if modern – will not suffice. A living financial system is not merely the endpoint of a transformation program. It is the beginning of a new operating model.

For every CIO, CTO, and CEO shaping the future of finance, the task is clear: Design systems not just to serve today's strategy, but to develop tomorrow's possibilities. That is how we build the bank of the future. That is how we make the core not a constraint, but a living foundation for growth, inclusion, and resilience.

Strategic Framework Box: Chapter 5 - The Core Transformed: From Legacy Systems to a Living Infrastructure

Key Insight

At the centre of every financial institution lies the core. But too often, that core is static, opaque, and decades old. The transformation of core banking infrastructure is not just a technical upgrade – it is a strategic imperative. Without it, agility is impossible and trust is brittle.

Strategic Takeaway

A modern bank's core must not only enable transactions, but also enable transformation. Infrastructure is no longer a back-office concern – it is a frontline strategy.

Core Element	*Traditional Banking Core*	*Transformed Core Infrastructure*
System Design	Monolithic, batch-based, vendor-locked	Modular, API-enabled, cloud-native
Time Orientation	End-of-day, lagged reporting	Real-time, always-on processing
Integration Logic	Hard-coded, point-to-point	Open, interoperable, plug-and-play
Security Posture	Perimeter-based, reactive	Embedded, zero-trust, resilient-by-design
Upgrade Cycle	Costly, disruptive, multi-year	Agile, iterative, service-oriented
Scalability	Fixed capacity, fragile under pressure	Elastic, dynamic, global-ready

This chapter makes the case that the "core" of banking must evolve into an invisible engine of trust. Its job is not to be seen – but to work flawlessly, securely, and intelligently in the background. Institutions that treat the core as a constraint will fall behind. Those who see it as a strategic asset will lead.

Bibliography

McKinsey & Company (2021). Modernizing Core Banking Systems: The Next Imperative for Banks. McKinsey & Company, Global Banking Practice.

6 The Power of Partnerships

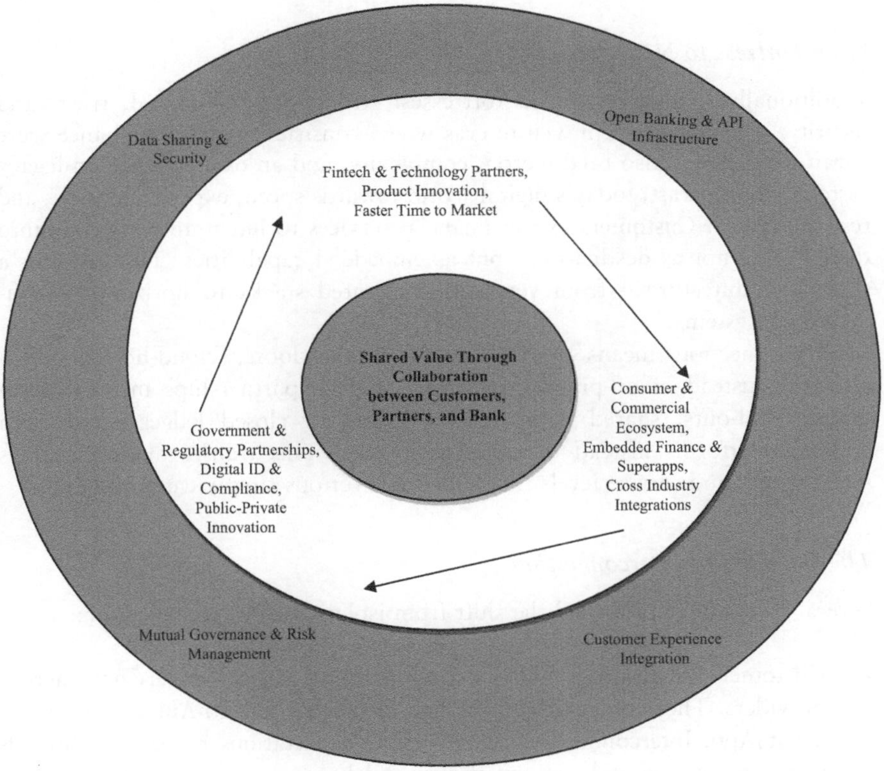

Figure 6.1 The future of financial ecosystems is driven by partnerships.

1 From Isolation to Interconnection

For much of the 20th century, banks operated as vertically integrated institutions. They owned the customer relationship, built and maintained their own technology, developed proprietary products, and managed services within

DOI: 10.4324/9781003737544-6

tightly guarded silos. This model was built on the logic of control – control over risk, information, regulation, and infrastructure. It was a world of isolation: of brand, of architecture, of process.

But the world has changed. The most competitive financial institutions of the 21st century no longer operate alone. They thrive through interconnection– with customers, with partners, with platforms, and with regulators. Instead of building everything internally, they increasingly orchestrate value across networks. In this emerging model, partnership is not a tactic; it is a structural shift. This section sets the foundation for understanding how the financial sector has transitioned from self-contained institutions to interconnected ecosystems – and why this transformation is not just technological, but cultural, strategic, and philosophical.

From Fortress to Network.

Traditionally, banks resembled fortresses: strongholds of capital, trust, and security. This served them well in eras where consistency and compliance were paramount. But it also bred inertia, complexity, and an over-reliance on legacy systems. By contrast, today's digital world rewards speed, experimentation, and responsiveness. Customers expect financial services to integrate seamlessly into their lives – not as destinations, but as embedded capabilities. This requires a shift in architecture – from vertically integrated stacks to horizontally connected ecosystems.

Interconnection means APIs instead of backdoors, cloud-hosted infrastructure instead of on-premise hardware, fintech partnerships instead of in-house build-outs, shared data models instead of closed ledgers, and open banking platforms instead of closed networks. This transformation enables scale, speed, and service levels that siloed institutions simply cannot match.

The Catalysts of Interconnection

Several forces have propelled the shift from isolation to interconnection:

- Customer Expectation: Users expect seamless digital experiences across providers. They compare banks not to each other, but to Amazon, Uber, or WhatsApp. Interconnection enables these expectations to be met through faster innovation and contextual service delivery.
- Technology Maturity: Cloud computing, microservices, APIs, and data interoperability have made it feasible to unbundle, externalize, and integrate functions. What once required a decade to build can now be partnered or licensed in weeks.
- Regulatory Pressure: Initiatives such as PSD2 in Europe and Open Banking in the UK have pushed institutions toward secure data sharing. Regulations increasingly favour collaboration over opacity, with built-in standards for authentication and privacy.

- Economic Logic: Cost-to-serve and cost-to-change are significantly lower in interconnected environments. Rather than replicating every capability internally, banks can plug into best-in-class services and focus on core differentiation.

From Pipelines to Platforms

The old banking model was pipeline-based: linear, provider-led, and product-centric. Banks manufactured products, distributed them via branches or digital channels, and controlled the end-to-end value chain. In contrast, today's most successful financial institutions think like platforms. They invite third parties to co-create value, enable plug-and-play services via APIs, expose capabilities as reusable components, and curate ecosystems of partners across verticals.

The platform mindset enables banks to act as infrastructure providers, aggregators, and orchestrators – not just service originators. This transition underpins everything from embedded finance to Banking-as-a-Service (BaaS).

Strategic Interconnection: Not Just Tech, But Trust

While APIs and platforms enable interconnection, trust sustains it. Strategic partnerships in finance require more than integration – they require shared purpose, governance alignment, and ethical clarity. This is especially true when customer data, payments, or identity verification are involved.

Banks must ask: Do we trust our partners to uphold customer protections? Are our incentives aligned, or is there hidden disintermediation? Is the relationship governed by transparent, fair, and enforceable terms? Do we have shared accountability when things go wrong? Interconnection without governance is a risk. But interconnection with strategic discipline is a multiplier.

Lessons from Other Industries

Banking is not the first industry to face this shift:

- Telecoms moved from vertically integrated operators to open carrier networks, enabling global roaming, mobile apps, and bundling with OTT services.
- Retail moved from controlling storefronts to partnering through marketplaces, affiliate models, and digital advertising.
- Media transitioned from owning broadcast channels to licensing content, distributing via streaming, and monetizing across ecosystems.

In each case, institutions that embraced interconnection flourished; those that clung to isolation were left behind.

Real-World Example: DBS and the Ecosystem Model

Singapore's DBS Bank is a global benchmark for ecosystem-based strategy. Rather than simply digitalizing existing services, DBS created over 1,000 APIs to enable ecosystem partnerships – across sectors such as ride-hailing, real estate, healthcare, and logistics.

This allowed DBS to embed financial services into third-party journeys, acquire new customers at lower cost, expand into new markets without building physical infrastructure, and offer contextual, data-enriched services with minimal friction. The bank's CEO, Piyush Gupta, famously reframed the institution not as a bank, but as a technology company in the business of banking.

Why Interconnection Is Now Inevitable

The idea that a single bank can do everything on its own is no longer credible. No institution, however large, can innovate at the pace of global start-ups, build every component from scratch, maintain compliance across every jurisdiction, or predict every customer need or niche. Interconnection is no longer optional – it is existential. It is how institutions adapt to complexity, how they accelerate relevance, and how they remain competitive in a world where speed and openness define advantage.

From Transaction to Transformation

The shift from isolation to interconnection is not just about how banks operate – it is about how they evolve: from siloed institutions to collaborative networks, from product creators to service platforms, from gatekeepers to enablers, and from owners of value to orchestrators of value. This transformation is fundamental. It redefines the nature of the financial institution – from a destination to a dynamic node in a larger ecosystem.

Conclusion: Partnership as Strategic DNA

Section 1 opens this chapter with a central proposition: The future of finance is interconnected. As banking moves further into an open, digital, and collaborative era, success will hinge on the ability of institutions to forge, manage, and develop partnerships. Not all partnerships are equal. But institutions that embed interconnection into their strategic DNA – not just their infrastructure – will be best positioned to scale innovation, meet customer needs, and uphold trust in a fast-changing world.

2 Ecosystem Thinking in Financial Services

The traditional bank operated within clearly defined boundaries – offering proprietary products, managing direct customer relationships, and competing with other banks in well-delineated sectors. But the age of ecosystems has changed all of that. No longer confined by rigid value chains, the modern financial institution is a node within a broader web of relationships – spanning technology platforms, data providers, consumer brands, government services, and fintechs. This is the essence of ecosystem thinking: not simply cooperating with external players, but co-creating value in a shared, dynamic environment.

Ecosystem thinking marks a clear shift from the isolated approaches of the past. It requires banks to shift their perspective – from institutions that own customer journeys to participants that enable them. The shift is not just strategic; it is cultural. It challenges banks to redefine control, trust, growth, and relevance in an interconnected world.

Defining Ecosystem Thinking

At its core, ecosystem thinking is the ability to:

- Recognize the interdependencies across sectors, platforms, and capabilities
- Identify and nurture mutually beneficial partnerships
- Orchestrate complex value delivery beyond the traditional boundaries of the bank
- Adapt to new roles – sometimes as provider, sometimes as platform, and sometimes as infrastructure

In contrast to transactional alliances or product reselling, ecosystems are built around shared purpose, sustained collaboration, and strategic integration. They are not just about plugging into others, but about curating and shaping environments where multiple players thrive together.

Why Ecosystems Matter in Financial Services

Ecosystem thinking is not a theoretical abstraction – it is now an operational necessity. Several forces are pushing financial institutions to adopt this mindset:

- Customer-Centric Demand: Customers no longer think in terms of sectors. They want frictionless experiences – whether paying for a ride, booking a home, or accessing healthcare. Financial services must be embedded in these journeys, not bolted on afterwards. Ecosystems allow banks to be present where life happens.
- Speed of Innovation: Fintechs, start-ups, and big tech players often outpace banks in specific innovations – from biometric verification to AI-driven credit scoring. Ecosystem thinking enables banks to integrate these innovations quickly rather than recreating them internally.
- Cost Efficiency: The cost of building and maintaining every product or service internally is prohibitively high. Ecosystem partnerships distribute risk and cost while enhancing scale.

- Regulatory Enablement: Regulators increasingly favour models that ensure openness, resilience, and transparency. Ecosystem designs – built around APIs, shared standards, and consent-based data sharing – align well with these principles.

Models of Ecosystem Participation

Banks can play different roles within ecosystems, depending on strategy and capability:

- Orchestrator: A bank curates and leads an ecosystem, setting standards and governing integration (e.g., DBS, BBVA).
- Participant: A bank integrates into another ecosystem, providing modular services such as payments, lending, or identity verification (e.g., Stripe integrating into e-commerce platforms).
- Enabler: A bank offers infrastructure for others to build on, such as Banking-as-a-Service (e.g., Solarisbank, Clear Bank).
- Aggregator: A bank pulls together offerings from multiple providers to deliver comprehensive value to end users (e.g., superapps and digital wallets).

The most effective institutions often play multiple roles simultaneously – depending on the use case, market, or segment.

Ecosystem Thinking Across Segments

Retail Banking: Ecosystems are enabling banks to embed financial services into lifestyle platforms – shopping, health, education, mobility. For instance, Standard Charterer's partnerships with ride-hailing and e-commerce platforms in Asia have allowed it to expand its reach without expanding physical presence.
SMEs and Corporate: Small businesses benefit from integrated ecosystems that combine banking, accounting, invoicing, payroll, and tax services. Solutions such as Tide (UK) and Khatabook (India) exemplify this model.
Wealth and Investment: Platforms now blend banking with investment, insurance, and advisory – accessible through a single digital interface. Robo-advisors, integrated insurance marketplaces, and goal-based investing tools are all part of this new ecosystem.
Public Sector and Infrastructure: Banks are also part of national ecosystems – supporting digital ID, e-governance, the Unified Payments Interface (UPI – India), and real-time tax collection systems. The role of public-private ecosystems is crucial for financial inclusion and resilience.

Governance in Ecosystem Models

Ecosystems are complex and require shared protocols for data exchange, including consent, standards, and encryption; service availability, such as uptime, fallback mechanisms, and SLAs; trust frameworks covering liability, audit trails, and breach handling; incentives and revenue sharing with clear models for value distribution; and brand control to manage customer experience across partners. Without governance, ecosystems can become fragmented and risky. With it, they become powerful, resilient, and scalable.

Ecosystem Case Study: BBVA's Open Platform

BBVA, a leading Spanish bank, has strategically embraced ecosystem thinking through the BBVA Open Platform. By offering APIs for payments, identity, accounts, and data aggregation, BBVA enables third-party developers to build financial services on top of its infrastructure.

Key results include lower cost of customer acquisition, faster go-to-market for new services, access to previously underserved markets, and stronger regulatory alignment with open finance goals. BBVA's ecosystem approach demonstrates how traditional banks can reconfigure their assets to become enablers of innovation, not just providers of services.

Common Pitfalls in Ecosystem Thinking

While the benefits are clear, ecosystem strategies can falter due to a lack of clarity on strategic intent, misalignment of partner incentives, overdependence on a single partner or platform, cultural resistance to openness and co-creation, and inadequate technology readiness. Banks must invest in internal capability building – not just in tech, but in mindset. Ecosystems thrive when leaders think in systems, not silos.

The Competitive Edge of Ecosystem Thinking

In a world where product advantages are short-lived and digital experiences commoditized, the real differentiator is ecosystem agility – the ability to connect, adapt, and grow through collaboration. Financial institutions that master ecosystem thinking can respond faster to change, serve customers in new contexts, monetize their capabilities beyond traditional boundaries, and build defensible positions in rapidly evolving markets. Most importantly, they stay relevant – not by doing everything, but by enabling everything.

Conclusion: The Ecosystem as Strategic Canvas

Ecosystem thinking is not a trend. It is a new logic for organizing value in a connected world. For banks, this requires more than technology adoption – it demands strategic intent, cultural shift, and operational redesign. The institutions that embrace this mindset will not only participate in the future of finance – they will shape it.

3 Embedded Finance and Seamless Integration

The financial world is no longer confined to bank branches, apps, or websites. Increasingly, it is invisibly woven into the fabric of our daily experiences – from paying for a ride with one click to receiving instant credit at checkout. This phenomenon, known as embedded finance, is reshaping how individuals and businesses interact with financial services. At its heart lies a powerful principle: finance should meet people where they are, not the other way around.

Embedded finance transforms banking from a destination into an enabler – delivering financial tools seamlessly through non-financial platforms such as e-commerce, transport, social media, healthcare, and education. Whether through a retailer offering by-now-pay-later (BNPL), a gig platform providing insurance, or an app offering savings goals within a fitness program; embedded finance creates a world where banking becomes intuitive, contextual, and invisible.

Understanding Embedded Finance

Embedded finance refers to the integration of financial services, such as payments, lending, insurance, and investment, directly into the offerings of non-financial brands or platforms. It allows customers to access financial tools as part of their existing digital journeys, without switching apps or dealing with banks directly.

Examples of embedded finance include embedded payments, such as Apple Pay and Uber in-app payments; embedded lending, such as BNPL services via Klarna, Affirm, or after pay; embedded insurance, for instance travel insurance bundled with airline bookings; embedded banking, such as debit cards offered by retailers or telcos; and embedded investment, such as micro-investing through shopping apps. This shift is powered by APIs, data analytics, and cloud-based infrastructure, enabling real-time decision-making and tailored financial experiences.

Why Embedded Finance Matters

For consumers, embedded finance brings unprecedented convenience, speed, and simplicity. For businesses, it opens new revenue streams and deepens engagement. And for financial institutions, it challenges the traditional model of customer acquisition and ownership. Key drivers of adoption include:

- User experience benefits from seamless transactions that enhance loyalty and reduce friction.
- Personalization through contextual offers increases conversion and trust.
- Distribution improves as embedding financial services into third-party platforms allows financial institutions to scale reach without scaling operations.
- Data access is enhanced because partner platforms offer richer, real-time data to inform underwriting, pricing, and fraud detection.

In short, embedded finance creates a triad of value – benefiting end users, platforms, and financial providers simultaneously.

The Global Landscape: Embedded Finance in Action

United States

The US has led the way in embedded finance through companies such as Stripe (payments infrastructure), Plaid (data connectivity), and Affirm (embedded credit). Amazon's integration with Affirm for consumer credit and Shopify's merchant lending illustrate how platforms can evolve into financial distributors.

United Kingdom

The UK's open banking regulations have facilitated secure data sharing and ecosystem integration. Start-ups such as True Layer and Railsr enable banking capabilities to be built directly into third-party apps. Retailers now commonly offer BNPL and micro-insurance at checkout, powered by embedded finance platforms.

Asia-Pacific

Superapps such as Grab (Southeast Asia), Gojek (Indonesia), and WeChat (China) embed everything from wallets and savings to investment tools. Banks collaborate or compete within these ecosystems – depending on their strategy.

Africa

Mobile money platforms such as M-Pesa have evolved into embedded financial ecosystems, offering lending, insurance, and savings. Fintechs such as Flutterwave now enable embedded payments for small and mid-sized businesses across the continent.

India

Platforms such as Paytm and Phonepe integrate insurance, investment, credit scoring, and gold savings into everyday commerce and lifestyle experiences – embedding financial services for over 400 million users.

Key Enablers of Embedded Finance

API-First Architecture

Banks and fintechs must expose core services via secure, flexible APIs. These interfaces enable third parties to build applications on top of banking infrastructure – bringing modularity, scale, and speed.

Regulatory Sandboxes

Jurisdictions that encourage innovation through sandboxes – such as the Financial Conduct Authority (FCA) in the UK or MAS in Singapore – have accelerated the development of embedded finance. These frameworks allow live testing without compromising consumer protection.

Digital Identity and KYC

Seamless onboarding is only possible if identity verification is quick, accurate, and low-friction. Digital ID systems – such as India's Aadhaar or Estonia's e-ID – are crucial for embedded journeys.

Consent and Data Governance

As finance moves into new contexts, consent-based data sharing and transparent algorithms become essential. Trust is the currency of embedded finance.

Strategic Implications for Banks

For traditional banks, embedded finance can feel like a threat. After all, they risk losing visibility, direct relationships, and brand presence. But this is also a moment of opportunity – for banks willing to shift from being the destination to being the engine. Three strategic options emerge:

- Build: Create your own embedded offerings (e.g., JPMorgan's acquisition of We Pay to offer payment solutions to merchants)
- Partner: Collaborate with platforms as infrastructure providers (e.g., Goldman Sachs powering Apple Card)
- Enable: Offer Banking-as-a-Service (BaaS) capabilities to fintechs and brands (e.g., BBVA, Solaris bank, Clear Bank)

These strategies require new capabilities – developer ecosystems, API documentation, uptime guarantees, and real-time compliance – which are not traditionally found in legacy institutions.

Designing for Seamlessness

Embedded finance must be invisible but powerful. The best integrations are intuitive, context-aware, and frictionless. This is achieved with the following design principles:

- Minimal disruption keeps the user in the flow with no redirection to external sites.

- Contextual relevance offers financial services when and where they make sense, such as insurance when booking travel.
- Speed and certainty are provided through instant credit decisions, transparent pricing, and clear terms.
- Failover systems ensure resilience, even when partner systems are down.

The embedded model is only as good as the infrastructure behind it. Uptime, latency, and customer service remain mission-critical.

Challenges and Risks

While embedded finance offers immense potential, it also introduces challenges:

- Compliance complexity arises around responsibility for KYC, AML, and data protection.
- Reputational risk occurs when a poor experience on a partner platform affects a bank's brand.
- Margin pressure results from revenue-sharing models that can reduce profitability per transaction.
- Over-reliance on partner platforms for distribution and growth can create dependency risks for banks.

Mitigating these risks requires robust contracts, shared governance models, and proactive monitoring.

The Future of Embedded Finance

Looking ahead, embedded finance will become more sophisticated: Future trends include hyper-personalized offers based on behavioural and contextual data, voice and gesture-based transactions within smart homes and vehicles, cross-border embedded services powered by blockchain and decentralized identity, and embedded ESG and impact metrics that enable users to see carbon footprints at the point of purchase. As financial services blur into the fabric of life, banks will need to reinvent not just how they deliver value – but where, with whom, and for what purpose.

Conclusion: A New Distribution Paradigm

Embedded finance is more than a channel – it is a reimagining of distribution, trust, and relevance. Banks that embrace it will expand their reach, relevance, and resilience. Those that resist may find themselves increasingly disintermediated. In this new paradigm, the most successful institutions will be those that think like platforms, operate like infrastructure, and partner like ecosystems.

4 Partnering with Fintech, Telco, and Retail

Strategic partnerships with fintechs, telcos, and retailers have emerged as one of the most powerful levers for transformation in the banking sector. No longer limited to traditional outsourcing or white-labelling agreements, today's partnerships are deeply embedded, co-designed, and value-driven. For banks navigating digital transformation and inclusion agendas, these relationships open new pathways to scale, relevance, and innovation.

The value of partnering with fintech companies is not limited to improvements in technology. It also includes speeding up innovation cycles. Fintechs bring advanced capabilities such as artificial intelligence, alternative credit scoring, and next-generation customer analytics. By integrating these technologies, traditional banks can reimagine how products are designed, credit is underwritten, and real-time insights are delivered to customers. Innovation becomes not an occasional event but a continuous process – fuelled by agile collaboration with players outside the core banking ecosystem.

Distribution is another critical value driver. Partnering with telcos, retailers, and superapps enables banks to reach new customer segments in ways that traditional branch or website models cannot. A telco can embed a savings product directly into a prepaid recharge journey. A retail partner can offer credit at the point of sale with a few taps. A superapp can host a digital wallet that doubles as a banking interface. These models unlock the power of distribution at scale – leveraging pre-existing networks and behaviours to bring financial services closer to daily life.

Operational efficiency is also dramatically improved through partnerships. Cloud-native fintechs bring modular SEA (software engineering and applications) solutions that allow banks to shift away from costly, rigid legacy infrastructures. With scalable platforms and plug-and-play integrations, banks can reduce IT overhead, streamline compliance, and launch new services at speed. This is not just cost saving – it is unlocking organizational agility.

Brand affinity is another domain where partnerships can play a catalytic role. Collaborating with digital-first fintechs helps banks modernize their brand perception, particularly among younger demographics and digital natives. When done well, these collaborations do not dilute the banks' identity – instead; they enhance it by signalling a forward-looking, customer-centric ethos. Strategic alliances with ethical brands or mission-driven start-ups also help align financial services with broader ESG narratives.

Perhaps most significantly, partnerships are increasingly instrumental in advancing inclusion and reaching underserved populations. Fintechs often serve as bridges into informal economies, rural regions, or digitally excluded groups – spaces where traditional banks struggle to operate viably. Telcos provide the digital rails, enabling transactions through mobile networks. Retailers serve as physical distribution points, especially in areas with limited banking infrastructure. Together, these actors co-create hybrid service models that deliver meaningful financial access at low cost.

It is worth noting that not all partnerships deliver equal value. Banks must approach this domain with strategic clarity, selecting partners who complement – not compete with – their vision and values. The most successful partnerships are those where each side brings differentiated strengths and where governance mechanisms enable shared decision-making and risk alignment. A strong partnership does not merely add value – it changes the very nature of what the bank can achieve on its own.

In the years ahead, we will see even deeper integration between financial services and everyday platforms. Banking will be increasingly embedded into retail checkout, telecom services, ride-hailing apps, social media, and government portals. To thrive in this landscape, banks must master the art of partnership – not as a procurement exercise, but as a core organizational capability. The future will be shaped not by those who have the best standalone systems, but those who can collaborate most intelligently across ecosystems.

5 Superapps and Everyday Interactions

In the next evolution of digital finance, superapps are fast becoming the primary battleground for user attention and loyalty. These multi-functional platforms – popularized in Asia and now gaining traction globally – are redefining how people engage with money. What began as messaging or ride-hailing apps has rapidly morphed into financial ecosystems, blending payments, banking, commerce, insurance, and lifestyle services into a single digital experience. For banks and financial institutions, the rise of superapps represents both a challenge and a transformative opportunity.

At the core of the superapp model lies a simple but powerful idea: the ability to integrate multiple everyday functions into a seamless, consistent interface. This integration changes user behaviour. Instead of toggling between apps for different services, users stay within a single environment – ordering food, paying bills, investing, or even applying for a loan. As the platform becomes a habitual part of daily life, it establishes extraordinary levels of trust, stickiness, and data visibility. Financial services offered within this context gain relevance not as isolated products but as logical extensions of everyday actions.

Banks that successfully partner with or embed into superapps can gain rapid customer acquisition, reduce friction in onboarding, and improve data-driven personalization. A user topping up a digital wallet to pay for groceries may be offered short-term credit or cash back on utility payments. A ride-hailing customer might receive dynamic insurance based on their usage patterns. A gig economy worker may be provided with instant access to earned wages via an in-app micro-savings plan. These are not just features – they are behavioural touchpoints that rewire how people perceive financial services.

Yet, for banks, the decision to partner with a superapp requires careful strategic consideration. Control over the customer interface often shifts to the platform, leaving the bank in a backend role. Branding, user insights, and cross-selling opportunities may be diluted. To mitigate this, some banks negotiate co-branded interfaces or establish dedicated micro-apps within the platform that retain their design language and customer flow. Others choose to build their own superapp-style ecosystems in partnership with telcos, retailers, and fintechs, offering bundled services that compete for the same customer moments.

In emerging markets, superapps have demonstrated immense potential to drive financial inclusion. In countries where banking infrastructure is sparse and smartphone penetration is rising, these platforms serve as an on-ramp to formal financial services. They offer vernacular language support, low-data usage interfaces, and familiar transaction flows. In India, Brazil, Indonesia, Nigeria, and beyond, superapps are becoming the de facto banks for millions of people who were previously outside the formal financial system. For global institutions seeking impact at scale, embedding in such ecosystems can be more effective than traditional expansion strategies.

From a risk and governance perspective, superapp partnerships demand rigorous due diligence. Issues of data privacy, algorithmic decision-making, customer consent, and cybersecurity become complex when services are layered across multiple providers. Regulatory regimes are still evolving to respond to the challenges of platform banking. Banks must ensure that their standards of compliance, KYC, and consumer protection are preserved even within third-party environments. It is no longer enough to manage risk within the four walls of the bank; risk now flows through code, interfaces, and shared infrastructure.

Perhaps the most important insight is that superapps are not merely a trend – they are a shift in digital behaviour. Consumers increasingly expect banking to show up where they are, rather than visit a separate app or branch. They want intuitive, contextual, low-friction experiences embedded in their daily routines. For banks, this means rethinking distribution not as a channel strategy but as a partnership strategy. It requires a mindset that places the customer's life – not the bank's structure – at the centre of service design.

As the ecosystem continues to evolve, we may see new hybrid models emerge – where banks co-create modular services, integrate open APIs, and participate in shared marketplaces, rather than compete as standalone entities. The success of such models will hinge on trust, alignment, and the ability to design experiences that feel native to the customer's world. In this future, banking won't be something for which you have to go somewhere. It will be something you are already doing – quietly, intelligently, and invisibly – inside the superapp you use every day.

6 Platforms That Scale with Purpose

In today's financial ecosystem, the ability to scale is no longer simply a question of infrastructure or capital – it is a question of purpose. Platforms that scale with purpose are those that combine technical capability with societal intent, commercial reach with inclusive access, and innovation with ethical design. In the post-platform era of digital finance, where banking is embedded into everyday services, partnerships must be evaluated not just on economic value but on the alignment of purpose and long-term vision.

At the heart of any scalable platform is the ability to serve millions – if not billions – of users in a modular, reliable, and context-aware fashion. Whether it is a digital wallet servicing gig workers across Southeast Asia, an AI-powered lending platform targeting underserved communities in Latin America, or an open banking API network spanning the UK and the US, these platforms act as connective tissue between banks, businesses, governments, and consumers. But scalability without direction can become a liability. The true power of modern platforms lies not only in how widely they operate but in the kind of financial experiences they enable.

Banks that create or join platforms today need to be clear about their purpose and effects. For instance, open banking platforms in the UK and EU were first required to boost competition and give customers control over their data. Yet, their real value has emerged in the way they enable fintechs and challenger banks to build personalized, cross-functional financial services – extending access, lowering costs, and simplifying user experience. The regulatory scaffolding provided the impetus; purpose-driven design allowed the ecosystem to flourish.

Contrast this with platforms built purely for commercial control – those that replicate existing hierarchies and gatekeeping through new interfaces. These may show early adoption but rarely sustain deep customer engagement or societal legitimacy. Today's customers – particularly Gen Z and millennial segments – are increasingly attuned to the values behind the services they use. They ask not just what a platform does, but who it empowers, who it excludes, and what norms it reinforces. Banks must therefore be deliberate in choosing platform partners and shaping the values that underpin shared infrastructure.

Some of the most successful platform models globally combine financial services with adjacent domains: health, education, agriculture, mobility, or identity. In Kenya, M-Pesa has long been more than a mobile wallet – it is a national platform for trade, welfare, and family support. In India, platforms such as India Stack and UPI are not just financial innovations – they are public goods that enable digital identity, seamless payments, and government disbursements across a billion people. These platforms scale not because they are technically superior, but because they solve deeply embedded societal challenges through partnerships between government, industry, and civil society.

In advanced markets such as the US and UK, purpose-driven platforms are now being shaped around ESG objectives. Green finance platforms that verify and track carbon impact, social lending platforms that direct funds to underserved neighbourhoods, and ethical investing apps that align portfolios with climate goals – they all signal a broader shift. These are not niche products. When platforms scale with purpose, they reshape what mainstream finance looks like.

Yet scaling with purpose is not automatic. It requires deliberate governance structures, transparent metrics, and a strong culture of inclusion. Banks participating in platform ecosystems must contribute more than capital or code – they must bring stewardship. This includes defining data governance norms, ensuring algorithmic fairness, embedding consumer protection, and maintaining resilience. Purpose is not a slogan; it is operationalized through design choices, partnership terms, service flows, and long-term accountability.

From a technological standpoint, scaling with purpose also demands modularity and openness. Closed systems may achieve short-term efficiency but stifle innovation and exclude smaller players. Open platforms – built around APIs, open standards, and shared protocols – encourage diversity of participation and resilience through decentralization. They allow local innovators to build on top of global rails, adapting services for cultural and linguistic context. Banks that support open ecosystems position themselves not as gatekeepers, but as enablers of broader economic empowerment.

The economics of platform partnerships must also evolve to reflect purpose-driven outcomes. Traditional ROI metrics – customer acquisition, transaction volume, fee income – remain important. But they must be complemented by measures of financial inclusion, digital literacy, sustainability impact, and user trust. Institutions such as the World Bank, the UN, and regional development banks are now pushing for standardized impact metrics in digital finance. As banks join platforms to scale services, they must also commit to tracking and reporting the societal value generated – at product, platform, and portfolio levels.

Another critical dimension is resilience. Platforms that scale without attention to governance and interoperability often become systemic risks. A failure in one component – payment rail, identity provider, cloud service – can ripple across millions of users. Designing for resilience means ensuring that platforms have redundancy, interoperability, and clarity of escalation. It also means ensuring that users – especially low-income or digitally marginalized groups – have recourse and redress when systems fail.

There is a growing call for banks and technology companies to co-create new governance models for platforms – ones that go beyond bilateral contracts and move toward shared stewardship. This may include co-funding public infrastructure, co-designing standards, or participating in digital commons initiatives. In the EU, the concept of digital sovereignty is pushing for infrastructure that is not just scalable, but locally governed and ethically anchored. In Africa and Latin America, regional alliances are emerging to build inclusive payment and data platforms tailored to their demographic and economic realities. Banks that engage with these movements not only gain market access – they help shape the next generation of financial infrastructure.

Ultimately, the question for banks is not whether to build or join platforms – it is how to do so in a way that scales with purpose. In the race for reach and relevance, it is easy to follow models that maximize short-term gain. But the long-term value lies in platforms that enable dignity, opportunity, and trust for all participants. As regulators, customers, and investors raise their expectations, banks must ensure that every platform they touch reflects not just strategic intent but societal contribution. In the years ahead, those who succeed will not be the ones who scale the fastest, but the ones who scale with meaning.

7 Public-Private Innovation Models

In the new architecture of contemporary finance, no single force is more determinative than public-private innovation. This collaborative way of working - – in which government, regulators, central banks, and private institutions work together to shape and provide financial services – has become essential to creating future-ready, resilient, and inclusive financial ecosystems. No individual actor, public or private, can address the systemic issues of financial access, digital revolution, or worldwide regulation on its own. The imperative is not cooperation but co-creation.

Public and private innovation models bridge the middle ground between free markets and full government control. They enable innovation to thrive in the context of public accountability, and they introduce agility to government-led infrastructure without compromising policy intent. If successful, these models provide exponential returns: economic formalization, penetration of digital identities, financial inclusion, data interoperability, clarity of regulation, and new forms of trust. But when not managed correctly, they can perpetuate monopolies, undermine public oversight, or kill off innovation through bureaucratic resistance. The nature of the partnership is thus as important as the partners.

A few of the most dramatic instances of public-private innovation are to be found in the emerging economies themselves, where structural restrictions have necessitated experiments of a bold nature. In India, the development of UPI provides a good example. Built by the National Payments Corporation of India (NPCI) – a non-profit organization shared by public and private banks – UPI established an interoperable real-time payment infrastructure, which is now the backbone of the nation's digital economy. Its mass adoption was made possible through government support, coupled with private fintech ingenuity. UPI today processes billions of transactions every month and enables services from microlending to government welfare payments. It has lowered the cost of payments, removed gatekeepers, and redefined the way banks and fintechs partner up.

Likewise, in Brazil, the Central Bank's introduction of Pix – a real-time payment system – was not only a regulatory measure but also gave rise to disruption. Pix was designed as a public good, yet the expansion of the system was initiated by private sector usage and innovation. Banks, wallets, retailers, and telcos embraced Pix to provide frictionless, instant, low-cost payments. The public sector developed the infrastructure; the private sector scaled it through use cases and distribution. This model of public foundational infrastructure accompanied by competitive service delivery is increasingly being adopted elsewhere in the world.

Open banking in the UK is another example of public-private interaction. Although derived from EU regulatory mandates (PSD2), the Open Banking Implementation Entity (OBIE) of the UK engaged in close cooperation with private banks and fintechs to develop secure APIs and data-sharing regimes. It has resulted in an expanding universe of services – ranging from personal finance utilities to SME credit analysis – that use data for which the customers have given permission. But open banking also shows the limitations of such collaborations: In some cases, an absence of government support and user-orientated design led to a limited take-up beyond early adopters. It underlines that there has to be cooperation not only at the level of technology, but also of behaviour, and that policies and communications must be aligned across sectors.

In the United States, public-private models tend to be more fragmented but equally impactful. The Federal Reserve's Fed Now initiative for real-time payments is being developed in parallel with private networks such as The Clearing House's RTP network. Difficulties arise in synchronizing public and private standards, ensuring interoperability, and preventing market bifurcation. In other areas – including cybersecurity, anti-fraud, and financial education – partnerships such as the Financial Services Sector Coordinating Council (FSSCC) offer a framework for strategic cooperation across regulatory and commercial divides. These frameworks highlight the value of institutional trust and common risk architectures when negotiating intricate ecosystems.

Public-private models are similarly essential when dealing with digital identity – an underpinning layer of any digital financial system. Estonia's e-residency initiative, Aadhaar in India, and the replaced GOV.UK Verify system are all examples where governments established identity infrastructure but used banks and fintechs to make it operational. The sustainability of such schemes in the long run does not only depend on scale but on governance, transparency, and trust. Banks become verifiers, intermediaries, or providers, whereas governments set data rights, protocols, and norms of accountability. In weak institutions, such models will have to be crafted with special sensitivity so that they do not lead to misuse and the exclusion of certain groups.

One of the most exciting areas of public-private innovation is ESG finance. As climate-related financial risk becomes a systemic issue, regulators and central banks are requiring disclosures, scenario modelling, and green taxonomies. But the real tools, platforms, and data analytics needed to make these shifts happen tend to come from private sector innovators. Public financing of climate data infrastructure, carbon registries, and green bond certification will need to be complemented by private sector uptake and innovation. Here, multilateral institutions – the World Bank, the IMF, and the BIS – have the crucial function of bringing the partners together. Initiatives such as the Network for Greening the Financial System (NGFS) illustrate how central banks are partnering with the private sector on climate alignment and resilience.

Another area of pressing importance is financial inclusion. Governments tend to subsidize or mandate inclusion initiatives – such as basic accounts, digital wallets, or priority lending – but their distribution tends to rely on private banks and fintechs. The best inclusion models align incentives: banks are incentivized to onboard and serve poor customers, and regulators simplify compliance and risk architectures. In countries such as Pakistan, Nigeria, and Bangladesh, collaborations between mobile operators, central banks, and private banks have brought services to millions. These are not isolated interventions but living ecosystems in which public regulation and private instruments evolve together.

But public-private innovation is not tension-free. Data ownership, commercialization, regulatory capture, and institutional responsibility are all issues that have to be carefully managed. Governments need to ensure they are not helping create monopolistic platforms, while the private sector needs to avoid treating public infrastructure as another growth tool. What is needed are respect for one another, transparency, and transparent governance models.

The key here is good governance. Successful public-private models create common objectives, open standards, independent audits, and participatory feedback loops. Some models foresee joint steering committees or public-interest boards to guide implementation. Others establish graduated regulatory sandboxes permitting experimentation with guardrails in place. The form doesn't matter; what is important is that both sectors have voice and responsibility. It is not sufficient for governments to only regulate or provide funding; they also have to remain involved in design and assessment. Likewise, fintechs and banks need to contribute more than lobbying and compliance – they need to co-invest in the system.

In the future, public-private models of innovation will play an increasingly important role. With AI, digital money, and cyber risks remaking finance, the speed and responsiveness of public and private institutions will determine whether systems remain secure, trusted, and inclusive. No technology is good or bad in itself; its effect lies in how it is governed and used. Through careful, open, and value-driven collaborations, governments and banks can construct financial infrastructure that is not only resilient but also regenerative.

The future of banking will not be brought in by one single party. It will be co-created – by public and private, centralized and distributed, institutional and grassroots organisations. The models we create today will shape the integrity, inclusiveness, and sustainability of finance for decades to come.

8 Governance in Shared Infrastructure

As financial services become increasingly interconnected, the question of governance – who steers, who safeguards, and who is accountable – becomes central to the sustainability of shared infrastructure. In an era of open platforms, cross-border data flows, API ecosystems, and collaborative innovation, governance is no longer a matter of internal compliance or regulatory submission. It is a strategic imperative that underpins trust, resilience, and long-term value. The deeper the interdependence between actors, the more crucial it becomes to design governance models that are transparent, participatory, and aligned to public interest.

Shared infrastructure in finance takes many forms: real-time payment networks, digital identity platforms, data-sharing protocols, regulatory sandboxes, open banking frameworks, and blockchain-based settlement systems. These are not merely technical constructs – they are socio-technical systems with multiple stakeholders, including banks, fintechs, telcos, regulators, developers, and consumers. Governance in such systems must accommodate diverse interests, distribute power responsibly, and embed mechanisms for dispute resolution, innovation, and evolution.

The governance challenge is especially pronounced when infrastructure is co-owned or co-managed. Consider open banking in the UK, where the OBIE was created to oversee API standards and industry-wide protocols. Initially funded by the nine largest banks, OBIE operated with technical autonomy but lacked clear accountability to end users. Over time, concerns around transparency, oversight, and inclusion prompted a governance review. The UK's FCA eventually intervened to strengthen public oversight, introduce independent board representation, and clarify the long-term transition plan. The lesson: even the most technically sound systems require governance structures that are inclusive, transparent, and adaptable.

In India, the governance of UPI under NPCI showcases a different model. NPCI is a non-profit entity owned by a consortium of public and private banks. While this provides a strong financial sector foundation, concerns have been raised about whether NPCI's dual role – as both regulator and operator – poses conflicts of interest. As UPI becomes foundational to India's digital economy, questions around neutrality, open access, and long-term innovation stewardship grow louder. Governance, in this case, must evolve beyond legacy bank consortia to include fintechs, consumer groups, and independent technologists.

In the United States, where real-time payment systems are emerging through both public (Fed Now) and private (RTP by The Clearing House) initiatives, governance fragmentation is a key concern. Without a unified governance framework or interoperability standards there is a risk that financial infrastructure remains siloed, limiting systemic efficiency and inclusion. The absence of a national digital identity system further complicates shared governance, leaving each institution to manage identity verification on its own terms, with varying degrees of security and friction.

In contrast, the European Union offers a more integrated governance approach through SEPA (Single Euro Payments Area), which harmonizes cross-border payments across member states. SEPA's governance is multi-layered, involving the European Payments Council (EPC), the European Central Bank (ECB), and national authorities. While this structure provides consistency and regulatory alignment, it can also be slow to adapt and limited in market responsiveness. Finding the balance between harmonization and innovation remains a central challenge in shared financial infrastructures.

As decentralized finance and blockchain networks emerge, governance becomes even more complex. These systems often claim to be "governed by code", yet behind every protocol lies a human decision-making process: who writes the code, who audits it, who decides on forks or upgrades. In the case of stable coins and central bank digital currencies, the governance stakes are even higher, with implications for monetary policy, financial stability, and international capital flows. Banks entering these domains must grapple with new forms of decentralized governance – voting mechanisms, token-holder decisions, smart contract immutability – while ensuring regulatory compliance and consumer protection.

The management of shared infrastructure also needs clear definitions of responsibilities. Who is accountable for data breaches in an open banking environment? Who resolves conflicts between API providers and third-party developers? Who manages onboarding and offboarding in digital identity federations? These are not just legal questions – they are design choices that impact user trust and ecosystem sustainability. A well-governed infrastructure includes:

- Representation: All key stakeholder groups – including smaller institutions, fintech start-ups, consumers, regulators, and civil society – must have a voice in governance structures. This prevents capture by incumbents and ensures that the infrastructure evolves in the public interest.
- Transparency: Decisions, rules, metrics, and changes must be communicated clearly and accessibly. Black-box decision-making undermines legitimacy and deters participation.
- Accountability: There must be mechanisms for appeal, redress, and performance review. Whether through ombudsman structures, independent audits, or regulatory oversight, shared systems must be accountable to their users.
- Adaptability: Governance must allow for evolution – of standards, security protocols, user expectations, and business models. Rigid structures risk obsolescence; flexible frameworks enable innovation.
- Security and Resilience: Shared infrastructure must be hardened against systemic risk, cyber threats, and single points of failure. Governance here includes incident response protocols, redundancy planning, and data sovereignty.

Emerging best practices include the establishment of multi-stakeholder boards, layered governance models (technical, operational, strategic), and governance sandboxes to test participatory frameworks. The Financial Stability Board (FSB), the Bank for International Settlements (BIS), and the International Organization of Securities Commissions (IOSCO) have all begun issuing guidelines on how shared financial infrastructure should be governed, especially in cross-border contexts.

One instructive example is Singapore's approach to digital infrastructure. The Monetary Authority of Singapore (MAS) has created a series of public-private frameworks – such as the Financial Industry API Register, Project Ubin (for blockchain settlement), and Project Orchid (for programmable money) – where governance includes consultation papers, public feedback loops, and industry-led implementation groups. These are not one-off initiatives but living ecosystems with built-in evolution pathways. They demonstrate that governance can be both rigorous and dynamic.

Ultimately, governance is a trust-building mechanism. In financial services – where the margin for error is slim and the cost of failure high – shared infrastructure cannot depend on informal norms or good intentions. It must be governed deliberately, inclusively, and with foresight. Governance is not about controlling outcomes, but about enabling shared purpose, managing complexity, and safeguarding the future.

For banks, embracing governance in shared infrastructure is not just a compliance exercise; it is a strategic posture. Institutions that engage proactively in governance design – rather than waiting to be regulated – will help shape the future financial system on their terms. Those that remain passive risk being excluded from the core layers of the ecosystem. As shared infrastructure becomes the operating system of modern finance, its governance will become a defining axis of competition, collaboration, and credibility. Banks that understand this – and invest accordingly – will not just survive in the future; they will help shape it.

9 Managing Complexity Across Borders

As financial institutions grow beyond national borders and digital ecosystems reach across borders, complexity management at the border is one of the defining issues of contemporary banking alliances. The infrastructure of today's financial services is not only highly interconnected but also embedded in different regulatory settings, technological architectures, cultural norms, and political economies. For banks, fintechs, and platform players, the ability to navigate this multi-layered complex reality is essential to sustaining growth, ensuring compliance, and building trust in international markets.

Cross-border complexity arises in multiple dimensions: operational, legal, technological, ethical, and strategic. Each jurisdiction brings its own set of licensing requirements, data privacy laws, cybersecurity standards, anti-money laundering directives, and financial conduct rules. In addition, the rules are never fixed – they change constantly according to political priorities, market disturbances, and new risks. For example, a model of partnership that excels in the UK may need serious adjustment in order to operate efficiently in the US, Singapore, or the UAE. This requires more than mere regulatory mapping – it takes organizational flexibility, local understanding, and cross-functional alignment.

Cross-border complexity mainly occurs in data governance and privacy. For instance, the General Data Protection Regulation (GDPR) in the EU sets a high standard for data consent, portability, and deletion. However, this is very different from data localization requirements in markets such as India, Russia, and China, where the regulators insist that financial data must be stored – and sometimes even processed – within national borders. For a bank that conducts business through international alliances, balancing these needs without bifurcating its digital architecture poses a significant challenge. Multinational fintechs tend to resolve this via region-specific data layers, modular APIs, and localized compliance teams. Banks need to learn how to operate with analogous architectural flexibility.

Cross-border payments and settlements add an additional layer of complexity. Even as real-time domestic systems such as the UK's Faster Payments, India's UPI, and Singapore's FAST have become increasingly popular, cross-border transactions continue to depend heavily on legacy infrastructure in the form of correspondent banking networks, SWIFT messaging, and manual reconciliation processes. These systems are opaque, slow, and costly. In turn, collaborative efforts such as SWIFT GPI, BIS Project Nexus, and private blockchain-based initiatives such as Ripple Net are trying to simplify and modernize cross-border flows. Successful integration, though, calls for harmonized standards, recognition of each other's identity protocols, and uniform risk perceptions.

Regulatory coordination is still uneven. The Basel Committee for Banking Supervision and the Financial Stability Board (FSB) have contributed to establishing international standards, especially on capital adequacy, systemic risk, and operational resilience. Enforcement and interpretation, however, diverge extensively. In the United States, for instance, the regulatory environment is divided among several agencies – OCC, Federal Reserve, SEC, and CFPB – with each of them having their own agendas. In contrast, the UK's twin-peaks model with the Prudential Regulation Authority (PRA) and Financial Conduct Authority (FCA) presents a more integrated interface. Banks dealing with both environments need to adjust their governance models to reflect this fragmentation, tending to replicate functions and legal controls to meet the requirements of each jurisdiction.

Cultural and behavioural complexity introduces another dimension. Customers, regulators, and partners' expectations can vary dramatically across markets. In East Asian economies, relationships are forged on long-term trust and relational depth, while in Western markets, commercial terms and speed to market capture decision-making. Contract negotiation, conflict resolution, and working with local market rhythms take more than legal expertise – they require cross-cultural proficiency and contextual intelligence. Global banks need to invest in local leadership, rather than merely legal presence, if they want the partnerships to remain relevant and robust.

Standards of technology and interoperability are also key. Various markets will have differing expectations of encryption protocols, interface standards, or methods of authentication. For instance, biometric authentication is the norm in India and much of Africa but remains contentious in parts of Europe because of privacy issues. Equally, cloud adoption strategies vary widely – with some regulators mandating – premise controls or local data centres, whereas others favour public cloud infrastructure. Banks have to build central systems that are both globally resilient and locally compliant – a requirement that demands modular architectures, API governance, and agile DevSecOps teams that are attuned to regional aspects.

With the increasing emphasis on ESG considerations, cross-border complexity is also turning into an issue about sustainability partnerships. For example, an EU green finance initiative needs to comply with the EU taxonomy for sustainable activities and disclosure regime under the Sustainable Finance

Disclosure Regulation (SFDR). But these standards need not necessarily conform to ESG frameworks in the US or Asia, where reporting is voluntary or sector-specific. Such fragmentation will influence investor confidence, reputational risk, and scalability of ESG-linked financial products across borders.

Cross-border risk management is particularly important in unstable regions or in times of geopolitical change. Sanctions regimes, currency controls, cyber-sovereignty rules, and emergent regulatory crackdowns will undermine even well-planned collaborations. The Russia–Ukraine war, for example, lead to a serious operational reassessment across financial networks as banks and fintechs needed to unwind collaborations, reset compliance models, and deal with reputational implications. All this emphasizes the necessity of real-time risk sensing and contingency planning for each cross-border interaction. In spite of all these difficulties, successful cross-border alliances are feasible – and increasingly vital. Here are a few strategies followed by successful institutions:

- Local anchoring, global orchestration: Top banks balance centralized strategy and decentralized implementation. They place regional partnership leads that have knowledge about local circumstances yet remain connected to the group's global design and values.
- Regulatory co-creation: Instead of awaiting clarity, active institutions involve regulators early – through consultation, pilot projects, or regulatory sandboxes. This fosters trust and enables the development of realistic frameworks.
- Scenario-based planning: Companies that simulate alternative regulatory, geopolitical, and technological futures are best equipped to evolve and shift their partnerships. Scenario thinking needs to become a mainstream boardroom discipline.
- Common language of standards: Cross-border partnerships flourish when there is a common vocabulary of trust – open APIs, ISO 20022 messaging, joint KYC practices, and mutual certification recognition. Banks need to drive convergence on these building blocks.
- Cultural intelligence as strategy: Cross-cultural communication, negotiation, and conflict resolution training is no longer a soft skill – it's a strategic facilitator to the success of international partnerships.

We are moving into an age in which no bank, no matter how big, can stand alone. Cross-border collaborations no longer sit comfortably – they are the scaffold of global financial inclusion, stability, and innovation. Navigating complexity through these arrangements is itself a discipline: one that mixes diplomacy, systems thinking, and operational discipline. While regulatory harmonization is an elusive goal and geopolitical volatility persists, the victors will be those that don't shy away from complexity – but understand how to navigate it with confidence, clarity, and collaborative purpose. Complexity management across borders is not merely a technical necessity – a bank which does it well will gain a strategic advantage for the future.

10 Designing Collaborative Advantage

In a world defined by interdependence, no bank can build the future alone. From fintechs and telcos to regulators, civic institutions, and global platforms, the emerging financial ecosystem is an intricate web of collaborations. Yet, not all partnerships are created equal. Some are tactical, time-bound, or narrowly functional. Others, however, are transformative – redefining not just what a bank does, but what it is. Designing collaborative advantage is about moving beyond transactional alliances to create lasting, value-generating ecosystems delivering shared benefits to all participants, including customers, communities, and future generations.

The starting point for collaborative advantage is strategic alignment. Too often, partnerships are pursued based on opportunistic value capture – launching a feature, accessing a customer base, or expanding reach. But truly generative collaborations require deeper alignment of purpose, vision, and time horizons. For banks, this means looking beyond immediate revenue goals and toward long-term impact metrics: financial inclusion, climate resilience, digital trust, and societal wellbeing. Collaborations should be assessed not only on ROI but also on their contribution to these broader objectives. ESG alignment, co-innovation potential, and mutual learning should be part of every partnership scorecard.

A key enabler of such alignment is governance by design. Traditional partnerships often struggle with misaligned decision-making, unclear accountability, and siloed execution. Designing collaborative advantage requires pre-agreed frameworks for data sharing, intellectual property rights, escalation protocols, and joint product lifecycles. Leading institutions now establish co-creation councils, embed cross-organizational teams, and use design thinking tools to ensure shared ownership. These structures are not bureaucratic add-ons – they are the operating systems of agile, equitable partnerships.

Technology also plays a central role. Open banking initiatives have shown how shared infrastructure – such as APIs, consent frameworks, and real-time rails – can allow multiple parties to innovate together without compromising on control or compliance. This principle must now be extended beyond payments and account aggregation to broader areas: SME lending, insurance distribution, carbon footprint tracking, and financial literacy delivery. The future lies in open ecosystems, where banks, fintechs, social enterprises, and even non-traditional actors co-create value at scale. Collaborative advantage is not about owning the platform; it is about shaping the network.

Trust remains the essential currency. In successful partnerships, trust is operationalized – through transparency, aligned incentives, and a shared commitment to risk and reward. In the UK, initiatives such as the Open Finance Working Group have created collaborative standards not just for technology, but also for conduct and ethics. In the US, public-private innovation hubs – such as those convened by the FDIC and Federal Reserve – have explored joint responses to cybersecurity, climate risk, and fintech regulation. In Singapore and the UAE, regulators have gone further, building sandboxes and digital corridors that make collaboration not just possible, but inevitable.

But trust cannot be mandated. It must be earned – and often re-earned – over time. This is especially true in cross-sector collaborations. When, for example, banks partner with telecom operators in emerging markets to deliver mobile money, questions of revenue sharing, customer data control, and brand attribution can create tension. When retail platforms integrate credit scoring into their offerings, consumer protection and algorithmic fairness come to the fore. Collaborative advantage depends on building principled partnerships, where shared purpose is matched by negotiated guardrails.

One of the more promising frontiers are purpose-led consortia. Rather than bilateral alliances, these bring together a diverse group of stakeholders to solve complex, system-wide problems. The Linux Foundation's FINOS project, for example, enables collaborative innovation across banks and fintech developers in building open-+-source financial software. The Green Digital Finance Alliance, backed by the UN and leading institutions, seeks to align digital transformation with environmental goals. These efforts demonstrate that collaborative advantage can transcend commercial competition – when the partners are united by a higher mission.

Designing for longevity is equally important. Many partnerships falter not because of a lack of initial intent but due to changes in leadership, strategy, or market dynamics. Resilient partnerships are those that are modular, adaptive, and values-based. They evolve with time, incorporate feedback loops, and invest in shared learning infrastructure. Some global banks now maintain partnership playbooks, capturing insights from past collaborations to inform future ones. Others run internal venture studios or ecosystem labs to pilot and scale new partnership models before full deployment.

Critically, the governance of collaborative advantage must include community voices. As banks expand into underserved geographies or deploy digital tools at scale, they must bring civil society, consumer groups, and academic institutions into the design process. This not only strengthens legitimacy but also leads to better outcomes. Co-designed financial products often show higher trust, uptake, and relevance, particularly among marginalized communities. A truly inclusive collaborative strategy requires banks to see communities not as markets, but as co-authors of innovation.

The path to collaborative advantage also involves rethinking metrics. Traditional KPIs – customer acquisition, conversion, and margin – are necessary but insufficient. Banks must also track ecosystem health indicators, such as speed of joint innovation, resilience of shared platforms, regulatory harmonization progress, partner satisfaction, and societal outcomes. Some institutions are now developing ecosystem scorecards, drawing inspiration from balanced scorecards and ESG frameworks, to measure the long-term impact and coherence of their collaborative networks.

From a talent perspective, collaborative advantage requires new capabilities. These include partnership design, systems thinking, behavioural economics, and cross-cultural negotiation. Many banks are now embedding ecosystem leadership training into their executive development programs. Some are also recruiting from adjacent industries – consulting, social entrepreneurship, technology platforms – to inject new thinking into how they build, manage, and evolve partnerships.

Looking ahead, the winners in banking will not be those with the biggest balance sheets, but those with the most trusted, adaptive, and generative partnerships. Collaborative advantage is not a marketing slogan; it is a design principle for institutional relevance in a shared future. As we design the bank of tomorrow, our greatest asset may not lie within our four walls – but in the strength of the partnerships we cultivate, the trust we earn, and the ecosystems we help steward. Collaboration, if intentional and principled, can become the foundation of sustainable advantage – not just for the bank, but for the world it serves.

Strategic Framework Box: Chapter 6 From Isolation to Interconnection: Banking in the Age of Ecosystems

Key Insight

The future of banking is not built in-house. It is built in collaboration. The most resilient and scalable institutions will be those that learn to orchestrate partnerships – not as bolt-ons, but as native parts of their value chain.

Strategic Takeaway

Banking partnerships are no longer optional. The institutions that thrive will be those that turn ecosystem design into a strategic competence – and collaborative advantage into lasting relevance.

Ecosystem Dimension	*Traditional Banking Model*	*Ecosystem Banking Model*
Strategic Posture	Self-contained, vertically integrated	Open, adaptive, co-designed
Partner Landscape	Selective, bilateral, controlled	Cross-sector, multi-party, modular
Platform Role	Product distributor	Ecosystem enabler and integrator
Technology Integration	Custom builds, limited APIs	Embedded finance, seamless APIs
Governance Structure	Internal compliance-– led	Shared accountability, trust protocols
Innovation Source	Internal R&D or vendor-led	Joint innovation with fintechs, telcos, governments

This chapter argues that scale is no longer a function of size – it is a function of connection. From telcos and retailers to fintechs and civic platforms, tomorrow's bank must learn to participate in and govern collaborative ecosystems. The goal is not ownership, but orchestration.

Bibliography

OECD (2020). *The Future of Finance: Open, Connected, and Inclusive Ecosystems*. Paris: OECD Publishing.

7 The Age of Intelligence

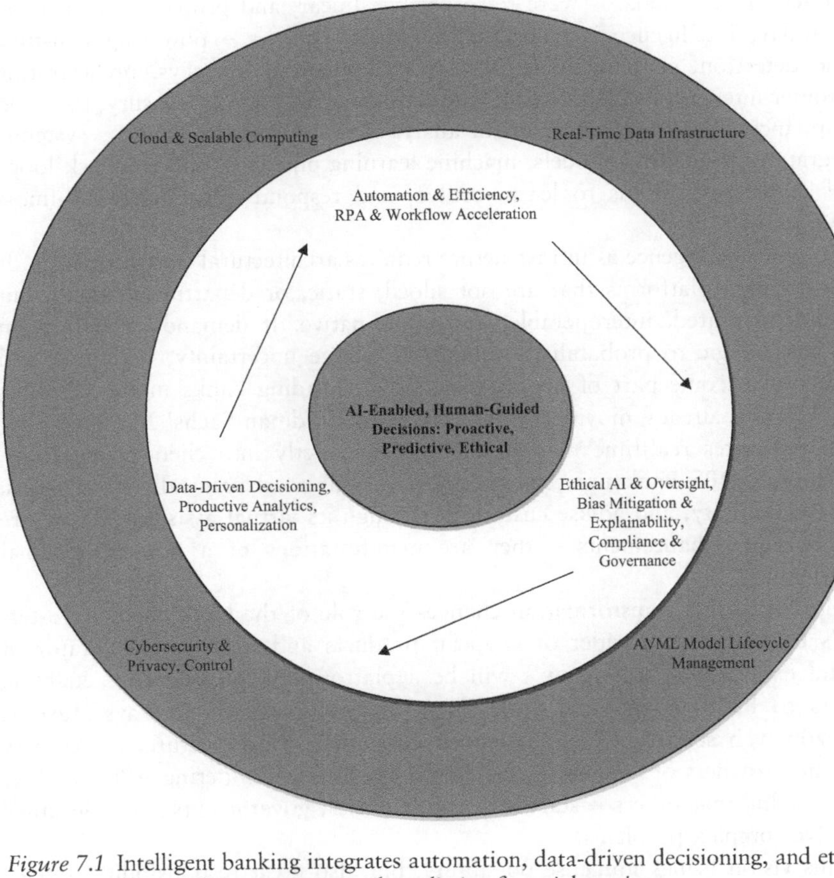

Figure 7.1 Intelligent banking integrates automation, data-driven decisioning, and ethical AI to deliver proactive and predictive financial services.

DOI: 10.4324/9781003737544-7

1 Intelligence as Infrastructure

AI is no longer a tool added to the financial institution – it is becoming its very foundation. In the same way that electricity and broadband became invisible utilities underpinning modern economies, intelligence – particularly machine intelligence – is now emerging as a core infrastructure layer for 21st-century banking. This shift redefines not just how banks operate, but what they are. Data is no longer a by-product of financial services; it is the raw material of insight. Algorithms are no longer decision-support tools; they actively participate in shaping the outcomes. In this age, intelligence is not a feature. It is the architecture.

The idea of "intelligence as infrastructure" marks a fundamental transition. Historically, banks invested in data analytics to extract value from historical transactions. Dashboards were retrospective, linear, and primarily descriptive. But today, intelligence is embedded across workflows – powering real-time fraud detection, enabling hyper-personalized financial journeys, orchestrating customer interactions, and driving autonomous operations in treasury, risk, and compliance. This is no longer about analytics as a layer. It is about a systemic integration of adaptive models, machine learning pipelines, and feedback loops that enable institutions to learn, evolve, and respond dynamically – almost biologically.

To treat intelligence as infrastructure requires architectural transformation. It calls for data platforms that are not siloed, static, or department-bound, but instead integrated, interoperable, and cloud-native. It demands a shift from rule-based logic to probabilistic thinking – where uncertainty, variation, and prediction become part of operational design. Leading banks in the US, UK, and Asia are already moving in this direction. Goldman Sachs' Marquee platform integrates real-time market intelligence directly into client-facing tools. Singapore's DBS Bank uses embedded AI models to dynamically price loans, manage liquidity, and advise customers through its virtual assistant. These are not bolt-on enhancements – they are manifestations of a new operational paradigm.

Moreover, this transformation changes the role of the bank itself. If yesterday's bank was a provider of financial products and today's is a curator of digital experiences, tomorrow's will be a platform of intelligence – enabling others to build, adapt, and scale financial logic in modular ways. Just as Amazon web services (AWS) redefined computing infrastructure, banks may become providers of "financial intelligence as a service," offering APIs, models, and insights that others – start-ups, communities, governments – can leverage to solve complex problems.

This vision brings immense possibility, but also great responsibility. Intelligence is infrastructure only when it is reliable, explainable, and accountable. Models must be monitored for drift. Biases must be tested and corrected. Outcomes must be auditable not just by regulators, but by society at large. The infrastructure of intelligence must be as robust and inclusive as that of electricity or water supply – serving all segments, not reinforcing existing inequities. For example, if AI models over-penalize certain communities in credit scoring or under-represent others in financial advice, then the system becomes not merely flawed but unjust. Treating intelligence as infrastructure demands that it be regulated, stewarded, and governed with a public-interest mindset.

This is where public-private cooperation becomes critical. Just as roads and telecommunications required standards and oversight, so too does AI in financial systems. In the UK, the Financial Conduct Authority (FCA) has initiated cross-sector sandboxes focused on explainable AI. In the United States, the Consumer Financial Protection Bureau (CFPB) has issued guidance on automated decisioning transparency. The EU's AI Act goes further, classifying high-risk use cases and proposing specific obligations. Financial institutions must not only comply with these frameworks but actively shape them – bringing real-world knowledge to the regulatory table and designing systems that reflect both technological excellence and ethical resilience.

Equally important is the internal transformation within banks. Intelligence as infrastructure changes talent models, team structures, and culture. Data scientists can no longer operate in isolation. They must collaborate with domain experts, compliance leaders, behavioural economists, and ethicists. Model governance cannot be the remit of IT alone; it must be a board-level priority. Investment in model operations (MLOps), responsible AI frameworks, and integrated risk management becomes essential. Banks that view intelligence as a series of experiments will struggle. Those that treat it as a core infrastructure pillar – designed, funded, governed, and developed like any other utility – will thrive.

The competitive implications are profound. In the past, banks competed on product pricing, physical footprint, or even branding. In the age of intelligence, they will compete on the quality, agility, and trustworthiness of their models. Who can detect anomalies fastest? Who can anticipate customer needs most accurately? Who can adapt pricing or personalize content in real time without breaching trust? These are not questions for the future - facing they are being asked today. Financial intelligence is becoming a differentiator which is more valuable than capital or distribution.

Yet intelligence alone is not enough. It must be coupled with wisdom. This means using AI not just to automate, but to elevate – to help people make better decisions, understand long-term consequences, and act in service of their goals and values. In retail banking, this might mean nudging users toward saving rather than impulsive borrowing. In corporate banking, it might involve advising clients on sustainable capital strategies or transition finance. Intelligence becomes infrastructure when it serves not just the institution, but the ecosystem – guiding individuals, businesses, and societies toward more resilient financial futures.

From a systems view, this also requires resilience in design. AI pipelines must be secure against data poisoning, adversarial attacks, and systemic drift. Just as we design physical infrastructure to withstand shocks – storms, floods, blackouts – so too must we design intelligent infrastructure to withstand algorithmic failure, misinformation loops, or coordinated fraud. This includes not just technological safeguards, but institutional reflexes: scenario testing, human-in-the-loop overrides, incident response mechanisms, and ethical escalation paths.

Looking forward, the infrastructure of intelligence will not be a one-size-fits-all solution. It will need to be contextual, localized, and evolving. What works in urban UK may not work in rural India. What suits a large pension fund may not suit a youth-focused nonbank. Banks must design intelligence systems that are sensitive to context – able to learn from local patterns, adapt to diverse user needs, and contribute meaningfully across socioeconomic boundaries.

In this new era, banks are not merely building smarter tools – they are becoming intelligent institutions. This shift is as much philosophical as it is technological. Intelligence is not simply what we build – it is how we listen, learn, and evolve. The infrastructure of tomorrow's finance is not concrete and cables – it is algorithms, values, and trust. And the institutions that thrive will be those which treat intelligence not as a secret weapon, but as a shared responsibility.

2 Automation with Human Intuition

As automation reshapes financial services, a profound question emerges: where does the machine end and the human begin? The banking sector has embraced automation with speed – from robotic process automation (RPA) in operations to algorithmic trading and AI-driven underwriting. But speed is not the same as wisdom. True progress lies not in replacing human judgment, but in harmonizing it with machine efficiency. The future of automation in banking is not about displacing intuition – it is about augmenting it.

At its core, automation is the use of technology to execute tasks with minimal human intervention. In banking, this initially meant automating repetitive, rules-based activities – such as form validations, reconciliation, and data entry. These early applications brought clear gains in speed, accuracy, and cost-efficiency. But as technology has evolved, automation now penetrates judgment-heavy functions: advising clients, detecting risk, making lending decisions, or allocating capital. Here, blind automation – absent of context or empathy – can do harm. What's required is a model of automation that recognizes the limits of code and the value of human insight.

Consider the example of credit risk assessment. An AI system can examine hundreds of data points in seconds. It identifies patterns that a human cannot see. It may flag a borrower as high-risk based on income volatility or payment history. But a human lender might notice that the volatility is seasonal, linked to agricultural cycles, and that the borrower has a strong local reputation for honouring debts. Without this human lens, the decision lacks context. In markets such as India, Kenya, or even rural parts of the UK, such nuance often makes the difference between exclusion and inclusion. Intelligent automation must therefore embed human intuition not as an afterthought, but as an active design principle.

The leading banks are already moving in this direction. JP Morgan's contract intelligence platform (CoiN) platform, for instance, uses AI to review legal documents, automating tasks that once took thousands of hours. But human legal teams remain central in interpreting outcomes, escalating edge cases, and refining models. Similarly, OCBC Bank in Singapore blends machine-led investment recommendations with human relationship managers who interpret client behaviour, cultural preferences, and financial aspirations. The result is a model where automation enhances trust rather than erodes it.

This blend is not accidental – it requires structural planning. Banks must invest in hybrid decision architectures, where machine outputs are transparently explainable and humans are trained to interpret, challenge, and override when needed. These are not just operational tweaks– they are philosophical shifts. Automation should not diminish human accountability; it should amplify human responsibility. When a model makes a recommendation, a human must still own the decision. When an anomaly is flagged, a human must still make the call. This is how we preserve ethical integrity in an automated age.

In retail banking, the automation-intuition balance becomes particularly visible in customer service. AI chatbots such as Bank of America's Erica or HSBC's virtual assistants handle millions of queries, saving time and increasing availability. Yet, customers still demand empathy when dealing with complex issues: a mortgage dispute, bereavement, a fraud incident. Machines can offer speed, but only humans can offer compassion. Smart banks don't see this as a limitation – they see it as an opportunity. They train AI to triage and learn from human responses, creating feedback loops that elevate both parties over time.

This feedback loop lies at the heart of human-in-the-loop (HITL) design. Rather than removing people, HITL systems include them in the model training, testing, and deployment phases. At Citi Bank, for example, fraud detection systems are constantly refined by analysts who review flagged cases, teaching the model to distinguish false positives from genuine threats. In this way, automation becomes a continuously learning system – not a static tool but a co-evolving partner.

This partnership requires cultural transformation. Traditional hierarchies, where decisions flow top-down, struggle to adapt to AI-enabled workflows where data scientists, compliance teams, and customer agents must collaborate in real time. Leadership must shift from command and control to orchestration and enablement. The most successful institutions build cross-functional pods that bring together technology and human insight – treating automation not as a project, but as an ecosystem.

Critically, automation with human intuition also redefines customer relationships. Personalization algorithms may identify spending patterns, suggest budgeting tips, or anticipate financial needs. But what builds long-term loyalty is the perception of being understood, not just being served. If automation makes a customer feel like a number, it fails. If it enables the bank to act with foresight and relevance, it succeeds. The distinction lies in the intelligent application of empathy, often delivered through well-trained humans who use AI as a tool rather than a crutch.

This is especially important in sensitive domains such as wealth management, insurance claims, or financial hardship assistance. A family facing foreclosure needs more than a repayment plan – they need compassion, flexibility, and options. Automating this process without human engagement risks deepening trauma and reputational damage. On the other hand, when AI is used to detect hardship early and flag it to empathetic human agents, the bank becomes not just a creditor, but a partner in resilience.

Of course, all of this depends on training. Human workers must be re-skilled to work alongside automation – not as passive overseers but as active contributors. This means developing fluency in AI tools, comfort with model outputs, and the confidence to question them. It also means upskilling data and tech teams to understand the human realities behind the code. A successful AI strategy is never just about algorithms – it is about people, their mindset, and their capacity to collaborate with machines.

One emerging model is the concept of augmented intelligence – where technology supports, rather than supplants, human capability. In this model, humans retain the final say in critical decisions, but are empowered by AI-generated insights. Think of it as having a super-analyst by your side: one who never sleeps, never forgets, and can surface relevant patterns from oceans of data – but who still relies on your judgment to act. This is the future of high-stakes domains such as financial regulation, strategic investment, or cyber defence. Machines advise. Humans decide.

Globally, we see growing consensus on this model. The OECD, World Economic Forum, and European Commission all promote human-centric AI as a guiding framework. In the UK, the Alan Turing Institute has led research into explainable machine learning. In the US, the National Institute of Standards and Technology (NIST) has released a framework for trustworthy AI. Banks must align with these principles not just for compliance – but for competitive advantage. Trust, after all, is the most valuable currency in financial services. And trust is built when humans, not machines, are seen as ultimately responsible.

The age of automation in banking is here – but it is not the end of human relevance. Rather, it is the beginning of a new partnership, where human intuition is amplified, not erased. Where machines take over the mechanical elements so that humans can focus on the meaningful. Where every decision made by AI is held up to the light of ethics, empathy, and real-world impact. This is not a return to the past, nor a blind leap into the future. It is a deliberate, thoughtful path – where automation becomes a servant of wisdom, not a substitute for it.

3 AI in Credit, Risk, and Personal Finance

The fusion of AI with the domains of credit, risk, and personal finance is not just a technological shift – it is a redefinition of core banking functions. From determining creditworthiness to pricing insurance, from managing wealth portfolios to protecting against fraud, AI is becoming the silent engine that powers financial decisions across the globe. Yet, as we embed AI deeper into these domains, we must ask: Are we merely accelerating old models, or are we reimagining them for a more inclusive and intelligent future?

In traditional banking, credit scoring depended largely on structured historical data, such as income statements, repayment history, and outstanding liabilities. Risk assessments followed actuarial tables and backward-looking metrics. Personal finance advice, if it existed at all, was generic and static. AI challenges all of this. It enables real-time evaluation, pattern recognition across unstructured data, and dynamic decisioning based on continuous learning. But with great power comes great responsibility. The deployment of AI must not only optimize accuracy and efficiency; it must also enhance fairness, accessibility, and transparency.

In credit, the most transformative shift lies in the move from scorecards to systems. AI can synthesize thousands of variables – from bank statements, utility payments, social media activity, geolocation data, and even smartphone usage – to build a multidimensional profile of a borrower. This has revolutionized credit access in markets previously underserved by traditional banking. In Kenya, start-ups such as Tala and Branch use AI-driven mobile data to underwrite micro-loans for millions without formal credit histories. In India, players such as CreditVidya and CASHe are redefining risk using digital behavioural patterns. In the US, Upstart has demonstrated that AI-based models can approve more loans with lower default rates than systems based on FICO, a measure of consumer credit risk used in the US – by learning continuously from borrower outcomes.

But this granularity raises concerns about bias. AI systems can inadvertently reinforce historic inequalities if trained on flawed data. For example, if in the past women or minorities were granted fewer loans, the model might "learn" to penalize these groups – unless explicitly corrected. This is not merely a theoretical risk. In 2019, Apple and Goldman Sachs faced scrutiny over the Apple Card's alleged gender bias, despite claiming algorithmic objectivity. The lesson is clear: AI in credit must be built with intentional fairness frameworks. Explainability, audit ability, and demographic impact analysis must become standard in all credit AI deployments.

Risk management has also undergone a paradigm shift. Previously, risk was calculated based on known variables – credit exposure, market volatility, and operational weaknesses. But today's risk landscape is fluid, interconnected, and increasingly nonlinear. Cyber threats, geopolitical instability, environmental disruptions, and behavioural anomalies demand a new approach. AI enables real-time monitoring of vast data streams, anomaly detection, and predictive alerting. For instance, HSBC's AI – enabled surveillance system analyses trading patterns across global desks to detect market manipulation and insider activity. JP Morgan's Global Surveillance Platform integrates natural language processing (NLP) to interpret trader chats and flag potential misconduct.

Even in regulatory compliance, AI is proving indispensable. Know Your Customer (KYC) and Anti-Money Laundering (AML) functions, once manually intensive, are now automated through intelligent pattern matching and network analysis. In the UK, Revolut has used machine learning to catch unusual transaction behaviours faster than traditional rules-based systems. In the US, MasterCard and Microsoft have collaborated to use AI to detect financial crimes at scale. The benefit is twofold: faster risk mitigation and reduced false positives. But regulators are watching closely. The EU's proposed AI Act classifies credit scoring and risk modelling as "high-risk" use cases, requiring strict oversight. Banks must therefore move from black-box algorithms to transparent and traceable models, with human accountability embedded at every layer.

In personal finance, AI is not just an assistant – it is fast becoming a coach. From budgeting tools to savings nudges, from automated investments to retirement planning, AI is personalizing financial journeys like never before. UK-based Monzo and Starling Bank use AI to analyse user spending and offer real-time feedback, encouraging healthier financial behaviours. In the US, apps such as Cleo and Digit use conversational AI to help users manage cash flow, set goals, and even challenge spending habits with wit and empathy.

But the frontier goes further. Robo-advisors such as Betterment and Wealthfront use AI to manage billions of assets, tailoring portfolios to individual risk profiles and adjusting strategies in response to market shifts. In Asia, platforms such as StashAway and Kristal.AI bring similar models to a growing middle class. These systems democratize wealth management, historically reserved for the affluent. Yet they also raise questions: What happens when markets crash? Will users understand that a machine is behind their portfolio losses? Will they blame the bank – or the bot?

To mitigate this, many hybrid models are emerging. AI handles the grunt work – asset allocation, tax optimization; rebalancing – while human advisors build trust, answer complex queries, and calm nerves during volatility. This augmented advice model recognizes what AI is good at (data processing) and what humans are good at (judgment and empathy). It also builds in resilience. When Blackrock's Aladdin system combines algorithmic portfolio analysis with human portfolio managers, it represents not just scale, but symbiosis.

As intelligent systems mature, the landscape of money itself is also evolving. The rise of cryptocurrencies, stablecoins, and central bank digital currencies (CBDCs) is redefining what institutions consider liquid, programmable, and trusted. These decentralized or tethered digital currencies, while still in regulatory flux, carry long-term implications for credit delivery, identity infrastructure, and algorithmic wealth allocation. The age of intelligent finance must account not just for how we score risk, but how we redefine money itself.

Importantly, AI in personal finance can also address long-standing challenges of financial inclusion. By understanding individual cash flows, AI can offer micro-savings strategies even to those on volatile incomes. It can recommend affordable insurance coverage based on lifestyle data. It can flag early signs of debt stress and propose interventions – before defaults occur. In Brazil, Nubank uses AI to serve millions of previously unbanked customers with tailored credit limits and contextual alerts. In Nigeria, Cowrywise leverages AI to provide low-cost investment advice to first-time savers. These models redefine financial literacy – not as a precondition for access, but as a product delivered in real time.

However, the ethical stakes are high. Personal finance is intimate. AI systems must handle sensitive data with care, comply with data privacy laws such as GDPR and the California Consumer Privacy Act, and be designed to empower rather than manipulate. If AI nudges a user to spend more, or upsell products without understanding the customer's long-term wellbeing, it becomes a liability. This is where AI ethics frameworks must go beyond compliance and embed human dignity at the centre of financial design.

Another overlooked dimension is mental health. Poor financial decisions are often symptoms of deeper stress, addiction, or instability. AI models must learn to detect patterns of financial self-harm – such as binge spending or payday loan cycles – and respond with care. Some fintechs are exploring partnerships with behavioural psychologists to make AI tools more supportive. For instance, the UK-based app Snoop encourages mindful spending through personalized alerts, while US platform Spring uses behavioural science to nudge users toward long-term goals. This fusion of AI and behavioural finance holds the promise for a more empathetic financial future.

Looking ahead, AI in credit, risk, and personal finance will become the default, not the differentiator. What will matter is how banks and fintechs use it – it should be to reduce harm, enhance inclusion, and build lasting relationships. Institutions must not merely deploy AI – they must steward its evolution. This means investing in explainable models, inclusive data sets, ethical oversight boards, and customer education. It means designing for trust – not just transactions.

The most successful banks will be those which recognize that AI is not about replacing human roles – it is about elevating human outcomes. A bank that uses AI to widen access, reduce risk, and improve financial health is not just modern – it is moral. This is the future the sector must build: one where intelligence is not just artificial, but purposeful, ethical, and deeply human.

4 Learning Systems and Dynamic Models

As the financial sector deepens its integration with AI, a crucial paradigm shift is emerging: from static models to learning systems. This evolution represents more than just technical sophistication; it reflects a fundamental reorientation of how financial institutions interact with data, clients, and risk. In the past, banks relied on rigid models – developed by so-called quants (quantitative analysts), locked in spreadsheets, and periodically updated. Today, leading institutions are embracing dynamic, adaptive systems capable of evolving with real-world feedback. These systems don't just process data – they learn from it continuously.

The reason for this shift is both simple and significant. The financial world is always changing. Customer behaviours evolve with economic cycles. Fraud tactics morph with technological exposure. Market volatility is triggered not just by fundamentals, but by narratives, tweets, and cascading sentiment. Traditional models, no matter how robust at inception, degrade over time. Learning systems, by contrast, improve. They absorb new patterns, recalibrate risk thresholds, and refine predictions in near real-time.

At the heart of this evolution are machine learning (ML) and reinforcement learning (RL) techniques. These models move beyond supervised training and toward contextual learning – where actions, outcomes, and rewards inform future predictions. In fraud detection, for example, anomaly detection algorithms improve as they encounter both false positives and confirmed threats. In credit scoring, reinforcement models can adjust approval thresholds based on loan repayment outcomes across customer segments, income brackets, or geographies.

Take JPMorgan Chase's COiN platform. Initially trained to read commercial loan contracts, it has evolved into a broader engine that learns from legal documents and regulatory shifts, reducing manual review time and improving compliance responsiveness. Similarly, Visa's real-time risk scoring engine uses dynamic model recalibration to continuously update transaction risk assessments, even incorporating global threat intelligence. These systems are not just tools – they are institutional memory engines, capturing organizational learning at scale.

The impact on operations is transformative. Learning systems make it possible to transition from batch-based processing to event-driven decision-making. Consider dynamic pricing in lending. A traditional bank might update interest rate models quarterly based on macroeconomic trends. A learning system can adjust risk premiums on a weekly – or even daily – basis based on real-time borrower signals, payment activity, and external shocks. This responsiveness improves portfolio resilience and enables more precise financial inclusion strategies.

Dynamic models are also critical in investment management. Hedge funds and asset managers increasingly use deep learning models that adapt to changing correlations, factor exposures, and volatility regimes. Man Group, a UK-based investment firm, has pioneered the use of reinforcement learning to optimize portfolio strategies in response to shifting market environments. In the US, firms such as Two Sigma and Renaissance Technologies treat their entire trading infrastructure as a living system – tuned, developed, and refined with every tick of data.

For retail investors, this intelligence is filtering into robo-advisory platforms. Companies such as Betterment, Nutmeg (UK), and Syfe (Singapore) use learning algorithms to dynamically rebalance portfolios, tax-loss harvest, and optimize allocations based on individual behaviour, not just static questionnaires. Over time, these systems learn not only about markets, but about the client's financial temperament. If a user tends to withdraw during downturns, the algorithm might recommend lower volatility assets – or offer nudges to build long-term discipline.

But with adaptability comes risk. Learning systems are only as good as their feedback loops. If these loops are incomplete, delayed, or biased, the model may reinforce false assumptions. A risk model that adjusts thresholds based only on approved loans, for instance, might fail to learn from missed opportunities – those applicants wrongly denied loans due to systemic bias. Similarly, if market sentiment models are trained solely on social media data, they may overvalue noise and amplify herd behaviour.

This raises a critical governance challenge: how do we validate and monitor systems that are constantly evolving? Traditional model validation relied on fixed parameters and known inputs. But dynamic models mutate. Their internal parameters shift with each iteration. Banks and regulators must therefore design new oversight mechanisms: real-time explainability tools, performance tracking dashboards, and "model health" alerts that flag drift, bias, or performance degradation.

The European Banking Authority (EBA) has highlighted this issue in its guidelines on model risk management, calling for continuous model monitoring and "change control" for machine learning systems. In the US, the Office of the Comptroller of the Currency (OCC) has begun examining how banks govern dynamic algorithms, especially in consumer credit. It is no longer sufficient to audit a model at the time of deployment – what is now also essential are ongoing validation and human-in-the-loop frameworks.

In addition, learning systems require a cultural shift. For decades, financial institutions prized model stability. Risk departments preferred conservative assumptions and strict documentation. Today's AI models thrive on experimentation, iteration, and agile deployment. This can cause tension. Data scientists may push for speed and novelty; compliance teams demand caution and accountability. Bridging this gap requires not just tools, but trust.

Leading institutions are responding by building cross-functional model governance teams – blending data engineers, behavioural economists, legal experts, and product owners. These teams do more than validate code – they debate ethical trade-offs, test societal impact, and embed customer protections into system design. HSBC, for example, has established an AI ethics risk committee to review dynamic models with potential societal implications. ING has integrated bias testing into every stage of model development. These practices signal a maturing discipline, where adaptability does not come at the expense of accountability.

Importantly, learning systems must be designed for diversity. If we feed them only data from affluent markets, urban behaviours, or dominant demographics, they will fail to serve the full population. This is particularly critical in global banks or fintechs expanding into new geographies. A personal finance AI trained on UK spending patterns may not generalize to India or Nigeria. Data localization, regional model calibration, and culturally aware design become vital.

Moreover, banks must acknowledge that some human behaviours are unpredictable. A model may learn that customers save more in December due to bonuses – until a crisis disrupts employment. It may learn that certain risk profiles default more during downturns – until government support changes the trend. In such cases, overfitting can be dangerous. Dynamic models must be controlled by human judgment, scenario analysis, and counterfactual testing. Learning should not be limitless – it should be disciplined.

From a strategic lens, learning systems offer a competitive edge not just with regard to speed, but also to resilience. A bank with adaptive credit models can respond faster to economic shocks. A wealth platform with dynamic recommendations can serve customers across life stages. A fraud system that learns from every failed attempt grows stronger each day. Over time, this advantage compounds – not unlike compound interest.

But the real potential lies in learning at the system level. Imagine a national financial grid where regulators, banks, and fintechs share data on scams, defaults, or behavioural trends – allowing everyone's models to learn faster, safer, and more ethically. In Singapore, the Monetary Authority is already piloting such shared utilities for KYC and risk scoring. In the UK, open banking frameworks could evolve into open learning ecosystems, where knowledge is not hoarded but pooled for public benefit.

In conclusion, learning systems and dynamic models are reshaping the financial industry into a living, breathing organism – one that senses, adapts, and evolves. But with this power comes responsibility. Banks must not only train algorithms – they must train themselves to think differently: about governance, ethics, inclusion, and long-term impact. The future of finance will not be static. It will be fluid, intelligent, and deeply human-aware. The institutions that thrive will be those that learn not only faster – but also better.

5 Ensuring Fairness and Transparency

As AI takes on a central role in financial systems, the potential for greater efficiency and predictive accuracy needs to be paired with a stronger focus on fairness and transparency. These are not ancillary concerns. In banking – where lives, livelihoods, and economic inclusion hinge on decisions made by unseen models – the moral burden is substantial. Fairness is no longer just a regulatory checkbox; it is a core element of institutional credibility. Transparency, likewise, is not merely about explained ability – it is about accountability, trust, and long-term sustainability.

Historically, financial decisions were mediated by human actors – bankers, underwriters, advisors – whose biases were at least visible and challengeable. With the advent of AI, those biases risk being obscured within code, perpetuated through data, and amplified by scale. An unfair lending officer could affect dozens of customers; an unfair algorithm can affect millions. When these models are opaque, even their creators may struggle to understand why a loan was denied, a fraud flagged, or an account frozen. For customers, this is more than frustrating – it is disempowering.

Fairness in AI begins with the training data. If the data reflects existing societal biases – gender disparities in credit history, racial imbalances in home ownership, income gaps tied to geography – then algorithms will reproduce and entrench those inequities. In the UK, studies have shown that postcode-based credit scoring systems disproportionately disadvantage minority communities. In the US, historical redlining practices are embedded in property value datasets that influence mortgage decisions. Without deliberate intervention, AI becomes a mirror to systemic injustice, not a mechanism of progress.

One global response has been the rise of algorithmic fairness techniques, which aim to detect and mitigate bias across protected attributes such as race, gender, age, or disability. Techniques such as counterfactual fairness – where a model's decision is tested against a hypothetical "if this person were of another gender, would the outcome be the same?" – are being adopted in ethical AI toolkits. Banks are using these to audit their models, especially in high-stakes domains such as credit and insurance. Monzo Bank, a UK-based digital challenger, has committed to publishing fairness audits of its decision models. In the US, Capital One has established fairness checkpoints at each stage of model deployment.

Transparency, meanwhile, demands more than technical explanations. It requires communication in plain language, accessible to regulators, consumers, and civil society. The EU's forthcoming AI Act explicitly calls for "meaningful information about the logic" of algorithmic decisions. In the financial domain, this has triggered innovation in explainable AI (XAI), where models provide not just scores, but reasons – "your loan was declined due to low income stability and recent delinquencies," for example. Start-ups such as Zest AI and Darwin AI offer financial institutions model interpretability tools that balance regulatory compliance with customer clarity.

But the frontier of transparency also raises hard questions: How much should be explained? To whom? And at what cost to intellectual property or security? A bank may hesitate to disclose exact model weights, fearing reverse engineering or manipulation. Yet withholding all reasoning erodes public trust. Striking this balance requires new norms – what we might call "institutional transparency hygiene". This includes tiered disclosure (one level for customers, another for regulators), robust challenge mechanisms (where customers can appeal or contest decisions), and regular third-party audits.

Globally, regulators are stepping in. In the UK, the FCA has launched an AI sandbox to enable safe experimentation with explainable models. The US Federal Reserve and CFPB have issued guidelines on the use of AI in lending, especially around adverse action notices. In India, the Reserve Bank is examining how digital credit scoring intersects with financial inclusion goals. These efforts signal a common realization: transparency and fairness are no longer optional – they are systemic prerequisites.

A powerful example comes from Brazil, where the Central Bank's open finance regulations require not only data portability, but transparency in how credit offers are produced. Customers can see which factors influenced their eligibility, and which data sources were used. This not only demystifies AI – it also empowers financial agency. In a similar vein, the Kenyan fintech Tala provides users with explanations of how their mobile repayment behaviour affects their borrowing capacity, helping build digital credit literacy in underserved communities.

But fairness and transparency cannot be engineered solely through software. They are cultural values – reflected in board decisions, hiring practices, and incentive structures. A diverse data science team is more likely to question biased assumptions. A governance board that includes ethicists, customer advocates, and behavioural economists is better at weighing long-term impacts. Financial institutions must embed these values across their operating models – not as separate "AI ethics" functions, but as integrated design principles.

This is especially critical as banks increasingly adopt automated decisioning at scale. From dynamic credit pricing to transaction monitoring, AI systems are being deployed without human touchpoints. In such settings, fairness cannot be an afterthought. It must be proactively designed into models – through representative sampling, debasing algorithms, and simulation testing. Fairness is not just a filter at the end of the process; it is a constraint in the optimization itself.

One emerging best practice is scenario-based fairness stress testing. Just as banks run capital stress tests under hypothetical economic shocks, they can now test AI models under fairness shocks – e.g., what happens to approval rates if certain demographics are disproportionately represented in the training data? How does model performance shift across regions, income bands, or educational backgrounds? These questions bring to the surface the latent vulnerabilities in seemingly neutral systems.

Another important development is the recognition that fairness is context-specific. A loan approval model may need different fairness criteria than a fraud detection model. In credit, the focus may be on demographic parity or equal opportunity. In fraud, false positives have real costs, and fairness might mean minimizing disparate impact. There is no one-size-fits-all metric – only fit-for-purpose evaluation. Regulators and developers alike must resist the temptation to reduce fairness to a single number.

Transparency, too, must be situated in context. For a retail customer, the most important factor may be an understanding of their score and how to improve it. For a regulator, it is traceability and auditability. For a bank executive, it is reputational risk and alignment with purpose. True transparency adapts to its audience, just as good financial advice does.

In the long run, banks that invest in fairness and transparency gain more than compliance – they gain strategic resilience. Customers trust systems which they understand. Societies support institutions that serve equitably. Regulators respect players who self-regulate responsibly. In an AI-driven era, reputation is not built through marketing – it is built through models. And the integrity of those models will define the legitimacy of tomorrow's financial institutions.

Ultimately, fairness and transparency are not endpoints – they are journeys. As models evolve, so must the questions we ask of them. As data grows, so must our vigilance against its embedded biases. As automation deepens, so must our human responsibility. In this age of intelligence, it is not enough to build smarter systems. We must build wiser ones.

6 Conversational Interfaces and Virtual Agents

The interface between customer and institution has always been central to banking. From the marble floors of grand branches to the call centres of the 1990s – and now to the ever-present screen of a smartphone – each evolution has changed not just how banks serve their customers, but how they are perceived by them. In the age of AI, that interface is increasingly conversational, intelligent, and, in many cases, invisible. Enter the rise of virtual agents and conversational banking, where speech and text interactions replace forms, menus, and even human tellers.

At first glance, this may seem like simple convenience. A chatbot can help reset a password or check a balance. But underneath lies a profound transformation: these interfaces are becoming the primary surface of the brand, the frontline of trust, and in some cases, the sole channel through which a customer interacts with their financial institution. They are no longer peripheral tools; they are central to how institutions listen, respond, and build relationships in real time.

In the UK, banks such as NatWest and Lloyds have integrated AI-driven chat assistants across the web and mobile platforms. In the US, Bank of America's Erica has become a widely used virtual financial assistant, handling over a billion interactions since its launch – ranging from transaction queries to proactive savings tips. DBS Bank in Singapore has deployed conversational AI across WhatsApp, WeChat, and other social platforms, enabling real-time customer support and even product origination. In all cases, these virtual agents are no longer simply reactive – they are proactive, contextual, and learning continuously.

But the rise of conversational interfaces is not just a technological upgrade. It is a redefinition of the user experience. Traditionally, customers had to learn the language of banking – navigating complex forms, financial jargon, and product silos. With AI-driven conversations, banks are now learning to speak the language of the customer. This reversal – or this shift in linguistic responsibility – is subtle but powerful. A mother in Manchester should be able to ask, "Can I afford to send my daughter to university next year?" and receive meaningful insight, not a redirected link to a student loan brochure.

This human-centric shift requires more than natural language processing (NLP). It demands semantic understanding, contextual memory, and the ability to synthesize data across domains. For example, if a customer asks, "Why is my credit score lower this month?", a truly intelligent assistant must not only understand the question, but access recent transactions, payment patterns, and external credit data – and then deliver an answer that is accurate, comprehensible, and emotionally intelligent.

Therein lies the next frontier: empathy in digital conversation. While AI cannot replicate human feeling, it can be trained to detect sentiment, modulate tone, and escalate appropriately. If a customer messages at midnight with the phrase "I can't pay my rent this month," the assistant must not reply with a generic late fee policy – it must recognize distress, express understanding, and guide the customer to support options. This is not just good UX – it is ethical design.

Transparency is critical here. Customers must know when they are speaking to a virtual agent, and what the agent can or cannot do. Clarity about escalation routes, data use, and response limitations builds trust. In markets such as the EU and UK, data protection frameworks such as GDPR require explicit consent when personal data is used to train conversational models. Banks must build not only smart systems, but responsible systems.

From an operational perspective, conversational interfaces are becoming centres of intelligence. Every interaction becomes a data point – an opportunity to learn about customer preferences, friction points, and unmet needs. Over time, virtual agents can move from transactional to advisory – nudging customers toward better financial behaviours, detecting signs of fraud or distress, and even offering micro-education. For example, India's Paytm and Brazil's Nubank have used conversational agents to explain financial products in vernacular languages, deepening inclusion in traditionally underserved segments of society.

There are strategic implications, too. Conversational interfaces enable scalability without loss of intimacy. A single AI assistant can engage millions, 24/7, across time zones and languages. This is particularly valuable for multinational banks looking to offer consistent service quality across geographies. HSBC, for instance, is deploying multilingual virtual agents that adjust their personality and tone depending on regional norms – from formal in Hong Kong to casual in the UK – maintaining brand coherence while respecting local nuance.

However, challenges remain. One is the risk of overreliance on automation. Not all queries can or should be handled by machines. High-stakes or emotionally charged conversations – such as bereavement, financial fraud, or legal disputes – require human empathy and judgment. Banks must design clear handover protocols, where virtual agents escalate seamlessly to human advisors without customer friction. These handoffs must feel continuous, not disruptive.

Another challenge is bias in conversation models. If training data reflects biased language patterns or stereotypes, the virtual assistant may replicate those biases. Examples of this are gendered assumptions in financial advice or culturally insensitive phrasing. Ongoing auditing, diverse training datasets, and inclusive design practices are essential to mitigate this risk.

Security is a further concern. Voice interfaces in particular raise questions around biometric authentication, impersonation, and data leakage. As banks move toward voice-first experiences – such as asking Alexa to transfer money – robust identity verification must be embedded into the interface itself. Multi-factor authentication, voiceprint matching, and anomaly detection can help ensure that convenience does not come at the cost of security.

Looking ahead, conversational interfaces will expand beyond phones and chat windows. We are entering an era of ambient banking – where your car might alert you to an upcoming insurance renewal, or your smart watch warns of a budget overspend. The boundary between financial interaction and daily life will continue to blur. In this context, voice, gesture, and even facial expression may become inputs into a bank's service logic. The conversational interface becomes not just a tool, but a companion – an always-on financial presence embedded in life's rhythms.

This raises fundamental questions about the future of the banker-customer relationship. As interfaces become more natural, does the emotional distance widen or shrink? Does the customer feel more known – or more under surveillance? The answer lies in how banks use the technology. Conversational AI can be a force for intimacy or intrusion, for empowerment or manipulation. The ethics of engagement will be as important as the mechanics of design.

Ultimately, conversational interfaces and virtual agents are not just about automation – they are about humanizing the digital experience. They represent a new literacy of finance, where speaking is enough, and understanding is assumed. For millions of people entering the financial system for the first time, a friendly chat on applications such as WhatsApp might be the first door to inclusion. That door must be opened with clarity, compassion, and care. As we design the age of intelligence, the best interfaces will not be those that feel the most robotic, but those that feel the most human. And in doing so, we may rediscover what banking was always meant to be: a conversation that helps people live better, more secure lives.

7 Predictive Tools for Proactive Banking

For much of its history, banking has been reactive. A customer deposits money, the bank records it. A customer misses a payment; the system alerts them. Even with the introduction of digital tools, the logic remained mostly the same: Systems observed what had already happened and responded after the fact. But in the era of AI and data intelligence, that paradigm is shifting. Predictive tools now enable banks to anticipate needs, pre-empt risks, and proactively guide customer behaviour in ways not possible before.

This is not simply about forecasting the future; it is about designing it, with intelligent nudges and real-time insights embedded across every financial interaction. At the heart of this transformation is the convergence of three forces: data abundance, algorithmic modelling, and customer-centric design.

Banks today have access to large datasets, both structured and unstructured. These come from transaction histories, behavioural signals, geolocation, and even sentiment analysis. Machine learning models can analyse this data to identify patterns, infer preferences, and detect anomalies with increasing accuracy. The result is a new class of predictive tools that do more than automate – they orchestrate financial lives.

Consider the shift from budgeting tools to predictive cash flow analysis. In the past, personal finance apps would help users track spending or set savings goals. Today, tools such as Cleo (UK), YNAB (You Need a Budget, US), and even mainstream banks are offering predictive insights such as: "You may run out of money by the 26th of this month," or "Based on past activity, your average electricity bill will rise next week." This moves the user from a state of financial awareness to financial preparedness.

In the UK, Monzo and Starling Bank have pioneered predictive transaction categorization and low-balance forecasting. These are not trivial features – they build trust at the point of anticipation, a fundamental shift from trust built through post-facto resolution. When a bank can reliably warn a customer about a potential overdraft five days in advance, and suggest action to avoid it, the bank is not just a platform, but becomes a partner.

At the enterprise level, banks are using predictive analytics to enhance credit models, detect fraud, and optimize operational efficiency. AI-powered credit scoring, for example, now incorporates alternative data such as rent payments, mobile usage, and social graph analytics – extending credit to underserved populations. This is especially powerful in emerging markets, where traditional credit history may not exist, but behavioural proxies can build financial identity.

One striking example comes from Kenya's M-Pesa platform and its evolution into full-spectrum financial services through M-Shwari and KCB M-Pesa. These platforms use mobile transaction data to predict loan repayment capacity with remarkable accuracy, enabling near-instant micro-loans to first-time borrowers. Similarly, India's BharatPe and Paytm use predictive models to offer working capital to small merchants based on daily digital sales – creating a real-time credit economy that bypasses paperwork and wait times.

In wealth management, predictive tools are enabling hyper-personalized investment advice. Robo-advisors such as Betterment and Wealthfront (US), Scalable Capital (Germany), and Nutmeg (UK) use algorithmic models to forecast market behaviour, assess risk tolerance, and adjust portfolios in anticipation of volatility. For mass-affluent and younger investors, this creates a dynamic relationship with wealth which is not static, but adaptive.

Yet, the power of prediction is not without peril. Over-prediction or false positives can erode trust. For instance, notifying a customer that their card might be compromised, only to later find it was a false alarm, creates friction. Banks must calibrate accuracy with empathy – ensuring that predictive tools do not trigger anxiety or decision fatigue. The goal is to be helpful, not hyperactive.

There is also the ethical dimension of nudging. Predictive tools can be used to encourage better financial habits – such as saving after payday or paying off high-interest debt – but they can also veer into manipulation. A well-timed notification can be a nudge or a push, depending on how it is framed. Transparency about model logic, user control over alerts, and clear opt-in mechanisms are essential for ethical deployment.

From a design standpoint, the challenge is to make predictions easy to understand. A sophisticated model may detect a pattern, but unless the insight is communicated in simple, actionable terms, it fails at the final hurdle. Saying "Your discretionary spend has increased by 14% in categories C1 and C2" is less useful than: "You've spent £120 more than usual on restaurants and shopping this month – consider reviewing your budget."

This is where explainable AI (XAI) comes into play. Predictive models should not operate as black boxes. Customers have a right to understand how a decision was made – especially when it affects credit limits, loan approvals, or fraud flags. Regulatory frameworks in both the UK and US are moving toward requiring greater algorithmic transparency. Institutions that embrace explainability not only comply with the law, but also build long-term credibility.

Importantly, predictive tools are becoming collaborative, not just prescriptive. Some banks now allow customers to adjust forecasting models – changing assumptions, toggling scenarios, or setting their own definitions of financial health. This interactivity fosters financial agency. It shifts the role of the customer from passive recipient to co-architect of their financial future.

The potential for proactive service is especially exciting. Imagine a bank that not only predicts that a customer will need travel insurance based on flight bookings, but also offers it seamlessly via a trusted partner – without any forms. Or a bank that notices a dip in salary payments and suggests a repayment holiday on a loan before the customer asks. This are not science fiction – these are emerging practices.

In institutional banking, predictive analytics is driving risk intelligence, allowing banks to flag early warning signs in client portfolios, monitor sectoral exposures, and stress-test balance sheets based on dynamic macroeconomic scenarios. During the COVID-19 pandemic, institutions that had invested in such capabilities were able to respond faster and more flexibly to unfolding risks.

The convergence of predictive AI with open banking will unlock even greater potential. As customers grant consent to share data across platforms, banks can build a richer picture of their financial life – predicting not just within the banks' own ecosystem, but across retail, telco, health, and education domains. For example, a student's university payment patterns and part-time income could inform a better understanding of repayment risk, enabling fairer loan pricing. But this future hinges on data ethics. Consent must be meaningful, not buried in terms and conditions. Predictions must serve the customer, not merely the institution. And algorithms must be continuously tested for bias, drift, and unintended consequences.

As we look ahead, the best predictive tools will not just be accurate – they will be adaptive, respectful, and empowering. They will serve not just the bank's efficiency, but the customer's wellbeing. They will help people move from reactive firefighting to proactive planning – from surviving financially to thriving confidently.

In designing the bank of tomorrow, prediction is not the goal. Better decisions are. And those decisions, made daily by millions of people in small but consequential moments, define financial health. By giving customers the power of foresight – delivered with clarity, care, and conscience – banks can transform not only services, but lives.

8 Ethical Boundaries of Machine-Led Decisions

As AI becomes deeply embedded within financial systems, banks find themselves confronting a profound question: not just what machines can decide, but what they should decide. In a sector governed by trust and regulation, where decisions often have life-altering consequences, the rise of algorithmic decision-making forces a redefinition of institutional ethics. The shift is not merely technical – it is moral.

AI systems nowadays influence a wide range of areas, including credit scoring, fraud detection, investment allocation, and personalized financial guidance. These systems promise efficiency, accuracy, and scale. But they also introduce new risks – opacity, bias, and the erosion of human accountability. As the boundaries between machine logic and human judgment blur, banks must draw a new line in the sand: one that protects fairness, transparency, and autonomy in a world increasingly governed by code.

At the heart of the ethical debate lies the issue of explainability. Machine learning models, especially deep neural networks, are often black boxes – generating outputs without revealing how or why a decision was made. For a retail customer denied a mortgage, or a small business flagged for fraud, this opacity can feel dehumanizing. In the UK and across Europe, GDPR enshrines the "right to explanation," compelling banks to offer clear reasoning for automated decisions. But compliance is only the starting point. True ethical leadership demands that institutions go beyond what is required, and instead build what is right.

This is where human-centred AI comes into play. The idea is simple but powerful: AI should augment – not replace – human decision-making, and should be designed with the rights and dignity of the individual at its core. In practice, this means embedding human oversight into high-impact decision flows, maintaining clear audit trails for algorithmic outputs, and allowing customers to contest or override machine-generated outcomes. It also means recognizing that not every decision should be automated in the first place.

Take credit approvals. AI can identify patterns in repayment behaviour more accurately than traditional models, incorporating variables such as mobile phone usage or utility bill payments. But if these models are trained on biased historical data, they may replicate – and even amplify – existing inequalities. For example, in the US, zip code-based proxies have been known to result in racial or socio-economic redlining, even when race is not an explicit feature. The solution is not to discard AI, but to design it responsibly, with rigorous fairness testing, diverse training datasets, and ethical guardrails built into every layer of the system.

Similarly, fraud detection systems must tread carefully between vigilance and overreach. False positives can lock customers out of their accounts, delay urgent transactions, or even trigger reputational harm. In an age of instant finance, where real-time detection is vital, banks must still ensure that their models are proportionate, reversible, and explainable. A bank that flags a customer's overseas transaction as suspicious should not simply block it without recourse; it should offer an immediate path to resolution, and ideally, learn from the customer's feedback to improve its future decisions.

In wealth management, robo-advisors promise low-cost, personalized portfolios for the mass market. But ethical dilemmas arise when AI nudges users toward certain products based on internal incentives or risk models the customer doesn't fully understand. Transparency becomes essential – not just with regard to fees and returns, but also about how recommendations are generated, what assumptions underlie them, and what potential conflicts of interest exist. Regulators in the UK, US, and Singapore have begun issuing guidance on algorithmic transparency in digital advice, recognizing that suggestions – when delivered by a machine – can carry undue weight.

Another frontier of ethical concern is emotional manipulation. As AI grows more sophisticated in analysing behaviour, mood, and even biometric data, banks may be tempted to optimize engagement using psychological levers – nudging users to save more, borrow less, or invest differently. While many of these outcomes are socially positive, there is a thin line between persuasion and manipulation. Ethical banks must ensure that nudges are aligned with the customer's best interests, not merely with product uptake or revenue targets.

This is especially important when serving vulnerable populations. For example, AI-driven lending platforms that target payday borrowers with high-interest products – even if technically approved by a model – risk reinforcing cycles of debt. Similarly, elderly customers interacting with virtual agents may not always realize they are not speaking to a human, raising issues of consent, comprehension, and emotional trust. Institutions must ask not just "Can we do this?" but "Should we?"

A growing number of banks are responding by developing AI ethics frameworks. These go beyond compliance checklists to define core principles – such as fairness, accountability, transparency, and non-malfeasance – and embed them into model development, governance, and deployment. For example, DBS Bank in Singapore has created a responsible AI charter that guides its use of machine learning across the enterprise. Similarly, BBVA in Spain has formed an AI ethics committee to review high-stakes use cases and ensure alignment with societal values.

Some institutions are even incorporating algorithmic audits – independent reviews of how AI systems perform across different demographics, geographies, and use cases. This is critical for detecting both bias and drift. A model that performs well today may become skewed over time as market conditions or user behaviour changes. Continuous monitoring, retraining, and version control are no longer optional – they are the foundation of ethical deployment.

Governance, too, must evolve. Boards and senior executives must be educated about AI risks and accountability structures. Decisions on AI implementation cannot be left to technical teams alone. Ethical oversight should involve multidisciplinary input – from legal, compliance, design, behavioural science, and importantly, the voice of the customer. Public consultation and engagement can help shape acceptable boundaries for automation in finance.

The question of responsibility also looms large. When an AI system makes a flawed decision, who is accountable? The developer? The model owner? The bank's executive leadership? Legal frameworks are still evolving to address these questions, but reputational risk is already real. Institutions that fail to take responsibility for AI outcomes – blaming "the system" or "the algorithm" – will quickly lose public trust.

International collaboration will be key. As financial systems globalize and AI supply chains stretch across borders, ethical standards must be harmonized. The UK's Centre for Data Ethics and Innovation, the EU's AI Act, and the OECD's AI Principles are steps toward a shared global architecture of responsible innovation. Financial institutions, especially those operating across jurisdictions, must align with both local regulation and global norms.

Ultimately, the ethical boundaries of machine-led decisions are not static – they must be continually re-evaluated in light of new capabilities, risks, and social expectations. Banks must build cultures that question, adapt, and learn, not just from compliance officers but from real people affected by their decisions.

In the bank of tomorrow, machines will be powerful. But ethics will be the compass. The institutions that thrive will not be those with the fastest models, but those with the wisest boundaries – designed not merely to protect profit, but to honour human dignity in a world increasingly governed by intelligence.

9 Governance in the Age of Algorithms

As AI becomes the main part of modern banking, the need for a strong and future-oriented governance framework is essential. In the past, governance revolved around human decisions, documented policies, and linear accountability. Today, it must also encompass decisions made – or heavily influenced – by algorithms, often in real time and at scale. This transformation needs more than a mere adjustment of existing frameworks; it calls for redesigning governance in a world where machines are the agents of institutional power.

Fundamentally, governance is about ensuring that the decisions an organization takes are in line with its values, strategy, and commitments – to customers, regulators, shareholders, and society as a whole. But in the algorithmic age, many of these choices can no longer be attributed to a solitary human agent. Machine learning algorithms can take in enormous sets of data, spit out suggestions, and implement automated actions with little to no direct human involvement. This introduces a new class of organizational risk: delegated intelligence without transparent accountability.

The first step in regulating algorithms is visibility. Banks and other financial institutions need to hold a register of all AI and machine learning systems used – whether developed in-house, sourced externally, or embedded through third-party APIs. This means the banks have to disclose not only what AI does, but how it was trained, what data it operates on, what its known limitations are, and who is accountable for ongoing monitoring. Without transparency, even high-level leadership might not know the magnitude or extent of the algorithmic impact on their own organization.

Once visibility has been achieved, the second challenge is control. Not all AI systems present an equal level of risk. A chatbot that suggests budgeting advice is essentially different from an algorithm that approves loans or identifies suspicious activity. Governance systems should thus incorporate risk-based categorization, mapping of systems across risk dimensions such as customer exposure, regulatory risk, data sensitivity, and model complexity. High-risk systems should prompt greater controls, such as pre-deployment examination, regular performance tracking, and independent auditing.

One of the main principles of algorithmic governance is explainability. Boards, regulators, and customers have to be able to comprehend – not merely accept – the justification of automated decisions. Although not all models can be fully interpretable, particularly in the case of sophisticated deep learning networks, banks have to invest in methods such as feature attribution, surrogate models, and natural language explanations to make decisions comprehensible. The European Banking Authority (EBA) and the UK's Financial Conduct Authority (FCA) both emphasize explainability as a cornerstone of trustworthy AI.

However, explainability is not sufficient. Banks also need to integrate responsibility structures into the AI lifecycle. This entails specifying ownership for model development, approval, deployment, and monitoring. Every model should have a named steward, rather than a development team. Model risk management (MRM) functions, first developed for quantitative finance models, are now being extended to cover AI systems, establishing lines of defence that merge technical knowledge with governance rigour.

In the US, the big banks have started incorporating AI governance into their enterprise risk management. JPMorgan Chase, for example, has established model governance councils that check high-impact algorithms for fairness, stability, and policy alignment. In the UK, major banks such as NatWest and Lloyds have created AI ethics boards consisting of members from compliance, data science, and customer advocacy groups. Such bodies exist not only to identify risk but also to create a culture where automation is considered from an ethical point of view.

Governance for the algorithmic age needs to rethink data accountability. Because AI models are only as good as the data they are trained upon, low data quality, buried biases, or defective labelling can result in damaging decisions. Banks need to have robust data governance policies in place to ensure that training data is accurate, diverse, representative, and governed by privacy principles. This applies to third-party data as well as synthetic data, which should have the same level of integrity and legality.

One of the most challenging hurdles is bias reduction. Despite the most positive of intentions, AI models can reproduce and amplify pre-existing disparities unless thoroughly tested. Governance groups need to deploy bias detection instruments – including disparate impact analysis and fairness scores – across protected traits such as gender, ethnicity, age, and location. Where disparities do occur, remediation needs to be incorporated into the model pipeline, and outputs need to undergo both technical validation and ethical audit.

As algorithms grow more autonomous, real-time oversight is paramount. Static governance structures – relying on sporadic reviews or post-deployment audits – will not be sufficient. Banks need to spend capital on dynamic monitoring systems that raise anomalies, identify model drift, and notify human overseers of performance deviations. Such tools not only make things safer, they also give confidence – ensuring that machine intelligence stays in line with institutional intent.

Most importantly, algorithmic governance cannot be left in the data science silo. Boards and executive management need to be involved. Just as cybersecurity is now a board-level topic, so too must AI governance. This involves upskilling directors, embedding AI risk within audit and risk committees, and ensuring that strategic decisions – including the launch of new digital lending platforms – take the algorithmic aspects into account from day one.

Globally, regulators are getting set to codify expectations. In the EU, the Artificial Intelligence Act will label some use cases in banking as "high risk" under a requirement for conformity assessments, documentation, and transparency. In the UK, the FCA and Bank of England have initiated a joint AI public-private forum to design governance norms. In the US, the Federal Reserve and OCC are considering supervisory strategies regarding AI. Governance, long regarded as a brake on innovation, is today recognized as an underpinning for accountable scalability.

For cross-border banks, this means an intricate matrix of intersecting standards and expectations. Harmonization by best practice is the solution, not regulatory arbitrage. Institutions that adopt high standards of algorithmic governance – regardless of the jurisdiction – are more likely to establish lasting trust with customers, regulators, and society.

It is also crucial to listen to the voice of the customer in governance. Governance has typically been internal. But in a world where customer data drives choices, and where impacts frequently appear to be black boxes to the end user, institutions need to create mechanisms to integrate public feedback. Such mechanisms could include transparency portals, grievance processes, design participation sessions, and public engagement around the launch of major algorithms.

It is just as important to ensure that organizational culture enables responsible AI. Governance is not merely rules – it is attitude. Data scientists need to be educated not merely in optimization but in ethics. Business executives need to view governance as a strategic accelerator and not as a chokepoint. Customer-facing employees need to learn how to describe AI-driven decisions with empathy and transparency. And technologists have to be rewarded for raising red flags, and not merely for producing output.

In the ultimate analysis, governance in the age of algorithms is a matter of defending institutional character in an era of digital decision-making. The question is not whether to automate, but how to automate responsibly and accountably while looking ahead. The institutions that will thrive will not simply use AI – they will govern it wisely.

10 Designing Intelligence with Integrity

As we arrive at the close of this chapter on the age of intelligence, one truth emerges above all others: intelligence is not just a technical construct. It is a human endeavour – shaped by values, stewarded through institutions, and judged by its impact on lives. Designing intelligence with integrity is not a slogan. It is a strategic and moral imperative for financial institutions navigating a world increasingly defined by data, automation, and digital decision-making.

We began this journey by exploring intelligence as infrastructure: the new foundation of modern banking. From conversational agents to predictive underwriting, from credit scoring to transaction monitoring, intelligent systems are no longer an add-on. They are embedded deep within the DNA of the everyday bank. But as these systems evolve in scope, autonomy, and complexity, a critical question arises: what governs the intelligence that governs us?

To design intelligence with integrity is to treat intelligence not as a neutral tool, but as a force with ethical, societal, and institutional consequences. In practical terms, it means ensuring that every step of the AI lifecycle – from problem framing to model development to deployment – aligns with the values and responsibilities of the bank. It also means recognizing the limits of automation, and building safeguards that emphasize human judgment, dignity, and discretion.

At the core of integrity is intent. What is the purpose of building a particular model? Whose interests does it serve? What outcome is it optimising for? In retail banking, these questions are not abstract. An algorithmic credit model that maximizes profitability but marginalizes low-income customers violates the principle of inclusion. A fraud detection system that disproportionately flags minority customers erodes trust. Intent must be articulated – and governed – just as clearly as accuracy or efficiency.

Transparency follows closely behind. Customers have the right to know when AI is being used, how it affects them, and what recourse they have. Yet, too often, AI operates as an invisible infrastructure, shaping decisions without disclosure. Designing with integrity means building explainability into customer journeys. Whether through summary explanations, decision rationale dashboards, or dedicated human support channels, banks must demystify machine intelligence.

Equally crucial is fairness. AI systems are deeply sensitive to data, and data reflects society – with all its historical inequities and structural biases. This means fairness cannot be assumed; it must be engineered. Banks must implement fairness-aware design frameworks, test models across demographic variables, and include diverse perspectives during development. Fairness is not the enemy of efficiency – it is a precondition for sustainable success in a diverse, global marketplace.

Consent and agency are also core to integrity. With the rise of embedded finance, banks now touch customers at invisible points – within apps, websites, and IoT (Internet of Things) devices. Data flows quietly, predictions are made passively, nudges are delivered algorithmically. In this context, banks must move beyond minimal compliance and toward genuine data dignity. Customers should be able to understand what data is being used, control how it is shared, and opt out of machine-based decisions without friction or penalty.

The challenge of integrity extends inward as well. Internal culture and incentives must support ethical AI. Data science teams should be trained not just in coding, but in consequence scanning. Product managers should be empowered to halt launches if ethical risks are unresolved. Risk, compliance, and audit functions should be equipped to engage with algorithmic systems meaningfully, not merely rubber-stamp them. And senior leaders must signal – through words, budgets, and behaviours – that integrity is a strategic priority, not a regulatory afterthought.

This shift is beginning to take shape. At DBS Bank in Singapore, "Responsible AI" is now part of the technology team's KPI structure. In the UK, HSBC Bank has launched an internal AI ethics academy to train staff on fairness and risk. In the US, Capital One has integrated AI governance into board-level reporting. These are not cosmetic changes. They are indicators of a financial industry reorienting around trust – not just performance.

Global standards are also evolving. The OECD AI Principles, the EU's AI Act, the UK's AI Assurance Roadmap, and emerging ISO standards all point toward a more consistent global understanding of responsible AI. Banks that embed these principles proactively will gain not just compliance advantage, but customer confidence. As regulation tightens, integrity becomes not a cost – but a competitive differentiator.

Designing intelligence with integrity also means planning for failure. No system is perfect. Biases can emerge over time. Data can shift. Models can degrade. Designing for integrity means anticipating harm, building fallback mechanisms, establishing redress systems, and continuously learning. Ethical resilience is just as important as technical resilience. When something goes wrong – as it inevitably will – institutions must respond with honesty, speed, and accountability.

A particularly pressing challenge is the rise of synthetic content and generative AI. As models become capable of producing text, images, advice, and even financial narratives, the line between human and machine blurs further. Banks must establish clear guardrails on the use of generative systems, ensure attribution of authorship, and protect against hallucinations or misinformation. What the model generates must not escape the institution's accountability.

To navigate all of this, we need a new generation of AI stewards – professionals who blend technical fluency with ethical insight, strategic foresight, and human empathy. These stewards will not be confined to IT. They will sit across product, compliance, customer experience, legal, and risk – forming a distributed architecture of intelligence with integrity.

And beyond individuals, we need institutions that take a stand, that commit publicly to ethical AI principles, that publish model audits, that engage openly with civil society, and regulators that treat responsible AI not as the subject of a press release but as a pillar of strategy, that choose the long-term trust of their customers over the short-term gains of opaque optimization.

Ultimately, to design intelligence with integrity is to design for humanity. It is to ensure that even as we scale automation, we never lose sight of empathy. That even as we optimize processes, we preserve human dignity. That even as we digitize finance, we humanize its impact. It is a profound responsibility, but it is also a profound opportunity. The future of banking is not just digital – it is ethical. Not just smart – but wise. And wisdom begins with intention, governed by integrity. Let that be our blueprint.

Strategic Framework Box: Chapter 7 - Intelligence as Infrastructure: Reframing AI in Financial Systems

Key Insight

AI is not a product – it is an institutional capability. The future bank will not just deploy AI; it will be intelligently governed, ensuring that predictive tools enhance decision-making without compromising trust, fairness, or human oversight.

Strategic Takeaway

AI is not just about automation. It is about institutional augmentation. The future of finance depends not only on smart algorithms, but on wise governance.

Intelligence Domain	*Legacy Financial Systems*	*Intelligent Financial Systems*
Decision Process	Manual, rules-based	Data-driven, probabilistic, contextual
Customer Interaction	Static menus, forms, FAQs	Conversational interfaces, virtual agents
Risk Management	Retrospective, report-led	Predictive, continuous, real-time
Credit Models	Credit score-dependent, opaque	Behavioural, inclusive, explainable
Governance Structure	Process-centric, audit posture	Algorithmic transparency, human-in-the-loop
Learning Capability	Institutional memory, slow to adapt	Dynamic learning, ecosystem-informed

This chapter reframes AI as a strategic layer that must be consciously designed – not just for efficiency, but for integrity. Intelligence must be explainable, auditable, and bias-aware. It must support – not replace – human judgment.

Bibliography

OECD (2021). *Artificial Intelligence in Society*. Paris: OECD Publishing.

8 The Architecture of Trust

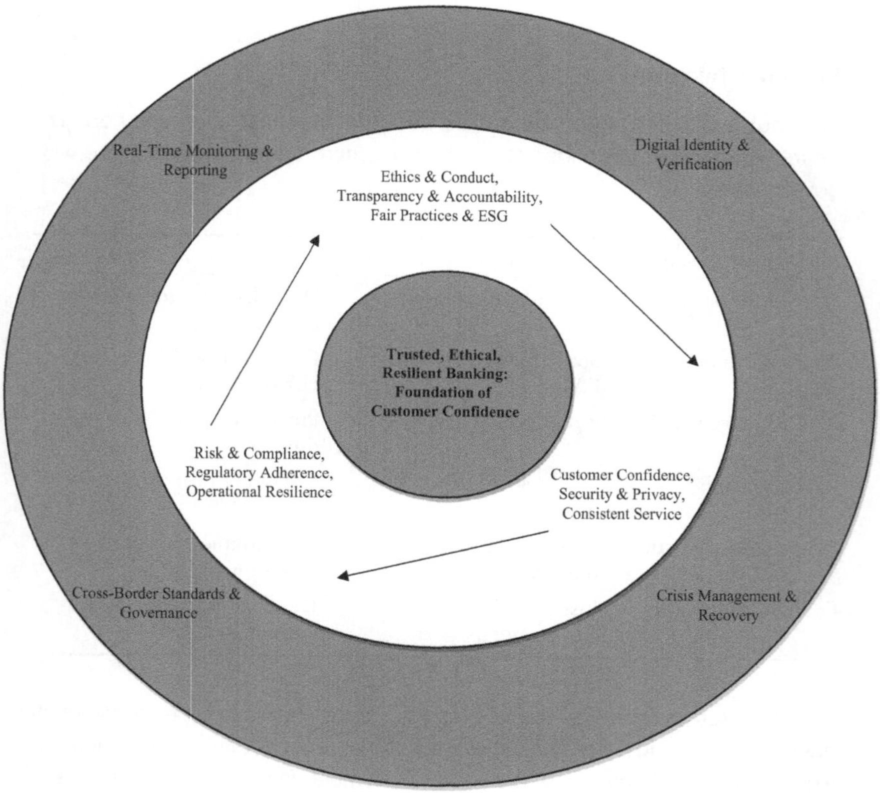

Figure 8.1 Institutional trust is built on ethics, risk management, and customer confidence – supported by strong governance and resilient infrastructure.

DOI: 10.4324/9781003737544-8

1 Trust as the Foundation of Finance

In the intricate machinery of global finance, trust is not a luxury – it is the engine. The very notion of banking, lending, saving, and investing is built on the premise that institutions will safeguard value, act in good faith, and operate in the best interests of those they serve. Unlike many other industries, finance operates without delivering a physical product. It deals in promises – of security, of access, of future outcomes. And so, trust becomes the intangible currency without which banking could not function.

Historically, trust relied on physical cues such as grand buildings, marble counters, vaults, and personal relationships with managers. Today, that trust must be established through digital interfaces, instant verification systems, and the silent integrity of algorithms. In this new era, where finance is increasingly invisible and intangible, the architecture of trust must be rebuilt from the ground up. And that process is not purely technical. It is ethical, cultural, psychological, and institutional.

A Crisis of Trust and a Call to Reinvention

The 2008 global financial crisis remains a defining moment – a rupture in the implicit contract between banks and society. Millions lost homes, savings, and confidence, not just in individual institutions but in the legitimacy of the financial system itself. Since then, banks have worked to strengthen capital buffers and comply with new regulations. Yet despite these efforts, public trust in financial institutions remains fragile.

What's more, we now see a new kind of risk: trust erosion via digital channels. A single data breach, a failed system update, or an unexplainable AI-driven loan rejection can destroy years of brand equity in seconds. In this environment, transparency, consistency, and accountability must be engineered into the core of every product and platform. The future of finance depends not just on new technologies, but on how those technologies are governed, communicated, and understood by customers. Trust is no longer a consequence of brand recognition – it must be a deliberate design principle.

Trust Is Not Static – It Is Dynamic and Must Be Earned

One of the most dangerous assumptions in banking is that trust is a stable asset. In reality, it is dynamic – constantly being earned, tested, and renegotiated. Customers evaluate their trust in an institution not once, but every time they engage with it. Did the app work when they needed it most? Did the bank notify them of fraud? Did a chatbot offer real support or just redirect them endlessly?

These micro-moments form the lived reality of trust in digital banking. And in an age where customers compare banks not just to each other but to super-apps, retail platforms, and digital-native experiences, the bar is set higher than ever. Trust is no longer a reflection of tenure or size – it is a reflection of empathy, performance, and clarity at the point of service. Trust must also be understood as multilayered. There is transactional trust (Did this payment go through?), relational trust (Does this institution treat me fairly?), and systemic trust (Does this institution behave ethically, even when no one is watching?). Rebuilding trust in finance means addressing all three simultaneously.

Designing for Trust in Digital Systems

So how do we build trust in environments where there is no face-to-face interaction, no physical presence, and no opportunity to "read" the human behind the brand? The answer lies in design. Digital trust is created through systems that are reliable, transparent, explainable, and aligned with customer expectations.

Reliability means systems that do not fail. Outages, bugs, or inconsistent functionality damage trust quickly. Transparency means users know what is happening with their data, their money, and their requests – without needing to dig through legalese. Explainability means that decisions, especially those made by algorithms, can be understood by humans. And alignment means that the institution's actions reflect the promises made in its mission and branding. This is where ethical design becomes a strategic differentiator. Institutions that proactively incorporate user consent, algorithmic fairness, and real-time communication into their platforms will outperform those that treat trust as an afterthought.

Global Perspectives: Trust Across Borders

Trust is culturally contextual. What builds trust in Germany may not suffice in India. In the UK and US, regulatory compliance and data protection frameworks such as GDPR and the California Consumer Privacy Act (CCPA) play a large role in shaping public confidence. In other regions, personal relationships and community banking models may dominate trust-building. Financial institutions operating globally must respect and respond to these nuances.

Moreover, trust is influenced by institutional memory. Banks that have demonstrated social responsibility – supporting customers during crises, waiving fees, or promoting inclusion – can draw upon that goodwill during difficult moments. But new digital entrants lack that legacy. For them, trust must be established from scratch – and every customer interaction becomes a test.

From Product to Principle: The New Mandate

Ultimately, trust must be elevated from a marketing message to a board-level priority. It is not something to be "earned" by advertising – it must be embedded in the institution's culture, governance, and product architecture.

This shift requires asking uncomfortable questions: Who audits our algorithms? Who represents vulnerable users at the design table? Do our KPIs measure customer wellbeing – or just short-term profitability? These questions are not peripheral. They are central to whether the public will continue to allow banks to serve in their essential societal role. In a world of rising scepticism, institutional trust is no longer assumed. It must be demonstrated, daily, and at scale.

Looking Ahead

As we look toward the future, trust will become even more essential – and even more complex. AI-driven decisions, decentralized finance, biometric authentication, and programmable money will challenge existing norms. Institutions that succeed will be those that view trust not as a historical asset, but as a strategic frontier. They will build not only systems that work, but systems that earn belief. In this new architecture, trust is both the foundation and the frame. It is not passive – it is actively constructed, maintained, and evolved. And in that construction lies the very future of finance.

2 Regulation in a Real-Time World

In a financial system that moves at the speed of algorithms, real-time regulation is no longer a futuristic concept – it is an urgent necessity. The traditional regulatory model, with its cyclical reviews, retrospective audits, and post-event compliance measures, was not designed for a world where trillions of dollars flow across borders in milliseconds, and a single line of code can affect millions of users instantly. Today's financial landscape requires a regulatory system that is as dynamic, flexible, and smart as the systems it oversees. The question is no longer whether regulation can keep up with innovation. It must lead it.

The Legacy Challenge

Historically, regulation has been a reactive function. New rules emerged in response to past failures – after fraud, after collapse, after crisis. Laws were drafted, compliance systems adjusted, and penalties levied. While this backward-looking model provided necessary guardrails, it now struggles to deal with the immediacy of digital transactions, the opacity of AI systems, and the complexity of global financial ecosystems.

Consider the compliance burden placed on banks after the 2008 crisis – Basel III, Dodd-Frank, MiFID II. Each introduced critical improvements but also added layers of process and reporting. In today's environment, those processes can create friction that impedes innovation and, paradoxically, weakens the agility needed to manage emerging risks. What's needed is a shift – from reactive regulation to anticipatory governance. From rule-based oversight to principles-based collaboration. From enforcement after harm to intervention before it occurs.

Supervising Algorithms, Not Just Balance Sheets

Modern financial regulation must expand its focus. It is no longer enough to examine capital ratios, liquidity profiles, or credit exposure. Regulators now need insight into how algorithms make decisions, how customer data is processed, and how digital products adapt over time. This includes understanding machine learning models, identifying biases, and ensuring that automated decisions are explainable and fair.

Real-time monitoring tools are emerging in jurisdictions such as the UK and Singapore, where regulators are piloting supervisory technologies – for example AI systems that analyse speech data to detect potential misconduct. These tools promise not just better enforcement, but smarter policy-making, informed by live data rather than quarterly reports. But they also raise new ethical questions: How much surveillance is too much? Can algorithmic oversight be trusted if regulators themselves don't understand the models? And how do we ensure accountability when decision-making is decentralized or AI-driven?

A Global Patchwork of Rules

Regulation in a real-time world is also complicated by its jurisdictional fragmentation. While finance is increasingly global, regulation remains largely national. A fintech operating across the US, UK, EU, and India may face four different sets of privacy laws, licensing rules, and reporting standards. This complexity can stifle innovation and create uneven playing fields.

To address this, international bodies like the Financial Stability Board and the Bank for International Settlements are calling for more regulatory harmonization. Initiatives such as the EU's Digital Operational Resilience Act (DORA) or the UK's FCA Digital Sandbox represent important steps. But global coherence remains elusive, particularly in emerging areas such as crypto assets, decentralized finance (DeFi), and digital identity. There is an urgent need for cross-border regulatory cooperation – not just in setting standards, but in sharing data, technologies, and supervisory strategies. The alternative is a race to the bottom, where companies arbitrage regulation and public trust erodes.

The Case for Embedded Regulation

A transformative idea gaining traction is the concept of "embedded regulation" – where compliance mechanisms are built directly into financial systems, platforms, and products. This mirrors the broader trend of "compliance by design", where controls are not bolted on, but integrated into the digital journey itself.

For instance, APIs can be designed to automatically log activity for audit trails. Smart contracts can execute regulatory rules within DeFi platforms. Customer onboarding flows can include real-time KYC/AML (know your customer/anti money laundering) verification without creating friction. In this model, regulation becomes ambient – ever-present but unobtrusive, like a seatbelt or antivirus software. Embedded regulation also offers regulators a window into live systems, enabling continuous supervision without constant intrusion. It marks a shift from regulation as an obstacle to regulation as infrastructure.

Financial Inclusion and Regulatory Balance

One of the dangers in overregulating is that it can inadvertently exclude the very people that modern finance aims to serve. Stringent compliance requirements often deter smaller institutions or underserved customers – those lacking traditional documentation or credit histories. Regulatory models must evolve to support inclusion as well as stability. This means adopting risk-based approaches that differentiate between low-risk and high-risk entities. It also means encouraging regulatory sandboxes, innovation hubs, and tiered compliance regimes that allow experimentation without compromising oversight. The FCA in the UK and the Monetary Authority of Singapore (MAS) are global leaders in this space, enabling fintechs to test products under controlled environments. Such models must now be scaled globally, particularly in regions where financial infrastructure is still developing.

Rethinking Accountability and Governance

Real-time regulation also challenges conventional governance structures. In traditional systems, there is a clear line of responsibility: decisions are made by people, guided by policy, and enforced by process. But when decisions are made by machines – based on dynamic inputs and evolving models – accountability becomes murkier. Who is liable for a biased algorithm? The data scientist? The CIO? The institution? What if the model learns an unintended behaviour after deployment?

New forms of governance are needed – ones that embed ethical review, continuous testing, and audit ability into the software lifecycle. Boards must become digitally fluent, not just to ask the right questions, but to understand the limitations of what even the best systems can provide.

The Next Generation of Regulation

Looking ahead, we are likely to see regulators evolve into platforms. Just as banks are becoming platforms for financial services, regulators may offer digital infrastructure that industry players can plug into – for example live reporting tools, risk assessment engines, and policy simulation models. Compliance will become real-time, not because of surveillance, but because of shared trust frameworks.

Blockchain technology may also play a role, enabling immutable records, shared ledgers, and decentralized oversight. But technology alone is not enough. Regulation is ultimately a human function, rooted in values, trade-offs, and social contracts. In a real-time world, we must ask: What kind of financial future do we want to build? Who do we protect? Who do we empower? And how do we ensure that speed does not come at the cost of justice?

3 Compliance by Design, Not Enforcement

In the traditional financial services world, compliance used to be viewed as an external overlay – a necessary evil to be dealt with, policed, and sometimes circumvented. Rules were usually added on top of a product once it was conceived and brought to market, resulting in inefficiency, user friction, and frequently unintended harm. In the digital-first world of today, this paradigm is unsustainable.

The new financial world requires a fundamental transformation: from enforcement-based to design-based compliance. It is not about digitalizing rules. It is about integrating trust into the very fabric of financial services and products. It is a transformation of the culture, technology, and strategy – one that changes how institutions design systems, provide value, and maintain integrity.

Compliance Is No Longer a Destination – It Is the Blueprint

To establish trust in an immediate, hyper-connected age, compliance must be intrinsic rather than procedural. This is to say that regulatory reason, ethical boundaries, and legal protections have to be incorporated into the code, the customer experience, and the data model – prior to a product's release into the market. This is what we observe in fields such as cybersecurity and user experience: security and design are no longer the domain of distinct departments – they're everybody's business, and they start at conception. The same has to be true of regulatory design.

Banks such as Monzo, N26, and Nubank have shown that a design-driven compliance can make interfaces cleaner, communication clearer, and the customer experience both more user-friendly and more regulator-friendly. Their success lies not only in product innovation but also in structural ethics.

Embedding Compliance in the Product Lifecycle

In a design-first compliance model, all phases of the product life cycle are influenced by trust requirements:

- Ideation and Planning: Compliance teams are engaged right from day one. Risk is integral to the creative process.
- Development and Prototyping: Regulatory sense is baked directly into systems architecture.
- Testing and Deployment: Compliance is stress-tested along with performance and UX.
- Monitoring and Learning: Continuous feedback loops make regulatory alignment adapt to changes in the marketplace.

This strategy is especially important in agile settings with fast iterations. Instead of the compliance being retrofitted every time a sprint closes, teams can create guardrails that incrementally grow as each deployment happens.

The Move Away from Policy Manuals to Compliance Infrastructure

Old-fashioned banks have tended to use policy books, audit roles, and yearly training to impose compliance. In the new paradigm, those stationary mechanisms are supplemented – or even supplanted – by compliance infrastructure: Security and compliance features encompass APIs to limit specific transactions based on geolocation or user profile, real-time monitoring software to mark anomalies or unusual behaviour, smart contracts to automatically enforce conditions such as loan amount or repayment conditions, and consent layers that are modular, transparent, and audit-friendly. This infrastructure is not merely quicker and more scalable, but also more in line with the assumptions of digital-native users, which are clarity, control, and accountability.

Behavioural Design and Trust Nudges

Compliance design is also designing for human behaviour. One of the behavioural science insights is that decisions about the user interface can make or break ethical outcomes. Simple changes to layout, text, or workflows can lower risky behaviour, make things more transparent, and improve understanding.

Examples are unambiguous opt-ins compared to unclear pre-ticked boxes, progressive disclosure of terms instead of overwhelming legalese, and contextual nudges reminding users of financial penalties before they act. Such behaviour, when following sound ethical principals, empowers users while minimizing regulatory risk. But when used maliciously – as it is the case with dark patterns – they break down trust. Therefore, ethical design needs to be deliberate, auditable, and rooted in user advocacy.

Compliance as a Competitive Advantage

There used to be a time when compliance was seen as a cost centre. Today, institutions that implement compliance by design are realizing its strategic value: Some of the most significant advantages are more rapid approvals by regulators and partners, reduced remediation costs and fewer operational hazards, greater brand equity with a foundation in ethics and transparency, and increased responsiveness to regulatory change.

Companies such as Alloy and Comply Advantage have built full platforms that facilitate banks and fintechs to automate, visualize, and tailor compliance workflows. They are not merely providing regulatory frameworks – they are design systems, allowing institutions to construct with trust from the ground up.

Global Standards, Local Execution

Financial institutions are more and more operating across borders, subject to a patchwork of local rules and international norms. Compliance by design needs to support this complexity by enabling modular, flexible structures that conform to the jurisdictional variation of regulations, such as GDPR in Europe, CCPA in California, MAS guidelines in Singapore, RBI norms in India, and FCA expectations in the UK. Leading platforms integrate compliance capabilities into their product design – not as fixed rules but as adaptive layers that may be turned on or tuned up depending on user location, account type, or product category.

Leadership and Governance for Embedded Compliance

Designing for compliance is impossible without leadership commitment. Boards have to move compliance from an operational afterthought to a design principle. Banks need to ask themselves: Are our systems built to safeguard the most vulnerable users? Are our auditors able to follow the reasoning behind each critical product choice? Are we hiring compliance engineers, not compliance officers? Progressive firms are developing hybrid positions – such as RegTech architects or product compliance strategists – that cross legal, technical, and design boundaries.

A Human-Centric Future for Regulation

Finally, the aim of embedded compliance is not merely to escape sanctions – it is to establish trust. It is to make sure that users are offered financial systems that are easy to understand, transparent, and serve their best interests. This is not merely a technology challenge. It is a cultural necessity. It requires a redefinition of compliance itself: transformed from a constraint into a catalyst; or from obstacle into a source of design simplicity. As capital systems grow smarter, more embedded, and more connected, the architecture of trust needs to be included in the blueprint – not merely the audit trail.

4 Digital Identity and Customer Verification

In the world of contemporary banking, few things are as fundamental – and as highly complicated – as digital identity. It is the keystone of trust in all financial transactions: how a bank identifies who its customer is, how risk is handled, and how services are provided securely across borders, platforms, and devices.

In a conventional world, identity was tied to physical documents and human authentication. Yet today's world of mobile-first interactions, remote onboarding, and cross-border payments means that the nature of identity has changed in a fundamental way. Banks now have the pressing challenge of reimagining digital identity – not as a compliance barrier, but as a strategic facilitator of trust, security, and inclusion.

Identity as the Foundation of Trust

Every sale of a financial product starts with one fundamental question to the customer: Who are you? If banks do not have a strong answer to this, they can't issue credit, open accounts, avoid fraud, or meet regulation. But identity is no longer fixed – it is dynamic, contextual, and multi-factorial. Digital identities must be:

- Portable and transferable across institutions and borders
- Verifiable, fraud-resistant and tamper-proof
- Respecting the users' privacy and allowing them to control it
- Inclusive and available to those without formal papers

This new identity model calls for a radical overhaul of the verification process, data structure, and user experience in financial systems.

The Transition from Document-Based to Data-Driven Identity

Classic KYC processes depended on passports, utility bills, and actual signatures. In the digital age, these artefacts are not enough. Banks today are looking to data-driven identity: using biometrics, device fingerprints, behavioural analytics, and government-issued digital credentials to build trust.

Digital-first banks such as Revolut and Chime have reimagined onboarding through video KYC, facial recognition, and immediate ID verification using smartphones. In India, Aadhaar has built a biometric identity infrastructure that supports low-cost, real-time verification for more than a billion citizens – significantly expanding financial access. Yet total reliance on biometrics is not risk-free. Spoofing attacks, data compromise, and algorithmic bias can derail trust if not adequately regulated. Therefore, a multi-factor solution – combining device data, location profiles, and biometric indicators – is rapidly becoming the gold standard.

Decentralized Identity and the Emergence of Self-Sovereign Models

One of the most significant innovations in this area is Decentralized Identity (DID). In contrast to systems that rely on the central storage of identity information by governments or banks, DID gives users control of their own credentials. In this model, customers may have a digital wallet with validated credentials – such as a driver's license, credit rating, or income verification – and they then selectively present them to financial institutions without divulging information they do not wish to share. The advantages of this framework are:

- Less fraud and phishing risk
- Better customer privacy
- More interoperability across platforms
- Onboarding at a higher speed
- Lower cost of compliance

Organizations such as MasterCard and Microsoft are actively pursuing decentralized identity networks that have the potential to change all transactions from the underwriting of credit to cross-border payments.

Regulatory Standards and Identity Interoperability

As digital identity becomes increasingly pivotal in financial systems, regulators are now starting to create global standards. The Financial Action Task Force (FATF) has issued recommendations on digital ID for use in KYC and AML. The eIDAS regulation in the EU and the UK's Digital Identity and Attributes Trust Framework (DIATF) will define the next stages of compliance.

In order for banks to thrive in this changing environment, digital identity infrastructures need to be auditable and regulator-ready, conform to developing standards for interoperability, and accommodate identity federation across jurisdictions and ecosystems. International banks with operations in a variety of different regulatory environments are particularly in need of this kind of consistency and portability of identity.

Identity and Financial Inclusion

Digital identity is not only an engineering problem – it's a door to inclusion. There are an estimated 850 million people in the world with no formal identification. Without a credible identity, they're excluded from financial systems, government services, and digital economies. Initiatives such as MOSIP (Modular Open-Source Identity Platform) and ID4D (Identification for Development) of the World Bank are facilitating low-cost, open-source identity infrastructures, which can be implemented in underserved communities.

Banks have a special responsibility – as well as the ability – to create onboarding systems that include individuals with non-formal credentials, such as community recommendations or the usage history of their mobiles. In doing so, they not only increase their own customer base but also support social equity in the wider society.

Identity Fraud, Deep Fakes, and Digital Risk

As verification systems become more advanced, so do the attacks on them. Synthetic identities, in which fraudsters merge actual and synthetic data to construct authentic-looking personas, represent one of the fastest growing types of financial crime. The advent of deep fake technology makes biometric verification even more challenging.

Banks thus need to construct layered, adaptive defences – using artificial intelligence, anomaly detection, and ongoing behavioural authentication to identify suspicious patterns without degrading user experience. In the US and UK markets, regulators increasingly want institutions to show evidence of proactive fraud prevention measures – not merely reactive forensic investigation.

UX Meets Identity: Frictionless but Secure

One of the biggest challenges in digital identity is achieving security and usability. Too much friction can push customers away; too little can leave them vulnerable to risk. Fintech leaders have innovated onboarding flows so that systems utilize document capture and AI to read ID data in real-time, offer real-time verification status with plain-language updates, and offer fallbacks, e.g., live chat with an agent, to prevent drop-offs. This combination of design thinking and compliance logic is the foundation of trust at scale. Identity needs to be viewed as an experience rather than a back-office process.

The Role of Public-Private Collaboration

There is no bank that can address the identity problem on its own. Public-private partnerships are necessary to construct national identity infrastructures, shared verification platforms, and trusted data exchanges. Examples include the BankID in Sweden, covering more than 90% of adults; Singapore's Singpass, facilitating digital access to government and financial services; and open banking and open finance architectures that are based on secure, verified identity flows for sharing data. These models illustrate the potential of collective infrastructure to lower onboarding expenses, streamline KYC, and build systemic resilience.

Conclusion: From Verification to Empowerment

Digital identity is more than a regulatory requirement – it is trust in the digital age. Done well, it facilitates frictionless onboarding, prevents fraud, increases privacy, and extends access. But it needs to be approached with sensitivity, imagination, and an unshakeable focus on the user. As financial services become increasingly digital, the Who are you? question will get even more complicated – and more meaningful. Those banks that create identity systems not only to authenticate but to enable their customers will determine the future of finance.

5 Embedding Risk into Digital Journeys

As the financial world shifts decisively into digital modes of delivery, the concept of risk must be reimagined – not as an external check imposed after the fact, but as an embedded, dynamic feature woven into the very architecture of every user journey. In the past, traditional models of risk governance relied heavily on periodic reviews, manual oversight, and lagging indicators. In contrast, digital banking demands real-time risk intelligence that operates invisibly but effectively throughout the lifecycle of a transaction or engagement.

Embedding risk into digital journeys means turning it into a first-class design consideration: built-in, not bolted-on. It requires banks to adopt smarter architectures, predictive analytics, and customer-centric interfaces that treat risk not merely as a constraint, but as a strategic differentiator.

From Reactive Control to Proactive Design

Historically, risk controls have been reactive. They were set up as barriers or interventions after specific thresholds were crossed. Whether it was a credit decision taken post-application, a fraud alert triggered post-transaction, or a compliance review scheduled post-activity, the approach was back-loaded.

In a digital context, this is no longer sustainable. Today's systems must detect and respond to anomalies in real time, with minimal disruption to the customer. Strategies to achieve this include integrating dynamic risk scoring into user journeys, using machine learning to predict high-risk behaviours before they materialize, and allowing interfaces to adapt based on the customer's real-time risk profile. When risk becomes ambient and intelligent, this enables a more fluid, personalized, and safe experience – especially in moments of transaction, onboarding, and authentication.

Risk-Aware Architecture: Code, Not Paper

Embedding risk means changing how systems are designed at the code level. Governance frameworks, thresholds, and exceptions must be codified within digital workflows, APIs, and decision engines – not managed manually or through static documentation. Key features which enable this transition include modular risk engines that integrate with digital platforms, real-time data ingestion from internal and external sources, auditability by design to ensure decisions are traceable and explainable, and cross-channel integration to provide consistent treatment across mobile, web, and backend systems.

A modern bank's architecture should treat every user interaction as a potential risk, which needs to be analysed, scored, and responded to on the fly. This also allows for differentiated controls: not every user needs the same friction; not every transaction carries equal risk.

Behavioural Biometrics and Adaptive Risk

One of the most promising innovations in embedded risk management is behavioural biometrics – analysing how users type, swipe, move their mouse, or interact with the interface to detect anomalies. For example, a customer logging in with familiar credentials but typing differently might trigger secondary authentication; a payment request made from a trusted device but at an unusual time or location might be flagged for review; and a sudden change in mobile device orientation during login could signal potential account takeover. These signals are subtle but powerful. When combined with AI, they enable adaptive risk mitigation – tailoring responses dynamically based on live context, not static rules.

Contextual Risk Scoring in Customer Journeys

Embedding risk means continuously scoring the context of a customer's actions. Risk factors include: location risk – whether the user is logging in from a high-fraud geography; velocity risk – whether they are making too many requests too quickly; device risk – whether the device is known, jailbroken, or behaving suspiciously; and time risk – whether the behaviour is out of sync with historical norms.

Modern systems use these signals to assign a contextual risk score at each key moment – login, funds transfer, password reset, or new product application. If the score exceeds a threshold, the journey adapts: extra verification may be required, transaction limits may change, or access may be temporarily frozen. This creates a non-intrusive risk posture – secure by default, but flexible in execution.

Aligning Risk with Customer Trust

Risk management has historically been seen as the domain of compliance and control. But in a digital bank, risk is also a trust mechanism. Customers want to feel protected – without being made to feel distrusted. That means being transparent about why certain steps are triggered, providing human fallback options when digital journeys are blocked, offering clear, real-time notifications if actions are denied or delayed, and enabling customers to see and manage their own risk settings, such as transaction limits and device authorizations.

These features build a partnership model – where risk is not a mysterious external judgment, but a shared responsibility. In today's open banking and API-driven environments, risk is no longer contained within the institution. It flows across partners, third-party providers, cloud services, and embedded interfaces. This creates an extended risk surface that traditional models were not built to handle. Banks must now:

- Embed security protocols into every third-party connection
- Continuously monitor for data leakage, privilege escalation, or credential misuse
- Conduct regular penetration testing and scenario modelling across digital journeys
- Establish incident response playbooks that are tested and rehearsed across the ecosystem

Embedding risk is also about being resilient – not just protected. When systems fail or threats emerge, the bank must respond instantly, transparently, and decisively to preserve customer trust.

Risk Culture Meets Digital Culture

A final challenge is cultural. Embedding risk requires a mindset shift – not just technology. Product teams, designers, and developers must be fluent in risk thinking. Conversely, risk leaders must understand digital architectures, user experience, and agile workflows. Some leading banks have created fusion teams where risk and product work side by side, embedded risk champions within agile squads, created risk pattern libraries akin to design systems that are reusable across journeys, and designed risk scoreboards that visualize risk dynamics in real time. These practices ensure that risk is not a bottleneck but a value creator – an enabler of smarter, faster, and safer innovation.

Conclusion: Risk as a Seamless Companion

The future of digital banking will not be defined by the absence of risk, but by the seamless choreography of risk throughout the user journey. The most trusted institutions will be those that embed risk invisibly – like oxygen in the air – present, adaptive, and indispensable. By designing systems where risk management is anticipatory, contextual, and user-aware, banks can protect not just their balance sheets, but their relationships, their reputations, and their relevance in a changing world.

6 Ethical Conduct and Accountability

Today, in the digital world, where banking increasingly occurs beyond contact with people, the moral centre of banks is more vulnerable than ever. No longer is trust established through face-to-face relationships or reputation heritage – it's assessed in milliseconds, at the point of service, when it's algorithm-driven and often invisible. Here, ethical behaviour and responsibility are not merely virtues – they are building blocks of digital trust.

As banking becomes increasingly sophisticated, automated, and data-driven, the task is not merely to prevent wrongdoing. It's essential to make sure institutions are actually being driven by ethical purpose. That involves infusing ethical principles into technologies, leadership behaviours, organizational structure, and customer-facing interactions.

Redefining Ethics in a Digital Age

Historic codes of ethics were crafted for human players – bankers, advisors, regulators. They established norms for behaviour, integrity, conflicts of interest, and fiduciary responsibility. But what does it mean when choices are made by AI, nudges are crafted by data models, and responsibility is hidden in stacks of code?

The ethics of the future will need to take into account what machine-driven decisions do to fairness, transparency, and human dignity; who bears the blame when algorithms generate prejudice or cause harm; if digital paths respect informed consent, privacy, and autonomy; and how rewards for money are compatible with the long-term flourishing of customers and communities. Digital banking does not exempt ethical responsibility – it magnifies it. Because damage can grow faster and be invisible and unrecoverable.

From Policy to Practice: Operationalizing Ethics

Ethical behaviour should not remain hidden in policy papers or training materials. It has to be operationalized – translated into real-world standards, measures, and design principles that shape everyday behaviour. This encompasses ethical design principles in product creation, such as avoiding dark patterns and favouring user clarity; including audit trails for algorithms that enable human review of automated decisions; building escalation channels where employees can bring up ethical concerns without reprisal; setting up cross-functional ethics committees that include tech, legal, risk, and customer advocacy; and using KPIs which measure conduct, not performance.

One of the world's top banks has introduced a "moral moments" approach – asking product teams to record the most difficult ethical dilemmas they faced during a launch and how they handled them. This encourages reflection and collective responsibility.

Culture as a Conduit

Ethical conduct derives from culture, not from compliance. In high-performing institutions, culture is not something on a poster on the wall – it is the way that individuals conduct themselves when they think that no one is looking. Infusing ethics into culture requires leaders to demonstrate ethical decision-making, particularly in high-pressure situations: Hiring and promotions should prize integrity as much as high performance; employees need to be comfortable to speak up, challenge groupthink, or voicing dilemmas; and examples of acts based on ethical principles need to be told, celebrated, and rewarded. A healthy culture treats ethics not as a cost, but as a strategic asset – a way to build trust, reduce risk, and attract long-term talent and customers.

Digital Conduct and Algorithmic Integrity

One of the most urgent frontiers of ethical conduct is algorithmic governance. Financial institutions increasingly rely on models to make credit decisions, detect fraud, personalize offers, or even determine pricing. Ethical issues crop up if algorithms perpetuate old biases, customers do not know that they have been scored or profiled, results are disparate in arbitrary ways on the basis of race, gender, or geography, and there is no way to appeal AI decisions.

The response is to implement AI ethics charters, compulsory model audits, and explainability features through which human beings can question decisions. The FCA in the UK and the Consumer Financial Protection Bureau (CFPB) in the US have indicated that ethical AI is a regulatory priority, not a luxury. Institutions need to be able to prove that their digital systems are fair, accountable, and transparent.

Accountability throughout the Value Chain

Ethical behaviour is not only an internal issue. It has to reach out to vendors, partners, cloud providers, and fintech collaborators. In an open finance ecosystem, third-party misconduct can harm the bank's brand as much as third-party failings. This necessitates due diligence systems that encompass ethical standards, codes of conduct for partners with enforceable norms, periodic audits of outside algorithms and data habits, and co-owned models of shared responsibility in which trust is not outsourced but co-owned. The aim is to create ethical ecosystems, not merely ethical institutions.

Crisis, Misconduct, and the Cost of Inaction

Recent global scandals – from algorithmic discrimination to mis-selling to rogue trading – have illustrated that the price of ethical failure is not solely regulatory. It's existential, cultural, and reputational. In the age of digitalization, news travels faster, customers leave faster, and employees speak out more.

The strongest defence against ethical breakdown is active architecture: systems that highlight oddities early, dashboards monitoring ethical metrics, internal modelling of moral challenges and management that becomes active ahead of the regulators' knock on the door. During times of crisis, stakeholders do not only hold institutions accountable for what went wrong, but also for how they reacted. This is where apologies, transparency, redress, and structural change play a vital role

Ethical Brand, Sustainable Trust

Ultimately, ethical behaviour defines the bank's character. The products of an ethical bank enhance lives without taking advantage; profits are chased with integrity; technology serves to enable, not deceive; employees are proud of what they create; and customers feel understood, respected, and safeguarded. This isn't about being perfect. It's about being principled, responsible, and human. As retail banks compete in a busy, digital-first world, ethics is a brand differentiator. It is the reason why customers remain loyal, why regulators grant the benefit of the doubt, and why top talent wishes to come aboard.

Conclusion: Making Ethics the Default

Ethical behaviour and responsibility cannot be reactive, defensive, or occasional. They need to be in the default mode – integrated in every line of code, every policy, and every leadership decision. Embedding ethics into systems, culture, and strategy enables banks to be institutions that not only do things correctly, but also do the right thing – even when it's difficult, even when nobody is looking.

7 ESG and the Institutional Conscience

Environmental, Social, and Governance (ESG) is no longer a peripheral consideration for retail banks – it is becoming the defining lens through which trust, relevance, and long-term value are assessed. ESG is not a marketing strategy or a disclosure checklist. It is, at its heart, a reflection of a bank's institutional conscience – how it shows up in society, how it impacts the world, and how it governs itself with integrity. For decades, banks measured success in financial terms – return on equity, shareholder value, and growth of assets. ESG shifts that calculus. It asks harder questions: What kind of value are we creating? For whom? At what cost? And with what legacy?

From Compliance to Commitment

The rise of ESG in banking started as a response to investor pressure and regulatory requirements. Banks were asked to publish carbon disclosures, gender pay gaps, board diversity metrics, and responsible lending policies. But the future belongs to banks that go beyond compliance – which treat ESG not as a burden, but as an opportunity to lead.

This shift includes proactive climate action, such as divesting from high-carbon assets or financing green transitions; inclusive finance strategies aimed at underserved groups and vulnerable populations; workplace equity with transparent pathways for advancement, pay parity, and psychological safety; and robust governance models where ethics, risk, and strategy are integrated – not siloed. Institutions with strong ESG commitments are beginning to outperform peers – not just in reputation, but in resilience, adaptability, and talent retention.

The E in ESG: Climate, Capital, and the Planet

Environmental responsibility is a direct expression of trust. Banks that finance destruction – whether knowingly or by omission – risk their social license to operate. The leading edge of environmental finance now includes sustainability-linked loans, where interest rates adjust based on climate performance; green mortgages that incentivize energy-efficient homes; carbon accounting for portfolios, with transparent scope 3 emissions tracking; and nature-positive investing, which supports biodiversity, conservation, and regenerative agriculture.

Global examples include major European and US banks setting net-zero targets, exiting coal financing, or committing billions to clean energy ecosystems. But ambition alone is not enough. The real challenge lies in the execution, accountability, and systemic coordination of these strategies.

The S in ESG: Social Justice and Financial Inclusion

Social equity in banking is about more than charity or PR. It is about recognizing that finance has always shaped the distribution of opportunity – and that history holds many examples of exclusion, redlining, and predatory lending. Modern retail banks must reimagine social responsibility through equitable credit models designed to remove bias and improve access; language and accessibility tools so digital banking works for the elderly, disabled, and neurodiverse; community reinvestment strategies, especially in low-income or historically marginalized regions; and crisis response frameworks offering relief during pandemics, disasters, or economic shocks.

In the UK, this aligns with FCA priorities around consumer duty and vulnerable customers. In the US, the Community Reinvestment Act (CRA) is undergoing reforms to hold banks accountable for their social impact. ESG, in this light, is about using the infrastructure of finance to serve the common good.

The G in ESG: Governance and the Heart of Trust

Governance is where trust becomes tangible. It shapes decision-making, allocates power, sets norms, and defines accountability. Weak governance creates blind spots – where ethical breaches, systemic risks, or cultural failures take root. Strong ESG governance includes diverse, independent boards capable of asking hard questions; integrated ESG oversight, not just annual reporting; remuneration policies aligned to long-term, sustainable outcomes; and scenario planning, including for climate, cyber, and geopolitical risks. In leading global banks, ESG is no longer relegated to a single team. It is embedded across risk, strategy, product design, HR, and operations. It is how the entire institution governs itself in an increasingly uncertain world.

Metrics, Transparency, and Accountability

One of the persistent challenges in ESG is measurement. What gets reported often shapes what gets prioritized. But not all impact is measurable in numbers. Nonetheless, banks must publish clear ESG scorecards, ideally with third-party assurance; disclose climate risk exposures and stress testing outcomes; monitor customer impact, especially for inclusion and ethical product design; and track internal equity metrics, including retention, representation, and well-being.

Emerging standards from the International Sustainability Standards Board (ISSB) and the Task Force on Climate-Related Financial Disclosures (TCFD) are helping banks align global reporting. Transparency is not about perfection. It is about honesty, progress, and a willingness to be held accountable.

The Human Face of ESG

Behind every ESG metric is a human story – a family securing their first home, a small business surviving a crisis, a community protected from displacement, a planet kept habitable for the next generation. Banks must reconnect with this human purpose. ESG is not a compliance burden – it is an invitation to serve differently.

Some examples include a UK challenger bank offering financial coaching to first-time savers; a US regional bank designing products specifically for black-owned businesses; and an Indian digital bank partnering with women's cooperatives to extend credit in rural areas. These are not just CSR projects. They are business strategies grounded in values – and they are changing what trust means.

Future Vision: ESG as the Default Operating System

Looking ahead, ESG will not be an add-on. It will be the default operating system for banks that want to survive and lead. This will require new leadership mindsets, investment in data, talent, and systems, partnerships with regulators, civil society, and customers, and a willingness to confront uncomfortable truths. Most importantly, it will require courage – the courage to go first, go deeper, and go together. Banks must decide: Are we merely ESG-compliant? Or are we ESG-committed? The difference is visible. And it will define which institutions earn trust in the century ahead.

8 Cross-Border Risk and Global Standards

In an age of instantaneous global flows – of capital, data, people, and ideas – retail banking is no longer a national business. It is inherently cross-border. Trust in one jurisdiction can be compromised by events in another. A cyber attack in Asia can trigger fear in Europe. A regulatory scandal in the US can impact investor confidence in Africa. The architecture of trust, therefore, must be designed to withstand cross-border risk and align with international standards. This section looks at how modern banks need to change from disconnected operations tied to specific areas to systems of governance, compliance, and assurance that are globally consistent and locally responsive.

The Nature of Cross-Border Risk

Cross-border risk in retail banking arises from several intersecting domains:

- Regulatory divergence: Different countries impose different expectations, from data privacy (e.g. GDPR in the EU) to capital adequacy (e.g. Basel III in Switzerland) to consumer protection (e.g. CFPB in the US). Banks operating in multiple geographies must navigate this complexity without sacrificing consistency or efficiency.
- Operational dependency: Outsourced IT functions, cloud infrastructure, and shared service centres often span continents. A failure in one region can cause cascading service outages across others.
- Cybersecurity threats: Global financial systems are prime targets for coordinated cyber attacks, ransom ware, and fraud networks. These are rarely confined to one geography.

- Political and economic shocks: Currency instability, sanctions, trade disputes, and policy shifts can upend previously stable banking operations.
- Reputation and trust contagion: In the digital age, trust is not geographically bounded. A scandal in one market can undermine customer confidence globally.

To build resilience, banks must embed global thinking into local operations.

Regulatory Harmonization and Its Gaps

Efforts to harmonize global financial standards have made progress, but inconsistencies persist. Some frameworks include the Basel Accords (I, II, III, and evolving IV), designed to strengthen capital and liquidity frameworks; FATF, a global standard for anti-money laundering (AML) and counter-terrorism financing; IFRS, international accounting standards slowly converging across jurisdictions; the OECD Common Reporting Standard (CRS), promoting transparency and tax cooperation; and TCFD and ISSB, for sustainability-related disclosures.

Despite these frameworks, application varies by region. For instance, the US has not fully adopted Basel III in the same way as the EU; India's data localization laws differ from UK/EU norms; and emerging economies may lack the capacity to implement or monitor compliance. Banks must build internal systems that are agile and capable of adapting to a mosaic of rules without fragmenting their own operations.

Data Sovereignty and Privacy

One of the most contested cross-border issues is data. As banking becomes digital-first, customer data travels across borders – but regulations don't. Examples include GDPR in the EU, which enforces rigorous consent and data protection standards; India's Digital Personal Data Protection Act, with localization and processing controls; and US state laws such as CCPA. Banks must map their data flows to understand where customer data resides and how it moves, maintain consent registries especially when using third-party services or AI, build sovereign architecture capable of storing and processing data within required jurisdictions, and invest in encryption, access controls, and audit trails. Trust in the digital economy begins with the question: Who owns my data – and how is it protected?

Managing Multi-Jurisdictional Compliance

Global banks increasingly face multi-jurisdictional audits, regulatory investigations, and enforcement actions. Managing these requires centralized compliance intelligence to track global developments in real time; local compliance ownership so regional teams are accountable and informed; integrated risk dashboards showing exposures by geography, product, and regulation; and cross-border coordination teams, especially for legal, audit, and risk functions. Digital RegTech platforms are helping to automate compliance tasks – from screening to monitoring to reporting – but human oversight remains critical, especially in grey areas.

Risk Aggregation and Enterprise Visibility

Siloed risk functions are a liability in global banking. Forward-thinking institutions are investing in enterprise risk architectures that provide unified views of market, credit, cyber, operational, and ESG risks; scenario planning across geopolitical, climate, and systemic dimensions; real-time alerts and controls, especially for conduct risk; and board-level reporting tools that synthesize complexity into action. Cross-border resilience is not about avoiding risk – it about having a clear understanding of your risk and responding decisively.

Shared Infrastructure and International Collaboration

To manage global risk, banks must also embrace shared infrastructure and collaborative oversight: SWIFT and ISO 20022 have created a shared language for cross-border payments; public-private partnerships support global Cybersecurity threat intelligence; supervisory colleges and cross-border resolution planning now feature in G-SIB (Globally Systemically Important Banks) regulations; and AI ethics and digital identity governance will be likely to require multilateral treaties in the future. This is particularly urgent as open banking and embedded finance grow – bringing new, unregulated actors into the global financial flow.

Ethical Imperatives in Global Governance

Trust in a global context is not only about risk mitigation – it is also about moral clarity. The questions banks must ask themselves include whether they are enabling extractive practices in emerging markets, arbitraging regulations in order to lower ethical standards, and supporting regimes or entities that violate human rights. Global banks must build ethical filters into their investment, lending, and onboarding processes.

Case Study: Reputation Travels Faster than Regulation –A Global Response to Fraud

In 2023, a coordinated fraud ring operating across Nigeria, the UAE, and the UK exploited weaknesses in digital KYC systems. The network could only be dismantled through the cooperation of several countries – including data sharing between regulators and banks.

This incident revealed three truths:

1. Cross-border threats require cross-border trust.
2. Systems are only as strong as the weakest link.
3. Customer confidence depends on proactive institutional coordination.

Vision Ahead: Trust in a Fragmented World

As geopolitical tensions rise, digital sovereignty grows, and protectionism resurfaces, the risk of financial fragmentation increases. However, trust does not thrive in isolation, but in openness with integrity. The future of banking lies in:

- Interoperable, ethical, and adaptive systems
- Smart regulation that balances innovation with protection
- Global collaboration, local accountability

The most trusted institutions in the future will not be the biggest or fastest – they will be the most coherent, resilient, and globally responsible.

9 Restoring Confidence After a Crisis

Crises are defining moments. They can fracture institutions – or strengthen them. For retail banks, restoring trust after a crisis is not merely about repairing a balance sheet or issuing public apologies. It is about rebuilding psychological and emotional contracts with customers, communities, regulators, and employees. It is about demonstrating, through action, that lessons have been learned, systems have evolved, and values have endured. In this section, we look at how banks around the world have dealt with trust breakdowns. We also discuss what it really takes to come out of a crisis stronger than before.

Understanding the Anatomy of a Trust Crisis

Trust collapses rarely occur overnight. They are typically the outcome of prolonged neglect, poor governance, systemic blind spots, or cultural erosion. But when the moment arrives, it is swift and severe – triggering customer flight, media scrutiny, regulatory probes, and employee demoralization.

Some common triggers include data breaches that expose personal or financial information; mis-selling scandals that betray customer interests; liquidity failures that threaten depositor security; leadership misconduct or ethical lapses at the top; algorithmic bias in credit, insurance, or fraud detection systems; and customer service breakdowns during high-stress events such as pandemic support or disaster relief. These events do not just affect numbers. They erode emotional equity – the belief that a bank is reliable, responsible, and on your side.

The First 72 Hours: Leadership in the Eye of the Storm

In any trust crisis, the first 72 hours are critical. This is when institutions define their posture – not only externally but also internally. Effective recovery begins with:

1. Radical transparency: Acknowledge the issue honestly. Avoid spin.
2. Visible leadership: CEOs and board members must be present and accountable.
3. Customer-centricity: Put affected individuals at the centre of all responses.
4. Speed and clarity: Act quickly, communicate clearly, and avoid jargon.
5. Listening and empathy: Understand not just what happened, but how it felt to those impacted.

Examples from recent history – such as TSB's IT migration crisis in the UK or Wells Fargo's account fraud scandal in the US – illustrate how poor early response can compound the damage, while authentic engagement can soften its impact.

Institutional Memory and Learning Loops

One of the most overlooked elements of trust restoration is institutional memory. After a crisis, many banks focus on external repair – regulatory settlements, rebranding, or new compliance policies. But unless lessons are internalized and operationalized, the same patterns may be repeated.

Key strategies include root cause analysis, going beyond symptoms to understand cultural or structural contributors; open forums and retrospectives, allowing employees and customers to share candid feedback; embedded feedback loops, integrating lessons into training, system design, and policy updates; and independent oversight, bringing in third-party evaluators to hold up a mirror to internal practices. Banks that genuinely evolve after a crisis often do so because they embrace discomfort and codify wisdom.

From Apology to Action: Rebuilding from Within

A public apology, however heartfelt, is not enough. Customers want evidence. Regulators want reform. Employees want hope. Action is the only currency that counts. Trust restoration must include policy overhauls that simplify terms, tighten controls, and improve fairness; tech remediation by fixing flawed systems, improving uptime, and bolstering cybersecurity; governance reforms to strengthen board oversight, risk committees, and audit trails; cultural resets that re-anchor the institution to its founding purpose and values; and restitution and redress by compensating those affected quickly and respectfully.

When ING faced money laundering investigations, it overhauled its internal AML frameworks and launched one of the most comprehensive compliance training programs in Europe. When Equifax experienced a massive data breach, it appointed a new CISO and restructured its cybersecurity function. The real test of sincerity is not the apology – it is the architecture that is introduced after the event.

Reputation Recovery and Brand Healing

Trust and brand are intertwined. Once lost, brand equity takes years – sometimes decades – to rebuild. But it is possible, with consistency and authenticity. A few examples of successful recovery efforts:

- Rebuilding from the inside out starts with employee trust and morale.
- Community investment supports local causes and restores social license to operate.
- Media re-engagement opens dialogue with journalists and thought leaders.
- Customer co-design involves users in the redesign of services or platforms.
- Transparent storytelling shares progress updates, setbacks, and wins.

The UK's Co-operative Bank, historically known for its ethical positioning and customer-owned roots, offers a notable example. It has now been acquired by Coventry Building Society, which will restore its mutual structure and use its ethical positioning and customer ownership model to recover from a major financial restructuring. It reframed trust not as perfection, but as transparency and values-led decision-making.

The Role of Regulators and External Oversight

Regulators play a critical dual role in trust recovery by enforcing accountability through fines, public censure, or operational restrictions, and by providing guidance to support remediation and rebuilding efforts through structured improvement plans. Forward-looking banks treat regulatory engagement not as a burden but as a strategic partnership. They view enforcement actions as signals for transformation, not mere compliance. Some even go further – inviting citizen panels, ethics boards, or digital rights advocates to co-create the next version of the institution.

Culture as the Core Determinant

Ultimately, trust restoration is not a technical challenge – it is a cultural one. If internal behaviours, norms, incentives, and power structures remain unchanged, all remediation is cosmetic. Banks must ask who gets promoted and why, what behaviours are tolerated, how customers are spoken about internally, and whether mistakes are used as learning opportunities or scapegoats. Culture is the soil from which both crisis and confidence grow. Restore the soil, and the institution can regenerate.

From Crisis to Confidence: A Future Vision

Every institution will face a crisis at some point. The difference between those that fade and those that rise lies in their response architecture. The banks of the future must build crisis playbooks embedded with empathy and agility, ethical risk sensors that detect early signals of erosion, continuous culture audits – not just compliance checks – and leadership training for resilience, humility, and moral courage. A crisis need not define a bank forever. But how a bank responds to a crisis always reveals what it truly stands for.

10 Building Institutions People Believe in

In the end, trust is not granted – it is earned, lived, and renewed. For banks, trust is not a logo, a PR campaign, or a quarterly metric. It is a relationship, a covenant, and often a legacy. As the financial system becomes increasingly digital, distributed, and data-driven, the human need for trust only grows stronger. This final section explores what it takes to build institutions that people believe in – not just during stable times, but through uncertainty, disruption, and transformation.

The Three Pillars of Belief

When people say they "believe" in an institution, they often mean one or more of the following:

1 Competence – "I believe they know what they are doing."
2 Character – "I believe they are guided by the right values."
3 Consistency – "I believe they will act the same way tomorrow as they do today."

These pillars do not come from mission statements alone. They are earned through a thousand small interactions, reinforced over time. They are destroyed by a single betrayal. And they are rebuilt through humility, accountability, and coherence.

Competence in a World of Complexity

Today's financial institutions are navigating extraordinary complexity: cyber risks, regulatory shifts, embedded finance, AI, geopolitical tensions, and generational change. In this landscape, competence is not a static skillset – it is the ability to keep learning. Trusted institutions invest heavily in technical and human capital, treat cybersecurity and risk resilience as essential to reputation, build cross-functional teams that blend compliance, technology, and customer insight, and create systems that adapt and evolve as complexity rises. Competence also means not to overpromise. Simplicity, clarity, and transparency are seen as competence in action.

Character in a Time of Public Scrutiny

Institutional character is forged in how decisions are made – especially when no one is watching. In the digital age, very little remains hidden. Character becomes visible in how a bank treats vulnerable customers, how it responds to social injustice or climate breakdown, whether it includes marginalized voices in innovation, and whether it can say "we were wrong" and course-correct.

Trustworthy institutions demonstrate moral clarity without being performative. They choose integrity over expedience, even when the cost is real. Their values guide behaviour, not just branding. As ESG scrutiny rises globally, character is becoming a board-level imperative, not just a CSR checkbox.

Consistency in a Fractured World

In a world of algorithmic bias, unpredictable markets, and polarized societies, people crave predictability. Consistency does not mean being rigid. It means being anchored – having principles that endure, even as strategies evolve:

- Consistency in customer experience builds emotional loyalty.
- Consistency in governance and audit reinforces credibility with regulators.
- Consistency in employee culture attracts and retains talent.
- Consistency in social impact grants a long-term societal license to operate.

The most trusted banks are those whose actions today feel aligned with their behaviour the previous year – and with the promises they made a decade ago.

Institutional Design for Trust

Trust is not just about people – it is about systems. Institutions must embed trust into the design of their technology stacks with explainability, control, and fairness; data governance with privacy, ethics, and portability; onboarding and identity flows with dignity and inclusion; customer support with empathy and empowerment; and risk frameworks with real-time intelligence and public accountability. Designing for trust means designing for the user's best interest, even when that interest contradicts short-term revenue. This is not altruism. It is strategy.

Leadership that Embodies Trust

Ultimately, trust is personal. Customers do not trust "a bank" – they trust the people who represent it, lead it, and serve through it. Banks that thrive in trust do so because:

- Their leaders listen more than they speak.
- Their boardrooms reflect the diversity of those they serve.
- Their ethics officers have real power, not symbolic roles.
- Their senior executives show up in crises – not just to defend, but to reform.

When trust is encouraged from the top, it flows throughout the organization. When it is outsourced to compliance or marketing, it dies quietly.

A Global Mandate

Trust is not a Western concept or a luxury of stable markets. It is a global imperative – especially in emerging economies where access to finance is deeply tied to dignity, aspiration, and survival. From digital identity platforms in India, to agent banking networks in Kenya, to inclusive credit scoring in Brazil, trust is being redefined through technology, participation, and proximity. Banks that build global trust do so by being locally embedded, yet globally compliant. They are digitally advanced, yet emotionally human, and financially strong, yet socially conscious.

Becoming a Legacy Institution

The final test of trust is time. Some banks aspire to be profitable. Others aim to be large. But a few seek to be trusted across generations. These are the institutions that transcend transactional relationships and become pillars of their communities and markets. They endure by embedding their values deeply, nurturing their people, and committing to social impact beyond mere profits. They earn respect not just through their size or success, but through their integrity, empathy, and long-term stewardship. To be a legacy institution is to be trusted by someone's grandparent, parent, and child. It is not only an achievement. It is a responsibility.

Final Reflection

In the architecture of trust, no detail is too small, and no decision is without consequence. Trust is not an outcome – it is the essence of banking itself. The banks of tomorrow will not be those that promise the most – but those that deliver the most consistently, listen the most deeply, and serve the most inclusively. They will be the ones people believe in.

Strategic Framework Box: Chapter 8. Designing for Belief: Trust as the Operating System of Modern Finance

Key Insight

In the digital age, trust is not a by-product – it is the product. Every financial interaction, digital signature, data flow, and automated decision is underpinned by a silent question: Can I trust this institution to act in my interest? Building trust today requires embedding it into every layer of the financial experience – not just declaring it.

Strategic Takeaway

Trust is no longer a reputational asset – it is a systems asset. Institutions that design for trust will not only comply more effectively; they will also lead more credibly.

Trust Dimension	*Traditional Trust Architecture*	*Future Trust Architecture*
Verification	KYC documents, episodic identity checks	Real-time digital identity, biometrics
Compliance Model	Audit - driven, after - the - fact	Compliance - by - design, embedded logic
Security Posture	Firewalls, passwords, static defences	End - to - end encryption, zero - trust architecture
Data Handling	Siloed, opaque, bank - owned	Consent - led, transparent, user - governed
Crisis Response	Institutional PR, delayed disclosures	Immediate action, open communication
Trust Signals	Brand reputation, physical presence	Behavioral consistency, ecosystem integrity

This chapter positions trust not as a sentiment but as an architecture – one that must be engineered across product design, regulatory systems, customer journeys, and ethical governance. It is not what institutions say, but how they behave when no one is watching.

Bibliography

Bank for International Settlements (2021). *Big tech in finance: opportunities and risks. BIS Annual Economic Report.*

9 The Promise of Inclusion

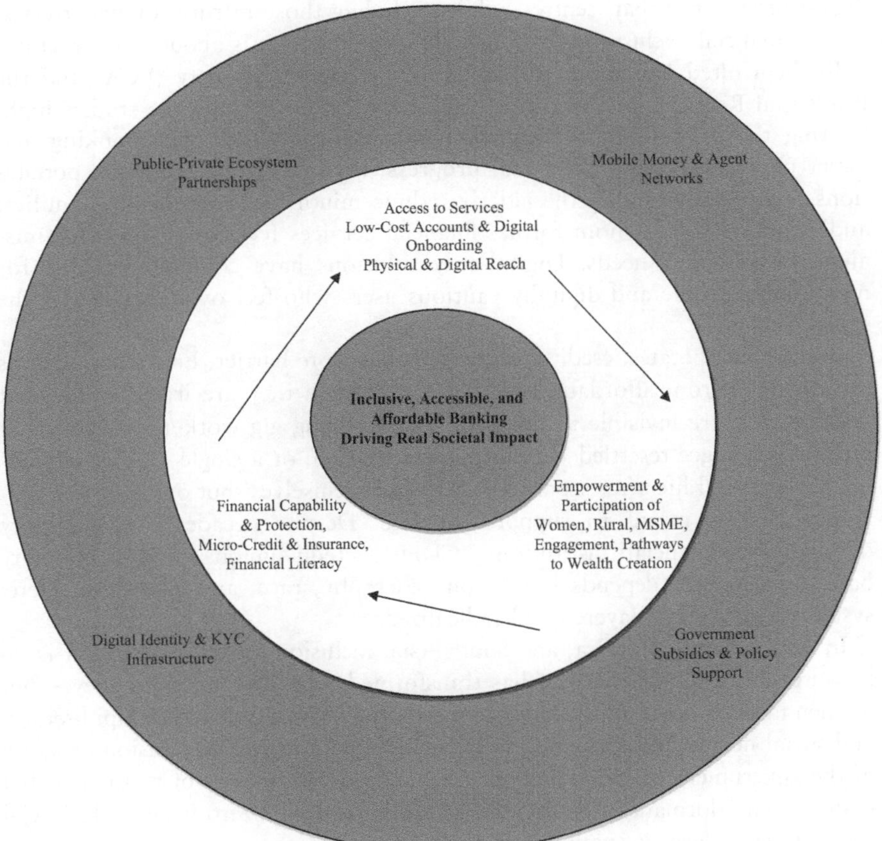

Figure 9.1 Financial inclusion is achieved through access, capability, and empowerment -enabled by technology, partnerships, and supportive policy.

DOI: 10.4324/9781003737544-9

1 Who Gets Left Behind

Inclusion in financial systems is often spoken of in terms of expansion – more customers, more access, and more technology. But before we rush to inclusion as an outcome, we must first sit with a more difficult truth: there are people, communities, and institutions systematically left behind. And in many cases, the very advances in finance that promise access and progress have unintentionally widened the gap.

Globally, more than 1.4 billion adults remain unbanked, according to the World Bank's Global Findex. But this number, as striking as it is, tells only a part of the story. Financial exclusion is not always total; it is often partial, conditional, or fragile. It takes the form of dormant accounts, products that do not serve real needs, predatory terms disguised as access, or services built for digital natives in urban centres, while excluding those in rural or underserved areas. Financial exclusion is as much about design as it is about infrastructure.

In the United Kingdom, the Financial Conduct Authority (FCA) and the Prudential Regulation Authority (PRA) have published multiple studies highlighting the persistence of financial vulnerability. While open banking and faster payment systems offer real progress, there are still significant populations – especially among the elderly, ethnic minorities, low-income families, and migrants – for whom formal financial services feel out of reach or misaligned with their needs. Digital-only solutions have compounded this for many older people and digitally cautious users who feel overwhelmed by the speed of change.

In the United States, credit scoring remains a core barrier. Entire populations are excluded from affordable credit – not because they are irresponsible, but because they are invisible to the data sets. A young gig worker with irregular income, a refugee resettled without documentation, or a single mother rebuilding her financial life after separation may find themselves shut out from the very system that is meant to support progress. Despite decades of community development financial institutions (CDFIs), credit unions, and community banks, access still depends largely on geography, race, and education. Here, systemic exclusion is layered and radicalized.

In Africa, Latin America, and South Asia, inclusion looks different but is no less urgent. In Kenya, M-Pesa has transformed access to mobile money – but women in rural areas still face usage gaps, driven by device ownership, literacy, and social norms. In India, the Jan Dhan Yojana, a financial inclusion program of the government of India, has opened hundreds of millions of accounts – but many remain dormant, used only sporadically or with a zero balance. Financial access in such cases is symbolic, not functional.

The core question is not just: Who has access? but: Who can meaningfully use the system with agency and dignity? That question changes everything. It shifts inclusion from a numeric metric to a lived experience. It asks us to listen not just to the people in the system but to those at the margins and to redesign the system based on their needs.

Inclusion failures also exist at the institutional level. Micro-enterprises and cooperatives are often underserved, especially in developed countries where mainstream banks find them too small to justify personalized risk models. The UK's credit union movement, while gaining traction, still remains under-leveraged in policy circles. National associations such as the Association of British Credit Unions Limited (ABCUL) have a critical role to play in shaping an ecosystem where cooperative finance can flourish – not as a legacy of the past but as a lever for the future. Similarly, the Bank of England and the FCA's collaborative frameworks on financial resilience and vulnerable customer strategies must now expand to meaningfully include such community-rooted institutions.

There is also the issue of people who self-exclude – those who choose not to engage with financial systems out of distrust, past trauma, or perceived irrelevance. For many refugees, formerly incarcerated individuals, informal workers, and low-income pensioners, the cost of engaging with formal systems outweighs the benefit. Here, inclusion is not a product to be marketed – it is a relationship to be built.

One of the biggest worries about exclusion today is algorithmic bias. With the rise of AI-driven underwriting, automated credit decisions, and robo-advisory services, we face a new generation of invisible barriers. Algorithms trained on historical data can replicate past injustices, denying loans to women, minorities, or applicants from certain postcodes without any overt discrimination. The systems are neutral only in appearance.

Furthermore, digital identity systems – often hailed as a gateway to inclusion – can exclude those without stable documentation or who live in grey zones of legal status. Biometric systems have been deployed with mixed results. In some countries, they have enabled access; in others, they have locked out the most vulnerable when fingerprint scans fail or names are misspelled in registration databases. Technology without human-centred design and fail-safes can amplify exclusion instead of resolving it.

Inclusion also intersects with education. Financial literacy is not a luxury – it is a prerequisite for inclusion. If people are onboarded into systems they do not understand, they are exposed to risks they cannot assess. Digital onboarding must be paired with meaningful, contextual education. And this must not be outsourced to marketing campaigns; it must be built into the user journey.

To answer the question: Who gets left behind? is to uncover a blueprint for reform. It means moving away from abstract statements about "underserved communities" and toward precise, actionable design choices: How do we build systems that serve someone who earns irregular cash income? Who doesn't speak English? Who has no fixed address? Who distrusts government but uses WhatsApp? Who lives rurally, or moves frequently, or earns less than £20 a day?

The answers require more than a fintech app or a CSR (corporate social responsibility) program. They require systemic rethinking of how products are priced, how credit is scored, how risk is assessed, and how dignity is preserved. They also require leadership. Boards and policymakers must stop treating inclusion as a compliance line and instead elevate it to a strategic imperative.

This section opens Chapter 9 with an unapologetic truth: Financial systems still leave too many behind. And while we have developed a language to talk about inclusion, the real test lies in design, delivery, and accountability. The rest of this chapter will build upon this foundation – showcasing strategies, ecosystems, and interventions that are shifting this narrative. But first, we must be honest about the magnitude of the gap. Inclusion, if it is to mean anything, must start with the recognition of who is missing, and why.

2 The Economics of Exclusion

Financial exclusion is not merely a social failure – it is a structural economic inefficiency. It distorts markets, entrenches inequality, and limits the productive potential of entire populations. At a macro-level, exclusion stifles demand, weakens social mobility, and exacerbates fiscal strain on public systems. At a micro-level, it increases vulnerability, deters savings, and forces households into high-cost informal arrangements. Understanding the economics of exclusion is fundamental to designing inclusive systems – not just because inclusion is ethical, but because it is economically rational.

Start with a basic premise: When individuals and small enterprises are excluded from formal finance, their ability to contribute to economic growth is curtailed. In emerging markets, the absence of accessible credit and secure savings mechanisms means millions of small businesses operate below capacity. They lack working capital, cannot invest in equipment, and face constant liquidity stress. This has ripple effects: underemployment, lower productivity, and subdued household consumption. The IMF estimates that financial inclusion could lift GDP by several percentage points in low- and middle-income countries, provided that access translates to usage.

But exclusion is not just found in informal economies. In developed economies such as the UK and US, financial exclusion continues to shape poverty cycles. Households without access to affordable credit are forced into high-interest payday loans, rent-to-own arrangements, or unauthorized overdrafts – paying a poverty premium that erodes their long-term stability. A report by the University of Birmingham found that low-income households in the UK pay £490 more per year, on average, for basic goods and services, simply because of their exclusion from mainstream financial products.

The economic burden is disproportionately borne by certain demographics: women, migrants, ethnic minorities, and young adults. When women lack access to financial services, their ability to participate in the labour force, manage risk, and invest in their families is significantly hindered. The World Bank's Findex data shows a persistent gender gap in account ownership, credit access, and digital payments. Closing this gap is not just a matter of justice – it is a growth strategy. Goldman Sachs famously estimated that closing gender gaps in credit and capital could increase global GDP by trillions of dollars.

Exclusion also undermines monetary policy effectiveness. If large portions of the population operate outside the formal financial system, central banks' efforts by central banks to influence interest rates, inflation, or liquidity conditions have diluted effects. Informality limits tax collection, distorts data, and creates blind spots in economic planning. The Bank of England, through its Financial Stability Reports, has acknowledged that financial exclusion weakens systemic resilience by making household debt profiles more volatile and less visible.

In addition, the exclusion of micro-, small, and medium enterprises (MSMEs) limits employment creation and innovation. According to the OECD, MSMEs account for over 60% of employment in most economies – but globally, they face a financing gap of over $5 trillion. Banks find them too small to assess individually, and fintechs often lack the data to underwrite risk appropriately. As a result, economic dynamism is stifled, innovation is capped, productivity remains flat, and structural inequality deepens.

Exclusion has a cost for the state as well. Governments that fail to integrate populations into formal finance systems often face increased welfare burdens, greater housing insecurity, and diminished tax compliance. Conversely, digital financial inclusion can improve cash transfer programs, reduce leakage, and increase the efficiency of public spending. In India, the JAM trinity (Jan Dhan accounts, Aadhaar digital ID, and Mobile connectivity) has reportedly saved billions of dollars in subsidy delivery through direct benefit transfers. But these gains depend on digital readiness and trust – which are unevenly distributed.

Financial exclusion also creates a drag on resilience. In times of crisis – such as pandemics, climate shocks, or financial downturns – those outside the formal system lack the buffers to absorb impact. They cannot access emergency credit, do not benefit from insurance, and are last to receive government support. This was evident during COVID-19, when millions of informal workers, especially women and migrants, were left without support despite being among the hardest hit. Inclusion is therefore not just about equity – it is about systemic shock absorption.

Inclusion improves the efficiency of capital allocation. When more people are integrated into the system, savings increase, deposits accumulate, and capital can be deployed more productively. Pension funds, insurance pools, and lending institutions benefit from broader participation. Economies gain not just in scale, but in resilience and adaptability. The idea that financial inclusion is merely a development agenda is outdated – it is central to financial system design.

At the level of infrastructure, digital public goods – such as interoperable payments systems, digital identity frameworks, and open banking APIs – are transforming the cost structure of inclusion. It is now possible to reach remote customers without building branches, to offer tailored products without manual underwriting, and to deliver financial literacy through mobile-first content. But unless these systems are governed inclusively, they risk recreating the same exclusion through new channels.

It is important to note that exclusion is sometimes embedded in pricing models. Risk-based pricing often penalizes those with thin credit files, low income, or erratic employment – creating a feedback loop where the cost of access reinforces exclusion. Without policy intervention, data innovation, or product redesign, this loop continues. Banks, insurers, and regulators must work together to develop risk-sharing mechanisms, alternative data models, and cross-subsidization strategies that do not burden the poorest customers.

The economic case for inclusion also intersects with sustainability and ESG. Investors increasingly assess financial institutions based on their inclusion metrics. The United Nations Principles for Responsible Banking require banks to align their portfolios with societal goals – including access and equity. Impact investors seek measurable outcomes in inclusion, and regulators are beginning to tie prudential incentives to inclusion strategies. The PRA and FCA have both signalled support for innovation in this space.

Inclusion, then, is not an act of charity. It is a lever for productivity, stability, and systemic integrity. Exclusion is not a symptom – it is a structural failure with cascading economic consequences. The cost of exclusion is borne not only by the individual but by the entire economy. The dividends of inclusion – when done with integrity – are not only measurable but transformative.

As we continue with this chapter, the economics of inclusion will be further explored through examples of low-cost innovation, behavioural insights, and ecosystem coordination. But the point is clear: inclusion is not optional. It is essential for the economy.

3 Gender, Identity, and Financial Access

In the drive toward financial inclusion, we cannot just concentrate on access. We need to know who is being excluded – and why. Gender, identity, ethnicity, and social norms are still among the strongest drivers of financial access globally. They intersect with structural inequalities to define the way individuals encounter the financial system. Whether in rural villages or urban financial hubs, conscious or unconscious of gender – financial access is influenced by product design, policy choices, and user experiences. This section delves into the intersections of gender and identity in financial access, not as peripheral issues, but as central design dilemmas when constructing inclusive systems.

Globally, the gender gap in financial inclusion has been remarkably resilient. Women are still six percentage points behind men in having a bank account, according to the World Bank's 2021 Global Findex report. The disparity is much larger in developing economies. The reasons are not just cultural – they are structural. Women do not have the identification that is necessary to open an account, particularly in countries where the national ID systems are weak or patriarchal naming conventions are used. They could have limited access to mobile phones, less financial control over the household budget, and lower financial literacy. These limitations, being based on tradition and infrastructure, form a cycle of exclusion that sustains gender inequality.

In most economies, women's work is part of the informal economy and sometimes invisible. Household work, care giving, and subsistence production are often not paid, but they underpin a household's resilience. When financial systems fail to acknowledge these types of contribution, they overprice risk and misallocate services. For example, conventional credit scoring systems punish women who are not formally employed or don't hold any assets – even if they are the financial managers of their families. This leads to reduced access to loans, insurance, and pensions, even when women's repayment behaviour has been demonstrated to outperform men's in micro-finance environments.

Growth in digital finance has provided new avenues to bridge these divides – but it also brings new dangers. Digital wallets and mobile money accounts have enabled millions of women to gain access to financial services without male intermediaries. It has been demonstrated, for instance, that M-Pesa in Kenya boosts women's savings, decreases intense poverty, and enhances household decision-making. However, digital inclusion calls for more than digital literacy using mobile phones. What is also needed are trust and cultural changes. In certain communities, women's use of the phone is governed by gender roles, so they cannot avail themselves of even minimal services. Further, digital onboarding procedures that are based on biometrics or AI-driven verification can codify and deepen prevailing biases, unless properly monitored.

Aside from gender, identity characteristics such as ethnicity, immigration status, and caste also have the potential to strongly influence access to finance. In the UK, for instance, research by the FCA has identified differences in the approval rates for credit and interest charges between ethnic groups. Black and minority ethnic applicants are disproportionately denied loans or charged higher interest rates even after accounting for income and employment. This is a reflection of more general trends of discrimination and imbalanced data representation within credit models. In the United States, too, the heritage of redlining and discriminatory lending continues to inform neighbourhood-level imbalances in financial opportunity.

For refugees, migrants, and stateless people, finance access is frequently restricted by the law. Without recognized IDs, evidence of address, or employment history, many cannot have an account, send money, or borrow. Fintechs have started to introduce creative solutions – leveraging alternative data, facial recognition, or blockchain identity systems – but these methods are patchy and usually hampered by regulatory ambiguity. Pilot programs with decentralized identity have started in the EU to establish channels for migrants to get access to financial services across borders, but large-scale models require coordinated policy intervention.

In marginalized and indigenous communities, the challenge tends to be one of trust. Historically excluded or exploited financial institutions carry a profound deficit of legitimacy. Inclusion here takes more than digital access but necessitates cultural humility, multilingual interfaces, and community-led design. In Australia, for example, First Nations groups have started to create their own financial instruments, rooted in cultural values and local governance structures. This bottom-up model is increasingly seen as a template for ethical inclusion.

Sexual orientation and gender identity further complicate exclusion. LGBTQ + people, and especially trans and non-binary individuals, are frequently subjected to harassment, misgendering, or outright exclusion when accessing banks and insurers. Mismatches between identity on documents and identity in life can activate intrusive examination in highly conservative regulatory systems. Financial inclusion in this case would mean facilitating identity flexibility, sensitizing frontline personnel, and designing processes that ensure equal treatment. Fintechs are starting to bridge this gap – through inclusive onboarding forms, recognition of pronouns, and community outreach – but systemic uptake is limited.

Policies and regulations play an essential role in bridging identity – related gaps. The Financial Action Task Force (FATF) and domestic regulators such as the FCA and PRA have published guidance promoting risk-based methods allowing for tiered KYC (Know Your Customer) obligations. This gives more flexibility when onboarding low-risk customers while not compromising on compliance. Yet in practice, institutions continue to apply blanket policies excluding those without formal documents. Policymakers have to commit to making inclusion a compliance strategy, not merely a social one.

Designing for a wide variety of customers with different identities involves embracing pluralism. Banks, fintechs, and regulators need to shift away from one-size-fits-all solutions and acknowledge the heterogeneity of financial lives. Research looking at users needs to feature women, migrants, LGBTQ+ individuals, and older people – not as edge cases, but as central constituencies. Product teams need to challenge assumptions about what is "normal" behaviour, and reframe measures of risk, value, and loyalty through inclusive prisms.

Financial literacy initiatives need to follow suit. Blanket workshops or one-size-fits-all apps tend to fall flat. Instead, collaboration with local NGOs, women's cooperatives, migrant rights organizations, and religious organizations can assist in the development of customized content. In the UK, Toynbee Hall and Fair4All Finance have spearheaded innovative work in community-based financial education that addresses identity alongside income.

Finally, inclusion is a social matter. Individuals interact with financial systems not only as rational agents, but as human beings. If a woman is rejected by a bank, or a migrant is overcharged, the message delivered is not merely economic – it is ontological: "You do not belong here." The work of inclusion is to turn that message around. To declare, in design, words, policy, and action: "You are seen.. You matter. This system was created with you in mind."

This part has explored the confluence of identity and gender with access to finance. In the next subchapter, we will examine the infrastructures that can make inclusion at scale possible – particularly for those who have long been excluded. From mobile money to civic registries, we'll consider how digital infrastructure can become the spine of inclusion when implemented with care, governance, and trust.

4 Digital Infrastructure for the Underserved

The conversation about financial inclusion often starts with access. However, access is only as good as the infrastructure that supports it. For underserved communities, infrastructure is not just wires, signals, or servers; it is the invisible scaffolding of possibility. Without identity systems, interoperable platforms, affordable connectivity, or trust-enhancing governance, inclusion becomes fragile and episodic. This section explores how digital infrastructure – when designed for equity – can serve as a platform for empowerment, resilience, and dignity.

At the core of digital financial inclusion lies a fundamental truth: people cannot enter what they cannot reach. For billions globally, particularly in rural and remote regions, connectivity remains elusive. According to the 2023 Mobile Connectivity Index by GSMA, a non-profit organization representing mobile network operators worldwide, over 3 billion people live in areas with mobile broadband coverage but remain offline due to affordability, literacy, or device barriers. Among these, women, older adults, persons with disabilities, and displaced populations are disproportionately represented. Solving this access paradox requires a shift in mindset – from coverage to usability, from availability to meaningful inclusion.

Governments have begun to recognize digital infrastructure as a public good. National programs in countries such as India (Digital India initiative), Brazil, and Ghana have demonstrated that state-led digital investment – when inclusive by design – can trigger dramatic shifts in access. India's Aadhaar biometric ID system, linked to bank accounts through the Jan Dhan Yojana scheme, brought over 450 million people into the formal financial system within a decade. While critics have rightly raised concerns around privacy and consent, the architecture itself created a national stack for identity, payments, and authentication that lowered transaction costs and enabled targeted benefits.

But infrastructure is not just about the state. The private sector, especially mobile network operators (MNOs), plays a pivotal role in enabling or constraining access. In much of Sub-Saharan Africa, mobile money platforms such as M-Pesa (Kenya), MTN MoMo (Ghana), and EcoCash (Zimbabwe) operate independently of traditional banks, reaching customers at the base of the pyramid. These platforms depend on agent networks – a human infrastructure which provides cash-in/cash-out nodes, educators, and trust anchors. Ensuring fair agent compensation, liquidity support, and regulatory clarity is essential to maintaining the viability of this last-mile infrastructure.

Interoperability is another cornerstone of inclusive infrastructure. Siloed systems limit scale and exclude users from ecosystems. The success of India's Unified Payments Interface (UPI), Rwanda's push for interoperable mobile money, and the European Union's digital wallet initiative all point to the power of shared standards. When platforms speak the same language, users can move funds, verify identities, and build credit across providers – without being locked into monopolistic networks.

Digital ID is perhaps the single most important infrastructure layer for financial inclusion. Without verifiable identity, individuals cannot open bank accounts, receive social transfers, or build a credit history. Yet nearly one billion people globally lack any form of official ID, with women and displaced populations at highest risk. Emerging solutions – including self-sovereign identity (SSI), blockchain-based credentials, and tiered KYC frameworks – offer promising alternatives. In Estonia, citizens can digitally sign documents, access e-health services, and open accounts using a national e-ID. In Sierra Leone, a blockchain pilot for digital ID verification has enabled rural populations to access insurance for the first time.

Cybersecurity and data protection are vital enablers of trust in digital systems. For underserved users – many of who are engaging with formal finance for the first time – data misuse or breaches can be catastrophic. Regulators such as the UK's Information Commissioner's Office (ICO), and global frameworks such as the EU's GDPR offer templates for responsible data governance. However, in many emerging markets, protection remains weak or unenforced. Infrastructure must be designed not only for access but for safety, empowering users to control how their data is collected, shared, and stored.

Digital literacy is also a part of the infrastructure. A smartphone in hand is meaningless without the skills and confidence to navigate apps, evaluate risks, and troubleshoot errors. Programs that embed digital skills into community centres, schools, cooperatives, and health clinics are proving most effective. In Bangladesh, the BRAC-led "Maya" initiative combines financial advice with women's health content through simple mobile interfaces. In Colombia, digital kiosks in rural areas offer agricultural price data alongside remittance services. Such hybrid models build familiarity and embed digital finance into everyday life.

Public-private partnerships (PPPs) are critical to building inclusive infrastructure. The UK's Lloyds Banking Group has invested in digital inclusion hubs in low-income communities, offering connectivity, skills training, and device loans. In Rwanda, the government's Smart Rwanda Master Plan integrates broadband deployment with e-finance and e-health services. These partnerships require careful alignment of incentives, with governments ensuring that commercial logic does not override public benefit.

At the international level, organizations such as the Better Than Cash Alliance, the Alliance for Financial Inclusion (AFI), and the Consultative Group to Assist the Poor (CGAP) have played a decisive role in setting standards and convening stakeholders. Their work demonstrates that inclusive infrastructure requires collective governance – not just market forces. The UK's FCA and PRA have also increasingly recognized infrastructure as a regulatory concern, especially in the context of financial resilience and systemic stability.

Incorporating underserved voices into infrastructure design is no longer optional. Participatory models – where users co-create tools, validate assumptions, and influence design – are proving more resilient and trusted. The Human-Centred Design (HCD) movement, supported by institutions such as IDEO.org and the Gates Foundation, has embedded empathy, iteration, and user testing into infrastructure projects. When the village is in the room, the outcome is not only more inclusive – it is also more sustainable.

Cooperatives and credit unions offer an important institutional lens here. While often overlooked in digital innovation narratives, they possess rich networks, community trust, and embedded social capital. National federations such as ABCUL provide a backbone for shared services, technology upgrades, and policy advocacy. In countries such as Canada, the Desjardins Group has led digital innovation within cooperative banking while preserving member-owned values. Their work illustrates that an infrastructure can be democratic, ethical, and technologically advanced.

Digital infrastructure for inclusion is not a fixed endpoint – it is an evolving journey. It must adapt to new threats (such as algorithmic exclusion), emerging opportunities (such as satellite connectivity), and shifting social norms. As we build, we must continually ask: Who is not yet here? Whose needs are not yet visible? Inclusion begins not with scale, but with seeing. And infrastructure – when designed with those questions in mind – can become the bedrock of a more just financial future.

The next section explores how mobile money and low-cost innovation have transformed access across geographies, revealing how simplicity, flexibility, and local relevance can sometimes achieve what grand infrastructure alone cannot.

5 Mobile Money and Low-Cost Innovation

Financial inclusion has often been stymied by the high costs of traditional banking. From brick-and-mortar branches to expensive compliance systems, the infrastructure of finance has historically been capital-intensive and urban-centric. But over the last two decades, a new paradigm has emerged – one that shifts the focus from infrastructure-heavy to infrastructure-light, from high-cost distribution to lean, agile, and mobile-first innovation. Mobile money has become the flagship of this transformation, enabling millions to access financial services through nothing more than a basic phone.

The success of mobile money is best illustrated by M-Pesa in Kenya, launched in 2007 by Safari.com. What began as a simple SMS-based platform for sending remittances has evolved into a fully fledged ecosystem, offering savings, loans, insurance, merchant payments, and government disbursements. By 2024, M-Pesa had over 60 million active users across Africa, with transaction volumes equivalent to over 50% of Kenya's GDP. The model's appeal lies in its simplicity: no bank account is needed, agents are embedded in local communities, and trust is built through daily interaction.

Other countries followed suit. In Ghana, MTN MoMo revolutionized domestic payments. In Bangladesh, bKash brought mobile finance to over 40 million people. In Pakistan, JazzCash and easypaisa now serve tens of millions of customers, offering QR-based payments, micro-loans, and digital wallets. What unites these platforms is not technological sophistication, but relevance. They work within the constraints of low bandwidth, low literacy, and cash-based economies – offering just enough digital technology to be powerful, but not so much as to be alien.

The effect on financial inclusion has been significant. According to the World Bank's Global Findex 2021, the gender gap in account ownership narrowed significantly in countries with mobile money penetration. Women, who often face social and logistical barriers to formal banking, found mobile wallets more accessible and less intimidating. Smallholder farmers began receiving payments digitally, reducing delays and leakage. Street vendors used mobile payments to build transaction histories that later supported micro-credit access.

One of the most striking aspects of mobile money is its ability to bootstrap an ecosystem. In many countries, mobile money agents outnumber ATMs and bank branches combined. These agents – often shopkeepers, teachers, or local entrepreneurs – are the critical human link in the system. They provide cash-in/cash-out services, explain features to new users, and serve as informal financial advisors. Their presence makes digital finance tangible. Policies that support agent networks – through liquidity, fair commissions, and protection against fraud – are foundational to inclusive mobile ecosystems.

Low-cost innovation extends beyond payments. In India, the rise of the Unified Payments Interface (UPI) has allowed millions to transact instantly with just a phone number or QR code. Built as part of the India Stack, UPI has enabled both fintechs and traditional banks to serve low-income populations with zero transaction fees and real-time settlement. The system's open architecture allows for competition, customization, and interoperability – lowering barriers for providers and users alike.

Micro-savings and micro-insurance platforms have also proliferated. In the Philippines, platforms such as GCash and coins.ph offer bundled products: Users can save as little as one peso, buy insurance for a few cents a day, or pay school fees digitally. In East Africa, firms such as BIMA have embedded insurance into telecom services, allowing users to get hospital cash or life cover by simply topping up airtime. These models rely on behavioural nudges, such as auto-deductions or gamified interfaces, to encourage participation in traditionally underpenetrated markets.

Another frontier of low-cost inclusion is the "USSD" interface – unstructured supplementary service data – often dismissed in high-income countries but crucial in contexts without smartphone or reliable internet. USSD codes allow users to dial simple numbers (such as 123) to access banking services, check balances, transfer money, or pay bills. Governments and regulators that mandate zero-rating (free access) for USSD transactions ensure that cost does not become a barrier to participation.

In Latin America, where banking penetration remains uneven, low-cost neobanks are making inroads. Brazil's Nubank, for example, offers app-based banking with no monthly fees, real-time control, and intuitive UX, reaching millions who were previously unbanked. In Mexico, fintechs such as Klar and Albo are targeting youth and gig workers. These platforms thrive by stripping away bureaucracy and focusing on user experience – mobile-first, low-touch, and high-trust.

The role of policy is critical. Regulators who embraced proportionality – designing rules that fit the risk and scale of low-value transactions – enabled innovation to flourish. In Kenya, Ghana, and Tanzania, regulators allowed mobile operators to offer payment services directly, later tightening oversight as the systems matured. In contrast, countries that insisted on full banking licenses for any financial activity saw innovation stall. The UK's FCA and PRA have also shown growing openness to tiered licensing and sandbox experimentation, offering lessons for other jurisdictions.

Credit unions and cooperatives have begun to adopt mobile-first strategies too. Their deep community roots make them ideal channels for digital outreach – especially when linked with interoperable platforms. Some, such as those affiliated with ABCUL, are exploring partnerships with fintech providers to offer mobile loans and savings products without requiring users to visit branches. These models retain the relational trust of cooperatives while expanding reach through low-cost technology.

Perhaps the most understated innovation is the invisible one: platforms that serve as infrastructure layers for others. In Indonesia, the Gojek platform started with ride-hailing but now powers digital wallets, bill payments, and microloans. In Nigeria, Flutterwave and Paystack provide backend rails for thousands of micro-merchants. These fintech utilities reduce the cost of entry for smaller providers, enabling a broader diversity of inclusion models. Yet challenges remain. Fraud, digital illiteracy, and exclusion-by-design (such as requiring a smartphone for access) continue to threaten gains. There is also a risk of dominance, where a few platforms entrench themselves as gatekeepers. Inclusion is not just about reach, but also about fairness, agency, and choice.

The success of mobile money and low-cost innovation shows us that the pathway to inclusion need not be paved with billions in capital expenditure. Sometimes, the greatest transformation begins with a simple code, a trusted agent, and a network of humans who believe that finance should be for everyone. The next section builds on this theme by exploring how credit, insurance, and financial education – when reimagined for context – can deepen the foundation of financial health for the underserved.

6 Credit, Insurance, and Financial Education

The promise of inclusion cannot be fulfilled by payments alone. While access to transaction services marks a vital first step, sustainable financial empowerment requires more: the ability to borrow with dignity, to protect against risk, and to understand and navigate financial choices. In low-income communities, the absence of formal credit and insurance has long trapped families in cycles of vulnerability. At the same time, traditional models of creditworthiness, risk pooling, and financial literacy have often failed to adapt to diverse realities. The future of inclusion demands a new synthesis – one that is context-sensitive, data-informed, and radically customer-centric.

Credit is still the hardest part of inclusion. Globally, over 1.4 billion adults lack access to formal credit, according to the World Bank. Even among those with bank accounts, many are excluded from affordable lending due to lack of collateral, employment records, or credit histories. Informal lending – often costly and exploitative – fills the gap, reinforcing cycles of dependency. The challenge lies not merely in offering loans, but in redesigning how creditworthiness is assessed, structured, and supported.

A growing number of fintechs and inclusive banks are reimagining credit through alternative data. Instead of relying solely on credit bureaus and income statements, these lenders evaluate digital behaviour – such as mobile phone usage, utility payments, transaction patterns, and even social network reliability. Tala, a fintech operating in Kenya, the Philippines, and India, uses smartphone metadata to assess loan applicants, with repayment rates exceeding 90%. Similarly, Brazil's Nubank and India's Paytm leverage customer engagement patterns to offer pre-approved micro-credit to millions previously locked out of lending systems.

Micro-finance institutions (MFIs) continue to play a pivotal role. Though often criticized for high interest rates, their presence in rural and informal economies remains critical. Many MFIs are evolving, digitizing operations and offering hybrid models that blend peer-group support with mobile convenience. In Bangladesh, BRAC's digital micro-finance pilot combines mobile wallets with AI-driven credit scoring to streamline loan disbursement. In Sub-Saharan Africa, MFIs such as ASA and FINCA are experimenting with app-based models that reduce operating costs and allow borrowers to self-manage repayments.

Insurance is another pillar of financial security that has historically eluded low-income populations. Traditional insurance products – complex, expensive, and paperwork-heavy – do not fit the lived reality of daily earners. The rise of micro-insurance and parametric models offers a breakthrough. In parametric insurance, payouts are triggered by predefined events (such as rainfall levels or earthquake magnitude) rather than claims processing, enabling faster and more transparent settlements.

In India, the Pradhan Mantri Fasal Bima Yojana (PMFBY) provides weather-linked crop insurance to millions of farmers. In Kenya, ACRE (Agriculture and Climate Risk Enterprise Ltd.) Africa partners with telecom providers to offer weather-indexed insurance bundled with seed purchases. In Ghana and Nigeria, health insurance apps are emerging that allow informal workers to contribute small amounts weekly, with coverage adjusted accordingly. These models are affordable, flexible, and often delivered through channels that people already trust – such as mobile money agents or cooperatives.

Financial education remains the most underleveraged lever in the inclusion toolkit. Too often, it is treated as a one-off intervention – a workshop, a brochure, a video. But financial understanding is not an event; it is a lifelong process, shaped by context, trust, and relevance. Studies by Innovations for Poverty Action have shown that abstract financial literacy has limited behavioural impact unless paired with timely, embedded nudges.

New approaches focus on "just-in-time" education – offering bite-sized learning at the point of need. A woman receiving a micro-loan may be guided through repayment planning via her mobile app. A smallholder farmer might receive a text message on budgeting just before harvest. A gig worker, onboarding with a digital bank, may be nudged to opt into savings with visual prompts. These micro-moments, when well-designed, can have more impact than formal classroom instruction.

Gamification is emerging as a powerful tool in this space. In Latin America, platforms such as Alfi and Zogo use quiz-style apps to teach budgeting, borrowing, and investing. In South Africa, the gamified platform "Smart Start" partners with employers to deliver financial education as part of salary payments. These platforms do not assume literacy or prior knowledge – they use storytelling, local language, and relatable scenarios to build confidence.

The UK has also been active in this arena, especially through the work of the Money and Pensions Service (MaPS), which coordinates national financial education efforts. Programs aimed at schools, vulnerable adults, and pensioners reflect a lifecycle view of financial capability. In parallel, regulatory bodies such as the FCA have called for clearer disclosures, better financial product design, and fairness in access – all of which enhance real-world financial understanding.

An increasingly important frontier is the intersection of financial education and digital safety. As mobile and internet banking become ubiquitous, so do phishing scams, digital fraud, and misinformation. Equipping users – especially first-time digital users – with the ability to spot scams, secure their accounts, and seek redress is now part of the core mandate of inclusion. In the UK, initiatives such as "Take Five to Stop Fraud" have combined public awareness with digital interventions. Globally, banks and fintechs must move beyond disclaimers and develop user-friendly safety by design.

Cooperatives and credit unions offer a unique pathway to integrate credit, insurance, and education in inclusive models. Their member-driven and community-embedded ethos make them trusted intermediaries. In the UK, ABCUL has supported credit unions in offering payroll-linked lending, insurance bundles, and financial coaching. Their digital transformation journey, though uneven, signals the possibility of combining ethical finance with scalable outreach.

Public-private partnerships also play a critical role. In Colombia, the "Banca de las Oportunidades" program collaborates with banks to deliver subsidized credit and insurance to rural women. In the Philippines, the government's Paleng-QR program enables vendors in wet markets to receive and repay microloans through QR codes linked to mobile wallets. In Ghana, a collaboration between MTN, Ayo Insurance, and the government provides funeral insurance to informal workers for a few cents a week, with claims paid instantly via mobile money.

To build real inclusion, these innovations must be interoperable, fair, and accountable. It is not enough to digitalize exclusion or automate prejudice. Regulators must ensure transparency in scoring algorithms, prohibit exploitative lending, and enforce simplicity in disclosures. Technology should be a tool for agency, not a barrier to understanding.

Ultimately, the goal is not just to bring people into the financial system, but to build a financial system that works for people. One where credit enables opportunity, insurance protects dignity, and education fuels choice. One where financial lives – however small in value – are treated with respect and designed for resilience.

The next section will explore how behavioural science – often overlooked in financial strategy – can transform inclusion from a compliance metric to a human journey, rooted in empathy, simplicity, and trust.

7 Behavioural Insights in Inclusion Design

At the heart of financial inclusion lies a human paradox: even when products are available, accessible, and affordable, many people still do not use them. A savings account may remain dormant. Insurance may be declined. A low-cost loan may go unclaimed. Why? The answer lies not just in infrastructure or affordability – but in human behaviour. To close the inclusion gap, financial systems must go beyond engineering and economics. They must integrate behavioural science – designing not only for what people need, but for how people decide.

Behavioural insights challenge the assumption that financial choices are always rational. In reality, people are influenced by emotions, context, habit, trust, and cognitive load. For low-income customers, these dynamics are even more pronounced. Scarcity – of time, attention, or money – tends to narrow mental bandwidth. Stress distorts decision-making. Past exploitation breeds mistrust. And cultural norms often shape expectations about money, risk, and obligation.

For decades, inclusion efforts largely ignored these behavioural realities. The focus was on product design, not user psychology. But in recent years, behavioural economics has emerged as vital lens – bridging gaps between access and use, between availability and action. Thinking about saving money, even putting away a little bit regularly can really help you build a safety net. Yet across multiple studies, people in low-income segments report an intention to save but struggle to follow through. Behavioural research suggests that setting defaults, enabling auto-debits, and providing social commitments can significantly improve outcomes.

In India, the "Save More Tomorrow" pilot encouraged factory workers to commit to future salary-linked savings increases. Uptake was three times higher than traditional opt-in models. In Kenya, M-Shwari experimented with locking mechanisms – preventing customers from withdrawing savings until a preset date – dramatically boosting average balances. In the Philippines, micro-entrepreneurs were offered labelled envelopes – each named for a specific goal such as "school fees" or "emergency fund." The act of labelling increased savings by over 30%.

Framing also matters. A product pitched as "earning interest" may appeal to a different psychological trigger than one framed as "avoiding loss." For low-income customers with volatile incomes, financial tools must accommodate uncertainty. Flexibility, liquidity, and transparency often matter more than returns. Behavioural design means aligning with the realities of everyday life – not idealized assumptions of budgeting and planning.

Trust is another behavioural cornerstone. Many underserved users have experienced past exclusion, hidden charges, or financial harm. A poor farmer sold crop insurance that never pays. A domestic worker charged fees for a supposedly free account. These memories shape behaviour. Once trust is broken, even the best-designed products can falter.

To rebuild trust, behavioural design uses simplicity, transparency, and human touchpoints. In Uganda, a study showed that when micro-loan officers visited clients at home and explained terms face-to-face, repayment rates increased and dropouts declined. In the UK, community banks that assign relationship managers to vulnerable customers – especially those in financial distress – see greater engagement and long-term loyalty. Familiarity and face-to-face reassurance often outperform slick apps and digital dashboards.

Choice architecture is central. Too many options can overwhelm. Presenting clear, curated pathways – with default selections and minimal friction – can help users act. In Bangladesh, the international development organization BRAC redesigned its micro-insurance enrolment forms, reducing options and simplifying language. Uptake rose sharply. In Latin America, savings accounts with pre-configured settings (e.g. "round up change" or "daily SMS balance reminders") significantly improved usage without requiring active decision-making.

Behavioural nudges can also support financial health. Text message reminders before bill payments, gentle encouragement to complete loan applications, or visual trackers for savings goals all increase follow-through. In South Africa, the "Kick Start" program used SMS reminders linked to personal goals – such as buying school uniforms or paying rent. Participants reported greater savings, lower stress, and higher financial confidence.

Importantly, behavioural interventions must be context-sensitive. What works in rural Nigeria may not work in urban Peru. Cultural norms, language, literacy, and social networks all influence what messages resonate. Co-design with users – not just for them – is essential. In the UK, the Behavioural Insights Team (BIT) has worked with regulators and banks to test interventions through A/B trials – ensuring that policies are empirically effective, not merely well-intentioned.

Inclusion is not only about access to tools; it is also about agency. Behavioural science helps uncover subtle barriers that block agency: fear, shame, complexity, and inertia. For instance, many women in patriarchal societies are excluded not by regulation but by household norms. Behavioural strategies – such as involving female peer groups, offering gender-specific messaging, and enabling private saving – can overcome such barriers.

Digitalization presents both opportunities and risks. On one hand, mobile platforms enable real-time nudges, personalized journeys, and behavioural segmentation. On the other, poorly designed digital interfaces can confuse, mislead, or frustrate users. Financial apps must prioritize clarity, not just features. Icons must be intuitive. Menus must be structured around user logic, not internal departments. Accessibility – for those with low literacy or a disability – must be built in from the start. Ethics is paramount. Behavioural techniques can be used to manipulate as well as support. Nudges must preserve autonomy. Defaults should not lock people into suboptimal choices. Disclosures must be honest and plain. Behavioural inclusion is about empowerment – not conversion.

Across the world, forward-looking financial institutions are integrating behavioural science into product design, customer journeys, and outreach. Some hire in-house behavioural teams. Others partner with universities or think tanks. In the UK, the FCA's "Consumer Duty" framework now embeds behavioural expectations – requiring firms to demonstrate that customers understand, engage with, and benefit from the products offered.

As behavioural insights become mainstream, inclusion strategy itself must evolve. It is not enough to build a digital bank for the poor. We must build systems that are emotionally intuitive, socially relevant, and cognitively kind. This is not about adding psychology as a feature; it is about rethinking finance from the human mind outward.

In the next section, we explore the ecosystem of actors – public and private, global and local – who are shaping inclusive systems through partnerships, platforms, and shared infrastructure. Because inclusion, at scale, cannot be achieved alone. It must be co-created.

8 Inclusive Ecosystems: Public and Private Roles

Financial inclusion cannot succeed as a solo act. It is not the responsibility of one institution, one government, or one technology provider. Rather, inclusion must be the outcome of an interconnected ecosystem – where public and private actors align, collaborate, and co-create structures that empower underserved populations. Just as a healthy financial system needs liquidity, capital, and trust, an inclusive system needs partnership, vision, and shared accountability.

Over the past two decades, the boundaries between financial actors have blurred. Traditional banks now partner with telecom operators. Governments deliver welfare through fintech rails. NGOs work alongside regulators to identify gaps in service. Development agencies fund sandbox experiments in blockchain or AI. In this ecosystem era, no single actor holds all the tools. Inclusion emerges when different institutions bring their capabilities together – and design with a collective purpose.

In most countries, public actors play the foundational role. Central banks, regulators, finance ministries, and national identity agencies set the tone for inclusion – through policy, infrastructure, and oversight. The creation of interoperable payment systems, the expansion of digital identity, the provision of credit guarantees, or the enforcement of fair lending practices – all of these sit in the hands of the state.

Take India's JAM trinity – Jan Dhan (bank accounts), Aadhaar (identity), and Mobile. It was a public initiative that unlocked access for hundreds of millions. But the real impact came when private fintechs, banks, and start-ups built services on top of this infrastructure. Similarly, Brazil's instant payment system PIX, designed by the central bank, now powers everything from corner-store QR codes to peer-to-peer transfers – thanks to private sector adoption.

In the UK, institutions such as the FCA and the PRA have championed inclusive design by embedding consumer duty, financial health, and vulnerability frameworks into regulation. The FCA's innovation sandbox allows both incumbents and challengers to test solutions in a controlled environment, while the PRA ensures stability and resilience. These bodies enable risk-taking – but within a responsible, citizen-centric frame.

It's extremely important that public infrastructure such as roads and buildings are made so everyone can use them without a problem. This means ensuring that APIs are open, pricing is affordable, access is equitable, and data rights are protected. Government schemes must not just digitalize services – but humanize delivery. Welfare payments, student loans, or pensions routed through digital rails should preserve dignity and choice.

The private sector, meanwhile, brings speed, innovation, and scale. Fintechs can rapidly test new models – from digital credit scoring to embedded insurance. Telcos can reach remote areas through agent networks. Banks bring capital, risk management, and brand trust. Retailers offer physical touchpoints. Together, they form the last-mile interface between the system and the citizen.

Some private actors adopt inclusive strategies as part of corporate social responsibility. Others embed it into commercial logic – realizing that low-income customers represent the next billion users. As ESG standards evolve, inclusion is no longer just a moral good – it is a business imperative. Investors now scrutinize financial institutions not only for profit, but for purpose.

Successful ecosystems are those that blur the false binary between profit and inclusion. They build models where serving underserved communities is economically viable. Examples abound. In Kenya, Safari.com's M-Pesa succeeded not just because of mobile wallets – but because of its agent network, customer support, and interoperability with banks. In Colombia, Daviplata became a leading digital wallet by partnering with government subsidy schemes and maintaining low transaction costs.

In the cooperative and mutual sector, inclusive ecosystems take a different form. Credit unions, building societies, and community banks often serve populations ignored by big finance. In the UK, national organizations such as ABCUL provide governance, training, and coordination. Though smaller in scale, these institutions play an outsized role in fostering trust, especially in marginalized or rural communities. Their federated model allows for local responsiveness backed by collective support.

Global development actors also shape inclusive ecosystems. The World Bank, UNCDF, the Gates Foundation, and regional development banks fund inclusion projects, advise on regulation, and support experimentation. Their role is catalytic – the aim is not to dominate, but to unlock local capability. The best global interventions listen first, adapt to context, and exit with dignity. Meanwhile, civil society organizations – ranging from women's cooperatives to legal aid NGOs – ensure that inclusion is not just technical, but ethical. They act as watchdogs, educators, and advocates. Their grassroots presence keeps the ecosystem honest – ensuring that marginalized voices are heard.

Ecosystem success requires more than coordination. It requires shared data, interoperable standards, and aligned incentives. For instance, if banks hoard credit histories, or fintechs build proprietary platforms, inclusion suffers. But when actors embrace open finance principles – where data is portable, identity is federated, and trust is mutual – innovation accelerates. This is why governance matters. Inclusive ecosystems need rules – about data use, platform access, customer redress, and algorithmic fairness. These rules must be co-designed and continuously improved. Sandboxes, policy labs, and consortiums can provide safe spaces for this collaboration.

Importantly, inclusion is not just about financial services. It intersects with energy, agriculture, education, health, and housing. Ecosystem thinking must be cross-sectoral. A solar lending platform may need to partner with micro-insurers, rural cooperatives, and climate funds. A gig worker app may need integration with tax authorities, pension schemes, and legal rights bodies. No actor, no matter how large, can build this alone.

Finally, we must acknowledge the risk of fragmentation. As more players enter the inclusion space, duplication, competition, and confusion can arise. Without a shared map, ecosystems become chaotic. A national inclusion strategy, backed by measurable targets, is essential. Such a strategy must include not only financial regulators but also tech ministries, postal departments, municipal leaders, and citizen groups.

The future of inclusion lies in ecosystem leadership. This means investing in convening power, cross-sector partnerships, and shared learning. Institutions must move beyond competition to cooperation – understanding that every inclusive journey is co-authored. In the next section, we turn to the crucial task of measurement. Because inclusion cannot be declared. It must be demonstrated – with data, evidence, and lived impact. Only then can ecosystems be held accountable – not just for growth, but for justice.

9 Measuring Real Impact

Inclusion is one of the most powerful words in finance today, but also one of the most misused. Institutions frequently speak of reaching the underserved, expanding access, and designing with empathy. Yet, without rigorous and transparent measurement, such claims risk becoming hollow. To truly advance financial inclusion, we must shift from intention to evidence – from metrics that flatter to metrics that matter.

Figuring out how included people feel is tricky; it's not just about hard numbers. It requires combining quantitative data with qualitative insight. It involves going beyond the number of accounts opened to asking: Are they being used? Are they affordable? Do they improve lives? At the most basic level, measurement begins with access. Regulators, NGOs, and multilaterals often track the percentage of adults with a bank account, mobile wallet, or credit profile. The World Bank's Global Findex database, for instance, has become a global benchmark for inclusion. But access is only the first step. What matters more is usage. Dormant accounts, ghost wallets, and unutilized credit lines may inflate numbers but fail to drive inclusion.

Usage metrics include frequency of transactions, diversity of services accessed (savings, credit, insurance), and consistency over time. For example, a mobile wallet used once for a government payment is different from one used weekly to manage household finances. Similarly, a small loan repaid on time is more meaningful than a pre-approved line never activated. But even usage has limits. The ultimate test is impact. Does financial access improve resilience, productivity, opportunity, and dignity? Does it help a farmer invest in better seeds, a small shop owner restock faster, a migrant worker send remittances securely? Does it reduce stress, enable planning, or buffer against shocks?

Impact is harder to measure – but it is not impossible. Surveys, ethnographic studies, and data collaborations can help. Randomized controlled trials (RCTs), though complex, offer gold-standard evidence. Organizations such as IPA (Innovations for Poverty Action) and J-PAL have conducted hundreds of such studies – linking financial access to health outcomes, education enrolment, or consumption smoothing. These insights have shaped policy in countries from Kenya to the Philippines.

Yet, measurement must also be contextual. A metric that works in urban London may be meaningless in rural Malawi. For instance, the number of ATMs per capita is irrelevant in a cashless ecosystem. Similarly, credit penetration without risk-adjusted pricing can create over-indebtedness rather than empowerment.

One useful approach is the financial inclusion index. These composite indicators bring together access, usage, quality, and impact into a single framework. Examples include the IMF's Financial Access Survey, the Alliance for Financial Inclusion (AFI) indicators, and regional initiatives such as the EU's Financial Inclusion Monitor. Countries can tailor these indices to reflect local priorities – gender parity, rural outreach, SME financing, or digital uptake.

Private institutions also need robust internal dashboards. Banks, fintechs, and insurers should track how many of their clients are first-time users, what proportion come from low-income segments, and how products perform over time. Do fees eat into benefits? Do customers churn after three months? Are defaults rising in certain regions? These insights can guide better design and accountability.

Crucially, measurement must include disaggregated data. Gender, geography, income, disability, migration status – these factors matter. Without disaggregation, averages hide inequities. A country may boast 85% inclusion, but still exclude its most vulnerable communities. Policymakers must ask: Who is not being served, and why?

The UK's FCA has made commendable progress in this regard, requiring firms to report on customer vulnerability and inclusion. Their frameworks encourage banks to identify at-risk groups, design for diverse needs, and embed inclusion into compliance – not just CSR. Similar approaches are emerging across Europe, with regulators demanding fair design and inclusive impact as part of operational licensing.

Beyond data, inclusion must be accessed through stories. A credit union in Birmingham might serve fewer clients than a digital bank – but offer deeper community resilience. A rural co-operative may have slower growth – but preserve local trust. Qualitative insights from customers, staff, and civil society can illuminate the human dimension of impact.

Technology offers new frontiers in measurement. AI and machine learning can detect behavioural patterns, track long-term outcomes, and flag unintended consequences. For instance, if loan apps are pushing aggressive repayments or causing digital stress, data analytics can surface early warnings. However, ethical safeguards are vital. Inclusion measurement must respect privacy, avoid surveillance, and be used to empower – not control. Measuring impact also requires time. Many inclusion interventions – such as youth savings schemes, SME upskilling, or climate insurance – show results only after years, not months. Funders and boards must resist the temptation for quick wins. Patience and iteration are part of the inclusion journey.

Institutions must also report impact transparently. Public dashboards, open datasets, and shared learning's build trust. Platforms such as the Inclusive Fintech 50, GSMA's Mobile Money Metrics, and the Better than Cash Alliance showcase what works. By sharing data across sectors and borders, we accelerate collective progress. Importantly, measurement must not become extractive. Communities should not be endlessly surveyed without seeing results. Measurement must close the loop – translating insight into action, feedback into change.

Finally, we must ask a deeper question: What is the purpose of inclusion? Is it to create more customers for financial services – or to enable agency, opportunity, and wellbeing? Metrics shape mindsets. If we define inclusion merely as market penetration, we may miss its moral core. True inclusion is not just about access – but about justice, equity, and dignity.

In the next and final section of this chapter, we bring all these strands together. We reflect on what it means to design not just inclusive products – but an inclusive system. A system that uplifts the many, not just the few. A system built not for extraction, but for empowerment. A system that keeps its promise.

10 Creating a More Just System

Inclusion, at its most profound level, is not about transactions, products, or outreach targets. It is about rebalancing the very structures of finance to serve all members of society – regardless of income, identity, geography, or history. After generations of exclusion and asymmetry, the task before us is not simply to extend access within the existing rules, but to redesign the rules themselves. The promise of inclusion is, fundamentally, a promise of justice.

A fair financial system? It must be one that looks at people struggling not as risks but as people with potential; views women not as collateral gaps but as agents of growth; does not dismiss rural communities, migrants, or informal workers as "unbankable" but asks instead: What do they need, and how can we serve them with dignity? This begins with reimagining the architecture of finance from the bottom up. We must ask: Who owns the institutions? Who sets the rules? Who benefits from scale, and who bears the cost of failure?

Credit unions and mutuals, for instance, offer an alternative to profit-maximizing shareholder models. In the UK, the movement led by umbrella bodies such as ABCUL represents thousands of members and billions in assets – but still struggles for visibility against commercial giants. These member-owned institutions, grounded in communities and values, prioritizes resilience over returns and can serve as anchors in underserved regions. A just system gives them the same digital tools, regulatory support, and growth opportunities afforded to fintechs.

Justice also means confronting the extractive nature of certain financial practices – overdraft fees that trap the vulnerable, payday loans with punishing interest, micro-credit without safety nets. True inclusion cannot be built atop exploitation. Regulators such as the UK's FCA and PRA are taking important steps through vulnerability frameworks, affordability assessments, and product governance standards. But enforcement must go further. A just system rewards integrity, not opacity.

Inclusion requires us to shift from a service-delivery mindset to a capability-building approach. Financial literacy is not just a consumer responsibility; it is an institutional duty. Banks must embed learning into every product – nudging behaviour, simplifying interfaces, and explaining terms. Schools must include financial education in core curricula, not as an afterthought. And employers can play role too – offering tools for budgeting, saving, and planning.

But financial capability alone is insufficient if the system itself remains biased. Algorithmic bias in credit scoring, for instance, can perpetuate discrimination even as digital channels grow. A just system demands transparent algorithms, auditable AI, and clear mechanisms for redress. Fintechs cannot claim inclusion while hiding behind black-box models.

Justice also requires redistribution – not just of capital, but of voice. Communities must have a seat at the table where products are designed and policies shaped. Participatory design, user-led testing, and co-creation with local actors are not just good practice – they are moral imperatives. Inclusion cannot be delivered from headquarters; it must be built through dialogue, humility, and shared power.

The international development community has long used the term "financial deepening" – implying a system that extends further into society. But depth without fairness becomes a form of control. The promise of inclusion is fulfilled not when everyone is connected to the system, but when the system itself reflects shared values: equity, sustainability, transparency, and solidarity.

One of the most powerful levers for creating a more just system is infrastructure. Public digital rails – such as India's UPI, the UK's open banking framework, or Africa's mobile money APIs – level the playing field. They allow small players, from cooperatives to community banks, to plug into national ecosystems without being crushed by the incumbents. A just system ensures open access, fair pricing, and data protection – so that trust is built and maintained.

Inclusion is also geopolitical. The global financial system often marginalizes smaller nations through correspondent banking de-risking, compliance overreach, and limited access to international capital. A just system empowers countries to build sovereign capabilities – domestic payment systems, regional settlements, and digital public goods. Cross-border collaboration must be based on mutual benefit, not imposition.

In climate finance, the inclusion lens is urgent. The communities most affected by floods, droughts, and displacement are often financially excluded. Yet green finance flows overwhelmingly to large corporate and urban projects. A just system bridges this gap – funding climate resilience at the grassroots, integrating environmental and social metrics, and ensuring that transition finance reaches the informal economy.

We must also acknowledge historical injustices. Colonization, redlining, gender discrimination, and generational poverty have left scars on financial access. A just system does not pretend neutrality. It proactively works to repair harm – through targeted outreach, reparative capital, and recognition of structural barriers.

Justice in finance is not only moral – it is strategic. Economies are stronger when all members can contribute. Innovation is richer when diverse voices are heard. Risk is lower when systems are transparent and fair. And trust – the most precious asset in finance – is built not through slogans, but through sustained inclusion.

At the close of this chapter – and of this sweeping journey through the architecture, culture, and possibilities of modern banking – we return to the human core. Inclusion is not an add-on. It is the test of whether finance serves its highest purpose. Not to accumulate, but to enable. Not to dominate, but to connect. Not to divide, but to empower.

In the final chapter, we look ahead – not just to the next strategy cycle or digital tool – but to the century ahead. What does a truly inclusive financial system look like in 2100? How do we build institutions that last, adapt, and uplift? And how do we ensure that the promise of inclusion, which is mentioned so often, will be finally fulfilled – not in words, but in practice? Let us now design a future worth inheriting.

Strategic Framework Box: Chapter 9. Inclusion by Design: Rewiring the Financial System for Equity and Access

Key Insight

Financial inclusion is not about access alone. It is about dignity, usability, relevance, and trust. A system that merely opens accounts but fails to empower is not inclusive – it is performative. True inclusion requires redesigning the entire financial architecture to work for the most invisible, underserved, and excluded.

Strategic Takeaway

Inclusive finance is not about who the bank can see – it is about who the system is designed to serve. Equity must be embedded from the infrastructure up.

Inclusion Dimension	*Conventional Model*	*Systemic Inclusion Model*
Access Strategy	Physical outreach, documentation - heavy	Digital rails, identity - light, mobile - first
Product Design	Standardized accounts, rigid conditions	Customized tools, behavioral adaptation
Cost Structure	Transaction - based, minimum balances	Low - cost, usage - based, subsidy - aware
Credit Philosophy	Collateral - based, score - gated	Cash flow - based, group or platform guarantees
Impact Measurement	Account openings, loan volume	Financial health, mobility, resilience

This chapter insists that inclusion is not a feature – it is a foundational design principle. It highlights how regulation, infrastructure, behavioural science, and ecosystem Governance must align to ensure that underserved populations are not just reached, but respected and resourced.

Bibliography

World Bank (2022). Global Findex Database 2021: Financial Inclusion, Digital Payments, and Resilience in the Age of COVID-19. Washington, DC: World Bank.

10 The Century Ahead

The Capstone of *The Future of Banking: A Global Blueprint for the Bank of Tomorrow.*

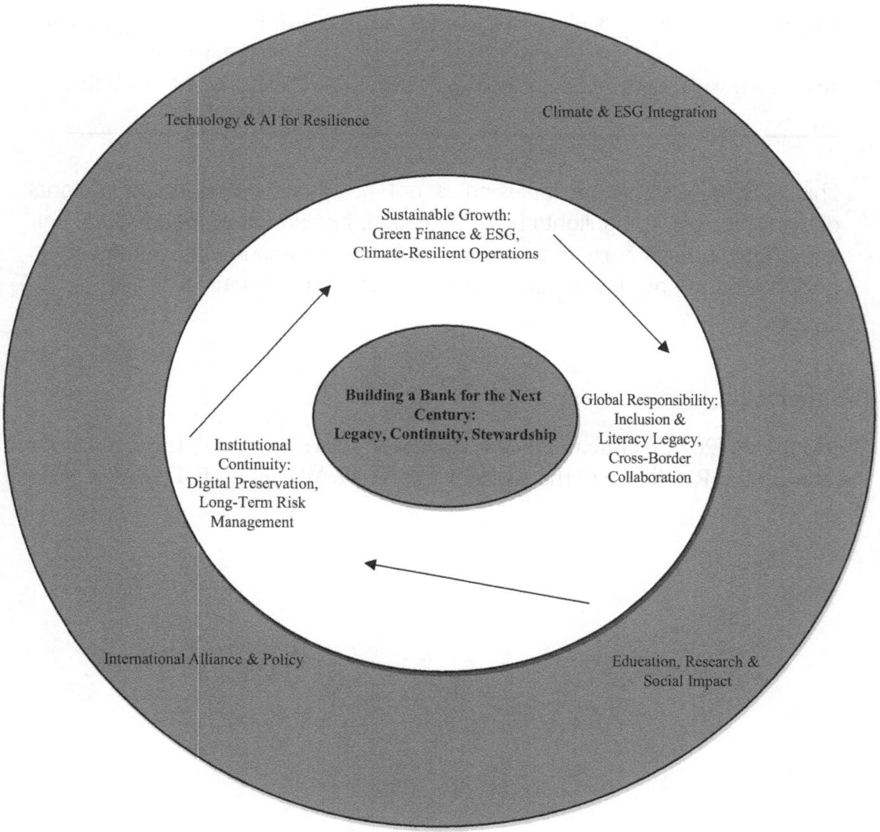

Figure 10.1 The 100-year bank balances sustainable growth, institutional continuity, and global responsibility – supported by ESG integration, technology, and education.

DOI: 10.4324/9781003737544-10

1 The Urgency of Long-Term Thinking

In a world obsessed with quarterly returns and short-term indicators, long-term thinking is not just rare – it is radical. Yet the future of banking, and indeed of civilization itself, depends on it. The financial sector, long driven by immediate performance, now stands at the edge of responsibilities that extend decades, even centuries, into the future. From climate risk to demographic shifts, from digital infrastructure to trust capital, the forces shaping tomorrow cannot be governed by the logics of today alone.

The urgency of long-term thinking arises not from distant unknowns, but from the compounding impact of decisions made in the present. When banks issue mortgages, they project decades ahead. When they invest in infrastructure or support industrial growth, they shape the future workforce, environment, and society. And when they deploy algorithms or fund innovation, they embed values and assumptions that may echo across generations. The tools of finance may operate in the present, but their consequences are disproportionately future-bound.

The COVID-19 pandemic revealed the fragility of short-term models and just-in-time thinking. It also demonstrated that institutions built with resilience, redundancy, and social purpose were far better equipped to adapt. The same holds true for banks. Those that had invested in digital infrastructure, ethical risk frameworks, and inclusive policies were able to maintain trust in the storm. The lesson is clear: preparing for the long term is not a luxury, but a necessity.

In the United Kingdom, long-termism is gradually returning to policy discourse. The Bank of England's climate stress tests, the Future Fund for innovative growth sectors, and the shift toward net-zero financing standards all reflect a more strategic orientation. But more is needed – especially at the operational level. Boards must ask not only what will deliver returns this year, but what will safeguard public value across decades. This is where the dual identity of banks – as commercial actors and public enablers – must be embraced in full.

In the United States, similar trends are visible. The emphasis on infrastructure renewal, decarbonization, and digital inclusion – whether through the Inflation Reduction Act or partnerships with fintech – signals a return to state-supported long-term investment. Yet even here, the private sector plays a pivotal role. Major banks and asset managers are being called upon to take positions not just on markets, but on planetary boundaries and social equity. The intergenerational lens is returning, slowly but unmistakably.

Globally, certain institutions already provide models of long-term banking. Japan's Government Pension Investment Fund (GPIF), for instance, has adopted ESG integration and stewardship codes that align capital deployment with sustainability outcomes. In Europe, the European Investment Bank and national promotional banks such as Germany's KfW are redefining financial intermediation through a mission-driven, century-oriented lens. These examples are not mere outliers – they are signals of a broader transformation underway.

And yet, there is a tension: How does a sector wired for short-term accountability embrace long-term responsibility without losing strategic clarity? The answer lies in changing what we measure, how we govern, and who we serve. Long-term thinking demands new key performance indicators – ones that track inclusion, environmental impact, resilience, and systemic health. It demands governance models that include not only shareholders but stakeholders. And it requires a service mindset that places society's future at the heart of today's decision-making.

Long-term thinking also requires institutional memory. Many banks are now younger in staff experience than in institutional history. As baby boomers retire and Gen Z enters the workforce, much is lost if wisdom is not consciously transmitted. Documenting transformation journeys, retaining ethical narratives, and embedding organizational learning will be vital. The banks that endure the next century will be those that understand their own past and prepare consciously for a future they may never fully inhabit.

Let's take a moment as we reach the end of this book. The future is not a distant destination. It is the result of choices which are made daily. Whether banks become part of the problem or the solution depends on whether they choose to operate in years – or in generations. Long-term thinking is not about prediction. It is about responsibility.

No long-term view of finance can ignore the monetary shifts underway. The growing influence of crypto currencies, central bank digital currencies, and digitally tethered currencies is reshaping the very architecture of global finance. These instruments challenge conventional models of central banking, cross-border regulation, and institutional trust. The future of banking will not only be defined by who holds the money – but by who defines what money is. This century is not waiting. Neither should we.

2 The Anatomy of a 100-Year Bank

What does it take for a bank to last 100 years – not just as a legal entity, but as a trusted institution, social anchor, and purposeful innovator? In a sector marked by disruption, consolidation, and shifting reputations, the idea of a "100-year bank" may seem nostalgic – but it is deeply forward-looking. Longevity is not a by-product of scale or tech; it stems from values, adaptability, and service embedded in the institution's DNA.

A 100-year bank is not necessarily the biggest or most profitable – it is the most resilient. And resilience goes beyond capital buffers or compliance. It includes moral, intellectual, and structural strength – the ability to evolve without losing identity and to sustain trust through turbulence. Such banks share key traits:

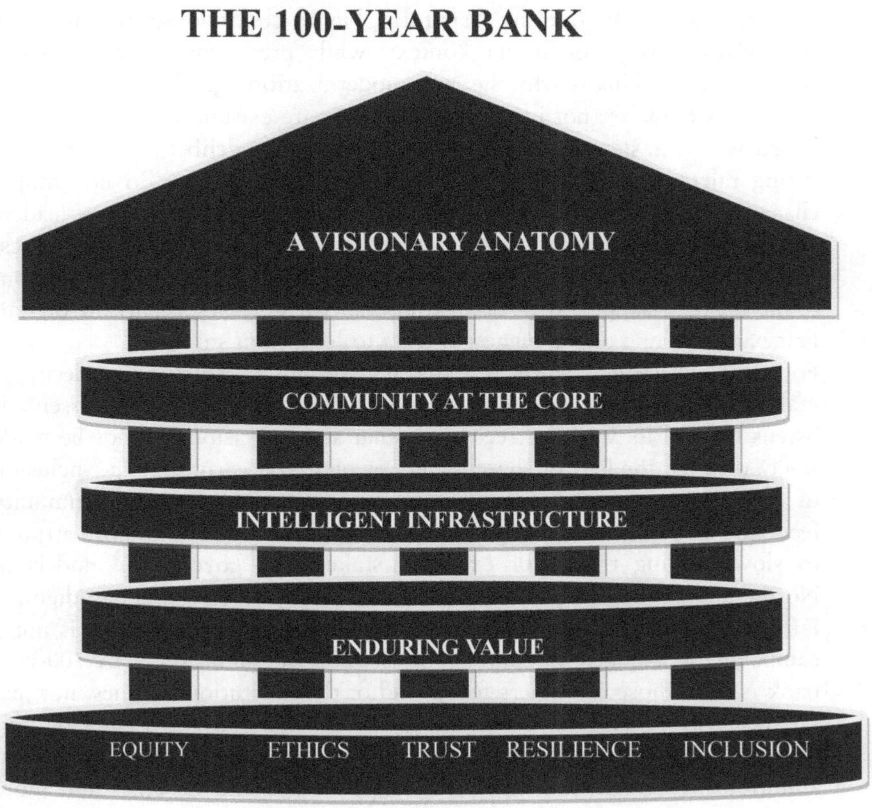

Design 10.1 The 100-Year Bank: A Visionary Anatomy

To make this vision tangible, the book introduces The Singh Framework for Long-Term Trust in Banking –a future-facing model that integrates inclusion, governance, ethical infrastructure, and resilience into a single blueprint. This framework is designed to help institutions move beyond short-term metrics and embed values, systems, and safeguards that can endure for generations. It brings together the essential pillars discussed throughout the preceding chapters, translating them into a cohesive architecture that can guide the design of the "100-year bank".

- First is clarity of purpose. A 100-year bank knows what it stands for beyond profit. Whether rooted in community, sustainability, or service, its mission holds steady despite market shifts. In the UK, the Co-operative Bank and the building societies movement have endured due to deep societal commitments. In Europe, mutual and regional savings banks remain relevant because they stayed true to their local missions – even as globalization accelerated.
- Second is architectural adaptability. A 100-year bank does not ossify around its systems or models. Instead, it invests in modularity, upgradability, and design that permits reinvention. Banks that have thrived across generations – such as JPMorgan Chase in the US, or DBS in Singapore –

have done so not by freezing their form, but by continuously reconfiguring themselves in response to the context, while preserving a stable institutional identity. This is why the core modernization agendas discussed earlier in this book are not just technical – they are existential.

- Third is talent stewardship. Long-lived banks are deliberate about cultivating talent with both character and competence. They do not simply chase the best engineers or analysts. They foster future stewards – leaders who understand the responsibility of banking as a public trust. They invest in mentoring, ethics, intergenerational learning, and deep knowledge continuity. The disappearance of institutional memory, especially in digital-first banks, is one of the biggest threats to long-term survival.
- Fourth is governance depth. A 100-year bank builds structures of decision-making that are not only agile but also reflective. It welcomes dissent. It listens beyond its walls. It recognizes that some decisions cannot be made solely through the lens of shareholders or quarterly earnings. The inclusion of civil society voices, of public interest perspectives, and of community feedback loops makes the organization more accountable and more attuned to slow-building risks. For example, stakeholder governance models in Nordic and cooperative banks offer valuable insights into this paradigm.
- Fifth is the bank's ability to embed trust across generations. Trust is not a campaign or a quarterly survey – it is an asset built slowly. A 100-year bank is one whose customers feel proud of the institution's values, not just satisfied with its services. It is an organization that earns trust not by perfection, but by consistent transparency, humility in failure, and ethical ambition in success. The regulatory response to the 2008 crisis and more recent compliance innovations such as "trust-by-design" systems are all steps toward this trust architecture.
- Sixth is alignment with planetary and societal systems. A bank cannot survive 100 years if the world around it does not. The existential risks posed by climate change, ecosystem collapse, rising inequality, and geopolitical fragmentation mean that every bank aspiring to long-term relevance must engage with ESG not as reporting compliance, but as institutional conscience. Climate risk is credit risk. Biodiversity loss is portfolio loss. Social fragmentation is default risk. The alignment of finance with planetary thresholds is not just prudent – it is foundational.
- Seventh is the ability to serve multiple economic layers without bias or exclusion. A long-lived bank builds systems to serve the underserved, not just to scale the profitable. It recognizes that inclusion is not charity – it is risk management, market expansion, and social contract fulfilment. Whether through partnerships with community finance institutions, support for SMEs, or universal access to basic financial services, the 100-year bank positions itself as an enabler of broad-based prosperity. In the UK, this ethos can be seen in the evolution of the Post Office network, as well as in modern credit union frameworks.

- Eighth is openness to collaboration. No bank can last a century in isolation. The most enduring banks are those that weave themselves into ecosystems – of fintechs, regulators, public institutions, academia, and civil society. They do not fear sharing infrastructure or enabling the innovations of others. They lead by convening. This open architecture of trust and collaboration will be central to the next century, where complexity outpaces control.
- Ninth is the courage to act with humility. Longevity does not come from arrogance, but from curiosity and care. A 100-year bank learns continuously, listens deeply, and leads responsibly. It asks not only: Can we? but: Should we? in matters of technology, policy, and societal influence. It invests not only in AI or block chain, but in wisdom.
- And finally, tenth is a 100-year bank preparing to outlive its founders. It institutionalizes values, not personalities. It builds structures that function ethically regardless of who is at the helm. It knows that leadership is a relay, not a throne – and that legacy is not reputation, but responsibility.

In the chapters that follow, we will explore how banks can build for climate resilience, ethical growth, memory in a digital world, and a future that is both regenerative and just. But all of these flow from a single premise: If we want banking to serve humanity for another hundred years, we must begin building as if we were going to live that long.

3 Building for Climate, Crisis, and Continuity

The next hundred years will be shaped not by financial forecasts or economic cycles, but by the escalating intersections of climate change, systemic crisis, and our collective capacity to endure. For banks, this is no longer a scenario on the horizon – it is the operating context of the present. Building for climate, crisis, and continuity means constructing institutions that are not only financially resilient, but ecologically embedded, socially responsive, and structurally adaptive.

Climate change is no longer an abstract environmental concern – it is a financial event. Floods destroy assets. Heat waves disrupt productivity. Droughts undermine food security and therefore creditworthiness across entire regions. The carbon transition itself, if not properly managed, poses both market volatility and reputational exposure. In this context, banks must move beyond carbon reporting to climate strategy. This includes assessing climate-adjusted credit risk, integrating environmental data into underwriting models, and supporting clients in decarbonization – not just penalizing them for lagging.

Resilience begins with scenario planning. Forward-looking banks are modelling climate outcomes not only in terms of risk-weighted assets, but in terms of supply chain disruption, geopolitical instability, and even population displacement. For instance, regional banks in countries vulnerable to sea-level rise – such as Bangladesh or parts of the Caribbean – are integrating relocation risk into long-term lending portfolios. Similarly, urban lenders are reconsidering infrastructure investments in cities facing extreme heat or energy grid stress.

Yet climate resilience cannot be siloed into risk functions. It must be embedded across every dimension of banking – from product design to capital allocation. Green bonds, climate-linked loans, and sustainability-linked instruments are all part of this financial innovation. But they must be paired with integrity: clear standards, verifiable impact, and meaningful alignment to planetary boundaries. Here, regulators such as the FCA and PRA are playing an increasingly important role, not only in stress testing banks for climate risk, but in ensuring that climate claims meet real-world scrutiny.

When things get tough, it's key to keep going by being strong online and in how you work. The COVID-19 pandemic exposed the brittleness of certain banking operations – particularly those overly reliant on physical infrastructure or centralized data systems. In contrast, institutions that had invested in cloud infrastructure, cybersecurity, modular platforms, and business continuity planning were able to adapt swiftly. In the century ahead, crises will not be episodic – they will be overlapping. Climate events, cyber threats, public health shocks, and social unrest may unfold concurrently. Banks must build systems that remain stable under strain, yet flexible enough to reconfigure as circumstances change.

This means rethinking service design. For example, mobile-first platforms that can continue operating in areas with disrupted transport networks or energy shortages. It means enabling distributed workforce models that can maintain continuity even when office access is compromised. It means securing core financial infrastructure not just against financial fraud, but against misinformation, political manipulation, and technological weapon. The concept of "always-on, crisis-ready banking" is no longer futuristic – it is foundational.

Yet continuity is not only about systems. It is also about trust. In moments of crisis, people turn to institutions they believe will act in their interest. This is where reputation, transparency, and fairness matter most. During times of hardship, banks must act not as extractors of value, but as enablers of stability. The response of many European cooperative banks during COVID-19 – extending forbearance, waiving fees, and increasing SME support – is instructive. It shows that ethical action in a crisis builds long-term loyalty, not short-term loss.

The concept of continuity must also encompass intergenerational equity. A bank cannot claim to be resilient if it sacrifices future stability for present convenience. This applies to credit expansion, natural resource exposure, and technological ethics. For instance, lending models that perpetuate unsustainable consumption or strip-mine ecosystems may appear profitable today, but they erode the very conditions under which banking can exist tomorrow. Similarly, AI systems that exacerbate bias or data systems that amplify inequality undermine the social foundations of finance.

Banks must begin aligning continuity strategies with the broader goals of regenerative economics. This means not merely doing less harm, but actively contributing to environmental repair, social cohesion, and systemic wellbeing. Investments in nature-based solutions, circular economy initiatives, inclusive infrastructure, and community wealth-building must be seen as continuity strategies, not side projects. They help create the kind of society in which banking itself remains viable.

The path forward demands new partnerships. No bank can build for continuity alone. Collaboration with government, civil society, academia, and global institutions is essential. The Bank of England's Climate Biennial Exploratory Scenario (CBES) is one such collaborative step. So are alliances such as the Net-Zero Banking Alliance (NZBA), the Partnership for Carbon Accounting Financials (PCAF), and localized climate finance coalitions.

But perhaps the deepest shift is cultural. Institutions that endure are those that embrace long-termism. This requires a departure from the tyranny of quarterly earnings and a reorientation toward legacy. It asks boards to think in decades, not in dividends. It requires leaders who see themselves as custodians, not only executives.

As we face an age of polycrisis, the challenge is not simply to withstand – but to transform. Continuity is not survival. It is stewardship. And for banks, that means asking: What kind of future are we funding? What kind of society are we enabling? What kind of world will we be part of, a hundred years from now? The answers to these questions must guide the next stages of design – not only for financial products or customer journeys, but for the institutions themselves.

4 Rethinking Growth in a Sustainable World

For centuries, the dominant narrative of progress has been defined by growth – linear, infinite, measurable growth. GDP growth. Loan book growth. Asset growth. In retail banking, this has translated into an ever-expanding customer base, relentless credit expansion, and a product logic driven by acquisition over alignment. But as the 21st century unfolds, it is becoming increasingly clear that the old metrics of growth are no longer sufficient. Worse – they may be distorting. Rethinking growth in a sustainable world demands a fundamental recalibration: one that shifts our attention from quantity to quality, from velocity to value, from extraction to regeneration.

The banking world is waking up to this, too. If the 2008 global financial crisis shook public confidence in financial systems, the decades that followed have gradually eroded the legitimacy of endless financial expansion untethered from social and ecological outcomes. Today, banks face a profound question: not just how to grow, but why to grow – and to what end?

The traditional model of growth has relied on expanding credit into new markets, layering new financial products on existing debt, or driving up fees and monetization through aggressive cross-selling. These tactics may offer short-term revenue, but they do not necessarily create sustainable value. In fact, they often deepen inequality, entrench overconsumption, and worsen financial fragility. The pursuit of growth for growth's sake can blind institutions to systemic risks – and to their own long-term role in society.

A sustainable reimagining of growth begins with redefinition. What if growth meant growing trust, rather than transactions? What if it meant expanding financial health, rather than just market share? What if success were measured not only in balance sheet size, but in the wellbeing of the communities a bank serves?

Across the world, we are seeing early signs of this shift. Some cooperative and mutual banks – especially in parts of Europe – are already reporting on "impact-weighted" growth: combining financial returns with social metrics such as improved savings behaviour, small business resilience, or reduced default rates among vulnerable segments. Institutions such as Triodos Bank in the Netherlands or GLS Bank in Germany are explicitly tying their credit expansion to ecological and social criteria, refusing to grow portfolios that undermine sustainability objectives.

In emerging markets, banks are redefining scale not by the amount of capital deployed, but by the depth of inclusion achieved. Mobile money platforms in East Africa, for example, measure growth through the number of unbanked people newly integrated into the formal economy – not just through profit per user. In India, Jan Dhan Yojana accounts have pushed the boundaries of what it means to serve scale, redefining national financial growth in terms of access rather than accumulation.

This new logic of growth does not reject profitability – but it insists on alignment. The core idea is that financial growth must be earned through contribution, not through arbitrage. That means rethinking products, incentives, and governance models. It means designing lending policies which prioritize sustainable enterprises over speculative capital flows. It means compensating bankers not only for how much they sell, but for how responsibly and with how much impact they do it. It means encouraging shareholders to see themselves as stewards of long-term value rather than short-term gain.

A major challenge lies in the metrics. The current financial reporting architecture remains deeply biased toward narrow indicators. Profit and loss statements do not capture environmental degradation. Return on equity calculations does not reflect societal wellbeing. For banks to truly rethink growth, they must invest in new accounting methods that integrate ESG performance, carbon intensity, biodiversity impact, and social inclusion outcomes. Initiatives such as the Task Force on Climate-related Financial Disclosures (TCFD) and the Value Balancing Alliance are beginning to lay the groundwork – but adoption is still slow, and integration into core bank decision-making remains nascent.

Rethinking growth also requires courage. It demands that banks walk away from profitable opportunities that contradict long-term sustainability goals. It requires confronting legacy business lines that may be lucrative but environmentally damaging. And it asks boards and investors to hold a longer view, resisting the temptation to sacrifice principle for short-term performance. The work of "degrowth" in harmful sectors must be matched by proactive investment in regenerative ones – from green infrastructure to financial literacy, from local cooperatives to climate innovation.

At the heart of this transformation is a simple truth: no bank can grow forever on a finite planet. There are planetary limits. There are social limits. And in the 21st century, the institutions that will thrive are those that operate within them – not those that try to bypass them. This is not a constraint – it is a design opportunity. Just as nature evolves in cycles, with balance and reciprocity, so too must finance. Growth, in a sustainable world, is no longer linear – it is circular.

It is also manifold. Instead of one single definition of success, banks must embrace diversity – of scale, of purpose, of impact. A small community bank that transforms the lives of a few thousand people may be just as valuable to society as a multinational institution that optimizes global capital flows. The goal is not to homogenize, but to humanize. And in doing so, to reclaim banking as a force for shared prosperity rather than systemic pressure.

As the century unfolds, regulators and policymakers will need to evolve as well. Institutions such as the FCA and PRA in the UK or the European Banking Authority (EBA) must begin embedding sustainability principles not only in stress tests, but in prudential guidance, capital adequacy rules, and innovation frameworks. Taxonomies, transition pathways, and carbon pricing will play a role – but so too will cultural signals, public expectations, and new forms of value recognition.

Ultimately, rethinking growth is not about abandoning ambition – it is about redefining it. It is about asking what kind of economy we want, what kind of society we seek, and what kind of role banks should play in shaping them. It is about shifting from an extractive mindset to a regenerative one. From growth at all costs to growth that matters.

In the final sections of this chapter, we will explore how this new philosophy of finance can be institutionalized – through regenerative banking, global collaboration, and a renewed sense of responsibility beyond the balance sheet. The future of banking is not smaller – it is wiser.

5 Regenerative Finance and the Green Transition

The 21st century will not be remembered merely for its technological leaps, nor solely for its financial innovation – it will be remembered for whether institutions rose to meet the defining challenge of our time: the climate crisis. And within that test lies a deeper question: Can finance become regenerative? Can banks move beyond mitigating harm to actively restoring ecosystems, empowering communities, and rebuilding a sustainable foundation for economic life?

Regenerative finance isn't just some buzzword. It is a paradigm shift. It calls on financial systems to evolve from being extractive to being life-affirming – from prioritizing short-term returns to enabling long-term resilience. For retail banking, this shift is particularly urgent. Retail banks are not just custodians of capital – they are architects of daily life. The products they offer, the incentives they set, and the values they reinforce shape the behaviours of millions. In embracing the green transition, retail banks must not simply follow – they must lead.

To understand the opportunity, we must first confront the gap. Despite the surge in ESG commitments, most retail banks remain misaligned with the pace and scale of the ecological transition. Green bonds and sustainable loans represent only a small fraction of total portfolios. Fossil fuel exposure persists through personal loans for petrol vehicles, mortgages for energy-inefficient homes, and credit flows to carbon-intensive industries. In many cases, the infrastructure for measuring environmental impact is weak, the data is fragmented, and the incentives remain perverse.

Yet change is underway. Banks across the globe are beginning to rewire their portfolios in line with planetary boundaries. In Scandinavia, banks such as Handelsbanken are pioneering climate-smart mortgages that reward customers for improving home energy efficiency. In Kenya, green asset financing is enabling the transition to solar and off-grid power solutions, particularly in rural areas. In the UK, institutions are partnering with housing associations to green social housing stock and embed sustainability into community regeneration.

The green transition is not just about technology – it is about reconfiguring value. Regenerative finance requires that banks look beyond traditional creditworthiness metrics to assess long-term environmental and social viability. A regenerative loan is not simply a lower-interest facility for a solar panel – it is a financial product designed to align incentives, reduce barriers to adoption, and create shared ownership in sustainable futures. This requires new underwriting models, new risk pricing, and new reward systems.

Retail banking can play a catalytic role in this transition. Through savings products that fund climate-positive initiatives, through micro-loans for green entrepreneurs, through payment systems that nudge carbon-conscious behaviours – banks can embed regeneration into the fabric of financial life. Embedded sustainability is not a niche feature – it is the next competitive frontier. Customers, particularly younger generations, are demanding it. Regulators are beginning to require it. The planet unequivocally needs it.

But regenerative finance also involves institutional transformation. It calls for a rethinking of governance, culture, and purpose. Many leading banks are now integrating sustainability KPIs into executive remuneration. Some are retooling their internal training programs to equip staff with climate literacy and green finance expertise. Others are creating dedicated sustainability units that operate across business lines, not as compliance departments but as engines of innovation.

The challenge is not merely to finance green things – it is to green the entirety of finance. That means aligning core systems – credit models, risk frameworks, branch incentives, product development – with climate science and ecological intelligence. It means adopting lifecycle thinking, ensuring that products do not just look green on paper but genuinely reduce harm and regenerate value in use. It means recognizing that environmental degradation and financial instability are no longer separate domains – they are converging.

The intersection of digital and green finance also offers powerful leverage. Smart contracts can enforce sustainability covenants. AI can detect green washing and model climate risks with greater accuracy. Digital wallets can reward low-carbon behaviours in real time. Open banking can enable consumers to track their ecological footprint across financial providers. In this landscape, sustainability is not a constraint on innovation – it is its most vital driver.

Globally, frameworks such as the EU's Sustainable Finance Disclosure Regulation (SFDR) and the UK's Green Finance Strategy are pushing institutions toward transparency and accountability. Yet the most transformative work is not happening in response to regulation – it is being led by values-driven institutions, by bold public-private partnerships, and by retail customers who are voting with their wallets. As financial citizens grow more conscious, regenerative finance becomes not just a moral imperative – but a business one.

Still, this is not an easy journey. Legacy systems, cultural inertia, and short-term pressures remain formidable barriers. Many banks struggle to define what counts as "regenerative". Taxonomies are still evolving. And the cost of the transition – technologically, operationally, and financially – is real. But the cost of inaction is higher. Climate change will not wait for institutional comfort zones. It will punish delay, and reward foresight.

In the coming years, banks that fail to embed regenerative principles risk becoming obsolete. Those that succeed will not only be future-proof – they will be future-making. They will become platforms for planetary resilience, engines of environmental restoration, and partners in the long arc of ecological justice.

The future of retail banking is not just about digital or data – it is about dignity. It is about ensuring that every pound, every rupee, every dollar entrusted to a bank moves us toward a healthier planet and a fairer society. Regenerative finance is not a fringe experiment – it is the banking system the 21st century demands. In the next sections, we will explore how education, collaboration, memory, and responsibility can extend this regenerative mission. We will examine how to embed it into the DNA of financial institutions and how to leave behind a legacy that outlives any single product, platform, or cycle.

6 Education and Financial Literacy as Legacy

In the architecture of a just and resilient financial future, education is not an accessory – it is the foundation. No transformation in banking, however innovative or inclusive, can be sustained without a corresponding uplift in financial literacy across society. As we design for the century ahead, the role of education – formal, informal, institutional, and intergenerational – must become central to the mission of every retail bank. Without a financially empowered public, the promise of inclusion, sustainability, and trust will remain out of reach.

Having a good handle on your finances is a seriously helpful thing that people just aren't using enough around the world. It determines the quality of decision-making in households, the effectiveness of credit, the resilience of savings, and the legitimacy of institutions. And yet, across both developed and developing countries, it remains startlingly low. According to OECD data, less than 30% of adults in many advanced economies demonstrate basic understanding of interest, inflation, and risk diversification. In lower-income economies, that number is often far lower. Even where access to financial services has improved, comprehension has not kept pace.

Retail banks must move beyond the transactional and embrace the transformational. Education must become a strategic pillar – not a side project or a regulatory checkbox. This means embedding financial literacy into every touchpoint of the customer journey: onboarding, product explanation, digital interfaces, and even customer support. It also means partnering with schools, universities, community organizations, and fintech innovators to reach wider and deeper into society, across all ages and stages of life.

Consider the models already emerging. In India, grassroots financial literacy campaigns have been co-led by banks and civil society groups, empowering rural women with the tools to manage microcredit and grow savings. In the UK, initiatives such as Young Money integrate financial education into school curricula, supported by banking foundations. In the US, digital-first banks have begun gamifying financial learning, blending behavioural nudges with short educational content inside apps. In Sub-Saharan Africa, mobile money operators are providing voice-based financial lessons in local languages, reaching populations once thought unreachable.

But scale alone is not enough. Relevance and trust matter even more. Education must be contextualized to local realities – culturally sensitive, linguistically appropriate, and designed for the lives people actually lead. A savings app in a multilingual market must go beyond translation to embed culturally attuned examples. A credit advisory program for first-generation users must start not with risk-adjusted returns, but with aspirations, fears, and lived experience.

Moreover, the future of financial education is not just in content, but in interaction. The most effective learning does not come from brochures or PDFs – it comes from human conversations, peer learning, digital simulations, and real-world experimentation. Retail banks must design not just materials, but experiences. They must create safe spaces – digital or physical – where questions can be asked without shame, where mistakes become lessons, and where the language of money becomes accessible rather than intimidating.

Crucially, this is not charity – it is strategy. Customers who are financially literate are more likely to use products responsibly, build long-term relationships, and contribute to financial stability. Educated customers are less vulnerable to fraud, less susceptible to misinformation, and more confident in navigating digital finance. For banks, this translates into lower delinquency, higher trust, and stronger reputational capital.

The intergenerational dimension is also vital. Financial literacy is not just about today's users – it is also about tomorrow's citizens. Children who grow up in financially literate households are more likely to save, invest, and avoid high-risk debt. When parents understand the basics of budgeting, insurance, and pensions, they create a culture of security and aspiration. Retail banks must see themselves not just as financial service providers, but as educators, mentors, and societal stewards.

To institutionalize this, many banks are now creating Chief Learning Officer roles within retail divisions – not just to educate their staff, but also to develop a customer-facing strategy. Others are investing in open-access knowledge platforms, sponsoring university chairs in financial inclusion, and forming coalitions with the media to deliver national financial awareness campaigns. Digital technology is a powerful enabler – but it must be paired with human empathy and long-term commitment.

The regulatory environment is evolving too. The FCA in the UK, for example, has embedded financial capability within its consumer protection framework. Globally, the World Bank and OECD are supporting national financial education strategies, recognizing their role in macroeconomic stability and social equity. But the work cannot be left to governments alone. Retail banks must co-own this mission – not reactively, but proactively.

As we look ahead to the next hundred years, we must also expand our definition of financial literacy. It is no longer just about understanding compound interest or reading a bank statement. It is about navigating digital wallets, protecting personal data, understanding climate risk in investments, and aligning money with personal values. It is about preparing individuals not just for transactions – but for transformation.

Education is legacy. It is the gift that compounds across generations. For banks, investing in it is an act of leadership, of accountability, and of deep purpose. The most visionary banks of the future will be known not by their assets under management, but by the lives they've empowered – the households they've uplifted, the small businesses they've educated, the communities they've made resilient. In the next section, we turn to collaboration. Because while education may begin within institutions, its true power is unlocked when banks join forces – across borders, sectors, and ecosystems – to elevate the financial capacity of entire societies.

7 Strengthening Global Collaboration

As the future of finance unfolds across borders, ecosystems, and emerging paradigms, one truth becomes increasingly evident: no bank, regulator, or government can solve the challenges of the next century alone. Whether the task is mitigating global crises, building inclusive infrastructure, or managing systemic risk, collaboration is no longer a choice – it is a foundational principle. And in this century, the quality of a financial institution's partnerships will determine its relevance, resilience, and reach.

Global collaboration in banking has historically been reactive – emerging in response to crises, regulatory arbitrage, or macroeconomic shocks. The 2008 financial crisis catalysed cooperation on stress testing and capital adequacy. The COVID-19 pandemic spurred emergency responses for liquidity and digital infrastructure. But as we enter an era defined by long-term structural shifts – climate change, digital decentralization, and demographic transitions – the nature of collaboration must evolve. It must become strategic, proactive, and purpose-driven.

Retail banks can really take the lead in this change. As institutions embedded in communities and wired into global networks, they straddle the local and the international, the human and the technological. Yet most banks have not fully activated this potential. Global collaboration is still often framed in terms of M&A, correspondent banking, or compliance alignment. But the future calls for something broader: ecosystems of shared innovation, platforms for cooperative resilience, and alliances that transcend commercial interest.

Consider the possibilities: Imagine a cross-continental coalition of banks pooling resources to create open-source digital ID frameworks, enabling secure and seamless onboarding in underserved markets. Picture regional financial literacy consortia that translate educational content into hundreds of local dialects, ensuring that digital inclusion respects cultural nuance. Envision a global fund – co-created by banks, multilaterals, and foundations – to derisk green finance in emerging economies and channel capital into climate adaptation at scale.

Some early signs are already visible. In the Nordic-Baltic region, banks and central banks have collaborated on real-time payment systems and joint cybersecurity defence. In Africa, platforms such as Mojaloop – backed by the Gates Foundation – are enabling financial institutions to interoperate and reach the unbanked. In Southeast Asia, collaborative credit registries and shared e-KYC systems are being piloted to enhance access and reduce duplication.

But these remain exceptions, not norms. What's needed is a shift in the mindset – from competition to co-creation, from proprietary thinking to platform thinking. Banks must realize that certain problems – such as financial exclusion, climate instability, or cyberrisk – are pre-competitive. Solving them benefits the entire sector, and indeed, the entire economy. It requires joint investment, shared governance, and trust across institutions that may otherwise be rivals.

Regulators have a key role to play in fostering this. In the UK, the FCA and the PRA have shown how innovation sandboxes and collaborative compliance can enable cross-sector experimentation without compromising stability. Internationally, the Financial Stability Board (FSB), the Basel Committee, and the IMF are increasingly encouraging regulatory convergence and collaborative risk assessments. These mechanisms must now be extended beyond capital ratios and liquidity buffers into the realms of digital ethics, sustainability disclosures, and inclusive access.

Technology can enable this transformation. APIs and open banking protocols offer a canvas for structured collaboration. Cloud infrastructure enables shared environments where institutions can co-develop solutions. Blockchain and distributed ledgers create transparent, immutable records that can underpin trust across borders. Yet the tech alone is not enough. Governance, interoperability, and shared vision are the glue that binds effective collaboration.

The private sector must also look beyond traditional partners. Collaborating with NGOs, academia, and civic tech organizations can unlock new insights and capabilities. Universities can act as neutral research hubs. Non-profits can offer access to vulnerable communities and user-centred design approaches. Cities and local governments can help banks pilot collaborative models of urban financial inclusion, digital ID rollouts, or emergency payments infrastructure.

The ambition must be nothing short of systemic change. A global collaborative compact for retail banking could include shared digital infrastructure, common ethical frameworks, coordinated climate finance initiatives, and mutual capacity building. Banks could co-invest in platforms for displaced populations, frontline community banking, and cross-border migrant remittances – reimagining inclusion on a planetary scale.

But such collaboration requires courage. It means acknowledging blind spots, embracing mutual accountability, and sometimes subordinating short-term gains for long-term shared benefit. It also requires humility – recognizing that wisdom may lie in unexpected partners, and that no institution has a monopoly on good ideas.

Crucially, this spirit of collaboration must be embedded into the next generation of banking leaders. From boardrooms to branch managers, from digital architects to frontline staff, the ability to work across boundaries – to listen, co-create, and partner – must become a core capability. Banks must train for it, reward it, and model it in how they engage with their own people and their external counterparts.

We are entering an era where the old dichotomies – public versus private, local versus global, profit versus purpose – are dissolving. What matters now is collective intelligence. The retail bank of the future will not be defined by the assets it owns, but by the partnerships it enables. Its greatest innovations may not be what it builds alone, but what it helps others build together.

In the next section, we explore how this spirit of collaboration must be grounded in memory and continuity. Because while the future may be digital and distributed, its soul lies in the lessons we carry forward – and the institutions we build to last.

8 Institutional Memory in a Digital Age

In the pursuit of agility, many organizations risk losing their identity. Legacy is often seen as a constraint to disrupt or modernize. But in finance – where trust is earned over time and past failures shape an organization's future resilience – memory is not a burden; it is an asset. A bank's ability to carry institutional memory forward – intentionally and dynamically – will define its authenticity, adaptability, and integrity.

Institutional memory is not nostalgia. It is the collective intelligence of an organization – its values, lessons, scars, victories, and the unwritten knowledge passed through mentorship, not manuals. For banks that have endured crises and served communities across generations, this memory runs deep – but it is fading.

As retirees leave, branches close, and systems are digitalized, vital knowledge embedded in relationships is being lost or abstracted. The result can be corporate amnesia: repeated mistakes, diluted culture, and shallow strategies in the face of digital speed.

To prevent this, organizations must rethink how they remember. It starts with the intentional capture of oral histories, legacy case studies, and retrospective reviews in order to strengthen the organization's culture, not just to satisfy compliance rules. Boards should treat memory as part of governance. After major transformations, "memory audits" should be routine – structured reflections on what was done, learned, and what is worth keeping – just like financial audits.

Next comes the embedding of memory into systems. Artificial intelligence can be trained not only on transactions but also on narratives. Decision support tools can include prompts based on historical precedent. Onboarding journeys can include legacy briefings – helping new joiners understand the institutional journey they are inheriting. In a hybrid banking model, where technology meets trust, digital platforms can carry forward human context.

However, memory is not just about data – it is also about meaning. Storytelling becomes vital. Institutions must curate and share stories that reflect their values, their turning points, their role in national or community development. Museums of banking history, like those maintained by the Bank of England or Germany's Bundesbank, are not vanity projects – they are repositories of institutional identity. Every major bank should consider creating its own "living archive", one that combines its history, culture, and vision.

Mentorship is another critical vector. As generational shifts reshape the workforce, structured mentorship programs ensure that wisdom is transferred with nuance. But this cannot be hierarchical alone. Reverse mentoring – where younger digital natives coach senior leaders on emerging trends – can fuse memory with relevance, the past with future. The aim is not to preserve the memory in amber, but to make it active and adaptive.

Leadership plays a central role in modelling memory. When CEOs reference the institution's founding principles, when board chairs invoke past dilemmas in current debates, when managers respect the cultural DNA of legacy teams – they are anchoring progress in continuity. This is especially critical during moments of crisis or reinvention, where memory can provide ethical grounding and historical perspective.

Globally, financial institutions are experimenting with tools to preserve memory while modernizing operations. The Monetary Authority of Singapore, for example, integrates regulatory history into policy dashboards. Scandinavian banks have created internal "heritage networks" to capture local practices before full digitalization. And some Indian cooperative banks maintain community oral records as part of their trust model – honouring multigenerational bonds that no algorithm can replicate.

Institutional memory also underpins accountability. It is what allows an organization to trace the origins of a failed product, a misaligned incentive, or a missed opportunity. In an age where reputational risk is existential, the ability to remember, analyse, and learn is core to survival. It also ensures continuity of purpose. A bank that remembers why it was founded – whether to serve farmers, rebuild after a war, or promote thrift – has a compass, even amid disruption. In the century ahead, where artificial intelligence may dominate transactions and where algorithms may mediate most customer interactions, human memory becomes a differentiator. The retail bank of the future must be digitally advanced but conscious of its history. It must move fast without forgetting why it exists.

As institutions evolve, so too must their definition of legacy. Legacy is no longer about bricks and mortar, or old IT systems. It is about principles, relationships, and institutional character. A forward-looking bank does not discard its past – it carries it forward, refined and reinterpreted, to guide new generations. In the next section, we expand this thinking even further – to consider the balance between financial performance and moral responsibility. Because in a world on edge, the bank of the future cannot be just a balance sheet. It must be a force for good.

9 Responsibility Beyond the Balance Sheet

In an era of planetary risk, political fragility, and social dislocation, the boundaries of what a financial institution is responsible for have expanded. No longer can banks define success solely in terms of return on equity or market share. The question confronting tomorrow's leaders is not merely how to grow, but how to grow responsibly – how to embed moral clarity into operational scale. Responsibility beyond the balance sheet is no longer a slogan. It is a structural shift in the role of finance in society.

Banks have always helped the economy. They provided credit, safeguarded savings, and allocated capital across sectors. Their legitimacy rested on fiduciary duty and regulatory compliance. But the crises of the last two decades – financial, environmental, epidemiological, and geopolitical – have reshaped expectations. Citizens now demand more than prudence. They demand purpose.

This shift is not idealistic – it is structural. Regulators, shareholders, and customers are redefining responsibility. Climate risk is now financial risk. Social equity affects creditworthiness. Governance failures bring instant reputational damage. Banks are judged not only by what they fund, but by what they stand for. This transformation demands a mindset shift. Responsibility must move from CSR departments to core strategy-shaping capital allocation, innovation governance, and growth priorities. Metrics must evolve: profit still matters, but so do planetary limits, community trust, and intergenerational fairness.

ESG frameworks have formalized parts of this shift. Banks now disclose carbon exposure, diversity stats, and governance practices. But compliance is not enough. The future belongs to institutions that design for responsibility – embedding ethics into algorithms and funding transitions, not just transactions. Global examples show this in action. Triodos Bank in Europe avoids fossil fuels and arms, funding sustainable housing and clean tech. Rural banks in India empower women through accountable microlending. In the US, community development financial institutions are redefining creditworthiness in underserved urban areas. In each case, the model is driven by inclusive, long-term value.

Redefining responsibility also takes courage – declining harmful but profitable deals, investing in neglected communities, and questioning unregulated technologies. It means asking not just: Can we? but: Should we? Boards and leadership teams must model this responsibility. It must be reflected in incentive structures, executive KPIs, and internal governance. Responsibility cannot be delegated – it must be owned. That includes facing up to historic harms. Many financial institutions have colonial legacies, discriminatory lending histories, or environmental footprints that require acknowledgement and redress. Transparency is not a reputational risk – it is reputational repair.

At the system level, regulators must support this shift. The FCA and PRA in the UK have already begun embedding sustainability into supervisory expectations. The European Central Bank and MAS in Singapore are experimenting with climate stress tests and green finance incentives. But true transformation will require global coordination – common taxonomies, shared ethical baselines, and cross-border ESG accountability.

Technology can accelerate or erode this progress. AI and digital tools can bring transparency, model fairness, and extend access. But without ethical architecture, they can amplify bias, extract value, and sever human relationships. The responsible bank of the future will be one that governs technology with integrity, not merely efficiency.

There is also an intergenerational dimension. Young employees, investors, and customers increasingly align themselves with values-driven organizations. Responsibility becomes a talent strategy, a reputational moat, and a resilience mechanism. Banks that ignore this trend may find themselves obsolete – not because of digital disruption, but because of ethical irrelevance.

Responsibility beyond the balance sheet also implies a civic role. During crises – whether floods, pandemics, or conflicts – banks become lifelines. They keep liquidity flowing, provide emergency support, and often coordinate with governments. This responsiveness must be institutionalized, not improvised. Scenario planning must now include not just economic shocks, but climate extremes, migration surges, and democratic instability.

Philanthropy has a role to play – but must be reimagined. Not as charity, but as catalytic capital. Strategic giving, blended finance, and community investment funds should become core competencies. The goal is not just to compensate for market failures, but to shape markets toward equity. Finally, this responsibility must be human. It must show up in how customers are treated, how complaints are resolved, how staff is supported during transformation. Culture is the carrier of responsibility. And culture is built day by day, decision by decision.

As we approach the final section of this book, we look not just to the bank of the future, but to the future itself. We ask: What kind of financial system is worth inheriting? What legacy will this generation of bankers, technologists, and policymakers leave behind? The answer must go beyond metrics, headlines, or awards. It must be visionary, enduring, and deeply human.

10 Designing a Future Worth Inheriting

The future has always belonged to the dreamers, but in this century, it will belong to those who design. Not design in the narrow sense of aesthetics or interfaces – but in the broader, more enduring sense of systems, intentions, and institutions that last. As we arrive at the conclusion of this journey across the landscape of tomorrow's bank, we are not merely closing a chapter. We are also opening a horizon.

In truth, this final section is not an ending. It is a beginning disguised as a reflection – a blueprint of ideas that will outlast the technologies we have praised, the trends we have explored, and the disruptions we have dissected. At this moment, the most important question we can ask is not: What will banking become? but rather: What do we want it to stand for in the lives of people, communities, and the planet?

This final section is built not as a summary, but as a strategic manifesto for long-term thinking. It is a culmination of everything the previous chapters have sought to illuminate: that banking is no longer a service. It is an infrastructure of trust, an architecture of values, and a mirror to society's hopes and flaws. And the way we choose to design this infrastructure today will determine the legacy we leave behind.

1 Legacy Is a Design Problem

Legacy is often misunderstood in financial circles. It is treated as a technical burden – obsolete systems, outdated policies, or non-cloud infrastructure that must be modernized. But the deeper challenge of legacy is not technological; it is philosophical. Legacy, at its core, is the answer to the question: What are we leaving behind that still makes sense, still serves purpose, still stands the test of time?

A 100-year bank cannot be built through quarterly thinking. It must be imagined through generational responsibility. Just as central banks shape monetary policy with a horizon beyond electoral cycles, so too must modern retail banks think in terms of societal continuity. They must resist the gravitational pull of short-term optimization and instead embed values – such as resilience, inclusion, stewardship, and dignity – into their very operating models.

2 Regeneration, Not Just Sustainability

The banks of the future will not merely be sustainable; they must be regenerative. Sustainability aims to reduce harm. Regeneration seeks to restore. This is a profound shift. It means viewing banking not only as an enabler of ESG compliance, but as a catalyst for environmental healing, economic justice, and long-term ecological health.

How might this look in practice? A regenerative bank does not just green its buildings – it finances the decarbonization of entire supply chains. It does not only issue ESG-linked loans – it co-creates ecosystems with circular business models and climate-positive impacts. It does not merely measure carbon – it measures contribution. In other words, regeneration demands that banks move beyond metrics and toward meaning. The real revolution is not in green bonds or carbon disclosures. It is in reimagining value itself – from extractive growth to shared flourishing.

3 From Risk Management to Stewardship

Throughout this book, we have returned to the theme of trust. But trust in the future cannot be earned by risk management alone. It requires stewardship – the idea that banks are caretakers of more than capital. They are stewards of possibility.

A future-facing institution must evolve from being a risk-averse entity into a purpose-driven steward of long-term outcomes. This shift requires a new mind-set; not: What could go wrong? but: What is worth protecting, nurturing, and scaling for the generations to come? Whether through climate financing, inclusive infrastructure, or digital literacy programs, the true question becomes: How are we earning our right to exist – beyond profit? To design a future worth inheriting, we must accept that accountability cannot end at the balance sheet. It must include the lives, environments, and ecosystems touched by every decision.

4 Time as the Ultimate Currency

In a world obsessed with speed – real-time payments, instant credit decisions, automated trading – there is a counter-intuitive truth we must embrace: The future is built by those who respect time, not rush it. Banks have a unique opportunity to reclaim time as a strategic asset. Not by slowing down, but by designing products, services, and systems that honour long-term thinking. Imagine a mortgage product that incentivizes sustainable building practices over 30 years. Or a youth savings program that builds financial capability across a generation, not just a quarter. The age of acceleration must not destroy our relationship with time. Designing a future worth inheriting requires us to think in decades, not just digital sprints.

5 Humanity as the Anchor of Technology

Technology has shaped the arc of modern finance, from core banking platforms to AI-driven advisory models. But the real test of the next century is not how intelligent our systems become – it is how human our outcomes remain. In the race toward automation, hyper-personalization, and quantum computing, we risk losing sight of the quiet truth that finance is still about people. It is about dignity in retirement, agency in savings, fairness in credit, and protection in times of vulnerability. Every algorithm, no matter how advanced, should serve the empathy that underpins trust.

To design a future worth inheriting, we must code values into our machines, not just logic. This means interdisciplinary collaboration between ethicists, engineers, policy-makers, and behavioural scientists. It also means questioning whose values are embedded – and for whose benefit. It is not enough to be digitally excellent. The future belongs to those who have moral intentions and are socially responsive in how they wield digital power.

6 *Institutions as Living Systems*

For too long, financial institutions have been built like machines – engineered for scale, standardization, and control. But the challenges of the 21st century demand a different metaphor: the living system. A living system is adaptive, regenerative, and interdependent. It learns from its environment. It evolves without losing coherence. It thrives not through rigid hierarchy, but through dynamic equilibrium. For banks, this means embracing models of governance that reflect shared intelligence, decentralized learning, and continuous renewal.

Consider how this reframing changes everything: compliance becomes a form of ethical metabolism; culture becomes a medium of adaptation; leadership becomes an act of ecological stewardship. Banks of the future will not survive as mechanical institutions. They will flourish as living organisms within a global financial ecosystem. Such thinking draws from biomimicry, complexity science, and systems design. But it also draws from indigenous wisdom, which has long recognized that the health of a system lies in its ability to honour balance, reciprocity, and renewal.

7 *Designing for Intergenerational Justice*

Most current financial frameworks are built on the premise of intertemporal transfer – moving money across time through instruments such as pensions, annuities, and sovereign wealth. But what if we designed not just for transfer, but for justice between generations? Intergenerational justice asks hard questions: Are we borrowing from our children's future to finance excessive spending? Are our lending models pricing in the ecological cost of extraction? Are our digital infrastructures inclusive of young, rural, and displaced populations?

Designing a future worth inheriting requires that we make the unborn visible in our policies, pricing models, and product architectures. It means aligning capital with consequences that will unfold not just in fiscal years, but in lifetimes. This is not a utopian concept. It is an ethical recalibration of the risk-reward equation – one that acknowledges that the beneficiaries of our financial decisions often cannot vote, speak, or are not even born yet.

8 *Narratives as Strategic Assets*

Financial institutions often obsess over data. But beyond the dashboards and metrics lies a deeper lever of transformation: the narrative. Narratives shape how people trust. They influence how institutions behave. They define what is seen as possible. The future will be designed not only by engineers and economists, but by storytellers, curators, and meaning-makers who can craft new myths of value.

The story of finance today remains dominated by scarcity, competition, and growth. But a new narrative is emerging – one of collaboration, regeneration, and sufficiency. Banks must become not only actors in this shift, but architects of the storylines that shape how society relates to wealth, time, risk, and care. Strategic narrative is not about branding. It is about cultural authorship. In a noisy, polarized, and digitalized world, those who define the story define the system.

9 The Return of Public Purpose

As we design the century ahead, a pivotal question emerges: What is the purpose of finance? Is it merely to generate returns for shareholders? Or is it to serve the evolving wellbeing of societies, economies, and environments? In the 20th century, the dominant logic of shareholder primacy reduced public purpose to a footnote. But the crises of the 21st century – climate breakdown, rising inequality, democratic fragility – are forcing a reckoning. Finance can no longer be indifferent to its consequences.

Banks must reclaim their public mandate, not as a compliance requirement, but as a strategic advantage. Institutions that embed public purpose at their core – whether through green portfolios, inclusion-first models, or ethical lending thresholds – will not just gain trust. They will gain resilience, talent, and long-term viability. Public purpose is not at odds with profitability. It is a deeper expression of it. It positions financial institutions as custodians of collective futures, not just as facilitators of private gain.

10 Transnational Collaboration as the New Normal

No single nation, company, or regulator can deal with systemic risks alone. Whether it is cyber-resilience, sustainable development, or AI governance, the solutions of tomorrow must be collaborative by design and global in scope. The banking system must now evolve into a networked infrastructure of trust, where public and private actors align on standards, safeguards, and strategy. This will require radical transparency, shared data protocols, and cross-border accountability.

Already, alliances such as the FSB, the Bank for International Settlements (BIS), and the Network for Greening the Financial System (NGFS) are showing what is possible when coordination transcends geography. But the future demands more: interoperable ethics, digitally verifiable consensus, and global commons of financial inclusion. The future is post-sovereign. It belongs to those who can build coalitions, platforms, and institutions that operate beyond borders and in service of shared futures.

11 Education as Infrastructure

Education is often treated as a separate sector, distinct from finance. But as we look ahead, it must be reimagined as a core component of financial infrastructure. Without financial literacy, digital access leads to exclusion. Without civic knowledge, algorithms deepen bias. Without systems thinking, innovation becomes extractive. To prepare for the century ahead, we must educate not only consumers and citizens, but also boards, engineers, and regulators.

This is not about training courses or onboarding modules. It is about designing financial systems that learn as they go, that reward curiosity, and that build capacity at every layer – from neighbourhood branches to multilateral banks. Open-source platforms, community co-learning, and embedded financial education in everyday services will be critical. In the long run, financial systems that educate are systems that evolve with dignity and purpose.

12 Cultural Legitimacy in the Age of AI

The last great currency in global finance will not be capital or data – it will be legitimacy. In a world shaped by machine-led decisions, cultural intelligence and ethical credibility will become the foundation of influence. This means that banks, regulators, and technologists must develop cultural fluency, not as a side effort, but as a strategic imperative. It also means designing AI systems that can respect, reflect, and respond to diverse moral frameworks, linguistic traditions, and social priorities.

Cultural legitimacy is built through dialogue, humility, and inclusion. It cannot be engineered – it must be earned. As AI begins to shape pricing, profiling, and policy, the institutions that will thrive are those that can answer not just: What works? but: For whom, and at what cost? And do so with clarity, courage, and compassion.

13 Institutional Memory in a Digital Age

In the rush to digitalize, automate, and optimize, one quality often forgotten is memory – not individual recollection, but institutional memory. The collective understanding of why decisions were made, what values guided them, and how they affected the real world. As leadership cycles shorten and technologies evolve rapidly, institutions risk losing the very narratives that anchor them. Without memory, banks drift toward amnesia – reinventing wheels, repeating mistakes, and disconnecting from the communities they serve.

In the century ahead, financial institutions must develop digital memory architectures – systems that don't just store data, but retain lessons, preserve ethics, and narrate purpose. This includes open archives of impact, transparent algorithms of change, and oral histories of transformation leaders. More profoundly, memory must be revalued as a strategic asset. Just as risk is priced, and trust is measured, so too should an organization's continuity of conscience be assessed.

14 The Moral Authority of Financial Leadership

Leadership in finance is no longer just about balance sheets and capital markets. It is about moral authority – the ability to act not merely because one has power, but because one holds credibility. The financial crises of the past decades, from subprime collapse to money laundering scandals, have eroded the public's faith in financial institutions. Regaining that trust demands more than rebranding. It demands leaders who are stewards of ethics as much as architects of growth.

The most influential banks of the future will be those whose leadership is known not just for business acumen but for integrity – leaders who can engage in complexity with humility, take stands in ambiguous times, and align institutional behaviour with broader societal values. This will require a different kind of boardroom: one where courage is a governance function, where dissent is encouraged, and where the long term is never sacrificed for short-term appeasement. Leadership must once again be a public good.

15 Intergenerational Design Principles

The future must not only serve the present – it must also be accountable to the generations yet unborn. For too long, banking strategy has prioritized quarterly earnings over planetary consequences, shareholder value over civic dignity. To correct this course, we must embed intergenerational design into the DNA of financial infrastructure. What does it mean to make a decision whose effects may be felt in 50 or 100 years from now? How do we price risk not just to investors, but to children?

Some pension funds and sovereign wealth vehicles have begun asking these questions. But the next leap forward is cultural and architectural: to build financial systems that optimize for continuity, equity, and sustainability across time. This is not utopian. It is existential strategy. The century ahead will judge us not by our innovations, but by the futures we enable – or foreclose.

16 The Rise of Mission-Driven Finance

A quiet revolution is already underway: finance is being reclaimed by mission-driven actors – institutions and individuals who view capital not as an end, but as a means to reshape the world. From community development banks to climate-aligned funds, from Islamic finance to circular economy platforms, new models are emerging that challenge the idea that purpose dilutes profit. Instead, they are showing that aligned finance can outperform, endure, and inspire.

This shift is not about charity. It is about strategic intention. It is about aligning capital flows with the needs of people and the planet, designing portfolios that reflect justice, and building services that uplift dignity. Mission-driven finance is not a niche. It is the blueprint for the next century. And those who understand this early – those who lead with clarity, invest with care, and govern with principle – will shape not just markets, but human possibilities.

17 Reconstructing Metrics of Progress

To design a future worth inheriting, we must rethink how we define progress. For over a century, financial systems have relied on metrics such as GDP, shareholder return, and credit ratings – tools of an industrial era focused on growth over balance, and profit over purpose. These numbers are now poor indicators of real well-being. They quantify the measurable, not the meaningful – ignoring climate resilience, mental health, social equity, and institutional trust. Increasingly, they're used to justify systemic harm.

The future needs new value metrics – ones that reflect human experience, environmental interdependence, and ethical financial responsibility. Frameworks such as the Doughnut Economy, ESG risk scoring, and community impact indices are steps in that direction. But tweaking old models is not enough. We must redefine the very language of finance – moving from extraction to regeneration, from competition to collaboration. What we measure shapes what we value. And what we value shapes what we build.

18 The Global Commons and the Financial Mandate

As climate change accelerates, geopolitical tensions rise, and digital systems scale globally, the idea of a shared global commons is resurfacing. Clean air, open data, biodiversity, and cyber resilience are now collective responsibilities. This reshapes finance. Banks, insurers, and funds can no longer act as neutral players. Their choices affect ecosystems, nations, and future generations. A mortgage in one country might drive deforestation in another; an algorithmic credit score can reinforce global racial inequality.

To respond, we need a new financial mandate – one that recognizes the interconnected, cross-border nature of risks and opportunities. Institutions such as the Bank for International Settlements and NGFS are starting this work, but a bolder vision is essential. Financial institutions must evolve from service providers to stewards of the commons. Their legitimacy will hinge not just on solvency, but on how they protect systems greater than themselves. This is not just about compliance – it is conscious engagement in shaping the global future.

19 Moral Imagination in Finance

At the heart of every transformation lies imagination – not the fantasy of escape, but the vision to see the world not only as it is, but as it could be. In finance, this power has long been neglected. We teach technical mastery, but not moral imagination. We reward innovation, but rarely introspection. And yet, the future will belong to those who can bridge both – who can model the path of a green bond with the compassion of a civil rights leader; who can design an inclusive payments system with the vision of a social reformer.

Moral imagination in finance is not a poetic luxury. It is a strategic necessity. It allows institutions to ask deeper questions: What kind of society are we funding? What stories are we reinforcing? What possibilities are we ignoring? The rise of ethical design, human-centred banking, and civic-focused fintechs signals the hunger for this shift. But for it to endure, it must be embedded not only in products, but in culture, governance, and leadership. To inherit a just future, we must first dare to imagine it clearly – and fund it boldly.

20 *Rethinking Capital Itself*

For too long, capital has been treated as abstract – fungible, mobile, detached from people and place. It has flowed toward extraction and speculation because the system rewarded it. To build a future worth inheriting, we must rethink the very nature of capital. Capital must become a means – not an end – to foster shared prosperity, community resilience, and planetary stewardship. This goes beyond CSR; it is a redefinition of value.

Movements such as mission-driven investing, community wealth-building, and cooperative finance show how capital can be rooted – circulating within ecosystems rather than draining them. From inclusive lending by local credit unions to climate-aligned sovereign wealth funds, the shift has begun.

New models – such as perpetual purpose trusts and regenerative finance tokens – prioritize long-term wellbeing over short-term yield. They don't reject returns, but reframe them: return for whom, at what cost, and toward what future? Capital must flow not just efficiently, but ethically – reinforcing the moral foundations of finance.

21 *Institutional Legacy and Intergenerational Duty*

Every great institution eventually faces a reckoning: Will it endure as an artifact of its time, or evolve into a steward of the future? For financial institutions, this moment is now. Legacy is no longer just a historical record; it is an intergenerational obligation. The decisions made today – in lending, in data design, in governance – will ripple through the lives of people not yet born. That knowledge must humble us. But it must also galvanize us.

Leading institutions such as the Bank of England, the FCA, and the PRA have started embedding climate risk and ESG mandates into their frameworks. But true legacy-building requires something deeper: a shift in institutional consciousness.

It means designing systems that can listen, adapt, and remain accountable across decades. It means documenting decisions transparently, so future leaders understand the intentions behind them. It means building cultures that honour dissent, welcome learning, and guard against amnesia. And it means asking, again and again: Are we acting in a way that our grandchildren would understand – and respect?

22 *Humanity as the Anchor*

In all the complexity of models, metrics, and machines, the danger is that we forget the human being at the centre. The customer. The worker. The vulnerable. The unseen. To design a future that is not just functional, but humane, we must return to humanity as the anchor of financial systems. This is not about nostalgia. It is about resilience. Systems that ignore human needs will fail – because they will lose trust, relevance, and legitimacy.

Designing with humanity in mind means considering the cognitive load of interfaces, the emotional dignity of service, the psychological impact of debt, the trauma of exclusion. It means building for people who are not tech-savvy, not well-banked, and not financially fluent. It means seeing customers not as data points, but as full human beings with stories, struggles, and dreams. In a world of hyper-automation and AI, the most radical act may be to slow down and listen. Technology can scale decisions. But only human-centred design ensures they remain just.

23 Finance That Listens, Learns, and Evolves

A living financial system listens deeply, learns continuously, and evolves wisely. This is the true test of institutions: Can they sense change, interpret it, and adapt fast enough to stay relevant? In this future, banks aren't static fortresses but dynamic ecosystems – open, porous, and co-creative. They evolve not just through tech upgrades, but by internalizing feedback from society. From customer complaints to climate stress signals, every input informs institutional intelligence.AI, machine learning, and behavioural economics matter – but not alone. Human insight remains vital. Algorithms find patterns; people find purpose.

A learning financial system must admit mistakes, course correct, and value reflection. It must empower people to speak up, question assumptions, and redesign with humility. This defines institutional integrity. Organizations that thrive will know this: learning is not a department – it is a culture.

24 The Role of Hope in Institutional Design

As we approach the end of this journey, one element becomes unavoidable – one that seldom features in whitepapers or strategy decks but underpins every enduring transformation: hope. Hope is not optimism. Optimism expects things to work out; hope commits to making them so. Hope is active, not passive. It drives people to innovate, collaborate, and endure.

Designing a future worth inheriting requires hope at scale – not blind faith in technology or markets, but an intentional, disciplined hope rooted in possibility and responsibility. We must build institutions that convey hope, not just stability. That tell customers, "You are seen." That tells young people, "Your voice matters." That tell future generations, "We were thinking of you."

Hope is what allows a community bank in a rural town to keep serving when the margins are thin. It is what powers a fintech founder to challenge outdated credit systems. It is what sustains regulators and reformers who believe that justice can be embedded into code and capital alike. And it is what sustains readers like you – who reach the final chapters of books like this one, looking not for a blueprint to copy, but a reason to act. The future we design is a mirror of the hope we carry.

25 The Next 1,000 Decisions

The future is not shaped by one grand decision – it is shaped by a thousand small ones. Policy tweaks, procurement choices, design defaults, hiring calls, risk tolerances, and vendor contracts. The architecture of tomorrow is embedded in the micro-decisions of today. A bank may issue a bold sustainability pledge – but if its lending criteria still favour carbon-heavy enterprises, the gap between rhetoric and reality grows. A fintech may claim inclusion as a value – but if its UX excludes non-English speakers or those without smartphone, the intent collapses under its own design.

What matters now are not declarations, but discipline. Discipline in aligning values to systems. Discipline in rechecking assumptions. Discipline in choosing what not to scale. Every small decision should be made in light of the world we want to build. And when these small decisions are made deliberately, consistently, and transparently, they become culture. No transformation is too small. And no institution is too large to forget this truth.

26 The Global Canvas of Responsibility

The responsibility of the modern financial institution is no longer confined to its jurisdiction. When a decision made in London ripples into liquidity in Lagos, or when a digital product launched in California affects livelihoods in Cambodia, the global interconnection of finance is no longer theoretical – it is personal, structural, and urgent.

In this new canvas, regulators, firms, innovators, and civil society must collaborate across borders. The FSB, IMF, BIS, and emerging coalitions of regional actors are already sketching new frameworks. But frameworks are not enough. We must co-design rules and relationships that reflect a shared future, not a divided past. This includes common taxonomies for sustainability, harmonized rules for data sovereignty, shared commitments to open access, and reciprocal respect for risk.

Finance has always had global reach – but now, it must develop global conscience. Institutions that operate on global infrastructure must also be bound by global ethics. And the future we inherit will depend on whether that ethical infrastructure proves stronger than any geopolitical rift, market crash, or technological disruption. We are, quite literally, in this together.

27 Leadership Beyond the Balance Sheet

The most impactful banking leaders of the future won't be remembered for profits alone, but for what they protected, transformed, and left behind. This moment calls for leadership that goes beyond transactions and into legacy.

Leadership that asks: Did we serve the whole community – or just the profitable part of it? Did we dismantle barriers – or just digitalize them? Did we build public trust – or exploit it for short-term gain?

Such questions require deeper, wiser leadership – not louder voices or more growth. Today, leaders who pair strategic clarity with conscience are not optional – they're essential. CEOs, board members, and policymakers must evolve into trust builders, system stewards, and legacy architects. Titles may stay the same – but their meaning must change.

28 *Creating a Moral Technology of Money*

Finance has always been a form of technology. Not just digital or algorithmic, but moral. How we design money, allocate capital, and enforce contracts shapes human outcomes as surely as laws or policies do. A bank is not neutral. A lending algorithm is not neutral. A payments network is not neutral. These are choices – and they embed values.

As we embrace AI, programmable money, and decentralized finance, we must recognize that code is never value-free. It expresses the priorities, assumptions, and worldviews of its creators. And so, the task ahead is not only to make finance faster, cheaper, or more efficient – but to make it just.

The next frontier of innovation is moral: How can we encode fairness into credit? accountability into smart contracts? equity into asset distribution? This is the moment to design a financial system not just capable of growth – but worthy of it. Because what we code today will define who gets to belong tomorrow.

29 *A World Worth Designing for*

In the end, banking is not about banks. It is about people:

- It is about the grandmother in Birmingham managing her pension on a mobile app.
- The young woman in Lagos using her first digital wallet to save for school.
- The migrant worker in Dubai sending funds home with a swipe.
- The climate entrepreneur in California raising capital through tokenized green bonds.

These lives – interconnected, vulnerable, and ambitious – are the real infrastructure of the future. To design the future of banking is to design for them. Not just for quarterly earnings, but for generational wellbeing. Not just for market share, but for shared futures. The responsibility is profound: We are shaping the architecture of economic life.

That architecture must be open. Resilient. Inclusive. Humane. Every policy, every platform, every product is a chance to build a world more worthy of our children. And we must ask ourselves: When they look back, will they say we chose wisely?

30 The Work Continues

This book ends – but the work does not.

The century ahead will be marked by crises and breakthroughs, by shocks and opportunities we cannot yet imagine. But the principles we embed today – trust, inclusion, intelligence, stewardship – will shape how resilient our systems become.

This is not a manifesto. It is a blueprint. A starting point. A provocation.

It invites leaders, technologists, regulators, and citizens to engage with the future not passively, but actively. Not fearfully, but faithfully. Not to predict, but to design.

And the work of design is never finished.

There is always more to learn.

More voices to hear.

More futures to consider.

Let us proceed – with humility, with ambition, and with a shared sense of responsibility.

Let us design a future worth inheriting.

Strategic Framework Box: Chapter 10. Legacy in Motion: Designing the 100-Year Bank

Key Insight

Most banks are built for quarterly results. The future demands institutions built for generational relevance. Designing the 100-year bank requires a shift from short-term optimization to long-term stewardship – across climate, continuity, education, and institutional character.

Strategic Takeaway

The bank of tomorrow will not be remembered for its app or its valuation – but for its role in building a just, resilient, and regenerative financial future.

Future - Building Pillar	*Legacy Bank Model*	*Century - Ready Bank Design*
Strategic Horizon	Quarterly, shareholder - focused	Multi - decade, stakeholder - anchored
Growth Philosophy	Extractive, scale - first	Regenerative, purpose - aligned
Climate Orientation	ESG as compliance	ESG as core infrastructure
Institutional Memory	Individual tenure, siloed records	Embedded learning, digital continuity

Future - Building Pillar	*Legacy Bank Model*	*Century - Ready Bank Design*
Financial Literacy	Outreach - driven, time - bound	Embedded, lifelong, tech - enabled
Responsibility Framing	Compliance - led, balance sheet - bound	Systemic, societal, intergenerational

This chapter argues that financial institutions must now evolve into stewards of economic, environmental, and ethical continuity. The banks that endure will be those that see beyond profit to planetary systems, policy design, and civic resilience.

Bibliography

World Economic Forum (2020). *The Future of Financial Services: Building Resilient and Sustainable Institutions*. Geneva:World Economic Forum.

Closing Reflections

As this book draws to a close, its message remains open. The future of banking – through its institutions, platforms, and ecosystems – is not a fixed destination. It is an invitation.The future is not the property of any one institution. It is a collective responsibility. A discipline. A design ethic that demands vision without ego, technology with conscience, and leadership with empathy.

Throughout these chapters, we have examined foundations for a stronger financial system – from modular cores to invisible architectures. Yet the theme central to all of them is something simpler, and more enduring: trust. Trust not only in banks, but in one another. Trust in our shared capacity to adapt, to build, and to serve.

We now stand at the threshold of a century where continuity will depend less on what we control, and more on what we cultivate. We must regenerate. Rethink. Reframe. Reconnect.The Singh Framework, introduced in these pages, rests on four enduring pillars:

- Trust that earns belief
- Inclusion that leaves no one behind
- Infrastructure that connects without barriers
- Governance that protects the common good

These are not design choices. They are promises to the future – embedded in every decision, every policy, and every act of service.

May this book serve not only as a reference, but as a reminder: that behind every system lies the seed of something larger, and behind every decision lies the possibility of a better world.The future will not design itself. We must design it – with intention, with care, and with courage.

Dr. Gulzar Singh
London

DOI: 10.4324/9781003737544-11

About the Author

Dr. Gulzar Singh is a globally recognised banking strategist, whose career spans the public, private, and policy sectors. Drawing on leadership experience across the UK, Europe, US, Africa, and India, his work focuses on designing financial institutions that centre trust, inclusion, and resilience.

He has led major programs across both high-street banks and global financial platforms, with experience in regulatory reform, operational scale, and innovation strategy. His writings and advisory work bridge practice and principle, seeking to guide the next generation of leaders through times of technological change and social expectation.

Now based in London, United Kingdom, he continues to shape conversations at the intersection of banking, ethics, and institutional design.

DOI: 10.4324/9781003737544-12

Index

Note: locators in *italics* refer to figures.